Refounding Democratic Public Administration

Refounding Democratic Public Administration

Modern Paradoxes, Postmodern Challenges

■

Edited by
Gary L. Wamsley
James F. Wolf

SAGE Publications
International Educational and Professional Publisher
Thousand Oaks   London   New Delhi

Copyright © 1996 by Sage Publications, Inc.

For information address:

SAGE Publications, Inc.
2455 Teller Road
Thousand Oaks, California 91320
E-mail: order@sagepub.com

SAGE Publications Ltd.
6 Bonhill Street
London EC2A 4PU
United Kingdom

SAGE Publications India Pvt. Ltd.
M-32 Market
Greater Kailash I
New Delhi 110 048 India

Printed in the United States of America

Library of Congress Cataloging-in-Publication Data

Main entry under title:

Refounding democratic public administration: modern paradoxes, postmodern challenges / editors, Gary L. Wamsley, James F. Wolf.
       p. cm.
Includes bibliographical references.
ISBN 0-8039-5976-1 (cloth: acid-free paper).—ISBN 0-8039-5977-X (pbk.: acid-free paper)
    1. Public administration. 2. Democracy. I. Wamsley, Gary L. II. Wolf, James F..
JF1351.R425 1996
350—dc20   95-50240

This book is printed on acid-free paper.

96 97 98 99 00 10 9 8 7 6 5 4 3 2 1

Sage Production Editor: Astrid Virding
Sage Typesetter: Marion S. Warren
Sage Cover Designer: Candice Harman

Dedication

In the last year and a half of his life Norton Long became intensely involved in the Refounding project. He left his retirement home in the Berkshires of Massachusetts and set off for Blacksburg with some of his belongings and his bulldog in a station wagon. He was in his eighties at the time; rather advanced years for such an adventure. He took up residence and began teaching at Virginia Tech's Center for Public Administration and Policy (CPAP) on a voluntary basis.

Norton became a respected and valued colleague at CPAP. He took great delight in teaching a course that put students in the field analyzing the causes of a fatal mine disaster in southwest Virginia, in organizing a conference on the importance of the burgeoning economies of the Pacific Rim to the American future, and in arguing with his colleagues on anything from perverse incentives in public organizations to the course of conflict in the Balkans and American policy there.

He involved himself enthusiastically in the development of this volume. From numerous discussions, we all assumed that he was working on a manuscript that would call for reestablishment of the Office of Management and Budget as the kind of office concerned, not with the partisan political well-being of the incumbent president, but rather with the well-being and interest of the institution of the presidency and of the government as a whole.

Every government ought to have such an office, he argued, and the old Bureau of the Budget had in fact been conducted in such a manner. Certainly we could resonate with the notion that such an office with such a mission should exist. Some of us expressed doubt that such an agency could be resurrected or find a constituency for itself in the present context. Those of us who expressed such doubts were subjected to withering criticism for our lack of imagination and our loss of idealism. We were assuredly vulnerable on those points, and assumed that he was working to answer some of our concerns in his chapter.

We were, therefore, surprised when his son brought us the nearly completed manuscript on which he had been working on the day he died. He had told his son it was for a forthcoming volume, which we presume was this one. Our surprise was that the manuscript was not about a "refound B.O.B." but the pernicious effects of perverse incentives in public organizations. We have chosen not to include the manuscript and to seek publication of it elsewhere. We do so not because it is without merit but rather because it is not typical of what we are developing in this volume, or, for that matter, what he seemed to be developing in his discussions. Instead it is vintage Norton Long and could have been written anywhere in the middle of his long career.

That editorial matter aside, this volume is dedicated to his memory and as an acknowledgment of his profound impact on the works of all of us and on the field of public administration.

Contents

Acknowledgments

This project builds on the support and works of our colleagues at Virginia Tech's Center for Public Administration and Policy during the past 18 years. They provided the necessary atmosphere of support and challenge that made it possible for us to sustain the Refounding project. To the same extent, the ideas and perspectives presented herein were continually enriched by the stimulation of the students and graduates of the Center. Some say that students make good classes. We believe that students make us good teachers and researchers. We appreciate their contribution to our development.

We also acknowledge the contributors of chapters in this volume. All the writers were either teaching faculty and/or students at the Center for Public Administration and Policy. We consider ourselves fortunate to be associated with an institution and group of colleagues where it is even possible to conceive of a continuing project like the one represented by this book.

Finally, we are both grateful to Monisha Murthi's editorial assistance during the final compilation of the book. Only someone who completes such a task or directly benefits from the fruits of editorial assistance can fully appreciate the significance of such a service.

Gary Wamsley and Jim Wolf

Preface

An outstanding government administrator once remarked that "administration must have a soul." . . . It needs to be added, however, that administration should contribute to the fuller development of the soul of the state. I have tried to point out that the administrative machinery and the political and philosophical principle together determine the system of government; that a democratic state must be not only based on democratic principles but also democratically administered, the democratic philosophy permeating its administrative machinery and being manifested in its relations both with the citizen outside the government and the citizen inside the government, the public servant; that administrative procedures are more important in effectuating the basic principles of government than is substantive law; and that these procedures must therefore be constantly reexamined in terms of the ends they serve and changed when the changing social and economic milieu requires different means to attain these ends.

David M. Levitan, *Public Administration Review,* Winter 1943

Our constitutional democracy rests on the basic notion of the inviolability of human dignity, and the justifications for our governmental system and the public policy process rest solely on the extent to which this categorical imperative of democracy is defended and enhanced. While every public official can legitimately be held accountable to this peremptory and absolute duty, it is the public administrator for whom this notion of duty has particular importance since it is the individual bureaucrat who stands opposite the individual citizen on a face-to-face, day-to-day basis as the actual implementation of public policy unfolds. If individual public administrators are to move beyond the role of boundary guarding agents, engaged solely in the transfer of quantitative goods and things, they must—in the fashion of the early Federalist and early Agriculture Department administrators—become motivated by a commitment to a purposeful cause and a sense of duty which transcend the specific situational circumstance and extend beyond to the categorical imperative of democracy—that is, the enhancement of the quality of life of the individual citizen.

From "Bureaucracy and Constitutional Development: The Duty to Risk,"
by Louis C. Gawthrop, pp. 181-212, in G. Bryner & D. Thompson (Eds.),
The Constitution and the Regulation of Society, 1988,
Provo, UT: Brigham Young University.

Gloomy tendencies toward social entropy are all too visible in wide areas of American life today . . . they have been aided by the simplistic and misleading view that institutions are simply neutral mechanisms for enhancing individual and social unity. But fortunately, in human affairs the recognition of problems need not entail fatalism. Recognizing that a weakening of civic bonds stems from mistaken social choices opens the possibility of changing the situation for the better by working to enhance the strength of civic culture. Taking responsibility for the well-being of our institutional structure importantly aids the renewal of democratic life. Public discussion of the nature and civic role of institutions can itself be a step in that direction.

From "Institutions as the Infrastructure of Democracy," by
William M. Sullivan, in Amitai Etzioni (Ed.), *New Communitarian Thinking:*
Persons, Virtues, Institutions, and Communities (pp. 170-180),
1995, Charlottesville: University Press of Virginia.

Introduction

Can a High-Modern Project
Find Happiness in a Postmodern Era?

GARY L. WAMSLEY
JAMES F. WOLF
Virginia Polytechnic Institute and State University

In 1982 several contributors to this volume participated in writing a tract that came to be known as the Blacksburg Manifesto (Chandler, 1987). It was a normative declaration of what we thought was wrong with the American political system and what must be done in order that public administrators and the institutions with which they are associated might be perceived as legitimate actors in a process of governance. It would not be an exaggeration to say that we had come to have serious doubts about America's ability to govern itself unless it developed a new way of thinking about and conducting the activities called public administration. Those doubts remain and grow.

We felt that before a new conceptualization of public administration could emerge, America's political dialogue would have to shift from where it seemed centered in the early 1980s—focused not only on how to shrink the role of government in society, but whether or not there was *any* role for government. There was talk of "night watchman government" and how government "did not need the 'best and the brightest' "—merely "adequate" people would do less mischief. After all, the reasoning went, "anything government does is a burden or a detraction from the private sector" (Wamsley et al., 1990).

That kind of ideological "reasoning" remained a permanent feature of both the Reagan and the Bush administrations. With the election of Bill Clinton in 1992 there seemed to be hope, though not a great deal, that the antigovernment, antibureaucratic tide might ebb. Although some observers may feel that that hope was realized, we feel that any change was more surface than substance. The difference between Democrats and Republicans on negative

1

attitudes and rhetoric directed against government and career civil servants is essentially one of degree only, no matter how much Republicans try to stereotype Democrats as lovers of "Big Government."

Our perception that there is little difference between parties in their approach to the "permanent government" is constantly reinforced in myriad ways, but for one of us (Wamsley) this was brought home even more concretely through his experience in the transition between the Bush and Clinton administrations. His account of that experience follows.

The idea for the Blacksburg Manifesto had originally developed when I was involved in a small way in the transition between the Carter and Reagan Administrations. It was, therefore, ironic that in late 1992 I found myself again involved in a small way (my roles don't seem to expand—just recycle) in another transition in the very same agency; this time from the Bush to Clinton administrations.

A presidential transition is a fascinating phenomenon, especially when viewed from inside the government. In the months leading up to the election there was definite slowing of work, and major initiatives ceased forward movement by unspoken consensus. Following the election I watched one subdued Republican appointee after another quietly pack their belongings. Farewell parties with very little emotion in evidence (no one in the permanent government wants to seem too sad or too glad about the departures) became routine. On Inauguration Day, I was amazed at the magical disappearance of the pictures of Republican political appointees lining the wall of the agency in which I was working. Who took them down? Mice? And when? I had worked in the building till after midnight and was back early the next morning. All the government seemed to go on hold as phones fell silent and offices emptied.

With God knows how many thousands of other citizens who lacked political connections but had sense enough to go to their Congressperson or Senator, I obtained an impressive-looking ticket that entitled me to stand in a huge crowd a half mile from the rostrum. By jostling and straining, I believe I saw a tiny figure alleged to be the new president deliver a speech promising a new era. Afterward, working my way back to the office through the throng, I watched ex-President Bush's helicopter take one more swing around the Capitol and White House in the clear cold air before fading from sight in the direction of Andrews Air Force Base and a plane to Texas.

That experience led me to know and feel uplifted by something at a visceral level that I had known but only at a cognitive level for decades—the miracle entailed in nonviolent change of power in a democracy. We tend to take a nonviolent transition for granted and forget both its rareness throughout the world and how fragile a democratic republic—a constitutional republic—truly is.

But the miracle of American presidential transitions disappears like water into desert sand as the new crop of "strangers" arrive to begin occupying the institutions of governance. The Democratic Transition Team seemed intelligent, pleasant, and responsive to suggestions that the career staff would be invaluable to a smooth and swift transition if given an opportunity for involvement. But I could not help recalling that the Reagan Transition Team had left exactly the same impression before turning on the careerists and making a complete botch of the same agency 12 years earlier.

The Clinton Transition Team did make the ranking career administrator the Acting Director, and later left him in the agency's number three spot. And they did make overtures to the career cadre and in fact made better use of their talents than the previous administration. But they also were unrelenting in their determination to fill the incredible number of political appointments carried on the agency's roster (32 out of 2,300; 9 of the 32 being presidential appointments requiring Senate confirmation). Then, perhaps not all but most of the wasted motion I had seen in the Carter-Reagan transition began to unfold inexorably.

Program activity ground to a halt and everything went on "hold" lest something be done that would meet with the disapproval of the new political executives. There were wave upon wave of rumors—some hopeful and some demoralizing. Real or imagined "hit lists" ratcheted anxiety higher and higher. Less visible political appointees of the previous administration schemed somehow to stay on or "burrow in" to the career service. Some high-level careerists were "induced" or got themselves assigned to "administrative Elbas" until things sorted out or were more propitious for a resurfacing. The few new appointees who found their way through the torturous process of clearance by the White House Personnel Office and/or Senate confirmation began the long process of understanding their jobs, a process that would never reach fruition for some, but that would be the longer for most of them because of their mistrust of the career personnel who could help them. At this writing, 28 months into the Clinton administration, some of the political positions have not yet been filled. The extent of wasted opportunity due to lack of knowledge on the part of most political appointees and lack of trust between political and career executives is appalling.

A president's de jure term may be 48 months in duration, but de facto it may be closer to 24 or possibly 18, depending on: (1) how long it takes to fill key positions and for those appointees to settle in and figure out their jobs; and (2) how early campaigning for a second term begins and the extent of involvement of political executives in that enterprise. All in all, it was the depressing similarities of the Carter-Reagan and Bush-Clinton transitions that stood out for me. It may be a cliché, but the words of that immortal philosopher, Yogi Berra, come to mind—it was "deja vu all over again."

The Clinton Administration and "Reinventing Government"

With Clinton's inauguration, open bureaucrat bashing did in fact seem to slacken a bit in Washington even though it continued in full swing in numerous states. But in some respects it merely assumed another guise. The Clinton administration used Osborne and Gaebler's (1992) book *Reinventing Government* as its centerpiece symbol for "fixing" a government that was declared to be "broken." Washington became either preoccupied, bemused, or aggravated by "reinventing government" in the form of a National Performance Review (NPR) directed by none other than Vice President Albert Gore.

The assessment of the NPR effort continues (see Green & Hubbell, Chapter 1, this volume). Surely it has done much that is good, and no one would wish to detract from its accomplishments. Though it is, like all preceding reform and reorganization efforts, a partisan political game dressed in the clothes of nonpartisan, "objective" management, it nonetheless has been conducted with more sophistication and high-level political support, and with less inflammatory, antigovernment bombast than its predecessor, the Grace Commission (Goodsell, 1984). At least the NPR generally distinguished between those problems created by congressional and interest group lawmaking and oversight and those created by inadequacies and pathologies of administration. This distinction was conveniently or stupidly ignored by the Grace Commission.

NPR was also aimed more at the processes within agencies than tilting at the windmill of "reorganizing the government," a futile exercise of rearranging the boxes on the executive branch organization chart, one that public administration academicians have been too quick to buy into and elected politicians too ready to bail out of at the first sign of weakening voter interest and congressional opposition (Dudley & Wamsley, in press).

The NPR was largely staffed by career public administrators, and surely this was a plus. Still, those outside the NPR team might be forgiven if they felt they had survived more than a decade of bashing by what Charles Fox (1993) has called "primitive libertarian philistines" only to find themselves engulfed by well-meaning colleagues of the reinvention project—who, one tired and cynical veteran claimed, were possessed of naïveté, zeal, and a proclivity for hoopla that had not been seen since the Children's Crusade. But all this aside, the greatest harm done by NPR is its reinforcement of that fundamental myth of American political culture: that government is "broken" on a technical/managerial level and can be fixed by "good management techniques borrowed from business" and by a good dose of "entrepreneurship" to overcome bureaucratic lethargy (Urban, 1982).

Those of us in the Blacksburg project do not see the problem as a "broken government" that can be fixed by a good dose of patent medicine borrowed from business. Given the constitutional design bequeathed us by our Founding Fathers and the way we have developed, our government works about as one might expect—which is not to say that we necessarily think it works well. The problem as we see it is fundamentally one of the lack of legitimation for a key component in the governance process—public administration. By legitimacy in a democratic and constitutional republic we do not mean legality. Some of us are all too quick to equate the two. In a constitutional republic that espouses democratic principles, the legitimacy problem for public administration becomes a severe one. The problem only worsens as public administration becomes more essential to the system.

We tend to assume that legitimacy can only stem from election—for example, "Who the hell elected Paul Volcker?" But as John Rohr (1986) reminds us, there are 16 ways to become an officer of the government and election is only one of those ways. We must find a way to legitimate those who become officers by another means. Our concern with legitimating public administration was certainly present in the first refounding volume, but it grows steadily as the problems of our political system grow. We have sought to express that growing concern in the title of this volume.

We must refound public administration in governance, the public interest, and its democratic character. One of our current students, on seeing the title for this volume, wondered aloud how we could refound democratic public administration. "When," he asked, "was it ever democratic?" After complimenting his perceptivity, we answered that we (the field of study and the practice) had assumed that we did in fact have "democratic public administration," that is, that problem was solved in what Redford (1969) has labeled "top-down democracy." That is to say, that by popular election of the president, governor, or strong mayor (making them plebiscitary) and claiming that we are centralizing administrative responsibility under these elected officials (making them managerial), we have seemingly solved the legitimacy—or the democracy—problem for public administration. Unfortunately, we have not. Public administration must find ways to create democratic legitimacy for itself that are not elective in nature. There are several facets to such an effort— among them a new conception or identity for ourselves, and from there a revisualization of the relationship between public servants and the citizens they serve—and among public servants, appointed or careerist in the governance process. And, all of this hinges on not only seeing ourselves as part of the governance process, but learning to think of governance in a different way (see Wamsley, Chapter 13, this volume).

Although we insist that the shifts in antigovernment rhetoric and attitudes may be discernible, they are not significant. The problem is much larger than these marginal adjustments can address. Neither this rhetoric nor our feeble responses to it have affected the status of public administration's legitimacy. Now, midway through the 1990s and late in the Clinton administration there is unfortunately little reason to alter our rather bleak view of the place of public administration in the American political system. Even as we write, the president is still trying to capture the political middle's support by reciting a litany of "downsizing government" accomplishments and plans. And in the Commonwealth of Virginia we have a Governor who seems to feel the only purpose of government is to protect citizens from one another—Thomas Hobbes must be smiling somewhere. *Plus ça change, plus c'est la même chose.*

The 1994 Mid-Term Congressional Election

If what we have said up to this point has not been persuasive, we offer the 1994 election as further evidence that the political system remains in a deep crisis and that attitudes toward public administration remain central both to that crisis and any potential amelioration of it. Republicans understandably chose to try to extract from the election results a mandate for a massive "turn to the Right." Speaker of the House Newt Gingrich showed great talent and skill in this effort. By crafting a "Contract with America" and promising a dramatic 100 days of change, he was able to seize center stage from the president in an unprecedented manner. But within a few months the cameras and reporters no longer beat on his door and the limelight shifted elsewhere. Partisan defenders of the so-called revolution pointed to the clever clause in the Contract with America that promised only to bring the issues it defined "to a vote." Passage by both Houses, they maintained, was never part of the contract. At this writing his ratings in polls have plummeted, and he speaks of quietly getting on with his work as Speaker. And political commentators express doubt that the "turn to the Right" was or will be a very sharp one, if in fact there is any at all.

We did not see the 1994 election as a turn to the Right, and we do not believe we are slipping into partisanship when we say so. The sources of the 1994 election returns lie much deeper than the current partisan clichés with which both parties fill the air.[1] Indeed we argue that the clichés, rhetoric, and symbols of both parties regarding the place of government in society and the role of public administration in governance have become antiquated remnants from an era that has passed (Luttwak, 1994; Reich, 1991).

Neither party is connecting with the very real fears, mistrust, and hopes, but mostly fears, of the American public. When trust in government falls from three in every four citizens in 1960 to only one in four trusting it today, something has to be seriously wrong. Indeed, we think a number of things are seriously wrong. The end of the Cold War, the collapse of the Soviet Union, the massive changes that are eminent in China and the rest of Asia, the emergence of a global economy and the decline of America as an industrial and monetary power, the steady erosion of real family income, the loss of any social contract between employers and employees, and the exploding media and computer-based telecommunications technology have changed our world so fundamentally and so rapidly since 1991 that our political institutions and leaders have not been able to adapt.

Both the public and partisan political leaders are still in a state of trying to place blame, either on partisan opponents, on the institution with the least legitimacy (public administration, a.k.a. "bureaucracy"), on the federal government in Washington, on welfare recipients, Big Money, Big Corporations, Minorities, Immigrants, Jews, Corrupt Unions, the Radical Right, the Radical Left, or the U.N., and on and on. The list grows and becomes more fantastic as one moves to the radical or reactionary ends of the political spectrum. This kind of blame placing is nothing new in American politics, and it has always become more strident and fantastic when social and economic dislocation and angst have run high. We are once again in such an era (Morrow, 1991, pp. 14-15).

Poll after poll has shown that Americans feel anxious and insecure to a degree unmatched since the Great Depression. We have lost confidence in our economy and in our ability to achieve or hold on to "the American Dream." We do not believe that our children will be able to live as well as we have, we do not believe in the integrity and worth of our major institutions and leaders (public or private, secular or religious), and we believe that we are only a few paychecks, a serious illness, or a pink slip away from financial disaster (Luttwak, 1994). At one time only the lower reaches of the socioeconomic scale suffered that kind of insecurity, but now corporate mergers, takeovers, and downsizing have made even the middle class and an occasional vice president of a bank insecure. In sum, we have lost the belief that is most fundamental to modernism—the belief in progress—that every day and in every way things (and we) are getting better and better. And we have lost two things most vital to a self-governing people—hope and confidence. We believe, therefore, that the 1994 election was not a Right reaction, but an ad hoc reaction—a reaction based on general economic fear and political frustration.

To use a phrase from the vernacular—"What's wrong with this picture?" What's wrong with it is that interest group liberalism has reached its fiscal limits, and our politicians are too reluctant, lacking in political imagination and skill, or too irresponsible to help us come to terms with the change (Axelrod, 1988; Lowi, 1979). Interest group liberalism can thrive only in a high-growth economy; its pathologies emerge and flourish in a declining or a zero-sum society (Thurow, 1980). The results are inevitable: cut entitlements, but not *my* entitlement; build prisons, but don't build them in *my* "back yard"; reduce deficits and debt, but, above all, don't raise taxes. The examples are endless at every level from national to local. This kind of unreality or—some would say—irresponsibility, after due discounting for the rapidity of change that we have experienced, must ultimately be placed at the feet of our parties and political leaders. This is not to say that public administration has no responsibility in all this; it does—we do; and this volume tries to speak to that responsibility.

The Oklahoma City Bombing

Finally, one last aspect of the contemporary political context cannot be allowed to go by without examination. That is the tragic bombing of the federal office building in Oklahoma City in the spring of 1995. An early draft of this chapter was written only days after its occurrence and as body parts of civil servants and their children were still being dug from the rubble. It seemed that to discuss it so soon was to risk being egregiously wrong about something. Political columnists must run such a risk daily, but we academics can usually avoid it. However, the enormity of that event seemed to warrant the risk. The tragedy could have been and could still be a defining point in our political dialogue about government, public administration, and public administrators. The operational words, of course, are *could be*. As a final draft of this chapter is written 3 months later, it has virtually disappeared from the news. One is left wondering which is worse—overheated rhetoric and blaming or no discourse at all.

The bombing was the inevitable and logical conclusion of events since _____. *Please provide your own date or event marking the loss of our national innocence (or is it the dawning of national maturity and realism?)* The list of possibilities is endless: assassinations?—JFK, RFK, MLK; Vietnam?—please specify the particular aspect of Vietnam; scandals?—Watergate, Irangate, Whitewater; CIA dirty tricks?—Mossadegh, Diem, Allende, Bay of Pigs, Nicaragua, El Salvador, and on and on; horrendous revelations?—JFK's sex life, unauthorized radiation tests, pollution by atomic weapons plants, the savings and loan debacle, and on and on. The point is: We Americans with our many faults were innocents trying clumsily to develop a "great society" and simultaneously play the role of dominant world power in the first-ever period of history when the end of humankind was both possible and probable. We felt on the verge of achieving the former and had come through the worst of the perils involved in the latter, only to find that we had not even come close to a great society and that, in world affairs, the worst keeps coming. Moreover, at any of the points above, each of us lost some of our belief that our government would not lie to us, hide the truth from us, or consciously do anything to harm us. But whether we simply know more now as a result of a tabloid news media, or Vietnam followed by Watergate were simply too much disillusionment for us to absorb, or things were done in a Cold War climate that should not have been done, our trust is gone, and among people of the political fringes that loss of trust has crossed a threshold into paranoia.

But there is more to this. For decades we have been told by both parties that government is wasteful, a burden on the economy, and a drag on the market. We have been told by both parties with careless disregard for facts that we are overtaxed, underserved, and rudely treated by the same government in which we have lost our trust. We have been told that the nonelected officers of that government, whom we used to call civil servants and in whom polls showed we once placed a great deal of trust, are overpaid rejects from the business world concerned only with their "turf," "perks," and pensions. Given our continued angst, our growing distrust, and the identification of objects (no longer seen as fellow citizens or even human beings) to blame for our condition, the only thing surprising about the Oklahoma City bombing is that it was so long in coming.

As of this writing it seems that the tragedy will not lead to a change in discourse. If such a change is every to occur, our political leaders must refrain from partisan blaming of one another and from depicting such tragedies as some consequence of ideology—Left or Right—and we as citizens must hold them to such conduct. Given their, and our, track records that is asking a lot. If we and our leaders can recognize the consequences of overheated rhetoric, blaming, and stereotyping, there may be a chance for healing and growth. If our political leaders can begin to recognize and help us recognize that most of those people they (the politicians) and the press identified as the "heroic rescue workers" in Oklahoma City were the same people they had derided as "pointy-headed bureaucratic jack-asses,"[2] then there may yet be hope for restoring legitimacy to government. If we can grasp that such rescuers were the same people whose raises and cost-of-living allowances have been denied, budgets cut, and ranks downsized, and who have been told repeatedly by growing layers of political appointees above them that they "must do more with less," then it will be a significant step toward lowering the ideological fervor associated with discourse about the place of government in our society

(Barr & Kamen, 1993). If our political leaders can help us understand that the rescuers and the victims work (we used to say "serve") in "bureaucracies" like FEMA, the FBI, the Oklahoma City Fire Departments, the U.S. Marshals Service, and the Oklahoma State Police, it will mark a beginning of new understanding. And if they will remind people that the broken bodies pulled from the wreckage belonged to people who worked, loved, and suffered life's ups and downs like the rest of us, but also once issued social security and disability checks, helped veterans obtain the benefits due them, made farmers loans to improve soil conservation, pursued federal law violators—in other words served us—then perhaps some good can yet come from such evil.

■ The Blacksburg Manifesto and Refounding Public Administration: Still Under Construction

The Blacksburg Manifesto was first published in 1984 in a self-proclaimed non-journal called *Dialogue* issued by the Public Administration Theory Network. Later it was published in *The Centennial History of the American Administrative State* edited by Ralph Chandler (1987). Another version written in the language of political science was published in *The State of Public Bureaucracy* edited by Larry Hill (1992). Finally, the original authors, joined by Camilla Stivers, Robert Bacher, and Philip Kronenberg, expanded on the ideas in the Manifesto in a book titled *Refounding Public Administration* (Wamsley et al., 1990).

Some refer to the Manifesto or the *Refounding* volume collectively as the Blacksburg Perspective, or to us as "constitutionalists," "discretionists," "neo-institutionalists," or "institutionalists." Reviews have been respectful or polite, but neither highly critical nor effusively laudatory (e.g., Marshall Dimock, Ralph Hummel, Laurence O'Toole, Philip J. Cooper, and Herbert Kaufman). It has been deemed to be "significant," "very important," "original," "refreshing," "worthy," and the like. We have preferred to interpret these as something more than damning with faint praise, but can never be sure.

We are disappointed, however, that more people have not chosen to dialogue with us on the issues we sought to raise. But from our viewpoint the most important thing to be said is that "it" is still unfinished. So far as we are concerned the refounding of The Public Administration is an ongoing project, a work "under construction" that hopefully will never be "finished." A steady stream of our students have gone on to become our colleagues in the "Refounding Public Administration" project and as they have interacted with us, they have critiqued our work and extended it or prompted us to do so. Other more senior colleagues, like Norton Long, have simply found the project important and volunteered to join us or have encouraged us.

To us, each publication, iteration, or presentation of the ideas has changed the corpus of our ideas in subtle but important ways. Indeed, the changes are running far ahead of any publication of them. For example, we cannot argue with some criticisms because they are justified insomuch as they were based on what we had published 3 to 6 years ago (Fox, 1993). Nonetheless, in reading them they strike us as odd because we often have moved on, sometimes to much the same position as the critic—but not in print (Fox, 1993). We have decided that when this sort of thing begins to happen it is time to say something more in print.

Space considerations preclude the presentation of even a concise summary of the concepts that are associated with the original Blacksburg perspective. However, for readers who have not read the Manifesto or the first *Refounding* volume, some foundation will be required in order to place this next phase of the ongoing project in its proper context (Wamsley et al., 1990).

One essential characteristic of the Blacksburg perspective is that it is explicitly normative theorizing about public administration. It prescribes a way of understanding public administration that explicates the practice as a legitimate partner in the governance process. It redefines concepts and roles for public administration that had fallen into disrepute—the agency, the public administrator, authority—and infuses new meaning into the practice of citizenship as that would or should be fostered by public administration. It restores the concept of the common good or the public interest and of the vocational quality of the public service to their appropriate places among our democratic values. And, although it can be said that the new conceptualizations provided by the Blacksburg authors are either just plain unrealistic or altogether too idealistic, like most models, they give the field a target to aim for, acknowledging all the while that we will almost always fall short.

The Blacksburg perspective contends that the legitimacy of public administration is derived from the founding debate that led to the formulation of the Constitution. Thus the oath that binds public servants to the Constitution is a valid and significant sign of the legitimacy of their roles in governance and can, and most often does, exert a powerful influence on the actions of those to whom administrative power and discretion have been entrusted. The first necessary step for this connection to be made involves a critical examination of the orthodox history of the field to refute the common notion that public administration was a product of 20th-century reform and demonstrate instead that it was an integral part of the founders' vision.

The Historical Backdrop for the Development of Public Administration Theory and Practice

Why bother to take an excursion, however brief, into history? Because we think public administration is incredibly lacking in a historical perspective. And why is that cause for alarm? Because we see the field as misfounded historically. Its conscious founding in the reform era was a part of a partisan political stratagem camouflaged as social movement and the inexorable march of science and progress (Urban, 1982). In other words, it was socially and politically "constructed." As Mary Douglas (1986) puts it, history "has very little to do with the past at all and everything to do with the present" (p. 69) and, we would add, with "the future." And therefore, if we are to more fully understand what we are about in the present, we must *re*found our field, that is, deconstruct and reconstruct our founding as a field. What follows is meant to be a mere historical sketch that emphasizes points *we* feel are important in understanding the development of public administration as a field of study, practice, and praxis.

Public administration did not begin at the turn of the century in America with Wilson's essay, the Progressives, the Urban Reform Movement, and Frederick Taylor. It is as old as mankind. E. N. Gladden (1972) had it right when he said it was the second oldest profession or identifiable occupation, preceded only by shamanism. The English colonies in America and the new states that grew out of them had well-developed administrative systems, as did the mother country from which they separated (Beach et al., in press). As John Rohr has shown us, the word *administration* most likely did not appear in the Constitution because the Founding Fathers assumed it to be so fundamental it needed no more mention than did oxygen (Rohr, 1986).

During the period following the Revolution, two major perspectives as to what a national government ought to be like and what purposes it would serve began to take shape. One was the Anti-Federalist, which grew out of "the Rousseauean tradition, emphasized trust in social dialogue and collaboration as a means for human interaction" (Caldwell, 1943, 1944; Marshall, 1994, p. 12; Ostrom, 1974; Stillman, 1984). Its public spiritedness manifested itself as a result of "small decentralized cohesive communities where access to the governmental function was immediate and direct" (White & McSwain, in press). (On a clear day Jefferson could almost see the Albemarle County courthouse from Monticello.) George Mason's thoughts on representatives captures the spirit of the Anti-Federalists: "they ought to mix with the people, think as they think, feel as they feel, ought to be perfectly amenable to them, and thoroughly acquainted with their interest and condition" (Rohr, 1986, p. 40).[3]

The perspective that predominated, however, was the Federalist or Hamiltonian—one that held that state and local governments notwithstanding, the republic needed a stronger central government that could defend it against both external and internal threats; assume its war debts; and foster expansion, commerce, and manufactures. Thus, instrumentalism prevailed over communitarianism.

At one time we might have said that practicality trumped romanticism, but that was too glib and lacked a real appreciation of the Anti-Federalist position. Anti-Federalism's concern for community was essential to Jacksonian Democracy in the early 19th century, to the Progressive Movement almost a century later, and remains an important dimension of American life down to this day. Many, and we now count ourselves among them, consider that perspective more important than ever. And though it may be ironic, it is not simply a triumph of romantic myth over practical reality that has led us to honor Jefferson in a temple on the Tidal Basin but remember Hamilton with a small statue, standing until recently at what had come to be the rear of the Treasury building amidst wooden tables for brown baggers.

We should also add that the political theory of James Madison has been equally important in propping the myth of what Herbert Croly (1914) would later call the Automatic Society. It was Madison who laid the basis for the belief that our system could handle, indeed would thrive on, "factions" as he put it (Nigro & Richardson, 1987). Hamilton's ideas, which helped build and justify a commercial republic, would have fallen on barren ground without Madison's brilliant theory (Green, 1987). We might never have survived as long as we have without the fortuitous convergence of those two bodies of thought, and paradoxically we might not have found ourselves in such a perilous state today had their ideas not been so successful.

We will skip over the end of administration by Federalist gentlemen and the changes that came with Jacksonian Democracy, and cut to the turn of the 19th century when the forces the latter had earlier set in motion came to a critical culmination (Mosher, 1968). As both industry and agriculture mechanized, as the economy grew in size and complexity, as the society steadily urbanized and diversified with the influx of tens of millions of immigrants, and as political entrepreneurs organized their votes into corrupt machines, it became painfully apparent that our society could no longer be held together or continue to grow and prosper on an erroneous assumption of some natural harmony.

This harmony was assumed to exist among natural wealth and factional interests and individual freedom. But hope for such harmony faded with the rise of large corporations and their ability to limit competition to their own ends, and the development of political machines capable of helping integrate immigrants and systematize corruption but not effectively plan and build infrastructure. The claim of a natural harmony could not justify the government handing out huge subsidies to railroads, but then refusing to intervene on behalf of the farmers, small shippers, and merchants that those same railroads were charging extortionist prices. The assumption became increasingly untenable that some invisible and unfettered hand (ignoring, of course, government subsidies and provision of infrastructure for industry) would lead to prosperity and freedom for all (Croly, 1914; Haber, 1964; Marshall, 1994).

Similarly, the Jacksonian assumption that democracy would always lead to better government and more freedom was challenged by politicians who organized the new urban poor, particularly immigrants, into machines complete with incredible corruption and incompetence. Meanwhile interstate commerce needed regulation, our national defense establishment required overhaul, and cities desperately needed infrastructure commensurate with their tumultuous growth. In this incredible socioeconomic and political turbulence the automatic society was simply no longer a tenable myth (Haber, 1964).

It was in an atmosphere of feverish reform, of devotion to progress, worship of science, and quest for efficiency, that self-conscious public administration was born. As Gary Marshall (1994) puts it,

> In this environment of rapid industrial expansion and the failure of democratic politics, public administration provided an institutional framework through which the disparate tensions of the national community could be resolved. The dominant feature of the progressive movement was the emerging administrative arm of government, serving to mediate the tension between the Federalist doctrine and the Anti-Federalist principles. (p. 5)

Although most of the things undertaken by the Progressives had a Hamiltonian thrust, and some of the reformers called themselves "Neo-Hamiltonians" (Huntington, 1957), the movement nonetheless drew heavily on principles of Anti-Federalism. For example, they argued for the "improvability of the human condition and a responsibility . . . for one another and a willingness to use all government and social institutions to give that responsibility legal effect" (Shafritz, 1988, p. 447, in Marshall, 1994). Importantly, the independent regulatory agencies and the delegation of legislative power to them survived crucial court challenges and set the stage for the future evolution of administrative discretion, rule making, and adjudication. In general, we still operate very much within that reform tradition and from its perspective on our political system (Dudley & Wamsley, in press).

As America moved into the Great Depression, the Progressive movement branched in many directions and eventually evaporated as an identifiable social movement. But its reform traditions merged with scientific management became "administrative management," the intellectual mainstay for the vast expansion of the federal government that came with the New Deal. Administrative management, sometimes called "classical administration," may have owed much to scientific management and Progressivism, but it also drew heavily on Henri Fayol and other theorists from abroad who had extensive experience with organizing large-scale organizations (Urban, 1982).

Where scientific management had aimed largely at organizing work at the shop-floor level, administrative management sought to develop principles for the organization as a whole. And some of its chief proponents, like Luther Gulick (1937), unhesitatingly sought to apply the ideas to the executive branch of government as a whole, though not without objections from some colleagues (criticism in Dudley & Wamsley, in press). The landmark of administrative management was the publication by Gulick and Urwick (1937) of the *Papers on the Science of Administration,* and its most notable achievement was the report of the Brownlow Commission in 1937 (Gulick & Urwick, 1937). It prescribed the 1939 reorganization of the executive branch and set the pattern for government reorganizations in federal, state, and some local governments for at least the next four decades. Some would say it is still doing so to this day (Dudley & Wamsley, in press).

Its main ideas will surely be familiar to every reader of this book, so we will not take great care to be thorough in their mention: the famous acronym *POSDCORB,* standing for the functions of the chief executive—planning, organizing, staffing, directing, coordinating, reporting, and budgeting; distinctions between line and staff functions; span of control; unity of command; organizing by purpose, function, or geographic location; politics-administration dichotomy; extension of the civil service; executive budgeting; concentration of responsibility in the chief executive; staff support for the chief executive; and centralization of key management processes under the chief executive—planning, budgeting, personnel, purchasing, and so on (Gulick & Urwick, 1937).

It is at least debatable whether ideas developed for application to organizations can be usefully applied to the entire executive branch of a government composed of separate branches that share power; or whether they can be so applied without altering the Constitution. But this is not a matter to be discussed here (Dudley & Wamsley, in press). Rather, our present purposes dictate that we focus on the years between 1939 and 1948 and the intellectual struggle within administrative management and between it and behavioralism in the social sciences.

It should be noted that in the early years of administrative management there were two distinct perspectives that reflected the Federalist and Anti-Federalist traditions. One held that the remedy to the excesses and lapses of the political system could be best supplied by more democracy through such things as home rule, proportional representation, and community development. The other favored a planned society with strong central administrative agencies. As administrative management evolved, however, its enthrallment with science and rationalism grew while concern for democracy and a relationship between administrators and citizens receded (Waldo, 1984).

Administrative management was riding high. In retrospect it would become clear that administrative management and public administration were not synonymous (although with the foundation of the American Society of Public Administration in 1939 they tended to be thought of as one and the same). Paul Appleby (1949), for example, asserted that "government was different" and stood in stark contrast to Gulick and Urwick (1937) who maintained that "there are principles which can be arrived at inductively from the study of human organizations. . . . These principles can be studied as a technical question, irrespective of the enterprise" (p. 49).

There were, among those who challenged the rationalist bent of administrative management, several voices of dissent. Dwight Waldo's dissertation at Yale in political philosophy amounted to a penetrating critique of administrative management's lack of consciousness, an analysis that should have caused its proponents to pause and reflect; that they seemed to have paid it little heed is no reflection on him. He said as bluntly as can be said in a dissertation that the proponents of administrative management were expressing nothing less than a political philosophy—a theory of the state or politics masquerading as management or organization theory (Waldo, 1984).

Also, there was Norton Long (1949) who emerged from wartime service in the Office of Price Administration to challenge orthodoxy with his classic essay, "Power and Administration." There were others as well—Emmette Redford, Wallace Sayre, Herbert Kaufman, Robert Dahl, Philip Selznick, Marshall Dimock, Charles Hyneman, and more, all of whom demurred from the orthodoxy of administrative management either just before, during, or after World War II (White & McSwain, 1990). Their dissents focused most heavily on challenging the separability of politics and administration, the reduction of democracy to only an implicit role in public administration, and the emphasis on rationalism and science.

White and McSwain have labeled these dissenters from the orthodoxy of administrative management as "traditionalists"—traditionalists in the sense that these scholars were true to the tradition that the Federalists and Anti-Federalists had in common: that administration was a fundamental part of governance. Whether we like their label or not, the analysis by White and McSwain (1990) of this group's shared perspective is compelling. They found that although all the perspectives did not appear uniformly in all the works of these writers, nonetheless the body of work as a whole could be said to contain three key tenets: (a) an emphasis on the normative view of the public interest; (b) an informed pragmatism; and (c) a communitarian ethos. They also developed four axioms from their survey of the works of the Traditionalists. First, "the realities of history served to place administrative action at the center of a government responding to a society in crisis. Second, that this could provide a line of action in a context of contending social forces" (Marshall, 1994, p. 27). Third, that institutional leaders "give expression to institutional imperatives" (White & McSwain, 1990, p. 27). And, finally, that a structuralist perspective provides the clearest insight into administrative events (p. 27).

White and McSwain set forth six "working principles" they maintain can be derived from the above: (a) the idea of the public interest can guide administrative action; (b) the public weal and the well-being of public agencies are synonymous; (c) the Congress and the political executive can effectively control agencies; (d) the case study method is the most effective way to learn the correct sensibility of a public administrator; (e) effective administration is achieved through a pragmatic, experimental approach to action; and (f) collaboration achieved through dialogue is essential to effective administrative action and policy making (White & McSwain, 1990).

Those of the Traditionalists were not the only voices raised in dissent from orthodox administrative management. There was another voice that had significant impact: Herbert Simon (1957) in his book *Administrative Behavior*. His dissent, however, was decidedly different from the Traditionalists', and through a combination of the power of his ideas and the vector sum direction of other forces at work in academia and in society, his line of thought would become dominant and that of the Traditionalists would be marginalized. Although we are sure he would not agree, we find great irony in the fact that he would ultimately win a Nobel Prize in Economics for his work on organizations and organizational decision making.

How did this turn of events come about? First, there was a "behavioral revolution" that swept the social sciences in the wake of World War II with all the advances made in the so-called hard sciences (physics and the A-bomb or engineering and aviation), as well as extensive behavioral studies like Stouffer's *The American Soldier* (1949). All seemed eminently worthy of emulation. Simon's (1957) ideas were cast in the mold of modern behavioralism, those of the Traditionalists were not. Second, there was the fact that

Simon did not so much as try to question the purpose or identity of administrative management—its ontology. Rather, he attacked it on epistemological grounds—the basis for its knowledge claims. In a devastating critique titled "The Proverbs of Administration" he showed that the Traditionalists could not meet the standards of modern behavioral science. Dwight Waldo saw immediately the relationship of Simon to administrative management and labeled Simon's work as "neo-classical."[4] Its end was the same as the classical, to structure and maintain effective and efficient organizations. If this effectiveness, economy, and efficiency served some higher purpose, its nature was assumed to be obvious by both the classicists and Simon.

Simon's organizational theories were built on the concept of bounded rationality, in other words, that it is a universal characteristic of human behavior that we tend to satisfice rather than maximize. But to Simon this seeming liability can be an asset in organizations if decision makers throughout those organizations are supplied by a variety of means with the premises for decisions by the "controlling group." It brilliantly draws on a verifiable finding of social psychology (bounded rationality) and uses that as a basis for structuring organizations and decision making so as to enhance effectiveness and efficiency. This approach has its limitations and pathologies, and a host of normative, ethical, and even behavioral questions can be raised about it, but that is not the task at hand.

What we want to highlight is the difference between Simon and the Traditionalists. From the perspective of 1995 we can see differences that were not apparent when these two perspectives on public administration originally collided. Clearly, Simon builds on the Progressives' infatuation with rationalism, science, and technology, but in the garb of modern behaviorism, logical positivism, and functionalist social science. The Traditionalists, on the other hand, saw the need for a normatively grounded public administration that played a key role in governance, and they combined their concern for efficiency with the Anti-Federalists' concerns for collective responsibility, dialogue, and community.

We can now also see that Simon's (1957) logical positivism carried with it the assumption that words carry specific meanings that are readily discerned by all in the same fashion, and that these words can be used to describe a "natural world," an objective, empirically verifiable reality independent of human existence, and thus "facts." In contrast, the Traditionalists' concern for collaboration through dialogue (authentic communications leading to authentic relations between people) was closer to what Burrell and Morgan (1979) would label the interpretivist paradigm and its assumption that reality is socially constructed. As Marshall (1994) puts it: "where the Simonian perspective seeks to control dialogue and thereby limit social process, the

Traditionalists [saw] the special dialogue that can be created within an agency as the basis for expanding social process and the community of shared meaning" (p. 28). Marshall (1994) offers as an example that Simon saw the public interest as a metaphysical concept irrelevant to the practice of good public administration and a value outside the purview of a scientific approach (p. 31).

The thing we wish to distill from this discussion is that Simon's ideas were in harmony with a dimension or branch of Progressive thought that had become preeminent (rationalism/technicism), and with the body of thought that led the "behavioral revolution" in political science. Thus it appeared as a new and exciting approach to the perennial problems of efficiency, economy, and effectiveness in business administration and to those in public administration who wanted to be part of the "behavioral revolution" and who felt that the public sector should mimic the private with all fealty possible.

In contrast, the Traditionalist perspective embodied many of the ideas that were marginalized with the dominance of the Simonian perspective. Among these were: (a) collaboration; (b) a moral perspective on the public interest; (c) a concern for democratic administration; and (d) experimental action. Marshall compiles an interesting table showing the ideas that became dominant under the Simonian perspective and those that were marginalized as the Traditionalists were swept aside (see table in Marshall, 1994). Marshall (1994) maintains that:

> Until this point in the history of public administration, a dynamic tension had always existed between the communitarian ethos of the Anti-Federalists and the tendency toward centralized control of the Federalists. The ineffability of many of the principles of the Traditionalists weakened their argument in the face of the scientific certainty of Simon's rational model. Yet by moving away from the path of the Traditionalists, the field of public administration became dislocated from its place in the governance process and fell into an inescapable search for the certainty of technique. (p. 30)

But it did more. It redefined public administration as scientific technique in the service of instrumental rationality rather than as a locus for dialogue between public administrators and citizens that could lead to a definition of the public interest (Marshall, 1994, p. 31). The discourse of public administration could scarcely have been defined in a more narrow and sterile way.

Professional politics of the discipline of political science and the field of public administration drained away energy in internecine warfare and forced choices in research interests or where to "reside" physically and intellectually—choices that cost both the discipline and the field dearly. Consequently, there was no intellectual "center of gravity" for public administration. Persons teaching public administration today are likely to come from political science, economics, sociology, planning, and God only knows what else. Only a third of them indicate that their degrees are in public administration, and that in itself can mean anything. Many of the latter were educated in interdisciplinary schools and studied organization theory under organizational sociologists who were oblivious to the difference between public and private organizations, had scarcely thought about the environments of organizations, and wouldn't have recognized a normative concern if they stumbled upon one.

Within this context, The New Public Administration that was identified with Minnowbrook represented a significant level of discontent on the part of a number of then-younger scholars with public administration theory, or a lack of it. The Minnowbrook Conference of 1968, sponsored by Dwight Waldo, was a more complex phenomenon than we can discuss here; we devoted some space to it in the introduction to the *Refounding* volume. We do not mean to slight it now, but will only repeat our impression stated in that earlier work.

The aims of most of the participants were to criticize extremes of functionalism and logical positivism in the study of public administration and more importantly to urge attention to social concerns in the practice of public administration. Those of us involved in the Refounding project resonate with those aims, we merely feel that the ends might have been better realized if they had been grounded in what we call neo-institutionalism, or for that matter grounded in anything other than good intention or social concern. We will discuss neo-institutionalism shortly. What we wish to get to here, is that we feel that The New Public Administration was an important manifestation of a felt need, a serious lack in American public administration. It marked a turning point for those persons thinking and teaching about public administration, but its impact on the practice and praxis has been less than earthshaking. Minnowbrook II 20 years later not only couldn't recreate that moment, it failed to produce a statement with any coherence unless one counts a kind of "dissident voices" text edited by Mary Timney Bailey and Richard Mayer (1992). This we think is attributable not to lack of serious and good intent but rather to a lack of grounding in (a) normative concerns; and (b) institutions of governance.

We have admitted earlier that we stumbled into serious public administration theory building. We need also to say that we have come to realize that we have unconsciously assumed the role of the Traditionalists in our evolving theoretical stance. (Would it make any sense to call ourselves Neo-Traditionalists?) Some of us knew that we felt a great deal of intellectual resonance with the works of the Traditionalists, but until White and McSwain's (1983) historical analysis we could not fully comprehend the connection. It is not so much a matter of embracing their stance as the only one and discrediting all others as misguided. Rather, it is that we recognize the value of their perspective alongside others in developing the field of public administration and are attempting to restore that perspective again to a position of equal importance and intellectual stature.

The Threads of Discourse Within the Refounding Project

The original authors involved in the Refounding project have always been amazed at the degree to which they have been able to agree despite their differing paradigmatic commitments, personalities, and views of human nature—to name only a few of their differences. On the other hand there were, and remain, very real differences among the authors. We have always been amused when colleagues outside the project would descend on us in person or in writing and point triumphantly to those differences as though they somehow vitiated the whole project. Our reaction, to use the vernacular, is that such persons "just don't get it." We never intended to present a comprehensive, logically integrated, and internally consistent—? What? A theory? Ideology? An explanation? We intended only to start a discourse we thought was long overdue. The project continues on the basis of our relationship to one another and a shared concern for the need of an effective public service as a part of effective governance, which in turn hinges on a legitimate public administration if this republic is to remain constitutional and democratic. The project does not depend on our shared points of view, paradigmatic convergence, or some interlocking of perspectives. In the increasingly postmodern world that may be the most meaningful way for the project to cohere: our relationship growing out of a shared concern. If that remark seems cryptic, we hope what follows will make it less so.

For now our intention is to keep that discourse going. The members of the original Blacksburg group have no more nor less agreement among themselves now than they did at the start of this journey, and the same must be said of this new and expanded group of project members. At the risk of oversimplifying, we think the chapters that follow engage one another, and hopefully the reader, around a central theme: *Given the challenges and problems confronting the American political system, it needs a public administration that can be accepted not only as an efficient implementor of policy, but as a legitimate actor in the governance process. The necessary legitimacy can come in a variety of ways, but ultimately it must come by deepening the democratic character of public administration.*

The deepening of public administration's democratic character involves forces of both coherence and emergence in a state of tension. The forces of emergence and coherence are to be found in the changing world around us and they are reflected in the pages of this volume. A discussion of the way the tension between coherence and emergence is being worked out in public administration generally and in this volume particularly may therefore be useful.

A High-Modern Identity Faces a Postmodern Era

The first *Refounding* book was reactive and instinctive, responding to the delegitimation and decapitalization of government by the Carter and Reagan administrations. Although, as noted above, such self-destructive activity on the part of politicians continues in subtler guises, this Refounding book is more measured and reflective. It benefits in perspective from the passage of epic events and changes: the collapse of the Soviet Union and the Iron Curtain; the end of the Cold War; the internationalization of capital and trade; the emergence of chaos/complexity theory; the development of media-driven, plebiscitary political institutions and processes; and the growing awareness that we have entered a new era to which the label postmodern has been applied.

The bewildering context in which today's public administration must operate is indeed as postmodern as MTV or "surfing" through "52 channels with nothin' on." The central tenets of modernity—linear, instrumental rationality; Cartesian science; and a faith in progress—are under siege. Their absolutism is being shaken by cynicism, hyperpluralism, and nihilism at worst, and criticality, playfulness, tentativeness, and openness at best (Rosenau, 1992). For better and for worse, values, morals, and social and economic institutions and ways of thinking at the center of Western civilization for centuries seem to be crumbling under the combined onslaught of individualism run amok; consumer capitalism; an economy that creates social instability and too often social wreckage; feminism; hyperpluralism; and proliferating technology, particularly exploding communications technologies, as threatening as they are helpful.

Among the many unsettling aspects of postmodernism, the fragmentation of our political system should not be a surprise. For decades we have been watching this occur, as de Tocqueville (1990) feared it might, and as observers from Herbert Croly (1914) to Theodore Lowi (1979) have described and predicted. We have not, however, been prepared for the pace of this fragmentation, disintegration, and kaleidoscopic change that has somehow taken a quantum leap in postmodernism. It is the Context from Hell for traditional public administration as we have known it up to now. Finding and maintaining some kind of coherence while accommodating, and indeed being urged to foster emergence sounds to many like some sort of cruelty joke designed for public administrators by Sisyphus.[5]

The Blacksburg project has been described as "high modern," which, we suppose, could be interpreted as a kind of "last gasp of modernism" (Marshall & White, 1989). That is perhaps a fair enough description of the original output of the project. Administration, especially public administration, is quintessentially modern. The notion of "reform" and the belief that great deeds for the collective good can be accomplished by instrumental rationality is as modern as thinking gets. It may also be that we have taken that kind of thinking close to its limits without a major change in consciousness. Modernism encompassed the digging of the Panama Canal, the eradication of yellow fever and polio, creating the interstate highway system, and many other great accomplishments that make our lives better. But it has also resulted in thermonuclear weapons, the Cuban Missile Crisis, the Vietnam War, jeopardization of the planet's ecological balance, and organizations and institutions that at times seem not only to be unable to accomplish what they intend but to be harmful to the physical and mental health of those within them and those with whom they interact. At the very least, it seems fair to say that to continue to operate solely within the consciousness of modernism presents as much hazard as benefit. In that the early products of the Blacksburg project reflect an attempt to alter the political discourse in a way that would reduce the hazard and increase the benefit of operating within a modern consciousness, it could fairly be described as "high modern."

But the world moves on inexorably and apparently so must we. Library shelves groan under books and journals bearing the term *postmodern* in their titles, and we do not intend to enter an extended discussion of it here. Let us simply state that for us it connotes a world in which technology develops with exponential speed while community declines and the notion of progress becomes increasingly precarious; and where subjectivity abounds, the notion of objectivity becomes increasingly antiquated and amusing, but the need and potentiality for intersubjectivity proliferates (Rosenau, 1992).

The speed at which we can travel, at which information reaches us, precludes any easy transition among cultures or rapid and collective response to critical issues. Anyone who has spent time in rapidly modernizing Third World countries (or, for that matter, in rapidly decaying American cities or poverty-stricken rural areas) has experienced the jarring incongruities and disorientation that seems to be the hallmark of the postmodern condition—or perhaps, of the juxtaposition or collision of one encompassing worldview with another. Squalid slums appear adjacent to state-of-the-art high-rises and public buildings. Magnificent churches stand in parishes that once housed the wealthy but now are characterized by tenements and housing projects. Traffic noise, the disconcerting cacophony of different rhythms and musics, the pace of today's living combine discordantly to send us scurrying to our homes or, for some, provide a chaotic background for living in the streets. The postmodern world is a composite of opposites, of traditional institutions that are subject to deconstruction, struggling to keep pace with kaleidoscopic change and proliferating individual differences.

The discontinuous change evident in the postmodern world is unsettling to most of us, but ironically is also the pool from which the means for creative change and transformation can be drawn. The apparent chaos and contradictions we see around us—whether in Brazil or Los Angeles, in New York or Central Europe—can be viewed in either light. From the modernist side of the high modern/postmodern threshold, they represent problems that may be resolved through the application of rationality; from the postmodern perspective, the problematic aspect of chaos is accompanied by myriad potentialities and possibilities as well.

We contend that the world in which public administration (that most modern of institutions) must exist is postmodern, and increasingly so along the lines of the connotations the term holds for us as described above. Much will depend on us. Will we see the manifestation of the postmodern era as problems or as potentialities?

High modernism marks the apogee of an epoch, but can also be an ontological stance—a sense of being, an identity with which one faces the world and finds one's place in it. Clearly the Blacksburg project has its origins in an ontological stance that is high modern, an epistemological orientation that is varied but that might well encompass structuralism, and with its dominant metaphor either a very complex machine or the organism. As the Blacksburg project evolves, however, some of its participants increasingly lean toward an ontological stance that is postmodern, an epistemological orientation that is post-structuralist, and search for a new dominant metaphor perhaps in the brain/mind or mind/body relationship (Little, Chapter 12, this volume). The contributors to this volume are not all at the same place intellectually even if they occupy some of the same space relationally.

The Critical Threshold Between
Structuralism and Post-Structuralism

To grasp the importance of the tension between high modernism and postmodernism, as well as the tension between coherence and emergence, one must briefly examine structuralism and post-structuralism. Structuralism developed in Europe from linguistics and from literary and film criticism. But the discourse has expanded to encompass inquiries into the nature of the mind, culture, psychology, Marxism, and critical theory. One stream draws on Freud and Marx; another concerned with linguistics draws on Saussure, Jakobson, Lévi-Strauss, and Chomsky, to mention a few.

Structuralism sees the usual manifestations of coherence, from organization charts to rules and procedures and rational instrumentality, as inevitable manifestations of the mind's structuring process. But structuralists do not stop at those surface manifestations: Their interests are in the deeper structures—in language and other forms of human interactions and cultural expressions—structures deriving from deeper sources including the individual and collective unconscious. It is through the deep structures of meaning and communication that people understand how to order their daily experience through language, given that the meaning of language forms is itself socially constructed (Rosenau, 1992, p. 14). Thus, if we are to understand the relationships among people in a social construct, we must examine deep structures—the texts and subtexts of their oral and written language.

The relationship between structuralism and institutions and the body of literature known as institutionalism or neo-institutionalism is therefore readily apparent (March & Olsen, 1989). Institutions are social constructs in which surface appearances like organization charts, titles, and job descriptions are manifestations of the human mind's innate tendency to structure, but they are not always what they seem. Surer knowledge is more likely found in deeper structures—in myth, ritual, symbols, socialization processes, and apocryphal stories, in texts and subtexts. That level of meaning has come under extensive discussion and study in recent years by American institutionalists/neo-institutionalists; and ethnomethodology, so common in anthropology, has become increasingly of use in institutional analysis.

According to White and McSwain (1983), structuralism has several qualities that push it, if not beyond, then to the edge of modernism, and that make it important for the Refounding project and preferable for our purposes to institutionalism as it has been developed in recent years in American literature.

Structuralism places emphasis on understanding the parts in terms of the whole, something sorely needed by both academics and action professionals, who are constantly pressed by the nature of bureaucratic and organizational thinking to focus on the part—the specialized, particularized, differentiated, segmented, and the specified—at the expense of seeing and understanding the whole. Structuralism explicates understanding in terms of transformation rather than of explanation and prediction. Both coherence and openness matter more than a vain search for Truth with a capital T. This depth explanation is based on concrete, detailed analysis, yet it is open-ended and does not define so much as it "sets in motion a continuing dialogue about its topic" (White & McSwain, 1983, p. 19). Because of this openness, "structuralism holds the potential for creating a reflexive analysis that is in itself a form of consciousness raising" (p. 19). It also is liberating because to understand underlying structures in the way fostered by structuralism is to lessen their direct hold on us.[6] It offers a "hope for and a way of believing in, the operation of reason in human affairs"—a transcendent hope and a kind of reason. Not the negative bounded rationality of Simon, which seeks to put human limitations to effective use, but rather a reason that "posits an innate reason" and one that "can lead us to positive guidelines for action" (White & McSwain, 1983, p. 19).

There is another aspect of structuralism that makes it particularly valuable for the purposes of developing the kind of understanding we seek in public administration. Structural analysis moves from the more abstract to the more concrete, and that is both appropriate and valuable for an applied field like public administration. In addition, it is an approach that neither ignores nor objectifies the individual, "rather by presenting a broader picture of the whole and a deeper understanding to the individual, it has the capacity to alter consciousness and to liberate" (White & McSwain, 1983, p. 15). This, we submit, is the kind of approach that is essential if we are to overcome our false consciousness about where public administration fits in the governance process, the polity, and society. The characteristics of structuralism outlined above are compatible with a high modern consciousness; they continue to have great value for those persons who are on the high modern side of the divide from postmodernism.

*Post*structuralism sees language, more precisely text, as ontologically prior to relationships. Post-structuralism seems to follow inevitably from the use of deconstruction as a method of analysis. One goes into the structure of language to reveal the arbitrariness of some words being privileged in ways that shape meaning and consciousness, or to reveal and deny any privileged position to the narrator or the narrative. It is easy to see why deconstructionism has been so popular with various movements such as feminism that seek to liberate, overcome false consciousness, or to alter consciousness. But to deny privilege to one word or signifier is to raise questions about *any* signifier or narrative.

Utilizing deconstruction thus inexorably leads to an ontological threshold that requires passage from high modernism into postmodernist thought. To enter this realm requires a different consciousness. To deconstruct meaning and to deny privilege to any word, to deny the possibility of representing anything, to reject values as having any transtextual qualities, is to confront the reality that putting forth an alternative superordinate word can be nothing more than an arbitrary act of power on the part of the one who has "dethroned" one meaning only to at best "offer" another and at worst "impose" another.

Post-structuralism, which to the uninitiated may seem a nihilistic relativism, has potential to foster genuinely open dialogue and render ideologies impotent. Derrida, for example, recognizes it as a means to maintain the creativeness of philosophy and to generate effects. To the post-structuralists the meaning is not in the text or subtext but in that which emerges as meaning for the reader or each participant in a discussion of them.

Thus on the post-structuralist or postmodern side of the threshold between high modernism and postmodernism, the emphasis definitely shifts from coherence to emergence, from the search for capital T Truth and G Goodness to truth and goodness that are "partial, multiple, and momentary" to be discovered in discourse, experimentation, and relationship and grounded in specific situations and contexts.

We will be quickly beyond our intellectual depth if we try to go any farther than to point up how fundamentally important the threshold between high modern and postmodern is for the Blacksburg project, and more importantly for public administration in general. Our modernist ontology/consciousness/identity with its teleological nature and our location at the crucial nexus between thought and action in the governance process makes it inevitable that we will be the source of action, an instrument of will, or the source of coherence on behalf of some other institution, actor, or group (chief executive, legislature, interest groups, courts) or on behalf of our own institutional self-interest. If we would be something more or different we must assume a new identity/ontology/consciousness. Without such a change we cannot be the source of coherence and emergence, the evoker of the search for shared meaning, the creator of civic space, the catalyst for experimentation and experience that we feel are the essence of a democratic public administration serving a constitutional and democratic republic. If these potential characteristics of a public administration that is an integral part of a "thicker," deeper, or stronger democracy are puzzling or lack full meaning at this point, we hope that will be ameliorated in the chapters that follow.

It is small wonder that those involved in the project are on different sides of the high modern/postmodern threshold. It boggles the mind to think of the problems that the threshold presents to public administration as a field. And yet if we are in fact in a postmodern era, we must confront that threshold if the field is to remain relevant, not to mention being the last best hope of a constitutional and democratic republic.

Institutionalism and Neo-Institutionalism

The original Blacksburg project participants labeled themselves, and were labeled by others, as institutionalists or neo-institutionalists. Some who have interacted with us have clearly misinterpreted what institutionalism means (Fox, 1993).[7] Several of the original project members grow increasingly restive with that label or would no longer be willing to accept it; the same is true and more so among the newer and expanded project membership. But none of us would deny the centrality and the essentiality of institutions in society; nor would any of us deny the need for institutions to produce both coherence and emergence, or that viable institutions can and must encompass both in a state of tension. Some in the project put more emphasis on coherence, which they feel to be more important, and see emergence as a necessary but inevitable twin; others see emergence as that which warrants more attention because they see humans as inevitably tending toward coherence with little coaxing.

We will return to coherence and emergence momentarily, but first we must try to convey something of what we mean by an institution and neo-institutionalism. Confusion is sometimes created by the tendency of some writers to use the term *institution* interchangeably with *organization,* or because we also apply the term to a particular kind of social construct described by Philip Selznick (1957). Selznick spoke of an institution as an organization infused with value. He was making the point that we can think of a social construct as an organization—a collection of persons brought together largely on contractual grounds to achieve a common purpose through cooperation; a social construct in which we think and act organizationally—rationally, contractually, instrumentally, and in defined roles. *Or* we can think of a social construct as an institution in which people place value—upon which they displace hopes and fears—and in which we relate and act institutionally—ritualistically, symbolically, dialogically, by developing shared-meaning language, by socializing new members, engaging in elite selection, and by ostracizing those who violate institutional norms.

Although there is no clear point when an organization becomes an institution or vice versa, we can recognize differences in the two modes of relationship sufficiently to label social constructs as one or the other. Nor is there a clear point of demarcation between Selznick's early and rather limited conception of an institution and Bellah's (Bellah et al., 1985; 1991) or Giddens's (1990) more developed and encompassing conceptions.

Institutions are the major shapers of our individual and collective behavior. We live, work, and die in them. We create them; that is, they are social constructs created both consciously and unconsciously by humans. To a considerable degree, we reify them; and they in turn create and shape us. Giddens refers to this reciprocally constitutive process as "structuration." Institutions create coherence, stability, order and continuity, sanctioned behavior, and enforced meaning—qualities without which society cannot exist, but qualities that in excess lead to societal pathologies and collapse. Although we are less likely to think of them in this way, institutions also create, perhaps to an arguably lesser degree, emergence, change, openness, experimentation, and shared meaning—again, qualities without which society cannot exist, but qualities that in excess lead to societal pathologies and collapse.

The coherence side of institutions is captured by Robert Bellah et al. (1991): "an institution is a pattern of expected action of individuals or groups enforced by social sanctions, both positive and negative . . . [they] are normative patterns embedded in and enforced by laws and mores (informal customs and practices)" (pp. 10-11). The emergence side of institutions is best seen in the writings of Anthony Giddens. His concept of structuration, as he calls it, particularly emphasizes the role of humans in the constituting or creation of structures, and in their dynamism. Giddens (1977) states that to study structuration is to study "the dynamic process whereby structures come into being" and to "attempt to determine the conditions which govern the continuity and dissolution of structures or types of structure" (pp. 120-121).

Giddens is most critical of what he claims is structuralism's view of the " 'reproduction' of social relations and practices 'as a mechanical outcome, rather than as an active constituting process, accomplished by and consisting in, the doings of active subjects' " (Giddens, 1977, pp. 120-121). Structura-tion, he claims, overcomes these lapses of structuralism by showing how "social structures are both constituted by human agency, and yet at the same time are the very medium of this constitution—structures are constituted through action, and—action is constituted structurally" (Giddens, 1976, p. 161).

Given public administration's applied nature, one logical question we confront is the place for human agency in the structuring of meaning. Giddens answers that question by moving post-structuralism away from the text to ordinary "talk." It is not words themselves, frozen as cultural artifacts in text or other media, but rather the "process of *using* words and phrases in contexts of social conduct" (Giddens, 1987, p. 209) that constructs meaning in those contexts. It is not to the signifiers themselves that we look for meaning, but to the "intersection of the production of signifiers with objects and events in the world, focused and organized through the acting individual" (p. 209). This understanding offers hope for a continuing role for the public administrator as an actor in the process of creating meaning for governance.

We feel Giddens's thought is valuable to public administration on both epistemological and ontological grounds because he rejects both positivism *and* subjectivism. He sees social science as "neither a natural science, nor a non-science, but rather as a science with a character of its own that reflects its subject matter" (Bryant & Hart, 1991, p. 10). That resonates with our notions of the special character of public administration as an interdisciplinary applied field. Not only is it a social science (albeit not merely a social science of the positivist paradigm) with a character of its own, but it is inescapably an applied field as well. Trying to ignore this duality has been a source of great confusion and conflict in the study of public administration. No matter how much some students of public administration claim to be involved in studying it simply in order to understand it, they coexist with practitioners who are affected by their "findings" and who will use the findings for their own purposes in a world of action. What Giddens (1977) says of social science is even more true of the applied interdisciplinary field of public administration—"[it] has to accommodate a double hermeneutic—two 'frames of meaning' : (1) 'the meaningful social world as constituted by lay actors,' as well as (2) the second order understandings" (pp. 76-77).

Returning to the inherent duality of institutions (coherence and emergence), we can say that those aspects of institutions that promote coherence are: norms, values, rules, standard operating procedures, programs, management resources that mobilize and apply human and material resources to task accomplishment, mission, vision, rituals, and symbols. Aspects of institutions that promote emergence are: dialogue, relationships, accommodation, processes that bring people into relationships and to shared meaning, experimentation, mission, vision, rituals, and symbols.

No, there is no typing error in the above lines. It is an enduring paradox that some of the same things that promote coherence also have the potential to promote emergence—for example, mission, vision, and values. How can these things we think of as sources of coherence be sources of emergence? Through the ambiguities intrinsic to them and the inevitable differences over them. They emerge as contexts, and events change for members of a social construct who believed they held a measure of shared meaning on those matters, and as they themselves and their perceptions and consciousness change. And how can rituals and symbols promote emergence? When members of a social construct are struggling to find a new equation of shared meaning, the rituals and symbols of their institutional tradition can both legitimate the search for and expedite the acceptance of the new meaning. Much in the way that the symbol of *stare decisis* (How does this case compare to previous cases?) facilitates acceptance of change in the law by the claim that it is in line with previous cases and thereby legitimate. One of the important features of institutions is that they must evoke both coherence *and* emergence to be viable: One is defined by the other; one does not exist without the other; one achieves coherence by constant emergence; and emergence is not achieved without coherence.

Bellah et al. (1991) point out that Americans are intimidated by institutions and fear they will impinge on our individualism as "the classical liberal view [has] held that institutions ought to be as far as possible neutral mechanisms for individuals to use to attain their separate ends" (p. 10). But if there is anything institutions are not, it is "neutral." Our fear of institutions, paradoxically, does not lead us to examine them very closely when we are trying to solve problems. We tend to think of a problem as being with an individual, or if not, then with an organization (p. 11). Bellah et al. (1991) ask what is missing with this American view of society, and answer,

> Just the idea that in our life with other people we are engaged continuously, through words and actions, in creating and re-creating the institutions that make that life possible. This process is never neutral but is always ethical and political, since institutions (even such an intimate institution as the family) live or die by ideas of right and wrong and conceptions of the good. Conversely, while we in concert with others create institutions, they also create us: they educate us and form us—especially through the socially enacted metaphors they give us, metaphors that provide normative interpretations of situations and actions. (pp. 11-12)

It is through institutions that a society is both reproduced and changed from generation to generation. They provide both stability and transformation.

Process

Process is more important in some of the chapters that follow than others, perhaps depending on whether the author is relatively concerned with emergence or coherence as an institutional aspect that each feels best promotes the deepening of democracy in a given context and given institutions. The number of Blacksburg project participants concerned with process is growing, but describing, never mind defining, *process* remains difficult at best.

If there is a key component of process, it must surely be relationship—not of roles, but basically human relations. Dennard (1995) speaks of "recognizing the human other" in the person with whom one is dealing. It is not likely that role behavior will soon disappear from social constructs, or even that such a thing would necessarily be desirable in all instances. But the pathologies and problems of communication and cooperation can be greatly ameliorated and democracy enhanced by relationship—the fundamentally human relationship.

As part of this focus on relationship, we embrace Mary Parker Follett's (1965) concern that both the individuals and groups acknowledge their inter-relationship. One is defined by the other; one is only possible because of the other. Process requires that each accept the interrelatedness of human beings. Weinberg's use of family systems theory captures the special dynamics of this interrelatedness (see Weinberg, Chapter 10, this volume).

At the same time, a process perspective also accepts that solutions are not final but simply experiments on a journey through life. They are tentative, open, and emergent, and process theorists urge individuals to adopt these qualities consciously (see McSwite, Chapter 7; Stivers, Chapter 9, Weinberg, Chapter 10; and Dennard, Chapter 11, all in this volume).

Surely another key component of process must be discourse—not debate nor argument, but discourse—grounded in a shared problem, concern, or goal and made meaningful through its clarity, authenticity, and absence of manipulation. Veterans of the micro-political wars we create in our organizations and between them may arch a quizzical eyebrow at this description of discourse, but meaningful discourse is possible. We simply have done little to foster it. It takes a skill and dedicated effort hard to come by in the organizations we have created and the kind of management we practice in the modernist mode.

The important result of process so far as deepening or strengthening democracy is concerned, is that the networks of relationship among members of public organizations or institutions, between them and members of other agencies, and, most importantly, between public administrators and citizens are potentially transformative for all concerned. This transformative potential and its desirability stem from assumptions and beliefs about the nature of humans and specifically their need to mature, search for significance and meaning in their lives, and to be in community with others as well as developing their individuality.

Even if one were only concerned about task accomplishment, efficiency, and product output, process would still be important. Certainly Follett insisted that it is, and we would not quarrel with the point. But public administration, even though we erred in adopting business values on the assumption that we were merely "managers," is engaged in purposes much broader than business, and it is in these broader purposes that process is so important.

We must of course be able to manage—to accomplish tasks effectively and do so efficiently when feasible. We must, in other words, be instrumental. But we are part of a governance process—a democratic governance process—and that requires us to be self-consciously constitutive (Cook, 1992). By the way we relate to one another and to citizens as we serve them, individually and collectively, we take part with them in constituting ourselves as individuals and as a nation. We are participating in the cocreation of the kinds of persons we are and the kind of nation we are. Relationship thus becomes one of the key concepts in deepening and strengthening democracy and the legitimacy of public administration in the difficult and perilous times our constitutional republic now faces.

A Final Word . . .

Overall, this book will elucidate a theme we believe to be of supreme importance to public administration in the postmodern era: the necessity for a constructive dynamism in key institutions like public administration between forces of coherence and stability on the one hand and, on the other, the forces of emergence and change. The literature of public administration is curiously dichotomous on such matters; for example, the individual versus the organization, authority versus participation, stability versus change. Scholars either excoriate forces of stability and extol the virtues of change or vice versa. Few have dealt with these forces as necessarily and ineluctably related.

But just as the individual cannot achieve identity and fulfillment without reference to the collective or group, change is defined by, and must be grounded in, coherence and stability. Evolving, maturing humans do not seek either change or stability; they seek *both* change *and* stability. An effective public administration must strike a constructive balance between these two primal forces in human societies—act as a bridge between them—so that our democracy can evolve and mature. We feel that the chapters in this volume effectively make that point.

Notes

1. These words were first written in the fall of 1994. Most political analyses since then has tended to confirm our analysis. See especially a six-part series called the "Politics of Mistrust" published in the *Washington Post* between January 28 and February 4, 1996.

2. Senator Ernest Hollins, a Democrat from South Carolina, made this widely reported remark on the floor of the Senate.

3. Some may argue that we have presented a romantic and incomplete view of Anti-Federalist thinking here. It is, we think, no more romantic a view than is common in today's political dialogue. It could be pointed out, and we would agree, that the Anti-Federalists did not so much have a countervailing vision of national government to contrast to the vision of the Federalists, as they had a concern about the effects of *any* national government on the social and political communities of the states and localities. We want to acknowledge the fact that the Anti-Federalists significantly influenced the development of the Constitution, particularly in their successful battle

for a Bill of Rights. But more important, it seems to us, is the fact that echoes of their voices, although often ignored or marginalized, have persisted in reminding us of the necessity of meaningful dialogue and community if a democratic society is to prevail.

4. Dwight Waldo said this in a monograph published by the Comparative Administration Group.

5. For those unfamiliar with Sisyphus, he was condemned by the gods to roll a huge rock up a hill—only to watch it roll down again—for eternity. One of my puckish colleagues has proposed that he be made the "patron saint" of public administration.

6. The type of professionalism we feel must undergird a refounded public administration practice would need to be based on reflexivity as well as praxis. Its practitioners must be reflexive by self-consciously interacting with a "higher authority." The unconscious may be one possibility, but our first thoughts are of the Constitution and the values suggested in it. Through self-conscious reflexing with its very general values and the struggle to give them contextual and situational meaning, the professional not only discovers "the right thing to do," but also grows and discovers self and meaning for his or her life.

The ability to grow in maturity and self-awareness is extremely important for public administrators. Although John Rohr never uses the phrase *professional reflexivity,* it is essentially what he prescribes in *Ethics for Bureaucrats* (1989) and what Green, Keller, and Wamsley (1993) imply in their "constitutive professionalism."

7. Charles Fox (1993) offers an amusing if egregious example of how we have been misunderstood. Fox equates neo-institutionalism with the much maligned institutionalism of pre-behavioralist political science when scholars allegedly tried to understand the politics of a country just by reading its constitution. (My behavioral professors always told me about such antediluvian people, but I have never met one). In any event, I have not heard this kind of institutionalism mentioned since my days as an undergraduate long ago and far away in another galaxy, and certainly don't intend to advocate it now.

Fox (1993) suggests that "it leads the mind along well worn paths, amongst the monuments and museums of official Washington D.C.," and "focuses attention on such institutional categories as powers of the presidency, where do tax bills originate, who makes war, who confirms treaties"—"or buildings with brass name plates" (pp. 57-58). We had something else in mind, although Fox's graphic projections are admittedly more amusing.

■ References

Appleby, P. H. (1949). *Big democracy.* New York: Knopf.

Axelrod, D. (1988). *Budgeting for modern government.* New York: St. Martin's.

Barr, S., & Kamen, A. (1993, January 11). Transition momentum bogs down at sub-cabinet level. *Washington Post,* p. A4.

Beach, J. C., Carter, E. D., Dede, M. J., Goodsell, C. T., Guignard, R. M., Haraway, W. M., Morgan, B. N., Murthi, M., & Sweet, V. K. (in press). State administration and the founding fathers in the critical period. *Administration & Society.*

Bellah, R. N., Madsen, R., Sullivan, W. M., Swidler, A., & Tipton, S. M. (1985). *Habits of the heart: Individualism and commitment in American life.* Berkeley: University of California Press.

Bellah, R. N., Madsen, R., Sullivan, W. M., Swidler, A., & Tipton, S. M. (1991). *The good society.* New York: Knopf.

Bryant, G. A., & Hart, D. (Eds.). (1991). *Giddens' theory of structuration: A critical appreciation.* New York: Routledge & Kegan Paul.

Burrell, G., & Morgan, G. (1979). *Sociological paradigms and organizational analysis: Elements of the sociology of corporate life.* London: Heinemann.

Caldwell, L. K. (1943). Thomas Jefferson and public administration. In C. E. Hawley & R. G. Weintraub (Eds.), *Administrative questions and political answers* (pp. 7-15). New York: Van Nostrand.

Caldwell, L. K. (1944). Alexander Hamilton: Advocate of executive leadership. In C. E. Hawley & R. G. Weintraub, *Administrative questions and political answers* (pp. 16-22). New York: Van Nostrand.

Chandler, R. C. (Ed.). (1987). *A centennial history of the American administrative state.* New York: Macmillan.

Cook, B. J. (1992). Administration in constitutive perspective. *Administration & Society, 23*(4), 403-429.

Croly, H. D. (1914). *The promise of American life.* New York: Macmillan.

Dennard, L. (1995). Neo-Darwinism and Simon's bureaucratic antihero. *Administration & Society, 26*(4), 464-487.

Douglas, M. (1986). *How institutions think.* Syracuse, NY: Syracuse University Press.

Dudley, L., & Wamsley, G. L. (in press). Organizational design and government reorganization: Sixty years and we "still don't get it." *International Journal of Public Administration.*

Follett, M. P. (1965). *The new state: Group organization the solution of popular government.* Gloucester, MA: Peter Smith.

Fox, C. J. (1993). Alternatives to orthodoxy: Constitutionalism, communitarianism, and discourse. *Administrative Theory and Praxis, 15*(2), 52-70.

Giddens, A. (1976). *New rules of sociological method.* London: Hutchinson.

Giddens, A. (1977). *Studies in social and political theory.* New York: Basic Books.

Giddens, A. (1987). Structuralism, post-structuralism, and the production of culture. In A. Giddens & J. H. Turner (Eds.), *Social theory today* (pp. 195-223). Stanford, CA: Stanford University Press.

Giddens, A. (1990). *The consequences of modernity.* Stanford, CA: Stanford University Press.

Gladden, E. N. (1972). *A history of public administration.* London: Cass.

Goodsell, C. T. (1984). The Grace Commission: Seeking efficiency for the whole people? *Public Administration Review, 44*(3), 196-204.

Green, R. T. (1987). *Oracle at Weehawken: Alexander Hamilton and development of the administrative state.* Unpublished doctoral dissertation, Virginia Polytechnic Institute and State University, Blacksburg.

Green, R. T., Keller, L. F., & Wamsley, G. L. (1993). Reconstituting a profession for American public administration. *Public Administration Review, 53*(6), 516-524.

Gulick, L. (1937). Notes on the theory of organization. In J. M. Shafritz & A. C. Hyde (Eds.), *Classics of public administration* (pp. 80-89). Pacific Grove, CA: Brooks/Cole.

Gulick, L., & Urwick, L. (1937). *Papers on the science of administration.* New York: Institute of Public Administration.

Haber, S. (1964). *Efficiency and uplift.* Chicago: University of Chicago Press.

Hill, L. B. (Ed.). (1992). *The state of public bureaucracy.* Armonk, NY: M. E. Sharpe.

Huntington, S. P. (1957). *The soldier and the state: The theory and politics of civil-military relations.* Cambridge, MA: Belknap.

Long, N. E. (1949). Power and administration. In J. M. Shafritz & A. C. Hyde (Eds.), *Classics of public administration* (pp. 179-187). Pacific Grove, CA: Brooks/Cole.

Lowi, T. J. (1979). *The end of liberalism: The second republic of the U.S.* (2nd ed.). New York: Norton.

Luttwak, E. N. (1994, November 27). Will success spoil America? Why the polls don't get our real crisis of values. *Washington Post,* pp. C1, C4.

March, J. G., & Olsen, J. P. (1989). *Rediscovering institutions: The organizational basis of politics.* New York: Free Press.

Marshall, G. S. (1994). *Public administration in a time of fractured meaning: Beyond the legacy of Herbert Simon.* Unpublished doctoral dissertation, Virginia Polytechnic Institute and State University, Blacksburg.

Marshall, G. S., & White, O. F. (1989, April). *The Blacksburg Manifesto and the postmodern debate: Public administration in a time without a name.* Paper presented at the Public Administration Theory Symposium of the National Conference of the American Society for Public Administration, Miami, FL.

Morrow, L. (1991, August 12). A nation of finger-pointers. *Time,* pp. 14-15.

Mosher, F. C. (1968). *Democracy and the public service.* New York: Oxford University Press.

Nigro, L. G., & Richardson, W. D. (1987). Self-interest properly understood: The American character and public administration. *Administration & Society, 19*(2), 157-177.

Osborne, D., & Gaebler, T. (1992). *Reinventing government: How the entrepreneurial spirit is transforming the public sector.* Reading, MA: Addison-Wesley.

Ostrom, V. (1974). *The intellectual crisis in American public administration* (rev. ed.). University: University of Alabama Press.

Redford, Emmette S. (1969). *Democracy in the administrative state.* New York: Oxford University Press.

Reich, R. (1991, February). The REAL Economy. *The Atlantic,* pp. 35-52.

Richardson, W. D., & Nigro, L. G. (1987). Administrative ethics and founding thought: Constitutional correctives, honor, and education. *Public Administration Review,* 367-376.

Rohr, J. A. (1986). *To run a constitution: The legitimacy of the administrative state.* Lawrence: University Press of Kansas.

Rohr, J. A. (1978). *Ethics for bureaucrats.* New York: Marcel Dekker.

Rosenau, P. M. (1992). *Post-modernism and the social sciences: Insights, inroads, and intrusions.* Princeton, NJ: Princeton University Press.

Selznick, P. (1957). *Leadership in administration.* New York: Harper & Row.

Simon, H. A. (1957). *Administrative behavior: A study of decision-making processes in administrative organization* (2nd ed.). New York: Free Press.

Shafritz (1988) in G. S. Marshall (1994), *Public administration in a time of fractured meaning: Beyond the legacy of Herbert Simon.* Unpublished dissertation, Virginia Polytechnic Institute and State University, Blacksburg.

Stillman, R. J. (1984). The changing patterns of public administration theory in America. In R. J. Stillman, *Public administration: Concepts and cases* (3rd ed., pp. 5-24). New York: Houghton Mifflin.

Stouffer, S., Lumsdaine, A. A., Lumsdaine, M. H., Williams, R. Jr., Brewster Smith, M., Janis, I. L., Star, S., & Cottrell, L., Jr. (1949). *The American soldier* (2 vols.). Princeton, NJ: Princeton University Press.

Thurow, L. C. (1980). *The zero-sum society: Distribution and the possibilities for economic change.* New York: Basic Books.

Timney Bailey, M., & Mayer, R. T. (1992). Public management in an interconnected world: Essays in the Minnowbrook tradition. New York: Greenwood.

Tocqueville, A. de. (1990). *Democracy in America.* New York: Vintage.

Urban, M. E. (1982). *The ideology of administration: American and Soviet cases.* Albany: State University of New York Press.

Waldo, D. (1984). *The administrative state: A study of the political theory of American public administration* (2nd ed.). New York: Holmes & Meier.

Wamsley, G. L., Bacher, R. N., Goodsell, C. T., Kronenberg, P. S., Rohr, J. A., Stivers, C. M., White, O. F., & Wolf, J. F. (1990). *Refounding public administration.* Newbury Park, CA: Sage.

White, O. F., & McSwain, C. (1983, April). *A structuralist approach to organizational action.* Paper presented at the Annual Conference of the American Society for Public Administration, New York City.

White, O. F., & McSwain, C. (1990). The Phoenix project: Raising public administration from the ashes of the past. In H. Kass & B. Catron (Eds.), *Images and identities in public administration* (pp. 23-59). Newbury Park, CA: Sage.

White, O. F., & McSwain, C. (in press). *The legitimacy issue in American public administration: A discourse analysis.* Thousand Oaks, CA: Sage.

1

On Governance
and Reinventing Government

RICHARD T. GREEN
LAWRENCE HUBBELL
University of Wyoming

The Blacksburg Manifesto, circulated originally in the early 1980s, argued that the American public administration needed refounding in order to acquire legitimacy and efficacy. The principles and processes of administration and the science of management that have emerged during this century provide an inadequate foundation. The authors of the Manifesto called for a reconceptualization of public administration as a matter of "governance" (Wamsley et al., 1990).

Governance means "administering in a political context" and directing competence toward the "broadest possible public interest." This includes competence in sustaining "the agency perspective" and "the constitutional governance process" (Wamsley et al., 1990, p. 39). The agency perspective alludes to the institutional insight, policy-relevant knowledge, and authority of subordinate agencies in our constitutional system. The fact of their subordinacy conditions and restrains their authority, and yet they remain quasi-autonomous actors, in large part because of constitutionally divided masters. They are constitutional representatives in their own right as a result of this design (see Rohr, 1986, chap. 4). In this role, they share with their masters the obligation to uphold the integrity and balance of the constitutional system through all its policy formulation and implementation phases (Burke, 1986; Rohr, 1986).

Administering in a political context requires multifaceted "agential" leadership. The facets include (a) the ability to sustain dialogue among competing interpretations of our regime values, and to balance their inherent tensions within and among diverse policy contexts (Rohr, 1989); (b) steward-ship or trusteeship, which includes notions of representation and standing in for the people on decisions of public interest (Goodsell, 1990; Morgan & Kass, 1989; Wamsley, 1990); (c) conservatorship, which requires an articulate sense of institutional preservation and performance (Burke, 1986; Selznick, 1957, 1992; Terry, 1995); (d) a restraining or tempering influence over public opinion for the sake of preserving long-term as well as short-term public interests (Wamsley in Wamsley et al., 1990, p. 38); (e) protection of our fundamental rights, and maintenance of rule by law (Green, 1992; Rohr, 1986; Storing, 1981); (f) educators and nurturers of citizen roles in our democratic governing process (McSwain, 1985; Stivers, 1990); and (g) constitutiveness, which involves presenting (or perhaps confronting) citizens with choices that will define their character as a common people (Cook, 1992). The authors of the Manifesto want to refocus the dialogue within and beyond the public administration community around these basic characteristics of governance.

The obligations and competencies inherent to American governance make public administration a dramatically different endeavor from its private-sector counterpart. Yet the endeavor remains largely unappreciated and misunder-stood in public life. Much of our political speech still derides and degrades the public administration as a source of American infirmity. The public mind remains cynical about its role.

With the advent of the 1990s, however, public discussion seemed to be muting this cynicism somewhat. The Clinton administration, at least initially, engendered some new optimism about the potential contributions of govern-ment to society. It adopted a seemingly fresh approach, promising to "reinvent government" as a dynamic and productive force for America. The reinvention theme persists in the Clinton administration, and has received added emphasis by the new Republican Congress. In this chapter we analyze the implications of the "reinventing government" movement in light of the concern for re-founding public administration as governance.

▬ Reinventing Government

Talk of reinventing government abounds in the halls of national, state, and local administrations. As Charles Goodsell (1993) indicates, David Osborne and Ted Gaebler's (1992) best-selling book on the subject "is the talk of the town in Washington; [and] must reading for state and local executives" (p. 85). The Clinton administration, with Osborne and Gaebler's assistance, quickly produced the "Gore Report" (Office of the Vice President, 1993) in an attempt to institutionalize reinvention principles in the federal government. State and local officials trumpet them in the Winter Commission Report (1993) and in town meetings and campaigns (Cox, 1994). It is all the rage.

The popularity of this phenomenon can be attributed to many causes, not the least of which is good timing. Osborne and Gaebler's book was published immediately prior to the beginning of a new national administration that promised great changes and embraced reinvention principles as an integral part of their new policies. In addition, the book synthesizes a variety of ideas, concerns, and grassroots initiatives that had just begun to capture national attention. Furthermore, Osborne and Gaebler's approach introduces a refreshing change in attitude toward public officials. They argue that public officials can and do manage as effectively as their private-sector counterparts. They offer new hope to citizens and officials alike that governments can serve vital and constructive roles in American society.

The authors also offer solutions to growing and seemingly intractable crises in public funding. Tax revolts and failed "new federalism" policies have left all levels of government in difficult financial straits. Osborne and Gaebler promise that entrepreneurial efficiency and creativity fostered by reinvention principles will do much to resolve these difficulties.

Small wonder, then, that *Reinventing Government* should catch on as it has. Initially, public servants at all levels of government were encouraged that they would be empowered to contribute meaningfully to needed reforms. Since the Carter administration they have lived under a dark cloud of suspicion and accusation that they were "part of the problem," rather than worthy contributors to public life. Reinvention seemed like good news.

The good news has faded quickly, however, due to partisan wrangling and the ascendence of government-bashing conservatives in Congress. The public administration is once again the target, blamed by both parties for the ills of the country. The Clinton administration changed its approach even before Republicans took over Congress, using the public administration as a convenient excuse for many of its troubles. Reinvention has turned quickly from a method of reinvigoration of the public administration to a handy but dispiriting method of partisan attack.

Beyond this, the reinvention fad poses other troubling dilemmas that public officials will be forced to confront sooner or later. It is our hope that they confront them now and not later, because some of the problems we see could get out of hand rather quickly. Analysis of these dilemmas will proceed from the refounding perspective offered by Wamsley et al. (1990) and extended in this volume.

Reinvention and Governance

Osborne and Gaebler (1992) assert that they address an essentially new form of governance, pioneered by managers and academics living under intense pressure to perform effectively/with reduced resources. Necessity is the mother of invention, and Osborne and Gaebler brought all the innovation together in one handy resource book.[1] In the process, they presented an artful blending of the philosophies and insight of Peter Drucker, Tom Peters, James Q. Wilson, W. Edwards Deming, E. S. Savas, and a host of public choice theorists.

Their book is organized around 10 principles upon which their new model of governance is founded. Briefly, these principles involve (1) steering others rather than rowing; (2) empowering customers rather than serving them; (3) injecting competition into service delivery; (4) organizing by mission rather than by rules; (5) funding results, not inputs; (6) intense customer orientation; (7) encouraging entrepreneurial earning rather than bureaucratic spending; (8) focusing on prevention rather than cure; (9) decentralizing organizations and fostering teamwork; and (10) leveraging change through market-based incentives.

Osborne and Gaebler (1992) appropriately call their new model "entrepreneurial government." Borrowing from Jean Baptiste Say, they define *entrepreneur* broadly as anyone who "uses resources in new ways to maximize productivity and effectiveness" (p. xix). All public officials can do this, the authors believe, if the systems they work in are structured to encourage it. Accordingly, Osborne and Gaebler focus not on *what* governments do, but on *"how they operate."* "The central failure of government today is one of means, not ends" (p. xxi).

The authors argue that the development of our society around high-tech communications and knowledge-based professions during this century has created the capacity for radical improvement in the means of organizing and producing services. The increase in capacity is so great that our established ways of running governments are now outmoded and challenged by emerging paradigms that will enable us to make effective use of that capacity. Osborne and Gaebler claim to offer us a coherent, alternative paradigm upon which to reform our governments.[2]

We find this claim to a new paradigm somewhat amazing and ironic. Throughout their book, Osborne and Gaebler sprinkle little proverbs and anecdotes to show how they have departed from the overreactive Progressive and New Deal Era reformers with a new entrepreneurial model. Though some important differences exist in their approach, the similarities to these earlier eras are striking.

Osborne and Gaebler would have us believe that we face only two choices of how to organize government. On the one hand, we can have government that is wooden, rules-based, and inherited from earlier eras that focused too much on protection against patronage abuse and corruption. This is the "bureaucratic" option. On the other hand, they advocate a mission-driven, performance-oriented government that is attuned to the needs of its "customers." "Entrepreneurial government" focuses our attention more on getting the job done than on protecting against abuse. This translates into more flexible managerial powers to put people and processes where needed to get results. Results, after all, constitute an important form of accountability in their own right. All of this makes tremendous sense until one looks more carefully at these older eras.

Virtually every history or biography that can be found portrays these eras as preoccupied with making governments more efficient and effective (see Eisenach, 1994; Haber, 1964; Hays, 1975; Karl, 1983; Link, 1954; Noble, 1970; Orloff, 1988; Quandt, 1970; Rohr, 1986; Rosenberg, 1982; Skowronek, 1982; Wiebe, 1962, 1967; Zinn, 1966). Leaders of the Progressive Era, for example, heralded the successes of the "business model" and called for its emulation in government (see Hays, 1964, 1975; Orloff, 1988; Rosenberg, 1982; Taylor, 1934; Trachtenberg, 1982; Wiebe, 1962; Wilson, 1887; Zunz, 1990). The council-manager form for local governments was derived from that model and represents the pinnacle of Progressive organizational designs for effectiveness (see Boyer, 1978; Bromage, 1936; Childs, 1952; Dewitt, 1915; East, 1965; Eisenach, 1994; Hays, 1964; Howe, 1905; Keller, 1989). Pragmatism and the can-do, engineering mentality dominated the political and social culture of the nation. Results-oriented administrative theorists and practitioners wrought tremendous changes in governance worldwide, all in the name of efficiency and effectiveness.

The public identity of these eras centered around public spirited professions that espoused scientific knowledge and technical innovation. Reformers called for more reliance on these experts throughout government (Eisenach, 1994; Skowronek, 1982; Wiebe, 1967).

Many Progressive and New Deal leaders also asserted principles that are essentially identical to many of those offered by Osborne and Gaebler. For example, Osborne and Gaebler's steering versus rowing analogy is basically a restatement of the Progressive Era's politics/administration dichotomy. Those who make policy are steering, whereas those who implement policy are rowing. A strong resemblance also exists between Woodrow Wilson's (1887) assertion that the task of his generation was to learn how to run a constitution, and Osborne and Gaebler's penchant for *how* governments do things rather than *what* they do.

In addition, some Progressive and New Deal Era reforms reflected demands for empowerment of the average citizen and immigrant. Initiative and referendum, pluralist political theory, party reforms, legal reforms, Constitutional amendments, and several grassroots regulatory movements contributed to this effort. Nor can one ignore the emphasis during these periods on new missions, strategic planning, systems analysis (during World War II), rapid results, and enterprising government. World War I, the Great Depression, and World War II compelled innovation, planning, and entrepreneurialism.[3] Rapid and radical changes occurred throughout those decades.

In these respects, Osborne and Gaebler's work merely extends the paradigm of the Progressives and New Dealers. The authors even exhibit much of the moralistic tone of the Progressives, portraying their entrepreneurial reforms as the embodiment of goodness and the old bureaucratic ways as the evil to be overcome.[4]

Nevertheless, Osborne and Gaebler's work also falls far short of the comprehensive vision and agendas of these earlier reformers. The Progressives, at least, included in their reformist vision new notions of citizenship, common good, and institutional legitimacy in public life. Osborne and Gaebler embrace a very narrow and meager reform agenda by comparison. They meld aspects of managerial progressivism with principles of privatization and public choice that run absolutely counter to Progressive public philosophy (Eisenach, 1994; Moe, 1994).[5]

From our standpoint these legacies pose serious problems for governance in contemporary political society.

Osborne and Gaebler claim to offer effective remedies for our ills with their entrepreneurial form of governance. We argue that they neglect vital dimensions of governance. Given all the excitement over their model, this neglect may bring some results they never intended. They affect the following basic concerns of American governance: institutional relations in a system of separate powers, rule by law, institutional stability and integrity, distributive impacts, and maintenance of a viable political community.

Institutional Relations and Separation of Powers

Over the past 50 years or so, students of organization and government have fought to overcome the myth of the politics/administration dichotomy. It is a stubborn dichotomy, born of the Progressives, that provides an expedient political justification for management by neutral experts. The field of public administration discovered very quickly that such justification is bankrupt in practice because administration and policy operate as a seamless whole. Experts make policy, or steer while they row, even at street levels (see Lipsky, 1980). Nevertheless, it remains a convincing dodge used by a variety of actors. It is still *politically* acceptable and expedient for administrators to shift responsibility upstairs to elected officials. It also provides an excuse for political executives to expand their patronage. Over the long run, however, it erodes the public administration's effectiveness and legitimacy. It is a sham justification for avoiding responsibility for thinking and arguing about how ends and means relate in the art of governance. Ironically, Osborne and Gaebler have given the myth renewed vigor just when it seemed to be receding.

In conjunction with this problem, David Rosenbloom (1993, pp. 503-507) makes an important point: Calls for administrative reform "inevitably involve issues of the separation of powers and the distribution of burdens and benefits in the polity." He goes on to suggest, almost plaintively, that "surely the day is long past when proponents of change can act as if there are no tradeoffs, collective action problems, or fundamental disagreements over the means and ends of government." Unfortunately, Osborne and Gaebler prove him wrong. They blissfully ignore such matters.

They apparently assume, for example, that Congress, state legislatures, and local councils and boards will eventually see the light and simply ratify and delegate to managers the various techniques of financial flexibility they describe throughout their text. Nowhere do they mention the perennial political battles fought among legislators, executives, and courts over such powers. Nowhere do they acknowledge that legislative bodies are naturally jealous of such fiscal power—that they were designed to be so in order to preserve a prudent balance of powers. They seem oblivious, for example, to the interbranch battles fought over the Budget and Accounting Act of 1921, and then over subsequent introductions of more executive-oriented performance budgeting, PPBS, MBO, and ZBB at all levels of government. Nor do they acknowledge the amazingly diverse hybrids of budgeting processes that have emerged as compromises (Axelrod, 1989; LeLoup, 1988; Wildavsky, 1988).

A recent article in *Governing* gives telling evidence of Osborne and Gaebler's shortsightedness on such matters. Rob Gurwitt (1994, p. 40) details the political backlash that has occurred in the wake of Gaebler's entrepreneurial leadership as city manager of Visalia, California. "The balance of power has shifted" from the city manager's office to what is "now a very strong council."[6]

According to Gurwitt's interviewees, the entrepreneurialism got out of hand. Professional managers and staff were juggling too many projects and task forces, some of which (and one in particular) failed miserably and expensively. In the aftermath, citizens discovered that some of these entrepreneurial managers may have engaged unaccountably in underhanded dealings with a developer to secure projects.

Furthermore, many of the city's staff became increasingly inaccessible to the public. They were constantly in task force meetings and other entrepreneurial activities that interfered with access. The current city manager (and former police chief), Ray Forsyth, said "we crossed the line to becoming a self-serving organization. We became too wrapped up in what we wanted and not what the community wanted" (Gurwitt, 1994, p. 40). The citizens now want "frugal" and stable "delivery of basic services," and they have put new members on the city council to guarantee this with very traditional political and budgetary controls, including a line-item budget!

Osborne and Gaebler clearly fail to assess their prescriptions in terms of the roles of the three branches in administration. Their book reads as though legislative bodies and courts hardly matter at all in what they propose (Moe, 1994, p. 115). They fail to admit that each branch is predisposed to steer and row using different guides. They talk as if a single or unified rational actor controls one rudder, when in fact there are many rudders, and many pilots contending for control over each rudder. Battles among the branches form the stuff of constitutional and administrative politics. These battles remind us that all three branches participate in administration, and that decisions about means and ends are always connected and always institutionally mediated.

Furthermore, decisions are usually mediated through the subordinate public administration, where their powers are mixed into policy subsystems and unique programmatic blends (Keller, 1984; Miller, 1994; Wamsley, 1984, 1985; Wamsley & Zald, 1973). Osborne and Gaebler ignore these very important, administratively diverse entities and how they might be affected by a standard, market-based approach. They also overlook the fact that program administrators must often choose sides in the battles among the branches, not only for their own good, but for the purpose of preserving or restoring a rough balance of powers among the branches (Rohr, 1986).[7] Osborne and Gaebler's prescriptions may erode the complex and stable relations required between the public administration and the superior branches to preserve this balance (Fisher, 1975; Miller, 1994).

Throughout their book, Osborne and Gaebler speak of the virtues of decentralization and the empowerment of low-level public officials, who need flexibility and power to anticipate and deal with problems that confront them. At the same time, the authors call for abandonment of civil service restrictions on agency and program heads so they can move and remove employees as needed to respond effectively to market-styled incentives. Obvious problems exist here in determining how much and what kinds of power to delegate among these various levels within an agency. Freedom from civil service rules at the program-head level may mean compromising significant powers of street-level officials because they may be moved or removed at will.

The only way this problem could be minimized is if all members of an agency agreed on a single definition of their values, missions, problems, and means. As unlikely as that may be, we can assume for a moment that an agency has achieved such consensus. That means little regarding the agency's relationship to other members of the policy subsystem within which it operates. These include individual legislators and whole committees, powerful interest groups, rival agencies, the courts, executive offices, other levels of government, the press, and possibly many others. These actors often hold differing interpretations of the values, missions, and problems that apply to the agency. They do not hesitate to influence and manipulate the agencies' missions and processes to obtain the outcomes they desire (Keller, 1984; Miller, 1994; Wamsley, 1984).

More significantly, as power is delegated to lower levels, the ability of these external actors to interfere inappropriately increases dramatically. The empowerment of lower-level officials can never be sufficient to ward off completely the designs and intrigues of higher-level officials or of powerful interest groups. Osborne and Gaebler fail to account for this play of power, especially between agencies and their electoral superiors.[8] They disregard the long-standing tension that exists in our governments between responsiveness to elected superiors and quasi-autonomous professional judgment.

Unfortunately, Osborne and Gaebler's persuasive calls for flexibility with personnel come at the same time Congress has significantly relaxed Hatch Act restrictions on electoral political activity for many civil servants. This combination of changes in the relations among Congress, Executive, and the Public Administration amounts to a new license to engage in extensive partisan patronage practices (cf. Pearson & Castle, 1993, pp. 511-525). Rather than empowering professionals, these changes could make them dupes for partisan agendas in both branches.

Some features of the Gore Report (Office of the Vice President, 1993), lend credibility to our argument. Following reinvention principles, the report calls for elimination of many middle-management positions responsible for various forms of oversight, support, and protection. Then it calls for empowerment of lower-level officials, while exempting the Senior Executive Service (SES) political appointees from any cuts or restrictions. It is well known that the SES has been significantly politicized ever since its inception. If the Gore Report recommendations are implemented, these appointees and their superiors will be able to exert tremendous new power over low-level bureaucrats.[9] Competition will then arise between Congress and the executive for patronage fiefdoms within the bureaucracy as a way of preserving each branch's constitutional turf. Such competition could generate forms of corruption and abuse on a scale not seen since before the Progressive era. Competition is *not* always good!

These dynamics cannot be overlooked in calls for reform. Managerial flexibility and empowerment translate just as easily into patronage abuse as into organizational effectiveness. On this point Osborne and Gaebler's naïveté seems incredible. As James Fallows (1992) indicates, their book

> offers a view of government that defines away some of our largest, most difficult problems. The book's working assumption is that the American public, through its government, always means to do the right thing, and that it's held back only by specific failures and barriers—faulty information, bad incentives. . . . An implied faux optimism runs throughout the book: If only we knew all the facts, we'd never make these foolish mistakes. (p. 121)

Our system was designed, of course, in anticipation of much darker human motives and failings. It divides and checks powers in order to mute the effects of wrongheaded public opinion conveyed through directly elected officials, and simultaneously to provide diverse and stable sources of insight for public decisions. The diverse and stable sources could be secured through the 22 different methods of selection to public office (only 1 of which is direct election) provided in the Constitution (Rohr, 1986; Wamsley et al., 1990, chap. 2). Public agencies today rely on many of these selection methods, especially in the middle ranks, to secure the balance between electoral responsiveness and professional judgment (cf. Staats, 1988; Volcker, 1989). Reinvention principles, if followed, will likely destroy this balance—to our peril.

Rule by Law

American governance entails rule by law. The public administration shares a substantial role in this constitutional principle. The administrative process can turn it into a dead letter or give it life as the law in action. To rule by law means, at the very least, to conform one's policies and decisions to articulable standards that suffuse and transcend one's position. An official's subjective (or interpretive) convictions about appropriate policy must therefore agree persuasively with externally derived and protected legal standards, or be set aside.

Furthermore, legal standards typically include a mix of substantive values and procedural guides. Rule by law, as a matter of prudence, attends as much to means as to ends. This is born of the centuries-old realization that results by any means may be more noxious to a political community than no results at all.

In this context, Osborne and Gaebler's (1992) principles of "organizing by mission rather than by rules," and "funding results, not inputs" ought to make public officials very nervous, at the least. As translated into the Gore Report (Office of the Vice President, 1993), these principles amount to a "profound misunderstanding of the role of law in the administration of the executive branch." The report "suggests to the President on down to the line manager that culpable laws and regulations should be either ignored or not enforced with vigor" (Moe, 1994, p. 115).

This suggestion follows a litany of similar abuses under recent presidencies that have undermined public confidence in our governments far more than any bureaucratic bungling or stagnation. Presidential claims of public mandates for making changes too often lead to neglect and abrogation of existing laws. Perverting rule by law in this way induces tremendous public cynicism. Osborne and Gaebler seem unaware that their principles may encourage such abuse and cause such damage to the public psyche.

We do not mean to imply that missions and flexibility have no place in American governance. They certainly do. Their place, however, must be determined through collaboratively derived agreements (among the branches and agencies) that have the force and effect of law rather than through unilateral will. Many agencies have adopted missions through this process, and enjoy substantial flexibility for carrying them out. Yet Osborne and Gaebler write as though much of the collaborative process should simply be abandoned in favor of immediate results. The outcome transforms rule by law into a hollow fiction.

Another reinvention principle, "empowering customers rather than serving them," also presents a substantial threat to rule by law. Theodore Lowi's

(1979) classic work on interest group liberalism describes how many regulatory and service agencies have already delegated much of their power to the clientele they regulate and serve. These empowered "customers" effectively dictate much of our public policy, and with almost no accountability whatsoever. Lowi aptly describes the result as "policy without law."

Osborne and Gaebler neglect to tell us that some customers may be more powerful than others, and can therefore coopt agencies and policies for their own interests. The authors never admit that perhaps some customers should have their powers reduced or compromised to enable agency pursuit of the broadest possible public interest.

Institutional Stability and Integrity

Great danger lies in Osborne and Gaebler's lack of attention to institutional stability and integrity. Their fascination with market-driven incentives and structure for public agencies necessitates managerial and organizational flexibility, to which they give high praise. For example, in their discussion of market-based reforms in education they write enthusiastically about how schools that do not sufficiently please their constituents will simply shut down due to lack of enrollments. School administrators, therefore, require enough flexibility to adapt their schools to market demands. But flexibility of this sort is always double-edged.

First, there arises the problem of uncertainty, ambiguity, and dissension about what the constituents want. Osborne and Gaebler assume constituents know what they want and that significant consensus exists about it. But that simply isn't true in most cases, either among producers or consumers in this era of contentiousness over school curricula.

Littleton, Colorado, has been embroiled over this matter. Some parents want a traditional "back to basics" curriculum; others want a new "performance testing" approach; and yet many others want variations, or simply don't know what to think about it at all ("School Wars," 1993). As one might expect, those who favor one approach do not want flexibility, unless of course we're talking about flexibility *within* the premises of their favored approach. What's a responsive manager to do?

One answer is to choose sides. Another would be to make an independent judgment. Another might be to create schools for each approach. However, no matter which course an administrator thinks may be right, the "market" he or she now depends on may determine otherwise. In that case administrators, staff, and teachers are unemployed; a neighborhood loses its school; and the city has to deal with vacant structures, not to mention haphazardly erected facilities elsewhere. Some swapping of existing facilities may occur, but that is often problematic in terms of lease/profit arrangements, transportation routes, and possible conflicts between the curriculum philosophy and the building's structure or scale. The inevitable result is that community and professional infrastructures are rapidly gutted, with much the same impact as when a large business firm decides to move elsewhere.

Furthermore, it is quite conceivable that the chief administrator and teachers in this scenario reach a wise decision in terms of the value of one curriculum over another, while the "market" determines otherwise. Of course, the converse may also be true. In either case, we must still confront the issue of where the authority (or "flexibility") to decide these matters should lay— with a politicized majority, with a minority, with a board, with a single official, or with a mix of these? And then we might ask how we can protect the dissenters' rights and interests as well. These are classic questions of politics and governance.

Osborne and Gaebler assert rather unreflectively that the authority should reside in the majority, for that is what markets and democracies are based upon. They ignore our historic and institutionalized fears about abusive majorities, about the questionable dynamics of their formation, and about our concerns for protecting minorities and individual rights. Nor do they acknowledge the power some elite groups (corporate elites, professional elites, etc.) exercise behind majoritarian facades.

They also ignore the fact that, however elegant and desirable in theory, markets are often politically and socially disruptive.[10] The scope of such disruption, and corresponding instability, expands as we "reinvent" our political institutions (education among them) as market institutions. For example, the potential for racial and socioeconomic stratification of school populations is likely to increase through competition for wealthier, better-prepared students. Not all "customers" are equally desirable.

In the long run, market-based public agencies would instill in public administrators a *trained incapacity* to uphold the missions and integrity of these institutions. Powerful incentives to follow market pressures would lead them to disregard contrary professional judgments for the sake of market survival. This happens in business constantly, with the costs (monetary and social) typically borne by governments and the unemployed. Of course, it also happens in some of our agencies operating under more "traditional" political incentives. We could hardly afford to have our governments increase this tendency by joining the market fray. Osborne and Gaebler admit that our governments must provide a stable infrastructure, upon which social and economic life depends. Yet their reinventions serve more to erode that base than to strengthen it.

From the standpoint of governance, we all share an interest in a stable infrastructure of public institutions. These institutions include education, our transportation and communications systems, law enforcement, defense, and even more mundane services such as garbage removal. The citizens of Visalia, California, voiced a vital public interest in stability with their negative reaction to the entrepreneurial intrigues of some public officials. They wanted certain basic services undisturbed by the search for optimization.

This does not mean that those who govern must resist change. But it does mean that public officials should treat change more ambivalently than Osborne and Gaebler's entrepreneur. Ronald Moe (1994) suggests that they have elevated change to a point beyond question or challenge. Accordingly, they reject our constitutional order because it is "not flexible enough to permit change to occur at the speed considered necessary in the new, information-driven technological world" (p. 114). They bow rather blindly to the gods of technological and market imperatives.

In terms of the education controversy cited above, the concerns of governance mean that various forms of judgment and authority need to be preserved rather than reduced to market determinants (whatever those may entail). For example, the distinctive judgments of professional educators and administrators should be countenanced as a vital part of the unfolding political dialogue. Their contributions are indeed political in the sense that they rest ultimately upon "strategically crafted arguments" about our common educational interests (Stone, 1988). The political nature of their judgments, as well as their positions, ties their profession directly to our broader political process (Green, Keller, & Wamsley, 1993). This means that while forming their own judgments they should "listen skillfully and openly," not only to the dominant interests in the debate, but also to "the neglected voices" among the public. The resulting decisions should flow from reciprocally developed understanding of key values and appropriate strategies for realizing them (Stivers, 1994, p. 367). This process requires more time than entrepreneurs want to take. However, we believe the results will be more lasting and beneficial to all.

Distributive Impacts

A central tenet of total quality management (TQM) holds that the people an organization serves are its "customers." These customers should be listened to by members of the organization that serves them. Osborne and Gaebler fully subscribe to this view. The problem is that *listening* means different things depending on the strength of one's inducements and obligations to listen. In business, for example, "there are some classes of customers to which entrepreneurs listen attentively," responding quickly to their requests. "Other classes of customers they might listen to, but will not act upon their requests." And finally there are others they will simply ignore altogether. "A business cannot afford to be all things to all people." Using the terminology of Osborne and Gaebler, the managers "must establish a market niche" and cater to a select clientele (Hubbell, 1993, p. 420).[11]

Nobody really questions which clientele business managers decide to target for distribution of their goods and services. That critical choice is almost entirely up to them. They have very few, if any, external obligations to meet in this regard. They will simply serve those they think will supply them a good and stable living.

For government agencies it is a very different matter. Take the case of the federal agency ACTION during the mid-1970s. At that time the two most dominant domestic ACTION programs were Volunteers in Service to America (VISTA) and the Older Americans Volunteer Programs (OAVP). VISTA, at least during the Nixon and Ford administrations, suffered constant threat of being eliminated or drastically cut because its emphasis on community organizing was anathema to the ruling Republicans. OAVP, on the other hand, was a politically popular triad of programs that provided funding for more than 800 locally managed senior citizens' programs strategically located throughout the country. VISTA's primary constituency consisted of the politically impotent poor. OAVP's primary constituency is the politically empowered senior citizens' lobby. If ACTION managers were to adopt the attitude of the entrepreneur, treating the people served as customers and the environment as a marketplace, they would obviously favor OAVP over VISTA for the sake of organizational survival. Any consideration of a broader common good would undoubtedly come only as an afterthought, if that.

Transforming an agency into an entrepreneurial, market-based firm will cause managers to abandon those customers they consider less valuable or profitable to their existence than others. Some may even be considered a harmful liability. Public servants should always explore new ways to get tasks accomplished, but they should not necessarily emulate entrepreneurs. To do so would, in many instances, deny some basic values of American governance—serving disadvantaged minorities, restraining powerful groups, and protecting individual rights.

Another distributive problem arises from Osborne and Gaebler's fondness for user fees as a way out of financial trouble for many agencies. They reject the option of increasing taxes, even though Americans are among the least taxed people in the world.[12] This puts them squarely in the conservative camp for downsized government, intentions to the contrary notwithstanding. In pressing their case, the authors call attention to "all the public services that benefit individuals: the golf course, the tennis courts, the marinas. Typically, the taxpayers subsidize those services. Average working people subsidize the affluent to play golf and tennis or moor their boats" (1992, p. 199). Osborne and Gaebler "ignore the fact that the affluent usually opt for private golf courses, tennis courts, and marinas, and leave the public facilities for the less affluent" (Hubbell, 1993, p. 421).

Gaebler cites his own experience as city manager of the affluent community of Visalia, California. There he raised the fees charged to softball teams for using the city's softball fields from $25 to $400 (Osborne & Gaebler, 1992, pp. 199-200). This resulted in substantial profit to the city. "Naturally the softball teams at first complained, but then were convinced to recruit team sponsors and pass the costs on to them" (Hubbell, 1993, p. 421). Visalia allegedly benefited from this policy because its citizens are affluent and influential enough to absorb the passed-along costs. However, such policies "can have cumulatively devastating effects on less affluent communities dependent on government services" (Hubbell, 1993, p. 421). User fees are inherently regressive financial devices. As Milan Dluhy (1992) suggests:

> It may simply be easier to be successful in a middle/upper class community like Visalia, California than in East St. Louis, Illinois. It may be that we need to look at both failures and successes in order to understand the broader question of why some governments have more of a capacity to be entrepreneurial than others. (p. 191)

In that regard, Don Haynes and Patricia Florestano (1994) recently studied taxing alternatives in Maryland and discovered a corresponding problem. They found that many people in Maryland prefer user fee programs "that push the burden onto someone else, typically a small proportion of the population." These politically acceptable revenue sources, however, "often fail to produce the kinds of revenues required for balanced budgets." This creates yet another "fiscal pincher" that exacerbates the general fiscal dilemma of increasing spending requirements and inadequate revenue sources (pp. 465-466). Public officials have no choice but to confront the hard cases along with the easier ones.

Furthermore, even in affluent communities one of the responsibilities of government should be to foster a sense of inclusiveness and community. Osborne and Gaebler wholeheartedly agree. However, that sense of community dissipates somewhat when government charges user fees and thereby excludes some people on the basis of income, or has to stigmatize them with a discount or exemption system (Hubbell, 1993, p. 421). Osborne and Gaebler

(1992) describe it as an advantage that such fees "lower demand for public services" (p. 204). Such a statement becomes ludicrous, and possibly dangerous, in the context of poor communities. The authors are hardly oblivious to the tensions inherent between markets and communities. But we see very little in their prescriptions that nurtures and supports community-oriented institutions and practices. Their model of governance decidedly favors markets, entrepreneurs, and competition.

Finally, if we take reinvention principles seriously, another distributive nightmare arises from the changed nature of our labor force. Mak Khojasteh (1994) reviews statistics on the growth of the "contingent work force," which includes temporary and part-time workers. He shows that the number of temporary workers has increased 175% from 1980 to 1988, with no sign of abatement in sight. The number of part-time workers is increasing at 15% per year, and estimates show that one third of all work will be part-time by the year 2000. These changes reflect business as well as government decisions to cut personnel costs. The reinvention philosophy turns this strategy into a principle of good governance.

Nowhere, however, do Osborne and Gaebler or any of their influential followers confront the implications for labor, welfare, health care, and other social policies. What do we do with more than a third of the workforce and their families when they need health care, another job, and the like. Social welfare programs are being pared back across the country, not expanded. Nonbenefited, lower-paying jobs cut away a huge support infrastructure for these people. Such conditions change people's attitudes about work in unpredictable ways. Governments will be forced to deal with the ensuing problems at some point, and that will give reinvention a whole new meaning—as in *reinventing the wheel!*

The impact of increased personnel cutbacks and mobility in government ranks compounds these problems because of reduced institutional memory and capacity. Guy Peters (1994) observes that we are hollowing state capacity through (a) reduction of legitimate governmental roles; (b) decentralization, privatization, and the corresponding loss of accountability and effectiveness; and the (c) shrinking discretionary powers of public servants. We can add to that the increasing partisan politicization of the public administration. Through this combination of disinvestment strategies we are crippling our governments' abilities to prevent or even respond to future crises, much less plan for a better future.

Competition and Political Community

Given the United States' relative economic decline in the emerging global political economy, few rallying cries are more likely to appeal to Americans than the call for increased competition. Osborne and Gaebler have capitalized on that deep-seated emotional appeal. "They warmly embrace the spirit of competitiveness" (Hubbell, 1993, p. 421). Indeed, Osborne and Gaebler (1992) write, "Competition will not solve all our problems. But perhaps more than any other concept in this book, it holds the key that will unlock the bureaucratic gridlock that hamstrings so many public agencies" (pp. 79-80; Hubbell, 1993, p. 421).

They believe public agencies should compete with private organizations to provide public services. We agree that some agencies should compete more with the private sector. Such competition often provides indicators to the private sector about significant public dimensions of their services and products. Many other countries employ this tactic extensively, to great public benefit (Carnoy & Shearer, 1980; Lindblom, 1977).

We also support, to a limited extent, their neo-mercantilist orientation to government-business partnerships. Government can indeed support substantial public interests while businesses profit in the same venture. This is especially important in the area of long-term investment in strategic goods and services. Governments can do much to stimulate investment in new technologies that can be beneficial and profitable down the road (Cohen, 1991).

However, our penchant for competition also gets us into trouble when we fail to discern where competition is appropriate and where it is not. Osborne and Gaebler shed little light here. Rather, they tend to universalize competition as the key to all innovation and excellence. Again, they go too far. Consider the following points.

Over the past decade U.S. business has run full tilt into a new and formidable industrial structure based upon a radical new form of production. The Japanese developed both in their attempt to join the mass-production world after World War II. The new production method is now known by a number of names, one of which is "lean production" (Womack, Jones, & Roos, 1990). Lean production dramatically reduces production costs and boosts quality through a small-batch production process that wastes almost nothing.

Lean organizations rely heavily on trust and cooperation, not only among employees but among suppliers, regulators, and others. Using trust and cooperation, the Japanese developed a powerful, innovative industrial structure that produces the highest quality goods in the world. They build long-term interorganizational networks with suppliers and regulators, guaranteeing them access and stable markets. This neo-mercantilist structure now ranges across industries, and emphasizes coalition bargaining and long-run balancing of multiple stakeholder interests in contrast to our penchant for short-run profit maximization (Cohen, 1991; Ross, 1994; Womack et al., 1990).

Lean producers also treat employees as their most important capital asset, rather than as an operating cost. They invest heavily in broad education and training to enhance creativity, and to make their employees more easily transferable from one job to another, even outside the host organization. Virtually all of this training reinforces cooperation, trust, and teamwork, rather than competition (Womack et al., 1990).

Ironically, Osborne and Gaebler borrow innovations arising from this cooperative model of enterprise (including from TQM). Yet they say nothing about cooperation and mutual trust as core principles. They also fail to acknowledge the centrality of these values to the broader political community from which these institutions draw their existence. Moreover, although cooperation and trust are not as central to our political-economic system, they have always played key roles. One need only consult a history of business development in our country to see that. Alfred Chandler (1977), for example, showed how American business has always relied heavily on government support and cooperation to sustain its growth and development. Theodore Lowi (1979, chaps. 1-3) indicated that cooperative administrative organization gave American business its stability and made our modern corporate political economy possible.

Nevertheless, our popular mythology enshrines competition, and Osborne and Gaebler pander to it single-mindedly as their proverb for success. As a result they seem unable to ascertain its limits, especially in public life. They fail to recognize its divisive and destructive potential. Where does the public benefit from competition end, and the damage begin? Correspondingly, they fail to articulate any possible place for trust and cooperation. And yet these necessarily form much of the basis for a viable community. As indicated earlier, many of their prescriptions will erode trust and trade cooperation for blind obedience to partisan competition.

On a related point, Fred Thompson (1993) indicates that market-styled incentives and privatization "presume that the services provided to or for government are homogenous or fungible" in such a way that "identifying the most efficient supplying organization . . . resolves to a simple question of price search" (p. 309). In reality, many goods and services supplied to or for governments are "heterogenous" in character and therefore difficult to measure and extremely costly to evaluate. The practical result is that privatization and other competitive, market-based practices gravitate to more homogenous goods and services, which are primarily *custodial* in nature (Thompson, 1993, pp. 309-311). Where the goods and services aren't homogenous, they will try to make them so.

Governments, especially at local levels, are often preoccupied with custodial management responsibilities (e.g., picking up the garbage, filling potholes, etc.). Market practices will work there, but they skirt the broader, more heterogenous problems of governance, such as ensuring equal protection under the laws, educating citizens, preserving institutional capacity, and nurturing community leadership. Thus the spread of market competition induces myopia in local governments about the nature of their problems.

According to Theodore Lowi this is already a problem in urban areas due to the lack of communication and coordination among multiple, independent governing bodies. He aptly describes American communities as generally "run well, but poorly governed" (Lowi, 1979, chap. 7). Thus racial, educational, criminal, and other intractable public problems receive less concerted attention than provision of mundane services such as filling pot holes and collecting garbage. Osborne and Gaebler would only compound this problem with their pitch for more marketization and decentralization.

Because Osborne and Gaebler lack any sense of limits to the competitive impulse, they cannot help but follow its logic to ridiculous extremes. In the process, they fail to see where a tension exists between their prescriptions and the needs of the broader political community. They claim in several places that community is a vital dimension to public life, but they offer no place for the community-oriented individual or policy in American governance. Their model fails to comprehend a powerful institutional niche or set of roles upon which a viable communitarian tradition may stand and endure.

Reinvention: Panacea or Red Herring?

For many people, Osborne and Gaebler's entrepreneurial approach appears to offer a panacea for a governmental system that seems more representative of lethargy than of the citizens it is supposed to serve. In the "age of the customer," reinventors tell us the traditional, hierarchical, monopolistic, one-size-fits-all government organization increasingly resembles the extinct Brontosaurus, characterized by a large body and a small brain.

Osborne and Gaebler use this catchy imagery to make their approach seem fresh and invigorating by contrast. Their entrepreneur is a model of American excellence and vitality. Their stories always reveal amazing success when the entrepreneurial spirit is set free. But this Hobson's choice between stultifying bureaucracy and competitive entrepreneurialism is neither helpful nor realistic for serious students of good government. As James Fallows (1992) describes, "the tone of the book often reminds me of an Amway or a Dale Carnegie sales pitch, or a TV infomercial. Every story is a success story. Before the change everything is bad. After the change, everything is good" (p. 122). Such banality obscures more than it reveals. For example, if there is any apt description of this country's eighty thousand-plus governmental units, it is that they display remarkable diversity in size, structure, and operating philosophy. Many of them, in fact, are quite small, personable, and very responsive. Some are even highly entrepreneurial and have been so for many years. Furthermore, most agencies operate very effectively, especially if one compares them to counterparts in other countries and surveys the citizens who interact with them.[13] The one-size-fits-all, lumbering dinosaur image casts the wrong impression entirely. We agree with Milan Dluhy (1992) that Osborne and Gaebler's book is not very helpful for readers "looking for a balanced, careful, and comprehensive empirical review of the behavior of state and local governments in the last 20 years" (p. 191). The same is true of their treatment of federal agencies. To characterize them all as hulking monoliths in need of entrepreneurial reinvention amounts to sheer rhetorical flourish.

The same judgment applies to all 10 principles of reinvention. They amount to trite maxims that obscure more than they reveal, and that divert much of our energy for making real improvements in government.

Most of the principles have already been found wanting and will therefore only need summary treatment here. The others require little effort to demonstrate our point. The first principle, "steering others rather than rowing," perpetuates misleading aspects of the old politics/administration dichotomy. It presumes that we all agree on where we shall steer, and how we shall get there. Nothing could be further from the truth.

The second principle, "empowering customers rather than serving them," and the sixth principle, "intense customer orientation," could as easily mean abdicating official responsibilities as responding to genuine public needs. This is especially true for regulatory agencies suffering under the perversions of interest group liberalism (Lowi, 1979). Empowered customers can make public policy without benefit of law! Osborne and Gaebler give us no guide for judicious application of these principles, or their converse.

The third principle, "injecting competition into service delivery," and the tenth principle, "leveraging change through market-based incentives," go hand in hand. They can benefit some agency efforts and harm others. Osborne and Gaebler offer little insight on the limitations of these principles, and fail to recognize cooperation and trust as more fundamental axioms undergirding many of their prescriptions. They seek widespread substitution of market mechanisms for discretionary judgments by public officials, and thereby subject institutional stability and integrity to the perils of market instability.

The fourth principle, "organizing by mission rather than by rules," and the fifth principle, "funding results, not inputs" can also be treated together. These principles, as presented, engender antagonism toward rule by law and toward the constitutionally separate branches. Osborne and Gaebler write as if the executive branch is all that matters for effective decision making. When rules interfere, executives should abandon them. The authors forget that one person's "red tape" may be another's "due process of law." When other branches interfere, they act as "managerial nuisances" (Moe, 1994, p. 117). The authors accord to executives the real prerogatives over budgets and agency practices. They ignore the historical conflicts among the branches over these powers, and the results as evidenced even in Visalia, California—Gaebler's entrepreneurial city.

The seventh principle, "encouraging entrepreneurial earning rather than bureaucratic spending," too easily leads to the abuses cited in the wake of Visalia, California's entrepreneurial frenzy. Management becomes so preoccupied with acquisition for pet projects that it forgets it is a public institution. Ironically, responsiveness and stable provision of basic services diminish as a result. Acquisitiveness (getting) creates even more distractions than spending!

The eighth principle, "focusing on prevention rather than cure," is so trite it invites ridicule. James Fallows (1992) explains:

> For instance, in illustrating the (unexceptional) point that it's cheaper to prevent a problem than to solve it . . . they [Osborne & Gaebler] mention that thousands of young black men are killed or wounded by gunfire every year. It would be more sensible and efficient, they suggest, to get rid of the guns than to build more jails. You don't say! Hey, maybe it would also be more sensible if the Arabs and Israelis made friends, rather than fighting so much! But perhaps there's something involved in the Middle East, and in America's reliance on guns, that goes beyond faulty cost-benefit analysis. (p. 122)

We need say no more.

The ninth principle, "decentralizing organizations and fostering teamwork," says nothing new at all in management circles. Decentralization forms one side of a very old debate on the principles of organization. Most of the management literature now acknowledges that both centralization and decentralization are required in complex organizations. The real trick is to know where each is needed and when. Osborne and Gaebler give no hint that they are even aware of this. They side unreflectively with decentralization, and therefore encourage some classic problems. Decentralization easily frustrates accountability, not to mention responsible leadership. It may also compromise effectiveness when coordination among diverse programs is required.

Conclusion

In terms of governance, we must conclude that Osborne and Gaebler's entire reinvention thesis offers no more than a disappointing series of red herrings. Nothing in their model is really new, and most of it leads down blind alleys. They parrot much of our Progressive reform tradition, melding it to neoclassical economic philosophy as revived through public choice theory. In many respects they have simply reinvented our historic impulse to reform our governments and are bound to disappoint everyone because the problems they seek to confront remain intractable (O'Toole, 1984).

Entrepreneurialism has been present, if not dominant, in virtually all reform periods of our history. It panders to the American "can-do" attitude and to our extremely individualistic culture. It is therefore not surprising that principles such as competition and market should be so revered that they are thought by many to be equally applicable in both the private and public spheres of life.

Osborne and Gaebler, like so many before them, have tried to universalize these principles, blowing them out of all proportion to our broader political values and traditions. They suggest that by increasing entrepreneurialism, individualism, competition, and market we will solve most of our serious problems. The new leaders in Congress agree wholeheartedly, and furthermore wish to devolve the bulk of this activity to the states. They ignore the possibility that these basic American traits may actually contribute to many of our current dilemmas.

Osborne and Gaebler might reply that they offer a model of the entrepreneur that is much broader and therefore capable of engendering communitarian and other non-market-based causes as well. Indeed, they state that intention early on. But they cannot ignore the fact, as they later admit, that they have consistently joined the entrepreneur to his or her traditional business milieu, the competitive market, and sought to reinvent governance in that image. Any advantages attributable to a broader conception, therefore, remain abstract and unattainable.

This does not mean that many of Osborne and Gaebler's prescriptions aren't worth trying, at least in some quarters. Many of them have been tried before in our governments, with some success (Goodsell, 1994, chap. 7). But they hardly address the broader problems we associate with ineffective regulatory practices, demeaning service and personnel policies, shortsighted budgeting systems, and the like. These require approaches that comprehend appropriate relations among political, economic, and social institutions, and that embrace more than the economic sphere of American life.

Economic metaphors such as *market, monopoly,* and *customer* lack vital dimensions of meaning in public life. Nor do they operate the same way in government as they do in the private sector. For example, monopolies usually do not pose the same kinds of problems in public agencies as they do in business. They usually cannot restrict supply in order to drive up prices (for lack of profit motive), and they generally offer more opportunities and services to a much broader audience than competitive markets can.

Furthermore, we believe that monopolies per se are *not* the reason why some citizens receive poor treatment from the government agencies serving them. Monopolies, private and public, have often been very effective service providers. The problem has more to do with a lack of commitment, low esteem, and a dissipating sense of vocational responsibility in the public service.

Government officials should be inspired by a sense of duty and esteem that elicit desires to serve others. Market-styled incentives summon fears of obsolescence and direct the passions more toward one's own survival than toward service to others. Until recently the public service has been free of such fears and open to the possibility of distinction through service to others. Much of the work is inherently challenging and important—an essential reward in itself to public servants.[14] If we transform this setting into a market-driven one, we will speed the demise of the public service ethic and the substantial rewards that it offers.

Instead, we should be looking for ways to draw citizens and officials further into this public ethic and to make the rewards more apparent and accessible. We need to revamp personnel policies to reflect more trust and a positive view of human aspiration, while retaining the broader context of institutional protection against abuse. We need to explore more carefully where discretion and judgment will work better than rule and regulation, and vice versa, over the long run; where decentralization will work, and where it won't in our constitutional order; and where cooperation will work better than competition. In short, we need to learn where and when entrusted powers will more readily entice public officials to exercise them for public benefit.

It is most unlikely that the public sector in this country will ever rival the private sector in terms of salaries and related benefits. Members of the Senior Executive Service discovered this soon after its creation. Congress quickly reneged on its commitment to pay them at levels comparable to the corporate sector, despite the fact that the service had been redesigned under corporate principles. SES members now live under the sticks of that model, and find very few carrots.[15]

The same fate seems unavoidable for the rest of the public administration, especially if reinvention principles hold sway. Richard Kearney (1993) thinks labor-management relations are "probably at their lowest point since the early 1930s" (pp. 786-787), and blames much of this on management preoccupation with fads such as total quality management and reinvention. Public officials need not emulate the corporate sector. They should promote the distinctive responsibilities, challenges, and powers long associated with public service. However, they cannot do so successfully without broad public encouragement.

It is in this spirit that we continue to advocate *refounding* rather than reinvention of governance. Popular political discourse today obscures the stubborn and paradoxical nature of public affairs. It fails to convey any sense of the complex array of values, powers, decision methods, and administrative arrangements contemplated in our constitutional system for wrestling with them over long periods of time. We need to rediscover as a whole people the roots of our governing systems, and rebuild our efforts upon their firm constitutional foundation. That road will take us much further and in many more directions than marketization.

Notes

1. See Osborne and Gaebler's (1992) Acknowledgements and Preface, pp. xi-xxii.

2. See chapter 11, "Putting It All Together," Osborne & Gaebler, 1992, pp. 321-325.

3. In the wake of World War II, Joseph Rosenfarb (1948) described war as the laboratory of innovation and administration. Also, the extensive work of Marshall Dimock, before and after the New Deal, is especially relevant here because he advocated exactly the same kind of entrepreneurialism espoused by Osborne and Gaebler. For example, see his *Administrative Vitality* (1959), *A Philosophy of Administration* (1958), and *Law and Dynamic Administration* (1980). For an excellent discussion of the "Managerial Progressivism," which gave shape to much subsequent administrative development, see Eisenach (1994, Conclusion).

4. See Crunden (1982), Haber (1964), and Keller (1989) for discussions of the moralism of the Progressives. Many of the reviews of *Reinventing Government* call attention to its simplistic moralism. Cf. Dluhy (1992), Fallows (1992), and Moe (1994).

5. Ronald Moe (1994) provides an excellent analysis of how Osborne and Gaebler's approach perverts the Progressive agenda. Eldon Eisenach (1994) gives a thorough account of the Progressive vision.

6. We realize that the council-manager system does not follow the traditional separation of powers structure of national and state governments. Nevertheless, its powers are diffused and understood to be accountable in a similar fashion, as is evidenced in the remarks of Gurwitt's (1994) interviewees.

7. We agree with John Rohr that this role of choosing among the masters on any given issue constitutes a vital ethical and political obligation in American governance.

8. Ronald Moe (1994, pp. 111, 119, fn. 6) also alludes to this problem in his searching critique of the Gore Report and its reinvention principles. He suggests the Gore Report contains an unwritten objective of more rather than less politicization of the executive branch.

9. These points have also been made in some recent *PA Times* articles and letters. See Frank Sherwood (1993, pp. 11, 20) and Thayer (1993, p. 9). Moe (1994, p. 16) concurs as well. See Note 15, below, for citations on the politicization of the SES.

10. Theodore Lowi makes this point clear in his classic work, *The End of Liberalism* (1979, chap. 1). A wide array of works critical of the social damage created by our economic theories and practices now exists. A recent example is Wilber and Jameson's *Beyond Reaganomics* (1990). Any reader not familiar with this literature need only consult a history book to recall all the depressions, recessions, and social dislocations arising from market cycles.

11. Parts of this section (where indicated with cites) quote and/or paraphrase Larry Hubbell's (1993) review of *Reinventing Government.*

12. According to the *Statistical Abstracts of the United States* (1994, p. 867), the United States ranks eighth lowest in the world in terms of per capita taxation. In terms of tax revenues as a percentage of gross domestic product (GDP) it ranks second lowest.

13. This point is argued at length by Charles Goodsell (1994: passim).

14. Much of the voluminous empirical and motivational literature on organizational life confirms the dominance of such intrinsic factors as motivators in daily work life over extrinsic incentives. This is especially true for highly trained professionals. See Foster (1990), Guyot (1962), Kohn (1971), Nachmias (1984), and Rainey (1979a, 1979b, 1983, 1992) for empirical studies of motivations among professionals and bureaucratic organizations. For a concise summary of these and other studies, see Goodsell (1994, chap. 5).

15. A huge literature now exists that describes the SES's predicament in rich detail, but the basic problems were recognized very early in, for example, Ring and Perry (1983), and subsequently replicated in other studies such as Gaertner and Gaertner (1985); Staats's NAPA Report (1988); and the Volcker Commission Report (1989).

References

Axelrod, D. (1989). *A budget quartet: Critical policy and management issues.* New York: St. Martin's.

Boyer, P. (1978). *Urban masses and moral order in America, 1820-1920.* Cambridge, MA: Harvard University Press.

Bromage, A. W. (1936). *Introduction to municipal government and administration.* New York: Appleton-Century-Crofts.

Burke, J. P. (1986). *Bureaucratic responsibility.* Baltimore, MD: Johns Hopkins University Press.

Carnoy, M., & Shearer, D. (1980). *Economic democracy: The challenge of the 1980s.* Armonk, NY: M. E. Sharpe.

Chandler, A. D. (1977). *The visible hand: The managerial revolution in American business.* Cambridge, MA: Belknap.

Childs, R. S. (1952). *Civic victories: The story of an unfinished revolution.* New York: Harper & Brothers.

Cohen, S. D. (1991). *Cowboys and samurai: Why the United States is losing the industrial battle and why it matters.* New York: HarperCollins.

Cook, B. J. (1992). Administration in constitutive perspective. *Administration & Society, 23*(4), 403-429.

Cox, R. W. (1994). The Winter Commission report: The practitioner's perspective. *Public Administration Review, 54*(2), 108-109.

Crunden, R. M. (1982). *Ministers of reform: The progressives' achievement in American civilization.* New York: Basic Books.

DeWitt, B. P. (1915). *The progressive movement.* New York: Macmillan.

Dimock, M. (1958). *A philosophy of administration.* New York: Harper & Brothers.

Dimock, M. (1959). *Administrative vitality.* New York: Harper & Brothers.

Dimock, M. (1980). *Law and dynamic administration.* New York: Praeger.

Dluhy, M. J. (1992). Review of *Reinventing government. Policy Studies Review, 11*(2), 189-192.

East, J. P. (1965). *Council-manager government: The political thought of its founder, Richard S. Childs.* Chapel Hill: University of North Carolina Press.

Eisenach, E. J. (1994). *The lost promise of progressivism.* Lawrence: University Press of Kansas.

Fallows, J. (1992). A case for reform. Review of *Reinventing government. Atlantic, 269,* 119-123.

Fisher, L. (1975). *Presidential spending power.* Princeton, NJ: Princeton University Press.

Foster, J. L. (1990). Bureaucratic rigidity revisited. *Social Science Quarterly, 71,* 223-238.

Gaertner, K. N., & Gaertner, G. H. (1985). Performance-contingent pay for federal managers. *Administration & Society, 17*(1), 7-20.

Goodsell, C. T. (1990). Public administration and the public interest. In G. L. Wamsley, R. N. Bacher, C. T. Goodsell, P. S. Kronenberg, J. A. Rohr, C. M. Stivers, O. F. White, & J. F. Wolf, *Refounding public administration* (pp. 96-113). Newbury Park, CA: Sage.

Goodsell, C. T. (1993). Reinvent government or rediscover it? [Review of the book *Reinventing government: How the entrepreneurial spirit is transforming the public sector*]. *Public Administration Review, 53*(1).

Goodsell, C. T. (1994). *The case for bureaucracy* (3rd ed.). Chatham, NJ: Chatham House.

Green, R. T. (1992). Constitutional jurisprudence: Reviving praxis in public administration. *Administration & Society, 24*(1), 3-21.

Green, R. T., Keller, L. F., & Wamsley, G. L. (1993). Reconstituting a profession for American public administration. *Public Administration Review, 53*(6), 516-524.

Gurwitt, R. (1994). Entrepreneurial government: The morning after. *Governing,* pp. 34-40.

Guyot, J. F. (1962). Governmental bureaucrats are different. *Public Administration Review, 22,* 195-202.

Haber, S. (1964). *Efficiency and uplift: Scientific management in the progressive era.* Chicago: University of Chicago Press.

Haynes, D., & Florestano, P. S. (1994). Public acceptability of taxing alternatives: Evidence from Maryland. *Public Administration Quarterly,* 447-467.

Hays, S. P. (1964). The politics of reform in municipal government in the progressive era. *Pacific Northwest Quarterly, 55,* 157-169.

Hays, S. P. (1975). *Conservation and the gospel of efficiency: The progressive conservation movement.* New York: Athenaeum.

Howe, F. C. (1905). *The city: The hope of democracy.* New York: Scribner.

Hubbell, L. (1993). [Review of the book *Reinventing government*]. *American Review of Public Administration, 23*(4), 419-421.

Karl, B. D. (1983). *The uneasy state: The United States from 1915-1945.* Chicago: University of Chicago Press.

Kearney, R. (1993). Federal Labor Relations 2000: Introduction to the symposium. *International Journal of Public Administration, 16*(6), 781-791.

Keller, L. F. (1984). The political economy of public management: An interorganizational network perspective. *Administration & Society, 15*(4), 455-474.

Keller, L. F. (1989). Public administration, city management, and the American enlightenment. *International Journal of Public Administration, 20,* 213-249.

Khojasteh, M. (1994). Workforce 2000: Demographic changes and their impacts. *International Journal of Public Administration, 17*(3 & 4), 465-505.

Kohn, M. L. (1971). Bureaucratic man: A portrait and an interpretation. *American Sociological Review, 36,* 461-474.

LeLoup, L. T. (1988). *Budgetary politics* (4th ed.). Brunswick, OH: KingsCourt Communications.

Lindblom, C. (1977). *Politics and markets: The world's political economic systems.* New York: Basic Books.

Link, A. S. (1954). *Woodrow Wilson and the progressive era, 1910-1917.* New York: Harper & Row.

Lipsky, M. (1980). *Street-level bureaucracy: Dilemmas of the individual in public services.* New York: Russell Sage.

Lowi, T. J. (1979). *The end of liberalism: The second republic of the United States* (2nd ed.). New York: Norton.

McSwain, C. J. (1985). Administrators and citizenship: The liberalist legacy of the Constitution. *Administration & Society, 17*(2), 131-148.

Miller, H. T. (1994). Post-progressive public administration: Lessons from policy networks. *Public Administration Review, 54*(4), 378-386.

Moe, R. C. (1994). The "Reinventing government" exercise: Misinterpreting the problem, misjudging the consequences. *Public Administration Review, 54*(2), 111-122.

Morgan, D. F., & Kass, H. (1989). Constitutional stewardship, phronesis, and the American administrative ethos. *Dialogue, 12*(1), 17-60.

Nachmias, D. (1984, December). Are federal bureaucrats conservative? A modest test of a popular image. *Social Science Quarterly, 65,* 1080-1087.

Noble, D. W. (1970). *The progressive mind, 1890-1917.* Chicago: Rand McNally.

Office of the Vice President, National Performance Review. (1993). *From red tape to results: Creating a government that works better and costs less* (Report of the National Performance Review). Washington, DC: Government Printing Office.

Orloff, A. S. (1988). The political origins of America's belated welfare state. In M. Weir, A. S. Orloff, & T. Skocpol (Eds.), *The politics of social policy in the United States.* Princeton, NJ: Princeton University Press.

Osborne, D., & Gaebler, T. (1992). *Reinventing government: How the entrepreneurial spirit is transforming the public sector.* Reading, MA: Addison-Wesley.

O'Toole, L. J., Jr. (1984). American public administration and the idea of reform. *Administration & Society, 16*(2), 141-166.

Pearson, W. N., & Castle, D. S. (1993). Expanding the opportunity for partisan activity among government employees: Potential effects on federal executives' political involvement. *International Journal of Public Administration, 16*(4), 511-525.

Peters, B. G. (1994). Managing the hollow state. *International Journal of Public Administration, 17*(3 & 4), 739-756.

Quandt, J. B. (1970) *From the small town to the great community: The social thought of progressive intellectuals.* New Brunswick, NJ: Rutgers University Press.

Rainey, H. G. (1979a). Perceptions of incentives in business and government: Implications for civil service reform. *Public Administration Review, 39,* 440-448.

Rainey, H. G. (1979b). Reward expectancies, role perceptions, and job satisfaction among government and business managers: Indications of commonalities and differences. *Academy of Management Proceedings,* pp. 357-361.

Rainey, H. G. (1983). Public agencies and private firms: Incentive structures, goals, and individual roles. *Administration & Society, 15,* 207-242.

Rainey, H. G. (1992). On the uniqueness of public bureaucracies. In L. B. Hill (Ed.), *The state of public bureaucracy.* Armonk, NY: M. E. Sharpe.

Ring, P. S., & Perry, J. L. (1983). Reforming the upper levels of the bureaucracy: A longitudinal study of the senior executive service. *Administration & Society, 15*(1), 119-144.

Rohr, J. A. (1986). *To run a constitution: The legitimacy of the administrative state.* Lawrence: University Press of Kansas.

Rohr, J. A. (1989). *Ethics for bureaucrats: An essay on law and values* (2nd ed.). New York: Marcel-Dekker.

Rosenberg, E. S. (1982). *Spreading the American dream: American economic and cultural expansion, 1890-1945.* New York: Hill & Wang.

Rosenbloom, D. H. (1993). Have an administrative RX? Don't forget the politics! [Editorial]. *Public Administration Review, 53*(6), 503-507.

Rosenfarb, J. (1948). *Freedom and the administrative state.* New York: Russell & Russell.

Ross, D. N. (1994). Japanese corporate groupings (Keiretsu): A reconnaissance of implications for the future. *International Journal of Public Administration, 17*(3 & 4), 507-539.

School wars. (1993, December). *Sunday Denver Post,* pp. 12, 1A, 14A, 15A.

Selznick, P. (1957). *Leadership in administration.* New York: Harper & Row.

Selznick, P. (1992). *The moral commonwealth: Social theory and the promise of community.* Berkeley: University of California Press.

Sherwood, F. (1993). Ins and outs of National Performance Review. *PA Times, 16*(11), 11, 20.

Skowronek, S. (1982). *Building the new American administrative state: The expansion of national administrative capacities, 1877-1920.* New York: Cambridge University Press.

Staats, E. B. (1988). *The executive presidency: Federal management for the 1990s* (Panel Report). Washington, DC: National Academy of Public Administration.

Statistical abstracts of the United States. (1994). Tax revenues by country. Washington, DC: Government Printing Office.

Stivers, C. (1990). Active statesmanship and public administration. In G. L. Wamsley, R. N. Bacher, C. T. Goodsell, P. S. Kronenberg, J. A. Rohr, C. M. Stivers, O. F. White, & J. F. Wolf, *Refounding public administration* (pp. 246-273). Newbury Park, CA: Sage.

Stivers, C. (1994). The listening bureaucrat: Responsiveness in public administration. *Public Administration Review, 54*(4), 364-369.

Stone, D. A. (1988). *Policy paradox and political reason.* Glenview, IL: Scott, Foresman.

Storing, H. J. (1981). *What the anti-Federalists were FOR: The political thought of the opponents of the Constitution.* Chicago: University of Chicago Press.

Taylor, F. W. (1990). *The principles of scientific management.* New York: Harper & Brothers.

Terry, L. D. (1995). *Leadership of public bureaucracy: The administrator as conservator.* Thousand Oaks, CA: Sage.

Thayer, F. (1993, October). Reinventing government is really the spoils system—again [Letter to the editor]. *PA Times, 16*(10), p. 9.

Thompson, F. (1993). Matching responsibilities with tactics: Administrative controls and modern government. *Public Administration Review, 53*(4), 303-318.

Trachtenberg, A. (1982). *The incorporation of America: Culture and society in the gilded age.* New York: Hill & Wang.

Volcker, P. A. (1989). *Leadership for America: Rebuilding the public service* (Report for The National Commission on the Public Service). Washington, DC: Brookings Institution and American Enterprize Institute.

Wamsley, G. L. (1984). Policy subsystems: Networks and the tools of public management. In R. Eyestone (Ed.), *Public policy formation and implementation.* Greenwich, CT: JAI.

Wamsley, G. L. (1985). Policy subsystems as a unit of analysis in implementation studies: A struggle for theoretical synthesis. In K. Hanf & T. A. J. Toonen (Eds.), *Policy implemen-*

tation in federal and unitary systems: Questions of analysis and design (pp. 71-96). Boston: Martinus Nijhoff.

Wamsley, G. L. (1990). The agency perspective: Public administrators as agential leaders. In G. L. Wamsley, R. N. Bacher, C. T. Goodsell, P. S. Kronenberg, J. A. Rohr, C. M. Stivers, O. F. White, & J. F. Wolf, *Refounding public administration* (pp. 114-162). Newbury Park, CA: Sage.

Wamsley, G. L., Bacher, R. N., Goodsell, C. T., Kronenberg, P. S., Rohr, J. A., Stivers, C. M., White, O. F., & Wolf, J. F. (1990). *Refounding public administration*. Newbury Park, CA: Sage.

Wamsley, G. L., & Zald, M. N. (1973). *The political economy of public organizations*. Lexington, MA: D. C. Heath.

Wiebe, R. H. (1962). *Businessmen and reform: A study of the progressive movement*. Cambridge, MA: Harvard University Press.

Wiebe, R. H. (1967). *The search for order, 1877-1920*. New York: Hill & Wang.

Wilber, C. K., & Jameson, K. P. (1990). *Beyond Reaganomics: A further inquiry into the poverty of economics*. Notre Dame, IN: University of Notre Dame Press.

Wildavsky, A. (1988). *The new politics of the budgetary process*. Glenview, IL: Scott, Foresman.

Wilson, W. (1887). The study of administration. *Political Science Quarterly, 2*, 197-222.

Winter, W. F. (1993). *Hard truths/tough choices: An agenda for state and local reform* (First Report of the National Commission on the State and Local Public Service). Albany: SUNY, Nelson A. Rockefeller Institute of Government.

Womack, J. P., Jones, D. T., & Roos, D. (1990). *The machine that changed the world*. New York: Rawson Associates.

Zinn, H. (Ed.). (1966). *New Deal thought*. New York: Bobbs-Merrill.

Zunz, O. (1990). *Making America corporate, 1870-1920*. Chicago: University of Chicago Press.

2

Fencing in the Inherently
Governmental Debate

LARKIN DUDLEY
Virginia Polytechnic Institute and State University

Within our folk wisdom, proverbs oppose. "Good fences make good neighbors," says a farmer in Robert Frost's (1967) "Mending Wall," yet in the same poem the farmer's neighbor remarks that "Something there is doesn't love a wall." The history of the debate surrounding the definition of that which is public and that which is private is no exception to opposing proverbs. Whether to build a good fence of precise definitions of the activities belonging to each sector or to promote more penetrable, ambiguous boundaries among the sectors reverberates both through the literature and action surrounding the questions of public and private responsibilities. One of the basic aims of *Refounding Public Administration* (Wamsley et al., 1990) was to refocus dialogue in public administration from *whether* public administration to the *place* of public administration and the public administrator in the governance of the third century. However, omitted in that volume was ample discussion of the serious challenge to the place of the institutions of governing by what has been called third-party government, government by proxy, and government by contract.

The astonishing fact is that we have incrementally moved to a new manner of governing. Service provision by sources other than the originating government has been estimated to be up to half of all service delivery. At the local level, recent surveys indicate that all local governments experimented with at least one contracting arrangement and that no service seemed immune to service provision by other sources (Kettl, 1993). The authors of *Refounding,* with a special concern about the role of administrative action in our democratic society, have ignored the implications of this reality for governing, and, in fact, have seemed hostile to a consideration that "third-party government" is the reality. The special insight of the authors of the *Refounding* volume for the fate of public interest, active citizenship, and agential leadership should have been and should now be turned to this new way of governing.

Even in the 1970s, a shift in service provision from government provision to contracting was apparent, according to Alice Mosher (1980). That time period also saw a rise of the public choice paradigm in both academic and governmental services in the increasing prominence of the work of authors such as James M. Buchanan and Gordon Tullock, William A. Niskanen, and Vince and Elinor Ostrom. In the 1980s, President Reagan promoted tax policies and the formation of the Office of Privatization and a Commission on Privatization to emphasize the limiting of the federal government's role. Substantive public administration scholarship, such as that of Harold Seidman, Lester Salamon, Donald Kettl, Paul Starr, Steve Hanke, Ruth Hoogland DeHoog, and many others, raised questions about the limits of contracting services whereas others, such as E. S. Savas, saw privatization techniques as one answer to increasing efficiency of government. In the 1990s, states have even more firmly continued dialogue and action that favors privatization, and at the national level the effort to limit government has gained momentum. Yet in the 1990s, more questions have been raised about the true benefits of contracting as the difficulties in implementation have become more apparent (e.g., see John D. Donahue, 1989, and Charles R. Wise, 1990).

Issues are many. Concern with efficiency has driven most of the questions about contracting. Although many have seen contracting as a source of gaining needed expertise, flexibility, and cost-savings, others have noted the difficulties in writing complete solicitations, monitoring, and avoiding patronage, corruption, and poor performance. Questions about the effect of third-party provision on governing have been raised. One is increasing concern that privatization, predominantly contracting or outsourcing in the United States, will yield limited support for the collective through questioning the public goods status of services such as elementary and secondary education and welfare. The worry that administrative capacity to govern will be depleted and difficult to reinstate has also been a theme. Concerns about accountability, liability, and legitimacy have been raised.

Although the harbingers of contracting have painted a future of simpler, less costly provision of better service, the evidence has yet to support that assumption. As the pressures on the public sector have increased downward for political accountability, upward from a customer orientation, and competitively from contracting (Peters, 1993), governing has instead become even more complicated. Increasing calls for a mixture of individual citizens as "customers," for private businesses as "partners," and for more politically accountable, efficient government have left customary boundaries questionable. Perhaps one reason the authors of the *Refounding* ignored questions raised by contracting is that these questions not only challenge us intellectually in analysis of the role of government in a capitalistic society, but tear at the heart of the very identity of government and public administration in this last decade of the 20th century.

As John Rohr (see Chapter 4) explains in this volume, the concept of a state would make a difference. Without such in the American political system, the definition of what is governmental and what is not becomes problematic, and proponents of both sides can, and do, make arguments from the Founding. The question of the role of government is part and parcel of philosophical debates on the role of the state, arguments surrounding the founding of American government, and numerous treatises on the differences in public and private. As vital as it is to answer those questions directly, this chapter takes a more modest focus, an examination of whether and how some of the dimensions embedded in a concept of governmental are reflected in the struggle in practice to draw boundaries among commercial and governmental activities. This approach gives us one perch from which to identify the crosscurrents in steering a discussion on the place and nature of public administration.

Specifically, this chapter examines how dimensions of public functions described in the academic literature are reflected in the executive's efforts through the Office of Management and Budget to delineate what is meant by the concept of "inherently governmental functions." The activities defined as "inherently governmental" are activities that must be performed by government personnel rather than contracted out to the private sector. The federal management program in which the concept has historically been defined is that of Circular No. A-76 (Office of Management and Budget [OMB], 1983). More recent policy focusing on definition of the term is that of *Policy on Inherently Governmental Functions,* Policy Letter 92-1 of the Office of Federal Procurement Policy, Office of Management and Budget, September 23, 1992 (Office of Federal Procurement Policy [OFPP], 1992).

Circular A-76, initiated by the Bureau of the Budget under the administration of Dwight Eisenhower to establish federal policy regarding the performance of commercial activities, recognizes the principle that the general policy of the government is to rely on commercial sources to supply the products and services the government needs. After many revisions, the current Circular, last revised in 1983 and under consideration for revision now, requires competitive bidding between a government agency and private enterprise for a decision as to which should provide functions that previously have been provided by the agency. For agencies deciding what functions to contract out, the policy has been the authoritative source for the executive's definition of what is inherently governmental.

Cries of inadequacy of the definition for those attempting to decide what activities could be contracted out were widespread (e.g., see Comptroller General, 1961; General Accounting Office, 1991; Kettl, 1987). In response, the Office of Federal Procurement Policy (OFPP), Office of Management and Budget (OMB), released in 1992 a policy on "inherently governmental," OFPP 92-1. This policy's purpose is to delineate the term *inherently governmental* to provide guidance in contracting so that lines on transferring responsibility for tasks become clearer.

Just as drawing the lines among territories was one of the first orders of American government, agency personnel daily draw the boundary between what is governmental and what is not as they consider the limits of contracting. Government personnel have to operationalize Paul Appleby's (1945) contention that government is different. Thus, the effort to define the concept of "inherently governmental" is a good example for assessing how the federal executive does draw that line and what criteria are used. To examine both the descriptive and prescriptive elements of the debate, I will first briefly describe early attempts in the law and in the executive to define "inherently governmental" functions. Then I apply some of the concepts associated with "publicness" in the academic literature to the current policy on "inherently governmental" in Policy Letter OFPP 92-1. Finally, I explore how the definition of "inherently governmental" may be related to the self-images of government portrayed in the policies, and suggest implications of "defining inherently governmental" for the practice and field of public administration.

Lack of Consensus in the Law

Despite pleas from many agencies for a list of specific functions that are inherently governmental, both the law and executive policy have traditionally resisted such a task. In a recent article, Craig and Gilmour (1992) maintain that in the law there is no one discrete function that has historically been reserved for government. An understanding of why the courts resist a concrete definition can be gleaned from reviewing the reasoning that the Supreme Court has applied to defining governmental functions in the well-known case of *Garcia v. San Antonio Metropolitan Transit Authority* (1985). Although the functions in this case are those at the municipal and state levels, the functions in question, such as private provision of security, transportation, and utilities, are similar to a number of the functions considered for contracting at the federal level.

In *Garcia,* the Supreme Court ruled that extending the provisions of the Fair Labor Standard Act's 1974 amendments to states and their subdivisions would NOT "impermissibly interfere with the integral governmental functions of these bodies." Included in the reasoning is that determination of state immunity from federal regulation does not turn on judicial appraisal of whether a governmental function is "integral" or "traditional."

As a supporting argument for his final conclusion that the unelected judiciary should not make decisions about what functions are governmental, Blackmun skillfully rejects selected criteria for defining "traditional governmental functions." Tradition is rejected because it prevents a court from accommodating changes in the "historical functions of states, changes that have resulted in a number of once-private functions like education being assumed by the States and their subdivisions" (*Garcia,* p. 31). Besides, the historical criterion is unworkable in that it asks the Court to decide how long a function must have been provided before it becomes historical. In rejecting the criterion of "necessary" government services, Blackmun argues that simply because the market does not provide enough of a service does not mean the government has to provide it, because other means, such as procurement or subsidies, can be used.

Turning to tort liability cases as precedent, Blackmun rejects the criterion of "uniqueness" because it has proven unmanageable. Blackmun thus argued that the judiciary does not need to delineate "traditional" or integral governmental functions. The Supreme Court had already stated in 1945 that the distinction between "governmental and proprietary" was "untenable" (*New York v. United States,* 326 U.S. 572). However, the problem of defining governmental functions continuously reappears indirectly in the contracting arena as well as in other areas of the law (see General Accounting Office [GAO], 1991; Krent, 1990).

Still, pessimism abounds on the likelihood of a clear doctrine in the law about what constitutes a public function. Several scholars (Craig & Gilmour, 1992; Lawrence, 1986) maintain that the "public function" doctrine at the federal level appears destined to join the nondelegation doctrine in the graveyard of once powerful judicial doctrines. Because of the lack of consensus on governmental functions and the lack of emphasis on a public law framework in discussions of contracting out, scholars, such as Ronald Moe (1987; Moe & Gilmour, 1995), emphatically assert the need for the recognition of the importance of public law in the setting of criteria for assigning functions to the appropriate sector.

▬ Context of the Concept of Inherently Governmental

Without a clear definition in the law of what is "inherently governmental" and with no national policy, the most authoritative source of the distinction has been in the executive. The traditional definition of inherently governmental is that in Circular A-76:

> Certain functions are inherently governmental in nature, being so intimately related to the public interest as to mandate performance by Federal employees. (OMB, 1983, p. 2)

This definition appears both in the current Circular A-76 (revised 1983) and in OFPP Policy Letter 92-1 (1992) almost exactly as it appeared in the 1979 Circular. Consistently, both in Circular A-76 and OFPP 92-1, the definition has been tied to that of the public interest . . . so "intimately related to the public interest as to mandate performance by Government employees" (OMB, 1983). Implied in both documents is that functions related to sovereignty, to the discretionary exercise of governmental authority, and to making value judgments on behalf of the government are functions that are inherently governmental and, thus, functions in the public interest. Yet the concept of public interest is never fully explained and is mentioned again only briefly in the policy.

This treatment of the concept of public interest as a defining characteristic of inherently governmental functions lends credibility to Charles Goodsell's (1990) discussion of the concept of the "public interest" as a symbol. As a symbol, the definition of the public interest is obscure, only partially understood, and felt emotionally rather than known in a precise way (Goodsell, 1990). Yet according to Goodsell's discussion, symbols do carry value premises with them, premises he discusses as aspects of the public interest. Goodsell's premises will be combined with those of others to examine the inherently governmental concept later in this chapter.

In both Circular A-76 and in OFPP Policy Letter 92-1, governmental functions are referred to as those that require "either the exercise of discretion in applying governmental authority or the use of value judgments in making decisions for the government." Two specific types of functions are mentioned: those relating to the act of governing and those related to monetary transactions. Although examples of activities that are commercial, and hence not "inherently governmental," are specified in Circular A-76, no specific list of functions that are prohibited from being contracted ever appears in the Circular or supplements to it.

It is somewhat ironical that, in the executive, the definition of what is a governmental function has historically received some of the most prominent attention in Circular A-76, a circular whose purpose is stated as that of establishing federal policy regarding the performance of commercial activities. Since 1955, the national policy promulgated in Circular A-76 has been to rely on contractors in the private sector to provide the goods and services that the government needs to act on the public's behalf. In even this cursory review of the Circular, our attention is drawn to the fact that in the "Background," the first part of the substantive text, the following is stated:

> the Government should not compete with its citizens. The competitive enterprise system, characterized by individual freedom and initiative, is the primary source of national economic strength . . . it . . . continues to be the general policy of the Government to rely on commercial sources to supply the products and services the Government needs. (OMB, 1983, p. 1)

Continuing to the policy itself, the Circular reaffirms three main goals of the United States Government: to achieve economy and enhance productivity, to retain governmental functions in-house, and to rely on the commercial sector. Competition is highlighted both as enhancing quality, economy, and productivity and as the philosophy behind the preferred methods of determining whether a government agency or a commercial source should provide a service. Note that two out of the three goals reaffirmed are those supporting the private sector. The same pattern is observed in the definitions. What is a commercial activity is explained first, and the definition of a governmental function follows. What is governmental is defined in relation to what is commercial, not the other way around. No wonder public administrators have had such difficulty in delineating among tasks. Without a clear philosophy of the parameters of the public sector, delineation becomes discretionary. Only 6 years after the original circular appeared in 1955, General Accounting Office (GAO) reports chronicled the difficulties that both agencies and contractors have faced because of a lack of clear guidance in the definition (Comptroller General, 1961). Continuing into the 1990s, concerns in GAO reports include fears that contractors perform basic management functions and construct policy in areas as wide-ranging as Head Start and hazardous waste (GAO, 1991). Neither policy guidance, the academic literature, nor the law provide definitive guidance on what tasks are "inherently governmental," according to a 1991 report by the General Accounting Office (GAO, 1991).

Finally, the admonitions and pleas from those engaged in public administration are heard by the Office of Management and Budget (OMB). New guidelines for determining what is inherently governmental appear from the Office of Federal Procurement Policy (OFPP), OMB, September 30, 1992, as Policy Letter 92-1. At first glance, one believes the OFPP assertions that the new inherently governmental policy does not fundamentally change the guidance originally found in OMB Circular A-76. After all, the traditional definition of an "inherently governmental function" was retained as one that is "so intimately related to the public interest as to mandate performance by Government employees." Retained also is the familiar emphasis on limiting the use of discretion and restricting value judgments to government employees. The same stress on government functions as those involving the act of governing and those involving monetary transactions appears.

However, there are some significant changes. This policy is addressed to all non-personal services contracting, not just to those engaged in the functions that could be considered commercial activities under Circular A-76. By doing so, the importance of understanding contractual relationships for all governmental managers is acknowledged and, in fact, contracting comes to be defined as a management process. In the effort to clarify the inherently governmental definition, the general principles underlying the definition are stated—the importance of accountability: avoiding the appearance of private influence with respect to documents prepared for Congress, law enforcement agencies, or oversight agencies; guarding the use of discretion; and using a "totality of the circumstances" approach to discern from a list of factors whether a function reflects a transfer of official responsibility (OFPP 92-1). These factors include Congressional legislative restrictions: the degree to which official discretion would be limited; the degree to which contractors could perform wide-ranging interpretations or determine an award or penalty in claims adjudication; the contractor's ability to take action that significantly and directly affects the life or property of members of the public; the applicability of available special agency authorities to the situation, such as the need to deputize private persons; and whether the function is already being performed by private persons.

Within the body of the policy, the importance of good contract management is not only stressed, but seen as a necessary ingredient for accountability. Further, an illustrative list of some 19 tasks that are inherently governmental is attached. These include, for example, the conduct of criminal investigations, the performance of adjudicatory functions, the direction and control of federal employees, and the determination of budgetary policy. The policy also identifies the management controls that are to be implemented when the government contracts for functions that approach being in the category of governmental. An illustrative list of these almost inherently governmental functions includes budget preparation, services that involve evaluating other contractor's performances, and performances of analyses for the development of policy.

What is so significant here is that the context and content surrounding the definition of what is an inherently governmental function has shifted. In Circular A-76, the focus is on defining commercial activities and on contracting procedures for functions that could be commercial activities in a context of affirmation of the private sector. In the inherently governmental policy, the focus is now on defining the criteria for determining inherently governmental and for understanding the responsibility for all governmental personnel of governing in public-private relationships.

One way to assess the magnitude of the change of context in Circular A-76 from that of the inherently governmental policy is in juxtaposing the text of the inherently governmental policy against some of the characteristics that have been involved in our understanding of what is governmental. Three multidimensional concepts are chosen here—legitimacy, public management, and creation of a public dialogue. The concepts are not necessarily mutually exclusive nor are they inclusive of all the dimensions that should be considered in a discussion of *governmental*.[1] Instead, these concepts seem to represent some of the more important dimensions of publicness by which a concept of governmental could be evaluated. The dimensions represented in the concepts include the work of several authors, primarily the review essays of Charles Goodsell (1990) on the public interest and of Stewart Ranson and John Stewart (1989) on public management, as well as the work of Ronald Moe (1987), Gary Wamsley (1990), and James March and Johan Olsen (1989). Here, I have combined the insights of others to focus on the dimensions of the concern for respecting sovereignty and a defining of public goods in a concept of *legitimacy;* maintaining accountability and demonstrating a concern for effects in a concept of *public management;* and the necessity of defending a policy in terms of the public interest, displaying a discernible logic, having a spirit of responsiveness, and creating a shared language as dimensions of creating a *public dialogue.* I then use these dimensions to assess the treatment of the concept of inherently governmental functions.

Legitimacy in the Public Domain

The purpose of the public domain, according to Ranson and Stewart (1989), is to constitute the social and political preconditions that make society possible: to create those agreements that enable social life to proceed and develop. Whether a concept of the public domain makes sense in a pluralistic society and in an ethos characterized as postmodern has been a continuing controversy.[2] Because the focus here is on assessing how governmental is defined in practice, the assumption is made that there exists enough agreement upon preconditions in American society to enable dialogue, if not consensus, about the roles of government.

Legitimacy must be established and preserved if the policies of governmental representatives are to be taken seriously. March and Olsen (1989, p. 49) maintain that legitimacy can be established by showing that decisions accomplish appropriate objectives or by showing that they are made in appropriate ways. In the inherently governmental debate, legitimacy stems from both. One way is that of accomplishing appropriate objectives through adhering to a concept of the rights and obligations of government to perform certain duties in the interest of the general welfare or, in other words, a doing of the right things. Second, legitimacy also stems from ensuring that contract decisions are made according to procedural guidelines, or in making sure things are done right. In this section, the concept of legitimacy is limited to its first meaning—a concept of the rights and obligations of government. A second source of legitimacy, ensuring that decisions are made appropriately, is discussed in the next section as the dimension of accountability.

Legitimacy stemming from meeting appropriate objectives in Circular A-76 and in OFPP Policy Letter 92-1 reflects a concern with some of the dimensions of the concept of sovereignty. Ronald Moe (1987) would agree that sovereignty should be the determining dimension in deciding the appropriateness of private provision of service. Moe has argued that, "The single most important characteristic that separates the public and private sectors, particularly at the federal level, involves the concept of sovereignty" (p. 456).[3] The federal government possesses the rights and immunities of sovereignty, whereas private sector organizations do not (Moe, 1987, p. 456). Those rights and immunities include the legitimate right to use coercion to enforce its will, such as the right to tax and to go to war; immunity from suit except by permission; indivisibility; the right to disavow debt, but not to go bankrupt with obligations protected by the "full faith and credit of the Treasury"; and the right to establish rules for protection and transference of property, both public and private (Moe, 1987).

Adherence to a concept of responsibilities reserved for the sovereign is found in OFPP 92-1 in the insistence that the interpretation and execution of the laws of the United States prevent other than government personnel from: binding the United States to take or not take some action; advancing or protecting U.S. interests by military or diplomatic action, judicial proceedings, or contract management; affecting the activities of property of private citizens; or exerting ultimate control over the acquisition, use, or disposition of the property of the United States. Further, one of the criteria of OFPP 92-1 to be used in deciding whether any particular action is governmental includes the degree to which a contractor's actions may affect the life or property of members of the public or require the use of force. Thus at the federal level the policy indicates certain purposes should be reserved for those duly authorized.

In addition to adhering to a concept of the rights and obligations of the sovereign, the task of government within the public domain is traditionally defined as that of making authoritative allocation of values for the whole and of securing their implementation through lawmaking and regulation (Ranson & Stewart, 1989). To allocate value, some consideration must be made for what the differences are between public and private goods. Public goods traditionally have been defined as collective goods that are nonexclusive and possess indivisibility of benefit. However, no matter how technical the definition, what a public good is and which ones are needed in society are in the final analysis collective political decisions (Ranson & Stewart, 1989).

In accordance with an attempt to define public goods, both policies do designate certain actions as those that are considered commercial (Circular A-76) or those that are considered governmental (OFPP 92-1). The OFPP policy does give criteria for determining whether activities should be considered inherently governmental and does list examples of tasks that are considered inherently governmental. These dimensions of the policy certainly extend the traditional policy in Circular A-76. However, rather than using the economic criteria of nonexclusivity and indivisibility of benefit to define public goods, the policy relies on the standard that service provision includes a concern for official responsibility and accountability. Although the OFPP 92-1 policy makes important gains in delineating services and activities, it is disappointing that the policy, and the discourse surrounding it, do not give more consideration to the context of delivering services within a public framework, to a better discussion of the special conditions that make governmental service somewhat different from private provision. Ronald Moe's pleas for a better theory—or at least a set of criteria—to assist in designating functions as public ones (Moe, 1987; Moe & Gilmour, 1995) have not yet been completely answered. However, some of the progress that has been made toward establishing criteria for designating public functions are discussed in the next two sections on the dimensions involved in public management and the creation of public dialogue.

Public Management

In the literature, at least two fundamental concerns are associated with public management—a concern for accountability and a concern for effects. Emphasized most has been accountability through adherence to legality and morality (Goodsell, 1990) or in terms of what Stewart Ranson and John Stewart (1989) call "being held to account." "Being held to account" includes an emphasis on the carrying out of proper procedures and on being able to show that decision making has been carried out in the proper way.

According to OFPP 92-1, the determination of whether a function is inherently governmental in the guidelines depends on a totality-of-the-circumstances approach where the presence or absence of any one factor is not determinative. A concern for accountability is reflected in guarding against a transfer of official responsibility through consideration of adhering to Congressional legislative restrictions or authorizations and judging the degree to which official discretion is or would be limited. One other method of ensuring accountability is limiting the type of tasks that can be delegated to those outside government. The degree to which contractor's actions would be circumscribed in claims adjudication and the delegation of approval or signature authority should be considered, according to the policy. As summarized by Richard M. Ong of the Office of Management and Budget, the distinction between discretionary and ministerial is important.[4] According to Ong,

> [the] more a contractor would be bound by clear guidelines imposed by the prior exercise of government authority, the less concern we should have. Conversely, the more the contract would require the contractor to exercise judgment in matching means to ends, to permit him a choice where a desired result may be achieved in one of several ways, or to investigate and then decide and act according to his discretion, the greater the need for scrutiny. (private correspondence, 1993)

A second concern that has been part of the focus on public management is a concern for effects, a concern for the implications for all groups. Only through a concern for the implications for all can public managers participate in the governing of the collective in the public interest (Goodsell, 1990; Ranson & Stewart, 1989). Effects are often measured through agreed-upon values, usually efficiency, effectiveness, and evaluation (Goodsell, 1990).

Several provisions are in place to monitor effects in the inherently govern-mental policy. One effort to value the effects of the OFPP policy is through procedures that require positions that are inherently governmental to be identified prior to issuance of any solicitation. Further, review of contracting takes place at the agency level with the possibility of review at another level by the Office of Management and Budget. Also stressed are clear identifica-tion of contractor work, the importance of management controls, the mainte-nance of good contract management post-award, and independent review by government. An important addition to this policy is the delineation of "man-agement controls" for identified functions that may approach being inherently governmental because of the relationship between contractor and government. Further, in the assertion that the policy is complementary to, not a replacement of, Circular A-76, the inherently governmental policy retains an emphasis on efficiency.

▬ Creating Public Dialogue

How open the construction of policy is to public dialogue is another way of evaluating the public dimensions of a policy. Some criteria that would be important in ensuring that public dialogue can occur are whether the policy itself can be defended in terms of the public interest and whether there is a discernible logic—whether the policy appears to be responsive and to contrib-ute to creating a language that can be shared among government and citizens are other criteria.

Goodsell (1990) asserts that a policy in the public interest should be defensible in terms of what the public wants, in terms broader than naked self-interest. In addition, according to Goodsell, part of making public one's claims should be a concern for logic. The evaluation of logic includes ques-tioning the policy's connection to its underlying normative purposes, articu-lation for a concern for societal purposes, and substantiation of how these purposes will be advocated (Goodsell, 1990).

The purpose of the inherently governmental policy is defined as assisting the executive branch officers and employees to avoid an unacceptable transfer of official responsibility to government contractors. This expression of safe-guarding the public trust does articulate an underlying normative purpose. Further, the policy concretely links the criterion of prohibiting the exercise of substantial discretion, defined as committing the federal government to a course of action when two or more alternative courses exist, to specific examples, such as not having contractors support or oppose proposed legislation. As such, a concern for defining and circumscribing discretion in practice is substantiated.

Whether dialogue allows for a spirit of political responsiveness, enabling the participation of citizens, is also a concern (Goodsell, 1990; Ranson & Stewart, 1989; Stivers, 1990). One indicator of responsiveness is the process of soliciting external opinions and the weight they are given in the decision making in OFPP 92-1. Comments were solicited in accordance with federal procedures and explained with the publication of the policy.[5] Debates about Circular A-76 and OFPP 92-1 did attract representatives from agencies, unions, a variety of occupational interest groups, contractors, contractors' associations, and members of Congress. Yet a wide range of citizens in government and in society have not been brought fully into the dialogue of details about governmental accountability and discretion.

According to Goodsell (1990), the pursuit of the public interest should also include a focus on the interests of ignored persons, those who may have been too poor or too unorganized to become part of the agenda. Generally, within the Circular A-76 debate, attention has been paid to the possible effects on displaced workers, to concerns brought forth by different employee organizations. In the OFPP policy, however, the future state of public service is not given quite enough attention. In fact, in response to one commentator, OFPP maintains that concern for the future balance between official and contractor workforce is a matter for agencies themselves to determine and, thus, the policy does not elaborate on the retention of adequate personnel for oversight.

Finally, we should consider Ranson and Stewart's (1989) assertion that the political process is one in which groups are necessarily enjoined to "make public" their claims and challenges. "Giving an account," according to Ranson and Stewart, means creating and negotiating a shared language with which to talk about purpose and performance within government and between citizens and government. If the executive policy concerning inherently governmental is to become a part of a larger dialogue, then a concern for the appropriate relationships among government, commercial, and nonprofit sectors must move from a concern about being held to account to include an equally important focus on "giving an account." As of yet, this has not happened.

According to Gary Wamsley, having others share in the giving of an account performs an even more crucial function than increasing dialogue and a sense of consensus. Instead, whether all who have a stake in the matter at hand have had the opportunity to share in defining it is the key to the legitimacy of any criterion (Wamsley, 1990, p. 40). As discussed above, however, the inherently governmental policy has depended more on concepts stemming from authority, another source of legitimacy, than on inclusiveness.

Implications for Policy Development

Reflected above in the discussion of the "inherently governmental" policy are oft-repeated themes in both the academic and governmental literature of concerns about legitimacy, public management, and public dialogue. The general tone of the discussion is that the inherently governmental policy is a definite improvement in guidance over the earlier Circular A-76 guidelines. However, further policy development could include better guidance to the public service on how to determine a need for a cadre of personnel properly to contract for, evaluate, monitor, and use highly technical products from the private sector. Dialogue around an inherently governmental policy should address some of the possible pitfalls of disinvestment (Wolf, 1987) and emphasize that not retaining sufficient professional personnel may impede the development of future capacity to govern. Further, neither Circular A-76 nor OFPP 92-1 has much emphasis on how to increase the ability for the larger polity continually to evolve, learn, and debate the roles and values associated with a concept of what is governmental.

Another crucial omission is that the importance of preserving agency culture (Wamsley et al., 1990) is given somewhat short shrift. Maintaining a pervasive commitment to the mission and values of an agency is seen by Gary Wamsley (Wamsley et al., 1990) as crucial to agency performance and by Robert Denhardt (1993) as essential to promoting change. Yet little provision is made in contracting in general or in these policies to educate coproviders or contract personnel about an agency's mission and values.

There is some irony in the simultaneous promotion of third-party governmental relationships and the current emphasis on organizations committed to empowered relationships. Good public-private partnerships and creative contracting may indeed be one of the tools managers use to serve the public better, but these same tools make the engagement of the other values more difficult. How to empower all with a high level of involvement in efforts to improve the quality and productivity of the organization is a goal usually not addressed well in contracting situations. Incentives to increase innovation in public-private interaction are sorely lacking.

Further, Denhardt's (1993) ideas of pragmatic implementation echo a concept of process in which the manager pursues a wide variety of often unexpected opportunities. Change is seen as occurring through a free-flowing process. How one reconciles the orientation toward control and stipulated duties that are part of contracting, and implied in the OFPP policy, with that of a free-flowing process of management has not been addressed. Future trends where agencies and units of government will be working more and more with temporary and contract workers will necessitate addressing the distinctions to be made between internal and external management processes and will bring us back again to the difficulty of differentiating that which is inherently governmental. Also, specifications in policy are still difficult to enact in practice. Although adhering to congressional limitations seems a straightforward specification, a recent Department of Justice (Office of Legal Counsel [OLC], 1992) memorandum illustrates the difficulty of discerning whether certain functions should be performed only by governmental agencies. At issue in this situation are two different interpretations of Congress's intentions in 18 U.S.C. 3621 (b) stating the Bureau of Prisons "may designate any available penal or correction facility that meets minimum standards of health and habitability . . . whether maintained by the Federal Government or OTHERWISE" [emphasis mine]. The General Accounting Office (GAO, 1991) had interpreted *otherwise* as only local, state, and federal facilities based on their interpretation that, with a few exceptions, Congress has never contemplated housing prisoners in private facilities. On the other hand, the opinion of the Office of Legal Counsel is that the decision to use facilities is entirely up to the Bureau as long as such facilities meet the standards set in relevant statutes. The ever-present difficulty in interpreting congressional statutes has not been surmounted by this policy either.

▬ What Self-Image for Government?

Attempting to understand the confusion surrounding the concept of inherently governmental presents its own conundrum. Boundary drawing is not only difficult, but in many circumstances may have to be a local, episodic endeavor rather than a national, systemic task. Both the earlier Circular A-76 policy and the later OFPP 92-1 policy attempt to circumvent this difficulty through not giving exact standards by which to judge each situation. The inherently governmental policy in OFPP 92-1 does correct Circular A-76's omission of guidelines for determining what may be governmental, but these guidelines are to use a combination of factors and leave the initial decision to the local level with the possibility of review at the national level. Neither in the executive policy nor in the law do guidelines once and for all divide the world into governmental functions and nongovernmental functions. This lack of a high, solid fence between the two does not answer the critics who would like to see definitive standards that separate tasks nor does it completely satisfy practitioners who must daily decide what can and cannot be done by the private sector.

Why this condition exists may be better understood through the use of a different lens, through speculating on what sort of self-image of government is projected in the policies. In a recent article, Jerry Frug (1993) delineates three possible images of self that could underlie local governmental law: the autonomous self, the situated self, and the postmodern self. The autonomous self is a centered sense of self that would include defining self as radically separate from others. Applied to the Circular A-76 policy, the reflection of a sense of an autonomous self of government is found in the elements of the definition of governmental that stem from a concept of sovereignty. Examples include the stipulations that only duly authorized personnel can perform tasks to bind the United States to some action, have control over property, or perform actions that may affect the lives of citizens. Although many gray areas exist in matching guidelines to situations, a traditional notion of governmental as distinct from other sectors is sought but difficult to operationalize. It is clear that only duly authorized governmental personnel could be given the authority to use force against another country. It is not so clear what duties can be contracted out to private security firms.

Because of the lack of definitive guidelines and Circular A-76's emphasis on defining commercial activities and neglect of defining governmental activities, a search for an autonomous sense of self was intensified. Although the Circular does define those activities as governmental that have traditionally been associated with a concept of sovereignty, in the interpretation I have given here the overall image of what is governmental appears as a residue left over from defining commercial. This image of what is governmental seems at best neglectful, at worst very negative.[6] The policy appears to preserve the identity of the corporate sector, but no identity is given to the other, in this case, governmental.

In the later inherently governmental policy, the image of an autonomous self as reflected in a concept of sovereignty is still present. Spelled out more clearly is the self-assertion of governmental responsibility for ensuring that contracting takes place under standards that meet the requirements of ensuring accountability, avoiding the appearance of private influence, guarding the use of discretion, and discerning whether official responsibility has been transferred.

However, hints of what has been called a concept of the "situated self" as discussed by Jerry Frug (1993) appear.[7] These include a notion of a self defined through connection, of a multiplicity of opportunities to express self, and of an understanding that only through participation in a larger political dialogue can a definition of political identity occur. Elements of the inherently governmental policy that focus on a relationship with the commercial sector, the opportunity for defining what is governmental at the local level, and a concern for the image of government in the citizens' eyes within a concept of preserving legitimacy reflect dimensions of those associated with a situated self. Governmental self-definition is understood in a relationship with the commercial, but with both in relationship to a larger whole of the public sphere. Further, the policy recognizes that what is governmental has to be fashioned from a combination of factors within an understanding of local interpretation.

Yet just as a more completely articulated concept of governmental with elements of both an autonomous and situated self was emerging in the "inherently governmental" policy, the trend in American culture of adoration of business management accelerated again. *Reinvention* and *reengineering* became the buzzwords, as noted by Richard Green and Lawrence Hubbell (Chapter 1, this volume).[8] As contracting, partnerships, franchises, and vouchers have become common means of providing services, the political dialogue intensifies around which means are more efficient. This focus on means blinds us to the processes of redefinition of *governmental* itself that have accompanied the new experiments in service provision.

One of the effects of the focus on means only, has been to decentralize governmental services and to dislocate them from governmental provision to situations combining actors from public, private, nonprofits, and the citizenry. Such dislocation moves the self-definition of governmental from that of a situated self to a world in which the concepts applied to governmental are more arbitrary, to a world characterized as "postmodern."

In the world of the situated self, one may seek to act under a norm of appropriateness. Questions that would be asked would be the epistemological ones of how can I interpret the world and what is my identity in it, according to Jerry Frug's (1993, p. 310) discussion of Brian McHale's *Postmodernist Fiction* (1987). Further, Frug, following McHale, asserts that living in a postmodern world raises different questions, ontological ones of in which world is the subject, and what happens when boundaries between worlds are violated, when different kinds of worlds are placed in confrontation.

The postmodern world has been characterized as a world of a decentered self reading all events as texts in organizations of adhocracy (e.g., the work of Charles J. Fox & Hugh T. Miller, 1995; Jerry Frug, 1993). In this world of blurred boundaries, changing roles, and celebration of the eclectic, agencies and actors engaged in the efforts of governing express confusion and frustration at how to cope. Deciding how to move from an image of government as a monitor of business and the nonprofit sector to one of coproduction is not an easy transition (e.g., see the work of Susan MacManus, 1992, and Susan Bernstein, 1991, respectively). To answer the myriad questions surrounding who will have access to what information systems, or how to relate monitors and providers, places all in arenas fraught with opportunities for misunderstanding and puzzlement about which world is to be engaged.

The postmodern predicament of shifting worlds requires different mindsets for governmental decision makers. Given the complexity of governing in any time in American culture, but perhaps even more so in a "postmodern" culture, to answer exactly which functions are governmental for all times and all places in American culture is to attack the wrong question. Instead, the trend of organizational devolution, privatization, and decentralization could have at least two effects on the concept of what is "inherently governmental."

One alterative is that a postmodern world of fragmentation could lead to a concept of inherently governmental that is parallel to what has been called a "postmodern self." Through multiple sites, multiple roles, and authority distributed to multiple actors representing all sectors, a concept of what is governmental could lose meaning. According to Frug (1993), a self characterized as postmodern has no core, no self that separates from others. Instead, the act of attempting to define governmental functions through generalizations would be seen as an act of futility.

Building on the work of Jean-Francois Lyotard's *The Postmodern Condition: A Report on Knowledge* (1984), Frug (1993) notes that the situated subject longs for interconnection with others, for the experience of collective unity no matter how impossible it seems. By contrast, the postmodern subject denies this possibility; a nostalgia for the unattainable, a hope of bringing the "mysterious hidden core of self to the surface" is not even a dream (Frug, 1993, p. 308). Instead, Frug summarizes the situation as one in which, "For the postmodern subject, relationships with others—and with the world at large—is an experience not of consensus, totality, or oneness but of conflicting multiplicities" (p. 308). Following Frug's concept, to adopt an inherently governmental philosophy that fits with a concept of a postmodern self would rob a concept of governmental of its symbolic, unifying characteristics. In fact, the postmodern political climate attempts to level a concept of what is governmental to that of just another actor, as is illustrated in the concept of "DG" (Damn Government) as discussed by Charles J. Fox and Hugh T. Miller (1995).

Conclusion

An alternative response to the hazards of maintaining some sense of what is governmental in postmodern ambiguity does exist. Moving to a different level and pondering some of the more general values associated with a concept of publicness in a dialogue of inclusiveness is the other alternative, and a better strategy. The tried and true approaches of understanding the arguments over values in constitutional cases, appreciating the arguments of politics and administration in theory, as well as engaging the concepts of the renewed interest in empowering people, enhancing citizenship, appreciating diversity, and creating a consensual and/or discursive democracy, seem essential.

Also essential will be a constant defining and redefining of what is governmental in the multiple sites and with multiple groups of citizens, all within a spirit of a situated self knowledgeable enough to negotiate a postmodern world. Only through a dialogue about the parameters of publicness can the experiments with new ways of governing be responsibly undertaken. Such dialogue could contribute to a possibility of a learning polity of reasoned discourse as reflected in Habermas (1990), March and Olsen (1989), and the ideas of Charles Goodsell, Gary Wamsley, and Camilla Stivers in *Refounding Public Administration* (Wamsley et al., 1990). But such a dialogue can only take place if those at the table can understand when and why a sense of some of the more important, although penetrable, boundaries around what is governmental may be violated.

The necessity of an understanding of what *publicness* means and is coming to mean returns us to the poem "Mending Wall" (Frost, 1967) and connects us back to another time when the debate of the limits of government underpinned social and political ferment. In a speech at the University of Georgia in the 1960s, Robert Frost recalled the great debate on poetry between Carl Sandburg and himself. Frost had maintained that writing poetry without a sense of rhyme and rhythm was like playing tennis with the net down. Sandburg maintained that playing tennis with no net was more fun.

They are both right. The relationship between sectors is not totally symbolized by the neighbor in Frost's poem, the spirit of restraint, "which insists that conventions must be upheld, built up and continually rebuilt, as a matter of principle" (Untermeyer, 1967, p. 111). Nor is it totally symbolized by the rebel, the speaker in the poem, the spirit of rebellion, who wants to tear down the wall, who admits "Something there is that doesn't love a wall."

But, mending the wall—examining the gaps, the boulders, and loaves; building, rebuilding, every spring, in respect for understanding why loaves and boulders were there before—could be a metaphor for the process of discovering what is inherently governmental. Not to take seriously the necessity of a better understanding of that which is "inherently governmental" may mean an acceleration of experimentation beyond what is prudent, of being unable to discern where the balls are in the game. Taking down the net in some situations may be more fun, but only if we have a concept of a court and a memory of why a net was once thought important.

The neighbor's talk in "Mending Wall" reminds us of the importance of preserving a political community where holders of such opposite views can still find some ways of responsibly competing and some ways of cooperating in coproduction. The inclusiveness of those in the dialogue is important, but most important is the ritual itself—of calling the neighbor beyond the hill and walking the wall together. To go too far without coupling means and ends in an inclusive dialogue may indeed remove all the fences among the sectors. Citizens from all sectors will continually need to engage, and clarify, if only momentarily, those situations where there is a need to emphasize a difference in the sectors and those where we need to minimize differences. Not doing so may result in losing a sense of what is governmental, in a lack of a place from which public servants can speak and in which citizenry can come to understand and contribute to the meaning of that which is public.

Notes

1. Left out of the discussion are two bodies of literature that are intimately related to the question of what is inherently governmental, the studies distinguishing public and private organizations and the scholarship most focused on questions of administrative law, particularly administrative discretion. The literature on these distinctions is well treated elsewhere and because each would require introducing separate frameworks, they are not considered here.

2. See Calhoun (1992), Johnson (1994), Somers (1993), and Villa (1992) for the controversies surrounding concepts of public realm.

3. Others would disagree with Ronald Moe's use of the concept of sovereignty. Jerry Frug (1993) in a description of sovereignty for localities asserts that the connotation of the concept is that localities can do whatever they want; an ability to be selfish, like consumers, on a collective rather than an individual basis. Frug is addressing the possibility that self-interest may permeate the general legal frame. However, Ronald Moe here and in other works makes a plea that public administration not abandon the more traditional concepts of public law, particularly Constitutional questions, for those of only an economic framework. Resolving this debate is not possible in this chapter; here, I have instead chosen to look at sovereignty in terms of the responsibility of the national government to act according to the duties generally understood under the Constitution. Whether or not the concept behind those duties can be seen as a license for aggrandizement or whether there is protection in the system created from the Constitution has been and will continue to be a controversy in American scholarship. In the Conclusion, I do use concepts from Frug to better understand the progression of the debate around inherently governmental.

4. Another important source informing the dialogue of discretion is that of a 1990 memorandum of the Office of Legal Counsel (1990 WL 488475) addressing the constitutional limitations of contracting out. Citing as precedent *Buckley v. Valeo,* 424 U.S. 1 (1976), the opinion reaffirmed that the term *Officers of the United States* is a reference to those people who may exercise "significant authority" under the laws of the United States. The *Buckley* opinion stated that one set of duties that should be carried out only by duly appointed officers of the United States includes "broad administrative powers"—rule making, advisory opinions, and determination of eligibility for funds and even for federal elective office itself. Duties of an "investigative and informative nature" could be delegated to those not appointed as officers of the United States.

5. Comments included 19 from government agencies, eight from industry or trade groups, four from private individuals, two from employee organizations, and one from a research and development center.

6. Of course, coming out of two world wars and at a period in the 1950s when government's legitimacy was not so under siege, perhaps our observations should include that the power and authority of the government was assumed and, therefore, did not need to be expressed. That interpretation could also be a legitimate one.

7. To describe some of the dimensions of a concept of the "situated self," Jerry Frug (1993) combines writings from a host of authors, including Charles Taylor, Michael Walzer, Roberto Unger, Carole Gilligan, and Martha Minow.

8. The movement to reinvent and reengineer government has emphasized the need for efficiency in all three branches, but the main impact has been aimed at roles and functions in the executive branch. With some exceptions, the overall roles of the legislative and judicial branches do not seem questioned. In response, efforts by the executive branch to solidify what is inherently governmental are, in effect, efforts to seek legitimacy.

▬ References

Appleby, P. H. (1945). *Government is different.* New York: Knopf.

Bernstein, S. R. (1991). *Managing contracted services in the nonprofit agency: Administrative, ethical, and political issues.* Philadelphia: Temple University Press.

Calhoun, C. (Ed.). (1992). *Habermas and the public sphere.* Cambridge: MIT Press.

Comptroller General. (1961). *Civil servants and contract employees: Who should do what for the federal government?* Comptroller General's Report to the Congress (FPCD-81-43, June 10). Washington, DC: General Accounting Office.

Craig, B. H., & Gilmour, R. S. (1992). The constitution and accountability for *public* functions. *Governance, 5,* 46-67.

Denhardt, R. B. (1993). *The pursuit of significance: Strategies for managerial success in public organizations.* Belmont, CA: Wadsworth.

Donahue, J. D. (1989). *The privatization decision: Public ends, private means.* New York: Basic Books.

Fox, C. J., & Miller, H. T. (1995). *Postmodern public administration: Toward discourse.* Thousand Oaks, CA: Sage.

Frost, R. (1967). Mending wall. In *The road not taken: An introduction to Robert Frost—a selection of Robert Frost's poems with a biographical preface and running commentary by Louis Untermeyer.* New York: Holt, Rinehart & Winston.

Frug, J. (1993). Decentering decentralization. *The University of Chicago Law Review, 60*(2), 253-338.

Garcia v. San Antonio Metropolitan Transit Authority, 469 U.S. 528 (1985).

General Accounting Office. (1991, November). *Government contracts: Are service contractors performing inherently governmental functions?* (USGAO Publication No. GAO/GGD-92-11). Washington, DC: Government Printing Office.

Goodsell, C. T. (1990). Public administration and the public interest. In G. Wamsley, R. N. Bacher, C. T. Goodsell, P. S. Kronenberg, J. A. Rohr, C. M. Stivers, O. F. White, & J. F. Wolf, *Refounding public administration* (pp. 96-113). Newbury Park, CA: Sage.

Habermas, J. (1990). *Moral consciousness and communicative action.* Cambridge: MIT Press.

Johnson, J. (1994). Public sphere, postmodernism, and polemic. *American Political Science Review,* 427-433.

Kettl, D. F. (1987). *Third-party government and the public manager: The changing forms of government action.* Washington, DC: National Academy of Public Administration.

Kettl, D. F. (1993). *Sharing power: Public governance and private markets.* Washington, DC: Brookings Institution.

Krent, H. J. (1990). Fragmenting the unitary executive: Congressional delegations of administrative authority outside the federal government. *Northwestern University Law Review, 85,* 62-112.

Lawrence, D. M. (1986). Private exercise of governmental power. *Indiana Law Journal, 61,* 647-695.

Lyotard, J.-F. (1984). *The postmodern condition: A report on knowledge.* Minneapolis: University of Minnesota Press.

MacManus, S. A. (1992). *Doing business with government—Federal, state, local, and foreign practices for every business and public institution.* New York: Paragon House.

March, J. G., & Olsen, J. P. (1989). *Rediscovering institutions: The organizational basis of politics.* New York: Free Press.

McHale, B. (1987). *Postmodernist fiction.* New York: Methuen.

Moe, R. C. (1987). Exploring the limits of privatization. *Public Administration Review, 47,* 453-460.

Moe, R. C., & Gilmour, R. S. (1995). Rediscovering principles of public administration: The neglected foundation of public law. *Public Administration Review, 55*(2), 135-146.

Mosher, A. (1980). *The relationship between personnel ceilings and contracting out* (Congressional Research Service briefing paper). Washington, DC: Congressional Research Service.

New York v. United States, 326 U.S. 572. (1945).

Office of Federal Procurement Policy. (1992). Policy Letter 92-1, "Policy Letter on Inherently Governmental Functions," Office of Management and Budget. *Federal Register,* Vol. 57, No. 190, Wednesday, September 30, 1992.

Office of Legal Counsel, U.S. Department of Justice. (1992). *Constitutional limitations on "contracting out": Department of Justice functions under OMB Circular A-76* (WL 488475 O.L.C.). Washington, DC: U.S. Department of Justice.

Office of Management and Budget, Executive Office of the President. (1983). *Circular No. A-76* (Revised). Washington, DC: Office of Management and Budget.

Peters, B. G. (1993). Searching for a role: The civil service in American democracy. *International Political Science Review, 14*(4), 373-386.

Ranson, S., & Stewart, J. (1989). Citizenship and government: The challenge for management in the political domain. *Political Studies, 37,* 5-24.

Somers, M. R. (1993). Citizenship and the place of the public sphere: Law, community, and political culture in the transition to democracy. *American Sociological Review, 58,* 587-620.

Stivers, C. M. (1990). Active citizenship and public administration. In G. L. Wamsley, R. N. Bacher, C. T. Goodsell, P. S. Kronenberg, J. A. Rohr, C. M. Stivers, O. F. White, & J. F. Wolf, *Refounding public administration* (pp. 246-273). Newbury Park, CA: Sage.

Untermeyer, L. (1967). *The road not taken: An introduction to Robert Frost—A selection of Robert Frost's poems with a biographical preface and running commentary by Louis Untermeyer.* New York: Holt, Rinehart & Winston.

Villa, D. R. (1992). Postmodernism and the public sphere. *American Political Science Review,* 712-721.

Wamsley, G. L. (1990). The agency perspective: Public administrators as agential leaders. In G. L. Wamsley, R. N. Bacher, C. T. Goodsell, P. S. Kronenberg, J. A. Rohr, C. M. Stivers, O. F. White, & J. F. Wolf, *Refounding public administration* (pp. 114-162). Newbury Park, CA: Sage.

Wamsley, G. L., Bacher, R. N., Goodsell, C. T., Kronenberg, P. S., Rohr, J. A., Stivers, C. M., White, O. F., & Wolf, J. F. (1990). *Refounding public administration*. Newbury Park, CA: Sage.

Wise, C. R. (1990). Public sector configuration and public organizations: Public organization design in the post-privatization era. *Public Administration Review, 50*(2).

Wolf, J. F. (1987). Disinvesting in the administrative capacity for public action. *International Review of Public Administration*, No. 3.

3

Public-Institutional Processes and Democratic Governance

JOY A. CLAY
The University of Memphis

> Administration may be thought of as the major invention and device by which
> civilized men in complex societies try to control their culture, by which they seek
> simultaneously to achieve—within the limitations of their wit and knowledge—the
> goals of stability and the goals of change.
>
> Dwight Waldo, "What Is Public Administration?" (1987)

The contributors to the Blacksburg Manifesto (1983) and later to the *Refounding* (Wamsley et al., 1990), have attempted to initiate through their writings a dialogue that they hope will result in the further development of a normative theory of public administration. A careful reading of the Manifesto and *Refounding* is required because the authors use multiple abstract levels of analysis, ranging from societal to the individual public administrator. Although this chapter will address these levels, the focus of analysis will be on internal agency processes that assist public agencies to interact with their environment, specifically the congressional hearing process.

The analytical focus on agency processes offers a vehicle to test empirically how agency processes unfold, how agency processes shape and are shaped by institutional forces, and the effect of and on individual public administrator's perceptions as they participate in agency processes. As part of

AUTHOR'S NOTE: This book chapter incorporates and further develops ideas presented in "Public Institutional Processes: Beyond Conventional Wisdom About Management Processes," by Joy A. Clay, August 1994, *Administration and Society, 26,* pp. 236-251.

this volume's effort to reflect on governance in a postmodern world, the focus on agency processes provides insights into public administration's institutional context and public administration's challenge of achieving both stability and change in a world marked by increasing fragmentation and dissensus.

The conclusions presented in this chapter are drawn from a case study analysis of the congressional hearing process at the Department of Veterans Administration (VA). Extensive interviews were conducted of VA, veteran service organizations, and congressional committee staff members (Clay, 1991).[1] In addition, the VA made internal administrative documents about the congressional hearing process available for review.

The Challenge: Achieving Stability and Change

Mainstream public administration theory conventionally views management processes as instruments of rational control. In private-sector organizations, where managerial autonomy is relatively high, the conventional view is reasonably descriptive of management processes. In public organizations, however, where political and institutional forces constrain managerial autonomy, this view is inadequate to describe fully the various and crucial societal roles that management processes accomplish. Moreover, as we have become more knowledgeable about the complexity and ambiguity of management processes in public organizations and about the agency's public and institutional context, we also understand that decisions reached, positions taken, and relationships built are fragile and continue to be assaulted by forces of change.

To understand the essentially political and institutional quality of management processes in government agencies is to begin to understand what makes public organizations different from private organizations. Management processes in government agencies are important not only for the end products and finite decisions they produce (e.g., a budget document), but also for enabling agencies to interact with their interested publics, make sense of institutional and environmental forces, marshal resources, and serve the public interest. Such public-institutional processes become essential in democracy where governmental and public agency legitimacy rest on public perceptions of openness, expertise, ethical action, and public and political accountability. Public-institutional processes in public organizations provide a sense of stability as the people involved in them develop shared understandings and yet allow organizations to adapt to the forces of change. While recognizing that this sense of stability is fragile and fleeting, public-institutional processes provide the capacity for administrative action (see Wolf, Chapter 5, this volume).

In public organizations, the structure and flow of agency processes rest on a continual interpretation of the political-institutional context and the particular situation, analogous to Mary Parker Follett's notion of the "law of the situation." These interpretations become institutionalized into a socialized code[2] that guides both individual and agency behavior and in turn shapes the structure and flow of management processes. Although the interpretation of this socialized code of behavior remains open to individual public administrator interpretation, shared experiences and conversation around public-institutional processes shape and reflect definitions of the administrative context. As certain behaviors and processes tend to evoke certain responses and relationships, institutional expectations about what is "appropriate" for given situations begins to build and becomes part of the institutional context. Though fragile and open to conflicting interpretations, agency personnel will rely on their understanding about what is "appropriate" to the situation in order to guide and negotiate future action by the agency.

Public-institutional processes in public organizations serve to counteract the centrifugal forces existing in contemporary governance, for example, unstable policy coalitions, policy ambiguity, increasing specialization, and particularized perspectives. Consequently, public-institutional processes serve to help build order and a sense of stability and coherence. In so doing, public-institutional processes in public organizations help to legitimate (or delegitimate) agency activities and government in general. The remaining sections of this chapter describe the institutional features of management processes in public agencies, the congressional hearing process as a public-institutional process, and the importance of public-institutional processes to democratic governance.

An Institutional View of Management Processes

Management processes are at the center of our system of governance. They are not only techniques but are central to the institutional stability and legitimacy of public agencies. Management processes serve an important political-institutional function as they allow organizations and individuals to cope with environmental instability and ambiguity. Insights into the overarching qualities of management processes provide a framework that better describes the complexity and dynamic features of public administration, how public administrative practitioners go about meeting the everyday challenges of organizing, and how management processes shape and reflect the political-institutional system of governance.

The most clearly identifiable public-institutional processes are public budgeting and public personnel management. However, other organizational activities have public-institutional process characteristics: regulatory and rule-making processes; preparation and development of agency testimony for congressional hearings; major acquisition and contracting processes; congressional casework; and management of regularized meetings with special clientele, interest groups, and statutorily mandated advisory groups.

Wamsley (1992) writes that,

> Management Processes can be defined as regularized cycles of activities (formal or informal)[3] which bring people within organizations and between organizations into interaction in order to work through or "live through" the performance of some function or the solving of some problem.[4]

Thus various characteristics help define management processes:

1. regularity—a sense of recurrence around the task or function

2. cycles of activities—routines and subroutines and expectations about the routines form the activities that demarcate the management process

3. interaction—people, with their particular reading of the task or function, agency mission, personal agenda, and environment, come together to "perform" their respective tasks and functions

4. outcome oriented—some end product is identifiable with the management process, such as budget document, personnel action, regulation, congressional testimony

Although this definition begins to capture how public administrators structure social, administrative, and political interaction around administrative tasks, functions, and problems, it insufficiently captures the richness of the dynamics inherent in management processes. A view that integrates both the individual and institutional dynamics that impinge upon management processes is to use the "public-institutional process" lens.

To understand this lens, we need to understand three principal qualities of political and institutional dynamics that shape, and are in turn shaped by, public-institutional processes. The discussion of these qualities focuses on the important role that public-institutional processes play in our political system, the institutional sense making and relationship building, and in their capacity to accommodate and constrain individual differences.

Dynamic #1: Interaction Within the Political System

Through public-institutional processes, public administrators attempt to deal with the ambiguity and instability inherent in the political environment of public agencies. Although organizational ambiguity and instability have become the norm for most modern complex organizations, these factors are exacerbated for public organizations because they exist within and serve a political and social system that itself is in a state of flux.

It is through the interaction with political structures that administrative structures and public-institutional processes are sustained, directed, and limited (Redford, 1969). Not only does organization structure matter, but the form, structure, and dynamics of the public-institutional processes also matter. Thus organizational processes in public agencies must not only result in the desired management activity, such as produce a budget document, but the management process itself must be responsive to diverse, and often conflicting, political and social expectations.

Public-institutional processes serve as a vehicle for resolving conflict and developing a shared sense of meaning among involved parties. These dynamics occur within the agency as political appointee meets career official and congressional forces compete with the executive branch for the control of resources and the exercise of power. In addition, interest groups and issue networks attempt to influence activities at major points in the public-institutional process. Thus public-institutional processes affect the level of resources coming into an agency; policy formulation; implementation and evaluation processes; the relationships with powerful external agents, such as Congress, the Office of Management and Budget, the Office of the President, the media, special interest groups, and the public.

Public-institutional processes become an important vehicle for coordinating and controlling organizational activities and understanding political-institutional dynamics. Public-institutional processes tell the story of how an agency relates to other branches of government as well as within the executive branch; how an agency obtains policy input from its clientele or the general public; how an agency interacts with other levels of government; how an agency obtains internal input into and support for its policy positions; and how an agency responds to complaints, criticism, or requests for information. Knowing the answers to all these questions provides insight into an agency's openness to its clientele, sensitivity to its mission, understanding of its place within the overall system of governance, and responsiveness to public scrutiny.

Dynamic #2: Institutional Sense Making

Institutional sense making draws attention to the importance of institutional structures and processes. Institution-based theories describe the richness of interplay between public agencies and their environments as well as the effect that institutional structure has on these relationships and patterns of relationship (Selznick, 1949, 1984). The interplay within the public organization and between the public organization and its environment reflects and shapes a socialized code that guides organizational and individual behavior. March and Olsen (1989) write that, "Institutions are constructed around clusters of appropriate activities, around procedures for assuring their maintenance in the face of threats from turnover and from self-interest, and around procedures for modifying them" (p. 24).

Theorists who view reality as socially constructed and ordered (Berger & Luckmann, 1967; Burrell & Morgan, 1979; Pfeffer, 1981; Weick, 1979) shift attention to the creation and maintenance of organizing processes. Such an approach posits that, as patterns of action become repeated, shared social definitions of situations are produced. Also, emergent and situationally defined action affects, and is affected by, the social culture, history, and value systems. This conceptual framework adds to our understanding of organization-environmental interactions and processes and interpretation systems (Daft & Lengel, 1986; Daft, Sormunen, & Parks, 1988; Daft & Weick, 1984; Weick & Daft, 1983).

Weick (1979) variously defines *organizing* as "a grammar, code, or set of recipes"; as streams of collective and social action; as a means of "arranging processes to cope with the equivocal nature of streams of experience" (p. 47); and as "the conjunction of procedures, interpretations, behaviors, and puzzles" (p. 4). Public-institutional processes become the "visible" form of organizing. Visibility evolves as organizing procedures gain collective meaning, that is, as rules become interpreted and habituated.

Organizing is a social process. It is characterized by interdependencies and active interpretation of, rather than passive reactions to, events and situations. When people expend energy to reduce equivocality, the principal problem with which they must deal is not the lack of data, but the lack of clarity of the information they already possess. Although the rules that flow from the socialized code become independent of individual actors, a continued collective sense of shared meaning requires continuous dialogue to maintain it.

Through public-institutional processes, public administrators make sense of their world through institutional sense making, meaning negotiations, and relationship building. In addition, standard operating procedures and structures define and defend values, norms, and interests intrinsic to public-institutional processes. Thus public-institutional processes create and sustain standard operating procedures, conventions, and rituals that shape action. March and Olsen (1989) argue that routines allow coordination to occur

> in a way that makes them mutually consistent. Routines help avoid conflicts; they provide codes of meaning that facilitate interpretation of ambiguous worlds; they constrain bargaining within comprehensible terms and enforce agreements; they help mitigate the unpredictability created by open structures and garbage can processes by regulating the access of participants, problems, and solutions to choice opportunities. (p. 24)

Similarly, Douglas (1986) argues that institutions are not just rules but are founded upon analogy, with conventions (social rules) arising to reduce conflict and assure coordination. She states that,

> Individuals, as they pick and choose among the analogies from nature they will give credence to, are also picking and choosing at the same time their allies and opponents and the pattern of their future relations. Constituting their version of nature, they are monitoring the constitutions of their society. (p. 63)

Thus political actors are not just driven by calculated self-interest but also by their institutional responsibilities and roles (March & Olsen, 1989, p. 159).

Dynamic #3: Accommodating Individual Differences

The third principal quality of public-institutional processes—accommodating individual differences—emphasizes the importance of people as individuals. Public-institutional processes provide the means by which agencies and involved parties serve and shape the political system and come to shared understandings about the process. Just as important, however, public-institutional processes also accommodate and allow individual participants in the process to maintain their differences. This quality reminds us that development of a socialized code does not result in completely agreed-upon collective readings of the situation. Instead, differences continue to simmer within an overarching but fragile agreement on what is applicable to the particular situations or processes.

Rules and conventions that guide behavior are not inflexible, nor is compliance automatic. March and Olsen (1989) argue that "the fact that most behavior is driven by routines does not, by itself, make most behavior routine

(p. 24). Further, rules are codified incompletely and inconsistencies are common (March & Olsen, 1989, p. 22). Also, determination that a rule is applicable to the situation does not mean that other observers might not judge it to be stupid or foolish. Institutionalization can act to enhance organizational performance, but can also lead people to ignore what might be more efficient alternatives (Tolbert & Zucker, 1983; Zucker, 1987).

Weick carefully describes how behavior comes first and then is interpreted, the great latitude that exists in interpretation of situations and events, and the need for organizations to achieve a balance between stability and flexibility. Thus people become "extraordinarily talented at normalizing deviant events, at reconciling outliers to a central tendency, at producing typifications, at making do with scraps of information, and at treating as sufficient whatever information is at hand" (Weick & Daft, 1983, p. 87). Consistent with this analysis, Duncan (1987) finds that, "Extensive reviews of the literature indicate that managerial work is situational, characterized by diversity, involves making decisions, and negotiating" (p. 28).

Public officials and administrators attempt to codify routines and procedures to direct and control individual actions, hopefully within an ethical framework. However, any social process necessarily results in people shaping the process to reflect their institutional perspectives, their own personalities and styles, and their particular readings of the situation. Thus the process can never be fully elaborated or formalized. This results in a dialectical tension between explicitness and implicitness.

A tension also exists between the abiding and the fragile nature of the process of organizing. On the one hand, the experience of participants in a public-institutional process and the shared sense of understanding about that experience become internalized by the participants. This internalization process creates a sense of "permanence" and "continuity" concerning what is applicable—"this is the way we do things around here." Conversely, this shared sense of understanding is fragile. Continual interaction among participants invested in the process is required if this shared sense of understanding is to be maintained. Environmental instability and ambiguity magnify the fragile nature of shared understandings.

This third principal quality of public-institutional processes reminds us that development of a socialized code depends on a degree of trust, that is, that people will abide by the code being created. Goffman (1973) describes this as a fundamental social principle: Society is organized such that individuals can expect others to value and treat them in an appropriate way. Consequently, public-institutional processes become vulnerable to gaming if individuals become more vested in competitive conflict and engaged in bargaining over preferences and personal gain. From a normative perspective, this quality squarely places accountability not only on hierarchical structures but on people for their personal actions within the process.

Congressional Hearings as Public-Institutional Processes

A key feature of the political economy is the complex relationships of the agency's policy subsystems (Wamsley & Zald, 1973). Public hearings provide a mechanism for policy subsystem members to press for public agency action and to expand public support for their position (Jones, 1984; Kingdon, 1984). Consequently, congressional hearings provide a worthwhile vehicle for examining how policy subsystem interactions and structures shape and are shaped by an agency's institutional processes.

Background

Dodd and Schott (1979) describe "dual" legislative oversight subsystems, consisting of the authorizing committees and the appropriations subcommittee in each house. Their convincing conclusion is that the dual subsystem significantly affects legislative-agency relationships. For example, the differing norms of each subsystem create institutional tension and conflict that can in turn be transmitted to the agency, thereby making their relationship with Congress "more complex and difficult" (Dodd & Schott, 1979, p. 225). In addition, competing "mini-subsystems" can form within the authorization subsystem, as well as House subsystems competing for influence with Senate subsystems (p. 226).

Differing administrative levels play a key role in each subsystem: Political executives generally take the lead in relationships with the authorization subsystem whereas budget directors, both at the agency and department or bureau levels, usually high-level careerists, generally are relied on by appropriations subcommittees. Because political executives tend to have brief tenure, the appropriation mini-subsystem "may help to explain the effectiveness of oversight exercised through the appropriation subsystem" (Dodd & Schott, 1979, p. 225).

Another impact of the rise of "subcommittee government" has been the institutionalization of congressional liaison offices in public agencies to coordinate hearing testimony and congressional inquiries. The congressional liaison office "represents a part of the congressional culture transplanted into executive departments and agencies" (Dodd & Schott, 1979, p. 264). Some view the creation of such offices as an attempt by political officials to counter the influence of subsystem politics (Dodd & Schott, 1979, p. 265). Although this organizational approach to constraining informal agency-committee relationships has not been successful in containing subsystem politics, the congressional liaison office

> has probably done more to rationalize a process for facilitating agency responses to congressional requests and to provide a convenient point of access for congressional needs for information and service than to weaken the traditional ties of subsystem politics or to enforce an "agency" (as opposed to a bureau) position on the Hill. (Dodd & Schott, 1979, p. 267)

Although not conventionally viewed from an administrative perspective, congressional hearings provide a worthwhile vehicle for examining how policy subsystem interactions and structures shape and are shaped by an agency's institutional processes. The congressional hearing process is viewed as highly political and idiosyncratic. It occurs regularly, although sporadically, throughout a calendar year. The scheduling of a hearing produces frenzied activities that appear to come together only at the last minute. And, most importantly, it is the definitive example of the interaction and relationships among the members of a policy subsystem, especially between the executive and legislative branches, career officials and the agency's political leaders, and the three-way relationship among the relevant interest group with the legislative and executive branches. An examination of the congressional hearing process also addresses how agency processes address the question of agency accountability.

VA Congressional Affairs Office

The Veterans Administration—VA—offers an excellent opportunity to analyze how an internal agency process, the congressional hearing process, serves institutional purposes. The VA is one of the largest agencies in the federal system; has a significant impact on the national, as well as local, economies; and has a complex policy subsystem.[5] Major components of the policy subsystem include not only veteran service organizations (VSO) but also various professional associations, interest groups, and advocacy groups affected by VA programs and policies, who attempt to influence policy formulation and implementation at all levels of government—national, state, and local. Both the House and Senate Veterans' Affairs Committees (SVAC) and House subcommittees significantly influence VA policies and programs.[6]

Congressional concern with assuring constituent services to veterans predates the establishment of the VA as a single agency in 1930.[7] Staff in the Office of the General Counsel generally has had responsibility for legislative liaison. Within this office, a small staff, usually political appointees, handled the more "political" direct liaison contacts associated with constituent services and resolved congressional inquiries. The career lawyers who were assigned to specific programmatic areas—such as medical care, loan guaranty, and the like—coordinated the congressional hearing process and coordinated the agency's hearing statement and issues with the Office of Management and Budget (OMB) staff.

In 1981, the Administrator expanded the responsibilities of congressional liaison to include providing advice to VA top executives on congressional relations. The newly organized Congressional Liaison Service also supervised the Liaison Staffs located on Capitol Hill. Political appointees managed the office. In 1983, the Administrator decided to add career staff to the congressional liaison function for the first time. The political liaison staff believed that the agency was too large for them to coordinate all the liaison activities effectively. In addition, VA officials reported that they wanted careerist support in "translating 'bureaucratese.' "

Since this organizational policy change, the congressional affairs function continues to consist both of political appointees who perform the more partisan responsibilities, and of career staff who attempt to centrally coordinate relationships with congressional committees and staff. When the VA attained cabinet-level status, the incoming Secretary placed the congressional affairs function organizationally under the Deputy Assistant Secretary for Congressional Affairs, as a section of the Office of Congressional and Public Affairs. Staff in the Office of the General Counsel continue to play an important role in the congressional hearing process, but share responsibility with the Congressional Relations Service.

A VA top official distinguished between responsibility for policy and responsibility for internally administering the congressional hearing process. He described the Congressional Relations Service as responsible for the administrative aspects of the hearing process. For example, this responsibility includes an administrative liaison role that assures that timetables are met, activities coordinated, and policies clearly articulated. In contrast, this official described the Office of General Counsel and program offices as responsible for policy, integrating the process by working with program offices and assisting in drafting and overseeing the preparation of the agency's hearing statement. According to this distinction, both offices have responsibility for policing the congressional hearing process, but the Office of the General Counsel appears to be assigned the major responsibility for guiding and guarding the institutional aspects of the agency process.

Hearing Process

The congressional hearing process includes the scheduling of the hearing, selection of agency witnesses, development of the agency statement, and follow-up activities after the hearing. Each stage of the hearing process is marked by a great deal of negotiation and coordination. Informal contacts among the policy subsystem members are also the norm.

VA officials coordinating the hearing process considered a degree of cynicism about the value of congressional hearings to be the most appropriate attitude. Most agency officials who are career officials expressed suspicion of those who take too political a perspective. Officials frequently mentioned the need to determine the "real" agenda of the committee chairman and members. This finding supports Weick's (1979) notion of how organizations use scraps of information to make sense of their world, "retrospective sense-making." The analysis of VA's congressional hearing process found officials examining members' past communications, past questions asked at hearings, and past relationships with the agency, as well as explicitly discussing their memories of these interactions to elicit clues and hints about what to expect in the future (Clay, 1991).

Agency Review and Coordination

Internal review and coordinating procedures serve to self-police the creation of the agency statement; the rules guiding the process become internalized. Before top-level political officials see the document, agency officials have already cleansed the document of statements or information that might raise "red flags," such as requests for additional resources. Explicit coordination with officials at OMB becomes unnecessary when either program officials or officials coordinating the statement (the staff attorneys in the General Counsel's office serve this function in the VA) understand the boundaries of their discretion. Insights from Weick and from March and Olsen suggest that this understanding builds on past experience as participants retrospectively make sense of interactions and determine what is appropriate for inclusion in the statement.

Both the internal agency clearance process as well as an external process with the Office of Management and Budget serve to constrain agency requests for additional resources. Through this clearance process, the agency's statement receives careful scrutiny to ensure identification of potentially damaging problems with agency policies and congruence with presidential policies and priorities. Career officials anticipate that they initially will draft the agency's statement and that this draft will undergo a "metamorphosis." As such, the agency process supporting congressional hearings provides an event around which the political leadership and career officials negotiate agency positions, especially concerning resource allocations and priorities. Also, varying perspectives compete for influence in establishing the agency's position.

Congressional hearings present a formal, staged event that makes visible the maneuvering of the policy subsystem. The agency processes provide a means by which program officials engage in negotiations with political managers, bringing in their understanding of the political environment and the place of the agency within this context. Much of the negotiation and communications among policy subsystem members occur continuously. However, the scheduling of a congressional hearing serves to pinpoint and focus these interactions.

Many VA officials suggested that the hearing process especially serves to force a coordinated Administration position among the executive agencies, thus dealing with a subset of an agency's environment. The exchange of testimony among agencies not only provides information about what another agency plans to say at the hearing but provides clues to that agency's priorities and problems. More importantly, it formally substantiates perceptions and understandings that have been created during informal interactions, thus further reducing, relatively, areas of possible ambiguity and furthering the negotiation of meaning. Perhaps it is not too far a stretch to suggest that an administration perspective builds through this process and impinges on the agency's culture and perceptions of individual public administrators, as involved officials attempt to make sense of their institutional environment.

Hearing Characteristics

Members both in the organization and external to the organization have expectations about routines, norms, and responsibilities that will be followed by the organization. Norms govern witness selection, demeanor of agency witnesses, and style differences between the two chambers and among various Committee and Subcommittee Chairmen. Both subcommittee staff and veterans services organization officials expect agency witnesses not to ask for additional resources and to avoid forthright answers when the agency has answers it does not want to give.

Special characteristics of the congressional hearing process deserve consideration. First, the congressional hearing process is highly individual-driven. Personality, level in the hierarchy, experience level with a hearing topic, and management style influence the details of how the process unfolds. Attendance at pre-briefings and hearings and increasing levels of responsibility for the process provide a means of "anticipatory socialization" into the norms guiding the congressional hearing process (Goffman, 1973).

The issue history, as well as the history of relationships that affect the issue, appears to serve as an important determining factor for the agency response to congressional committee oversight and how participants make sense of the process. Issue history can affect the agency posture; selection of the lead witness; level of openness, trust, and information sharing among policy subsystem members; and amount of interaction among the policy subsystem prior to scheduled hearing. Most officials minimized the value of the actual hearing. Except for a few VA officials who commented on the value of establishing a public record of agency activities and an agency's formal statement of policy position, most officials suggested that any value from the effort expended in the hearing process results from the agency's preparation process.

Policy Subsystem Expectations

Because most officials in the policy subsystem expect policy decisions to be made prior to the actual hearing, officials universally consider pre-hearing communication as critical to exerting any influence. One VSO official explained, "Hearings are frosting on the cake; however, they have little effect since a congressman already knows what he wants to do." Although recognizing the importance of early intervention in the process, another VSO official cautioned that, "What one says is crucial. If a legislative proposal later parallels what was presented [during a hearing], how can the organization later oppose it? The witness has to be careful; you're on the hot seat."[8] The "show" and "performance" are important.

Acknowledging that relationships are not always marked by harmony, most officials explained that there is a great deal of rapport within the VA's policy subsystem.[9] Comparing the more adversarial relationship of the military and its significant congressional committees, one former high-level VA official suggested that this less adversarial relationship results from a shared sense of mission: "Both are interested in the same direction, high quality care for veterans." This shared sense of understanding supports continued interactions and relationship building among the participants in the policy subsystem. In another mark of uniqueness of committee norms, the two authorizing committees consistently include veterans service organizations as part of the hearing process. One SVAC staff official explained that, "The veterans service organizations in attendance are always asked to comment on VA's testimony." Another SVAC staff member suggested that inclusion of the veterans service organizations is unique: "I don't know of any other committee who consistently gives such opportunity to their interest groups. The Committee is interested in finding out what the VSOs want and to deal with their legislative agendas."

This norm of inclusion further supports continuous interaction among the policy subsystem members. The interactions promote the members' negotiation of meaning and institutional sense-making activities. Further evidence to support this conclusion is provided by congressional committee staff members who described four purposes that they believe congressional hearings serve: eliciting information to aid in decisions about major funding increases or decreases for programs, following up on agency promises, responding to the issues receiving public attention, and educating agency officials as to member priorities. This last purpose was repeated consistently. For example, one staff member suggested that congressional hearings are "Not about grading performance. It is a forum for VA and our subcommittee to let it be known what their concerns and priorities are." This provides further support for the recognition of the importance of congressional hearings as a means of negotiating meaning and building relationships.

The Individual and the Process

Importantly, the inclusion of the role of individuals in the congressional hearing process reinforces the realization of personal responsibility for system processes. As Weick (1979) so clearly describes, organizing results from the coordination and cooperation of people in organizations. The resulting organizational processes rest on creating and maintaining rules and conventions that, in turn, come together to produce the processes that become visible. Thus political leaders and career public administrators are responsible for the processes they create and maintain.

The congressional hearing process helps public administrators make sense of their world. Although perspectives vary about the value of the process, all appear to take their own responsibilities within the process seriously. The scheduling of a hearing presents an everyday challenge to an agency. However, the management process that it triggers intensifies and focuses the negotiations among members in the policy subsystem. Clearly, the congressional hearing process serves as a means of coping with ambiguity and instability in the environment of public agencies.

Agency officials must balance an organizational need to codify routines and procedures—which help to direct and control individual actions—with the need to allow individuals the freedom to shape processes to reflect their own personality and style as well as their professional reading of the situation. Participants in the process are socialized into the rules and procedures that guide the congressional hearing process, even though very few are written.

The "cookbook" procedures that guide agency activities in preparing for a hearing serve as a stabilizing factor in the proceedings. Most participants understand the process and their expectations are reinforced with each hearing. At the same time, staff member attention to the nuances of personality, style, and issue dynamics allows the hearing process to change to meet the needs of the situation.

The data show that the process is built in such a way as to handle unique situations routinely; variability within rules. Definition of *uniqueness* rests on the participants' understanding of the history and dynamics of the issue, the demands of the individual officials involved in the process, particularly the agency's lead witness, and the controlling style of the top managers.

As some agency officials noted with the rise to Cabinet status, program officials probably will be less likely to serve as the agency lead witnesses for hearings. Thus the norms change to reflect changed circumstances, but it takes time for participants in the process to understand and accept the shift.

VA officials suggested that individual personality and management style affect the congressional hearing process. For example, the quality of the relationship between the top agency leaders and other members in the policy subsystem affects the level of suspicion directed at the agency by Congress and the veterans services organizations. This, in turn, affects the treatment of the agency leadership at hearings; hearings tend to be more adversarial when the top political appointee is viewed negatively by Committee members, particularly the Chairman. The personality of the Committee chairman also affects the process. Officials described some committee chairmen, such as the two authorizing committees, as "friendly" to the agency. Expectations about how agency witnesses will be treated by the congressional committee become integrated into and shape the congressional hearing preparation process.

The personality and style of the lead witness also affects the process. One official responsible for congressional liaison activities, stated that "every situation is a little different, the process has to accommodate the witness. The witness drives the procedures and process." One program official suggested that who the lead witness is affects the amount of pre-briefing meetings, the amount and type of material that has to be prepared, and the length of the agency's statement. In the agency case, officials coordinating the process had to make sense of someone new to the agency, as well as someone who had not yet served as a lead witness at a hearing. During the preparation process, this sense of "discomfort" with the unknown was palpable. Consistent with the insights offered by Weick (1979) and by Goffman (1973), participants in the process watched closely for clues about the agency witnesses' ability to deliver during the pre-briefing sessions.

One former committee staff official suggested that personality also affects the performance of committee staff. This official noted that unfortunately it is easy to fall into an adversarial stance: "However, it is best not to make yourself an enemy; you might win the battle and lose the war." Partisan affiliation also affects the process, particularly witness and topic selection. One committee official observed that when the Republicans were the majority party in the Senate, the SVAC did not invite organizations representing federal employees to testify; in contrast, the Democrats tend to include union representatives. Thus witness selection reflects partisan philosophy, which itself reflects institutionalized patterns.

Some VA officials determine what their appropriate area of expertise is by making distinctions between policy and science. Several other officials made distinctions between policy and administration. However, most agency officials suggested that such distinctions, in practice, are fuzzy and difficult to make. Through experience, they begin to learn what is appropriate behavior on their part. Thus experience helps practitioners make sense of the politics-administration dichotomy, as a guide to action, albeit not a clear one.

In accordance with Goffman (1973), the "front" presented during pre-hearing negotiations concerning what is "appropriate" behavior becomes explicit during this "background" interaction. This interaction provides a "safe" opportunity to develop a shared sense of meaning about an upcoming hearing before the "performance" becomes publicly tested. The process accommodates differing perspectives although the "reality" of a team effort is delicate and fragile due to differing perspectives and agendas (Goffman, 1973). In addition, the pre-hearing process allows officials to make explicit their concerns about being too open or closed (too trusting or suspicious) about external forces. Weick (1979) describes this as a constant tension for organizations. Each of the perspectives attempts to take into account assessments of the political environment.

In summary, the pre-hearing process provides a vehicle for agency officials to create a shared sense of what is appropriate for this specific context, the hearing. In addition, each pre-hearing process provides clues for the participants to make sense of each other's attitudes and perspectives and to affect the current public "performance." However, this interaction also reinforces feelings about the appropriateness of each person's respective perspective. In addition, future interactions become affected as participants glean information that anticipates others' attitudes and behaviors.

Agency Processes and Democratic Governance

The congressional hearing process serves as an excellent illustration of the political, institutional, and social dynamics associated with public-institutional processes. Preparation for a hearing becomes a process of solving the puzzle presented by the scheduling of a congressional hearing. The process supports the authority of the various levels of political leadership, while also providing a vehicle for program officials to influence and shape the agency's policy statement. The hearing process thus legitimizes the expenditure of public resources; serves as a vehicle for institutional sense making between career and political officials, and among agency officials and other pertinent public agencies and other members in the policy subsystem; serves as a vehicle to contain conflict and reduce ambiguity; and provides information that participants can use to help them predict what leads to successful interactions.

The congressional hearing process also makes the agency's policy decisions public and the agency officials accountable for their decisions and priorities. Congressional hearings offer the possibility of public debate and democratic dialogue. Moreover, the hearing forum makes at least some of the private maneuvering of interest groups visible. Thus the congressional hearing process serves to make a public institution's management processes, and the outcome of these processes, visible to others. At the hearing, the mission of the agency becomes the focus of discussion as participants create a shared sense of expectations and priorities. Although other forums, informal and formal, are available for such dialogue, the congressional hearing has symbolic value and a degree of "publicness" not apparent in most other agency processes.

The analysis of the congressional hearing process evokes insights into public-institutional processes and their relationship to democratic governance. In summary, public-institutional processes

1. serve as an important means for meaning negotiation, both within the public institution and with its policy subsystem

2. build relationships within the public institution and among institutions

3. rest on a degree of trust among the participants

4. require both explicit and implicit rules and norms to guide performance and behavior

5. become institutionalized through the infusion of institutional values

6. require continual interaction to be maintained and yet have some degree of institutional "memory"

An appreciation of the public-institutional features of management processes provides insights into how public administrators shape and reflect their agency's institutional history and development and relationships within its political economy. While at one level public-institutional processes allow for a semblance of stability to develop so that administrative action can occur, the forces of change continue to exert pressure as the processes unfold.

Although management processes are conventionally thought to be internal control functions, those management processes that specifically help public agencies to mediate with their environment are essential to democratic governance. The insights gained about public-institutional processes have consequence at all levels of government, increasingly so as public agencies are being required to be more responsive to their community. Collaboration and cooperation from the public require public agency attention to processes that support interaction and dialogue, whether the interaction be around the review of zoning applications, citizen review of budgets, citizen participation in strategic planning, or a commission for developing the downtown area.

Public-institutional processes are a central feature of our political and institutional system. As public-institutional processes unfold, they shape and reflect their political-institutional context. Moreover, public-institutional processes serve as a stabilizing force for administrative action while maintaining openness to environmental forces. For public-institutional processes to result in democratic administrative action, participants must be attuned to their institutional context, take responsibility for the development of public-institutional processes, and make agency decision-making processes more open to the public.

━ Notes

1. Public administrators from several other agencies were also interviewed, specifically officials at the Department of Health & Human Services, Department of Agriculture, Environmental Protection Agency, and the Office of Technology Assessment.

2. In *Rediscovering Institutions: The Organizational Basis of Politics,* March and Olsen (1989) call this socialized code the "logic of appropriateness."

3. Rather than formal *or* informal, our understanding of the dynamics of public-institutional processes is enhanced if we view the cycles of activities as a collection of both formal *and* informal routines and subroutines.

4. Unpublished manuscript, Center for Public Administration and Policy, Virginia Polytechnic Institute and State University.

5. The Department employs approximately 245,000 employees, making it the second largest federal employer after the Department of Defense. The VA serves 27.3 million veteran beneficiaries and 53 million dependents and survivors of veterans. The VA has facilities in every state, the District of Columbia, Puerto Rico, and the Philippines. Physical facilities include: 172 hospitals, 233 outpatient clinics, 119 nursing home care units, 28 domiciliaries, 194 Vietnam Veteran outreach centers, 112 cemeteries, and 58 regional benefit offices (U.S. Department of Veterans Affairs, 1989). The beneficiaries of VA programs are not only numerous but well organized and active. For example, in 1990 the two largest organizations were the American Legion with 3 million members and the Veterans of Foreign Wars with 2.3 million members (U.S. Department of Veterans Affairs, 1990). The larger VSOs have permanent, professional staff in Washington, D.C., that lobby the president, Congress, and VA Central Office. Historically, top political appointees have taken leadership positions on the staff of the two authorizing committees or with veterans service organizations upon leaving the agency. Moreover, key agency appointments are often drawn from the committee staff or veterans service organization leadership. Staff serving both committees have extensive knowledge of VA programs and governing statutes.

6. In a study that recommended against elevation of the VA to cabinet status, the National Academy of Public Administration (NAPA) commented negatively on the high level of intrusion into the internal management of the VA. To illustrate, NAPA described the "report and wait" provisions that the agency must abide by before making decisions that affect management of field facilities. The agency must report to the House and Senate Veterans' Affairs Committees and wait an elapsed time before proceeding with reducing employment by 10% in a VA facility or transferring property valued at more than $50,000 (National Academy of Public Administration, 1988, pp. 17, 40).

7. The Senate commissioned a Senate Liaison Office in December 1922 and the House established a House Liaison Service in February 1925. With the establishment of the VA, these offices were attached to the Office of the Solicitor, a predecessor to the Office of the General Counsel. The Congressional Liaison Service was assigned to the Office of the Assistant Deputy Administrator from February 1975 until June 1977, when it was returned to the Office of General Counsel again in June 1977.

8. This same official observed that this is especially important during the annual legislative hearing when a VSO witness has only "four minutes to comment on thirty two Senate bills."

9. The House Veterans Affairs Committee conducts its affairs in bipartisan manner. One HVAC member suggests that this was due to the fact that the members were fairly unanimous about what the agency is all about. He also notes that it is unusual to have one agency as the sole focus of two congressional committees.

■ References and Bibliography

Berger, P. L., & Luckmann, T. (1967). *The social construction of reality.* Garden City, NY: Anchor.

Bower, J. L. (1983). Managing for efficiency, managing for equity. *Harvard Business Review, 61,* 83-90.

Burrell, G., & Morgan, G. (1979). *Sociological paradigms and organizational analysis.* Portsmouth, NH: Heinemann.

Clay, J. A. (1991). *Congressional hearings: A neglected management process.* Unpublished doctoral dissertation, Virginia Polytechnic Institute and State University, Blacksburg.

Daft, R. L., & Lengel, R. H. (1986). Organizational information requirements, media richness, and structural design. *Management Science, 32,* 554-571.

Daft, R. L., Sormunen, J., & Parks, D. (1988). Chief executive scanning, environmental characteristics, and company performance: An empirical study. *Strategic Management Journal, 9,* 123-139.

Daft, R. L., & Weick, K. E. (1984). Toward a model of organizations as interpretation systems. *Academy of Management Review, 9,* 284-295.

Dodd, L. C., & Schott, R. L. (1979). *Congress and the administrative state.* New York: John Wiley.

Douglas, M. (1986). *How institutions think.* Syracuse, NY: Syracuse University Press.

Duncan, W. J. (1987). When necessity becomes a virtue: Don't get too cynical about strategy. *Journal of General Management, 13,* 228-243.

Fayol, H. (1949). *General and industrial management* (C. Storrs, Trans.). New York: Pitman.

Gilmour, R. S. (1971). Central legislative clearance: A revised perspective. *Public Administration Review, 31,* 150-158.

Goffman, E. (1973). *The presentation of self in everyday life.* Woodstock, NY: Overlook Press.

Harris, J. P. (1964). *Congressional control of administration.* Washington, DC: Brookings Institution.

Harmon, M. M., & Mayer, R. T. (1986). *Organization theory for public administration.* Boston: Little, Brown.

Jones, C. O. (1984). *An introduction to the study of public policy* (3rd ed.). Monterey, CA: Brooks/Cole.

Kingdon, J. (1984). *Agendas, alternatives, and public policies.* Toronto: Little, Brown.

Koontz, H. (1977). The management theory jungle. In M. T. Matleson & J. M. Ivancevich (Eds.), *Management classics* (pp. 19-33). Santa Monica, CA: Goodyear.

Macmahon, A. W. (1943). Congressional oversight of administration: The power of the purse. *Political Science Quarterly, 58,* 161-190.

March, J. G., & Olsen, J. P. (1989). *Rediscovering institutions: The organizational basis of politics.* New York: Free Press.

National Academy of Public Administration. (1988). *Evaluation of proposals to establish a department of veterans affairs.* Washington, DC: NAPA.

Neustadt, R. E. (1954). Presidency and legislation: The growth of central clearance. *American Political Science Review, 48,* 641-671.

Nigro, F. A., & Nigro, L. G. (1976). *The new public personnel administration.* Itasca, IL: F. E. Peacock.

Pfeffer, J. (1981). *Power in organizations.* Marshfield, MA: Pitman.

Redford, E. S. (1969). *Democracy in the administrative state.* New York: Oxford University Press.

Schick, A. (1976). Congress and the "details" of administration. *Public Administration Review, 36,* 516-528.

Schick, A. (1983). Politics through law: Congressional limitations on executive discretion. In A. King (Ed.), *Both ends of the avenue: The presidency, the executive branch, and Congress in the 1980s* (pp. 154-184). Washington, DC: American Enterprise Institute for Public Policy Research.

Selznick, P. (1949). *TVA and the grass roots.* New York: Harper & Row.

Selznick, P. (1984). *Leadership in administration.* Berkeley: University of California Press.

Shafritz, J. M., Hyde, A. C., & Rosenbloom, D. H. (1981). *Personnel management in government.* New York: Marcel Dekker.

Stein, H. (Ed.). (1952). *Public administration and policy development: A case book.* New York: Harcourt, Brace & World.

Stoner, J. A. F., & Wankel, C. (1986). *Management* (3rd ed.). Englewood Cliffs, NJ: Prentice Hall.

Tolbert, P. S., & Zucker, L. G. (1983). Institutional sources of change in the formal structure of organizations: The diffusion of civil service reform 1880-1935. *Administrative Science Quarterly, 28*, 22-39.

U. S. Department of Veterans Affairs. (1989). *Annual Report*. Washington, DC: VA.

U. S. Department of Veterans Affairs. (1990). *Directory of veterans organizations* by the Office of the Deputy Assistant Secretary for Veterans Liaison, Washington, DC.

Waldo, D. (1987). What is public administration? In J. M. Shafritz & A. C. Hyde (Eds.), *Classics of public administration* (pp. 229-241). Chicago: Dorsey.

Wamsley, G. L. (1992). *Management processes*. A working document, Virginia Polytechnic Institute and State University.

Wamsley, G. L., Bacher, R. N., Goodsell, C. T., Kronenberg, P. S., Rohr, J. A., Stivers, C. M., White, O. F., & Wolf, J. F. (1990). *Refounding public administration*. Newbury Park, CA: Sage.

Wamsley, G. L., Goodsell, C. T., Rohr, J. A., White, O. F., & Wolf, J. F. (1987). In R. C. Chandler (Ed.), *A centennial history of the American administrative state* (pp. 291-317). New York: Free Press.

Wamsley, G. L., & Zald, M. N. (1973). *The political economy of public organizations*. Lexington, MA: D. C. Heath.

Weick, K. E. (1979). *The social psychology of organizing* (2nd ed.). Reading, MA: Addison-Wesley.

Weick, K. E., & Daft, R. L. (1983). The effectiveness of interpretation systems. In K. S. Cameron & D. A. Whetten (Eds.), *Organizational effectiveness: A comparison of multiple models* (pp. 71-93). New York: Academic Press.

Wildavsky, A. (1988). *The new politics of the budgetary process*. Glenview, IL: Scott, Foresman.

Wilson, J. Q. (1989). *Bureaucracy*. New York: Basic Books.

Wilson, W. (1885). *Congressional government: A study in American politics* (2nd ed.). Boston: Houghton Mifflin.

Wilson, W. (1887). The study of administration. *Political Science Quarterly, 2*, 197-222.

Zucker, L. G. (1987). Institutional theories of organization. *Annual Review of Sociology, 13*, 443-464.

4

What a Difference a State Makes

Reflections on Governance in France

JOHN A. ROHR
Virginia Polytechnic Institute and State University

Political scientists often observe that American government rests on a weak notion of the state, contrasting it with governments in countries like France that enjoy a strong-state tradition. The purpose of this chapter is to consider *concretely* the differences a strong or weak state might make for administrative governance. I stress *concretely* to distinguish my efforts from the analytical work of those who examine the meaning of the state as a philosophical or juridical concept.[1] If a refounding of American public administration is in our future, it may be helpful to examine the practical limitations our weak-state tradition imposes on administrative innovation. My focus in this chapter is descriptive, not prescriptive. I do not suggest that we jettison our traditions and imitate the French. I do believe, however, that an overview of administrative governance in a strong-state country, like France, stimulates the reformer's imagination and illuminates the need for reform.

The theme of this book stresses *democratic* public administration. American readers will find some French administrative practices derived from the strong-state tradition to be at odds with their own understanding of

AUTHOR'S NOTE: Certain sections of this chapter are taken from the author's forthcoming book, *Founding Republics in France and America: A Study in Constitutional Governance,* in press, Lawrence: University Press of Kansas. The permission received from the University Press of Kansas is hereby gratefully acknowledged.

democracy. At times, this will be because the practice in question—for example, the elitist system for recruiting high-level civil servants—is simply undemocratic, like the undemocratic federal judiciary in our own country. At other times, however, American puzzlement at the French and their administrative ways may be due to the very different meaning of *democracy* in the two countries. Our understanding of democracy is inextricably (and somewhat illogically) linked to our anti-majoritarian commitment to a constitutional republic anchored in our traditional belief in natural rights. It knows nothing of such salient institutions in French democracy as a sovereign parliament, national referenda, and the Jacobin tradition of ensuring majority rule through a centralized state. Consequently, it would be pointless to try to graft the French administrative system as a whole onto our democratic stock. This, however, does not preclude the possibility of finding here and there in the French system—at the retail level, as it were—certain practices that might suggest limited administrative reforms compatible with our understanding of democracy. This is what I mean by my modest hope to "stimulate the reformers' imagination."

In our quest for *democratic* administration we must not forget that the true friends of democracy are aware of the vulnerabilities of their favored form of government. If we were discussing electoral, rather than administrative, reform, we would surely agree with Aristotle that a lottery is a far more democratic way of selecting officers than an election. No true friend of democracy, however, would seriously advocate such a practice despite its impeccably democratic credentials. Electoral reformers willingly abide the inherently elitist nature of elections and wisely call for their improvement rather than their abolition. Administrative reformers should be no less sensible, again recalling Aristotle's sound observation that regimes are often destroyed by an excess of their own principles.

I am not so bold (nor so foolish) as to maintain that all the characteristics of French governance discussed below are *caused* by the strong-state tradition in France, but I do believe there is at least a plausible connection between those practices and that tradition. In choosing a mere handful of examples from the vast domain of French governance, I have tried to make my selection on the basis of the strength of the plausibility of the connection and the likelihood that the chosen examples will provide some insight—though not necessarily any guidance—to those who ponder the possibilities of refounding American public administration. Finally, I must warn the reader of my belief that the examples below range from the curious to the profound, but, needless to say, it is the task of the reader—and certainly not that of the author—to say which is which.

▬ Language

Language is a good starting point to examine some salient differences between the administrative practices in the two countries. In French the "state" (*l'Etat*) is nearly always capitalized and the same is sometimes true of "administration" (*l'Administration*) (Wilsford, 1991b, pp. 611-624). Although the French occasionally speak of "public administration" (*Administration Publique*), more often than not they omit the adjective as redundant because in French the word *Administration* alone nearly always means public administration. When the French speak of business administration, they prefer an entirely different word, *la gestion.*[2]

A telling illustration of these linguistic matters appeared at the establishment of an advanced school of administrative studies in francophone Quebec. Borrowing its name from the prestigious *Ecole Nationale d'Administration* (ENA) in Paris, the Quebec school was called *Ecole Nationale d'Administration Publique.*[3] Because of its North American location, it was necessary to add the adjective *publique* to convey accurately the nature of the institution as a school dedicated to preparing students for careers in government work as opposed to careers in the private sector.

Currently in American public administration circles, there is an animated linguistic debate over the merits of Osborne and Gaebler's (1993) use of *customer* to encourage the entrepreneurial spirit in the public sector. Although the idea of introducing business-like techniques into public administration is quite fashionable in France today, I cannot recall ever hearing a French administrator speak of his or her "customer" (*client*). They do, however, make an interesting distinction between *le citoyen* (citizen) and *l'administré* (an untranslatable word, literally meaning "one who is administered"—from the passive participle of the verb "to administer"). The same person is both *citoyen* and *administré*. He is a citizen insofar as he participates actively in public affairs—for example, when he votes. He is an *administré* when the state acts upon him—for instance, arresting him, calling him to military service, forbidding him from developing his property in a certain way, or conferring upon him a benefit grounded in public law. The closest English equivalent to the untranslatable *administré* is probably *subject,* but such a word has no place in a republican regime. In the United Kingdom, one speaks appropriately of British subjects because of the monarchy, but to speak of an "American subject" or a "French subject" would certainly be inappropriate and probably offensive. The fact that Americans have no equivalent for the French word *administré* is a good indication of the relative importance of administration as state activity in the two countries.[4]

In French, the "state" often has a strongly normative force that one hardly ever finds in English. Nowhere is this clearer than in the writings and speeches of General de Gaulle. For example, in the opening paragraph of his second memoir, de Gaulle links the state to the nation and its destiny in a most eloquent way:

> France has emerged from the depths of the past. She is a living entity. She responds to the call of the centuries. Yet she remains herself through time. Her boundaries may alter, but not the contours, the climate, the rivers and seas that are her eternal imprint. Her land is inhabited by people who, in the course of history, have undergone the most diverse experiences, but whom destiny and circumstance, exploited by politics, have unceasingly moulded into a single nation. This nation has embraced countless generations. At this moment it contains several. It will give birth to many more. But by reason of its geography, of the genius of the races which compose it, and of its position in relation to its neighbors, it has taken on an enduring character which makes each generation of Frenchmen dependent on their forefathers and pledged to their descendants. Unless it falls apart, therefore, this human amalgam, on this territory, at the heart of this world, comprises a past, a present and a future that are indissoluble. Thus the State, which is answerable for France, is in charge, at one and the same time of yesterday's heritage, today's interests, and tomorrow's hopes. (de Gaulle, 1971, p. 3)[5]

I apologize to the reader for inserting such a lengthy quotation, but I believe it is important for our purposes to let General de Gaulle speak for himself if we are to grasp his exalted vision of the state. Recall that this is the opening paragraph of the memoir and, as such, sets a tone for all that follows. For de Gaulle, the state is charged with nothing less than answering for the France he loves so dearly, and this for "yesterday's heritage, today's interests, and tomorrow's hopes." We Americans may have our heritage, our interests, and our hopes in mind when we speak of the "common good" or the "public interest," but we have no *institution* that is answerable for it. In de Gaulle's vision of France, the state is such an institution.

In his earlier memoir from World War II, the general had singled out "the feebleness of the State" during the years between the two world wars as a major cause for the humiliating defeat France had suffered in 1940. The state was enfeebled because it had been captured by various political parties, each of which necessarily had a limited view of the good of France as a whole. Hence, in writing about the liberation of Paris in 1944, de Gaulle says of that most solemn moment: "I myself had already determined what I must do in the liberated capital. I would mold all minds into a single national impulse, but also cause the figure and the authority of the State to appear at once" (Cook, 1983, p. 245). Before talking about constitutions, elections, and political parties, the state must first be restored. Significantly, at the time of his triumphal entry into Paris, de Gaulle first visited the prefecture of police before going to the *Hôtel de Ville* (City Hall) where the people awaited him. The purpose of this meaningful detour was to symbolize his control over the police as a crucial element of the apparatus of the state (Cook, 1983, p. 248).

Shortly after the end of the war, the French people approved a new constitution that created the Fourth Republic. De Gaulle had severely criticized the proposed document for its failure to provide a sufficiently strong executive to counteract the influence of the political parties in parliament. When the people rejected his advice, de Gaulle withdrew from public life and remained a private citizen until 1958 when he was called upon to lead his country once again in a time of crisis—this time the extremely divisive Algerian War, which brought France to the brink of civil war.

During his self-imposed retirement from public life from 1946 to 1958, de Gaulle continued to speak out against the weak governing structures of the Fourth Republic. His grand notion of the state held center stage in his arguments. Thus, in an important speech at Strasbourg in 1947, he urged his followers to work for "reform of the State" and 3 years later he told them to "hasten to establish the State," even though the busy men and women of the Fourth Republic would surely be forgiven for thinking that a state was already in place (Mauriac, 1966, p. 180). At the time of his return to power in 1958, de Gaulle (1971), not surprisingly, "pointed to the degradation of the State as the cause of the threatening calamity" (p. 23).

Even after the Fifth Republic had been established under de Gaulle's leadership in 1958, the general continued to emphasize the central role of the state. For example, in November 1962 he urged his fellow citizens to vote for loyal Gaullists in an upcoming parliamentary election for "the good of the State, the fate of the Republic, and the future of France"—thereby linking the state to the Republic and to France itself (Mauriac, 1966, p. 160).

In a particularly telling comment, de Gaulle revealed to his friend André Malraux his feelings when he assumed power in 1958:

> When I saw the politicians gathered together again for the first time, I felt at once, no mistaking it, their hostility to everyone. They did not believe in the slightest that I was a dictator, but they understood I represented the State. That was just as bad; the State is the devil, and if it exists, then they do not. They lose what they value most, and that is not money but the exercise of their vanity. They all loathe the State. (Malraux, 1971, p. 82).

This comment goes to the heart of de Gaulle's notion of the state. Politicians represent particular interests—farmers, unions, business enterprises, and so on—and therefore they fear de Gaulle, the man of the state, who sees in himself one who speaks for all of France. There can be no doubt that de Gaulle did see himself in this way. Speaking by radio from London in the darkest days of 1940, he gave hope to his dispirited countrymen by proclaiming, "I, General de Gaulle, French soldier and leader, am aware that I speak in the name of France" (Mauriac, 1966, p. 68).

At the end of the war, he referred to "exceptional powers I have exercised since June 18, 1940, in the name of the Republic" (Mauriac, 1966, pp. 108-109). In 1960 after he had become President of the Fifth Republic, he referred to "the national legitimacy that I have embodied for twenty years." In the same year, speaking of national unity, he did not shrink from saying: "I have no other *raison d'être,* as you know than this unity. I am in a sense its symbol and its guarantee" (Mauriac, 1966, pp. 91-92).

Such statements surely strike the American reader as startling and perhaps even as preposterous, but not so for de Gaulle's close associates. Witness François Mauriac's (1966) account of the origins of his allegiance to the general: "I was sitting opposite someone who did not distinguish himself from France, who said, openly, 'I am France' without anyone in the world saying he was mad" (p. 7; see also pages 35 and 88 for similar remarks).

This is heady wine. An American statesman saying "I am America" would surely be mad. I believe the strong-state tradition goes a long way toward explaining why a statement that would be sheer madness in the United States could be taken as authentic patriotism in France. De Gaulle claimed to speak for France as a whole and most of his countrymen believed him. No American statesman could speak for the United States "as a whole" because our institutions and traditions render meaningless any notion of "a whole" for our amazingly diversified nation. Indeed, the very grammar of the name of our country—a *plural* noun modified by an adjective—mocks the idea of a comprehensive whole. We have never had a Charles de Gaulle because, happily, we have never needed one.

One need not soar to the heights of Gaullist rhetoric to grasp the significance of the state in the French political tradition. At the mundane level of everyday politics and government in today's less stressful times, French politicians and administrators routinely pay homage to the centrality of the state. Thus a governmental decree of March 1990 permits the preservation in official files of highly personal information concerning those who are likely to present a threat "to the security of the State or to the public safety."[6] The text makes an interesting distinction between public safety on the one hand and the security of the state on the other. This implies that there is a state interest in its own security that is something other than the more general public safety, an implication quite consistent with the legal doctrine of the state as a moral person with its own rights and duties. A comparable American regulation would probably mention "national security" or possibly "public safety," but it would be a rare American text that would *add* a concern for the security of the state itself as an independent entity.

Every New Year's Eve, President Mitterrand customarily offers his best wishes to his countrymen in a televised address. In the course of his remarks on the last day of 1991, the president rehearsed a list of things badly needed in France. They included such high-priority items as "a healthy moral climate to mobilize our collective energy," "a greater equality in the sharing of the benefits derived from the labor of everyone," and "education of our youth for careers in order to diminish the curse of unemployment." Heading the president's list, however, was the assertion that "we have need of the State and of its authority in order to control private interests." It is simply unthinkable that a president of the United States would speak of the state in such a way in such a context.

In an address to the students at the prestigious *Ecole Nationale d'Administration* (ENA) in 1991, Socialist Prime Minister Michel Rocard assured the aspiring high-level civil servants that their careers in public service would soon regain the esteem in public opinion that they had once enjoyed. Conceding that during the 1980s "business careers rediscovered a legitimacy in the eyes of the French people," he confidently predicted that "the 90s will be the years of the rehabilitation of the public service." The reason for this confidence, Rocard tells his listeners, is his firm belief that "[t]he State is back" (*L'Etat est de retour*).[7] Presumably, Rocard's glad tidings found a warm reception at ENA because, according to Michel Debré, the founder of the school, its purpose was to instill in the students "a sense of the State."

Jacques Chirac, a former prime minister and prominent conservative leader, used a televised interview in 1990 to criticize his socialist opponents for using their official position for partisan advantage—hardly a novel complaint from the opposition in any democratic country. Chirac, however, in typically French fashion accused government officials of using major powers of the state—its fiscal powers, its police powers, and its administration of justice—to serve their own interests. An American might see in this unremarkable charge nothing more than another case of "corruption in government" or an "abuse of power," but Chirac phrased it as "a crisis of the State."[8]

In presenting these examples, I must not overstate my case. The French are by no means impervious to the danger of excessive regulation by the state—especially in economic affairs. Indeed, they have a clearly pejorative word for it—*étatisme* (statism). The recent failure of the proposed merger between Renault (a state-owned enterprise in France) and the Swedish company Volvo was blamed on the bad reputation of the French state as a major shareholder. Specifically, Volvo management took a dim view of the French government's order in September 1993 imposing on all nationalized industries a moratorium on firing any workers. This order may have been wise politically in view of the severe unemployment crisis in France, but Swedish businesspersons feared that badly needed organizational reforms at Renault would be sacrificed on the altar of French politics ("Renault-Volvo," 1993, p. 14).

I mention this merely to put my argument in perspective. Despite these correctives, however, it seems to me absolutely clear that an examination of French political discourse reveals the centrality of the state as the normative foundation for civic life in France.

▬ Practice

Having established the salience of the state in French politics, let us now consider what administrative practices might come in its wake. To do this, we will first examine the status of the civil service in France and then look at a series of representative administrative actions.

Civil Service

The French civil service is among the most powerful in the world. High-ranking civil servants—*hauts fonctionnaires*—enjoy a social prestige comparable to that of federal judges in the United States. No study of elites in French society would be complete without careful attention to high-ranking civil servants (Suleiman, 1974).

The prestige of the high civil service is due in no small part to the structure of the French personnel system, which places every civil servant of the state, that is, of the central government, in a corps. The most prestigious of these corps are called *les grands corps de l'Etat* (the great corps of the State). There is some dispute among personnel experts about just which corps merit the rank of *grands,* but there are some one finds on everyone's list:

- *Conseil d'Etat* (Council of State): specializes in administrative law but covers a remarkably broad range of administrative activities beyond questions of law; it has been aptly called "the great administrative corps *par excellence"* (Kessler, 1986, p. 208)
- *Inspection des Finances* (Financial Investigators) and *La Cour des Comptes* (Court of Audits): both of these corps monitor the regularity of the financial transactions of the state and its officers

■ *Corps des Ponts et Chaussées* (Corps for Bridges and Roads) and *Corps des Mines* (Mining Corps): technical corps staffed by engineers who deal with questions far beyond the narrow confines of roads, bridges, and mines

In addition to these five corps, one often finds the *corps préfectoral* (prefects' corps) and the *corps diplomatique* (diplomatic corps) included among the *grands corps* (Kessler, 1986, pp. 16-18).[9]

What these *grands corps* have in common is that most of their members are graduates of elite professional schools called, appropriately enough, *les grandes écoles—Ecole Polytechnique* for the engineers and ENA for the other *grands corps*.[10] Admission to these schools is determined by rigorous examination so that there is no doubt that the civil service ends up with "the best and the brightest" young men and women in France.

This recruitment system has been justly criticized as elitist, but repeated efforts to change it significantly have been to no avail. A prominent French executive put it well when he said, "Ninety percent of the population want to abolish the *Ecole Polytechnique,* but they all also want their sons to go there" (Barsoux & Lawrence, 1991, p. 64). As for ENA, an article in a socialist journal marking that school's 30th anniversary in 1975 rehearsed the familiar and thoroughly justified attacks on its elitist character but candidly acknowledged the brilliant performance of its graduates. The author then asked, "Must we abolish a professional school because its alumni are too good at what they do?" (Kessler, 1986, p. 81, citing *Unité* of October 31, 1975).

The elitism in the French civil service is nothing new nor did it come about by accident. J.-L. Boudigel tells of an official report from the era of the restoration of the Bourbon monarchy in the early 19th century whose authors saw that the great task at hand was to "justify rank by merit and wealth by talent and virtue." That is, if the privileged classes were to maintain their positions in society in the face of the rising tide of democracy, they would have to show that they earned it. Emile Boutmy, the founder of a school that trained many of the high-ranking civil servants during the Third Republic (1871-1940), justified the establishment of his school on the grounds that "the upper classes can only maintain their hegemony by invoking the rights of the most capable." Boutmy, like many serious Frenchmen before and after him, adopted a strategy intended to ensure that the upper classes, whose talents were believed to be so badly needed in public life, would achieve high position on merit, because they could no longer count on privileged birth or wealth (Boudigel, 1990, pp. 711-713).

The prestige of the civil service is due not only to its elite character, but also to its effective performance. It has often been observed that a strong civil service was necessary to bring stability to France because the political character of the country was notoriously unstable (see, e.g., Zeldin, 1973, pp. 113-130). As France lurched from one revolution to another, monarchies, empires, and republics—to say nothing of foreign armies—came and went with distressing regularity. Depending on how one defines the word *constitution,* France has had from 13 to 17 of them since the revolution of 1789. That France has survived and flourished under such circumstances as one of the world's great nations is owing in considerable part to its elite civil service. An eloquent testimony to its importance is the legal requirement imposed upon civil servants to obtain permission to leave their jobs (Braibant, 1988, p. 172).

The substantive contributions of the civil service have been many and varied. The Council of State, for example, which was created by Napoleon in 1799, provided an extremely useful integrating mechanism by bringing together in one deliberative body representatives of the prerevolutionary aristocracy and the new imperial aristocrats who owed their rank to the Emperor.

One need not reach back to the Napoleonic Era for examples of great statesmen relying on the civil service. Throughout World War II and its immediate aftermath, General de Gaulle frequently charged civil servants with serious responsibilities in organizing the activities of the Resistance Movement. Jean Moulin, the best known of these organizers, had been a prefect before the war. When the Nazis executed him, de Gaulle called upon Alexandre Parodi, a prominent civil servant who had refused to serve the Vichy government, to represent him at the meetings of the Resistance Council (Cook, 1983, p. 203).

De Gaulle's reliance upon the civil service as one of the major institutions in French public life was evident throughout his career. Shortly after the allied landing in North Africa, the general used the BBC to urge his countrymen to give what support they could: "French leaders, soldiers, sailors, airmen, *civil servants,* French settlers in North Africa, arise. Help our allies" [emphasis added]. Typical is the record of one of many important meetings during and after the Liberation in which the future of France was planned. Present at a meeting with de Gaulle at the Palais Chaillot on September 12, 1944, were representatives of "the unions, industry, commerce, the universities, the bar associations, *the civil service,* and, of course, the Resistance" (Cook, 1983, p. 254; emphasis added).

Not surprisingly, when de Gaulle returned to power in 1958 and needed a new constitution to rechart the course of the nation, he turned to the Council of State, the *grand corps* with special expertise in administrative law. Working under the direction of Justice Minister Michel Debré, himself a councilor of state, a small working group (*groupe de travail*) of young councilors drafted the text that eventually was approved by the French people in the referendum of September 28, 1958, and is still in effect today, some 35 years later. Not bad by French standards of constitutional longevity.

In governing the Fifth Republic as its first president, de Gaulle relied heavily on civil servants, appointing a substantial number of them to ministerial posts. He tended to prefer civil servants to the experienced politicians from the parties because the former were more likely to share his vision of the good of France as a whole, a characteristic de Gaulle looked for in "men of the State."

Reliance on civil servants to govern the Fifth Republic did not end with General de Gaulle. A study published in 1987 showed that throughout the Fifth Republic all the prime ministers (10 at that time) had been civil servants. Eighty percent of the Finance Ministers and 54% of all other ministers had also come from the civil service as well as 42% of the deputies elected to the National Assembly, the more powerful chamber of the bicameral French legislature (de Baecque, 1987).[11] Further, civil servants often serve as mayors of the towns wherein they reside.

In addition to civil servants holding political office at all levels, there is a marked tendency to turn to civil servants to head special investigatory or problem-solving bodies—as President Mitterrand did in the scandal involving the environmental group "Greenpeace" and the destruction of its ship *Rainbow Warrior,* which was monitoring French nuclear testing in the Pacific Ocean.[12]

The political role of civil servants is encouraged by a constitutional prohibition against ministers, that is, members of the government, holding seats in Parliament. A parliamentarian who accepts a minister's portfolio must resign his or her legislative seat—a practice much closer to an American-style presidential system than to a conventional parliamentary regime. Should the government fall, the parliamentarian-turned-minister could be out of a job, although, as a matter of fact, erstwhile parliamentarians have shown considerable ingenuity in circumventing this regulation.

Unlike parliamentarians, civil servants who accept a minister's portfolio can always return to their corps if they must leave their high office. A particularly dramatic example of a *grand corps* providing a safe haven for a cashiered minister concerned Prime Minister Michel Rocard. When President Mitterrand asked for his resignation in the spring of 1991, Rocard returned to his corps, Financial Inspectors, while he prepared his campaign (ultimately unsuccessful) to become the Socialist candidate for President of the Republic in 1995 (Bréhier, 1991).

To conclude this review of the importance of the civil service, let us consider three remarkable statements that confirm the point I have been making. The first came from Jacques Delors, a Frenchman who served as president of the Commission of the European Union in Brussels. In a lengthy interview on French television, Delors responded to the fear of French nationalists that the country's interests would be ignored in the larger European community. Delors said this would not happen. France would always be able to hold its own in European affairs. He gave three reasons for his confident prediction, the first of which was "the quality of our public service and of our bureaucrats. . . . There is no other administration which operates as well as the French administration."[13]

The second statement came from President Mitterrand at the customary ceremony in which he exchanges greetings with representatives from the major organizations in French society at the beginning of a new year. On January 3, 1992, he received the representatives of the civil service. After cautioning against yielding to a certain "caste spirit" that would offend democratic values, he assured the civil servants that they enjoyed his full support. He went on to complain that there are too many people who "for too long a time have wanted to destroy not only the State but also the public service, *which is the same thing*" (emphasis added). In view of the exalted French notion of the state, the president intoned a remarkable paean to the prestige of the civil service.

Third, Michel Debré, General de Gaulle's first prime minister under the Fifth Republic, went even further, when he said quite simply of "the administration as represented by 'the grands corps' ": "It is the state" (Debré, 1957, p. 9).

Administrative Action

The principles of administrative law developed by the Council of State provide a striking example of the importance of administrative action in French governance. The Council's strength lies in the fact that it is both the highest administrative court in France and the government's highest official advisory body. That is, it adjudicates cases brought against officers of the state and advises the government of the day on the suitability of proposed legislation. A British commentary on the Council captures nicely the essence of this dual role by describing the daily routine of a councilor of state:

> In the same afternoon, one person may act as a member of a judicial panel on tax cases and then come down the lift to advise on the drafting of a new law on privatizing a television channel. Far from creating a conflict of interests, the dual function is seen as enriching administrative adjudication. (Brown & Bell, 1989, p. 71)

In addition to their twofold role as judges and advisors, councilors of state routinely serve in various ministries as line administrators. Thus, French administrative judges enjoy a well-deserved reputation of being practical men and women who understand the problems and pressures of everyday public administration. This reputation is crucial for the morale of public administrators and aggrieved citizens, because there is no appeal from a decision of the Council of State. Unlike the United States, France has no Supreme Court where administrative decisions can be reviewed.

Throughout its long history, the Council of State has developed a reputation for independence and integrity that ranks it among the most respected institutions in France. On one occasion the Council defied even General de Gaulle by setting aside the conviction and capital sentence of dissident French Army officers in Algeria. The Council found legal flaws in the decree that the general, as President of the Fifth Republic, had relied on to establish the military tribunal that tried and convicted the officers.[14]

Perhaps the most striking example of the Council of State's importance appears in its relation with the Constitutional Council (*Conseil Constitutionnel*). Here a brief background explanation is in order.

As noted above, there is no Supreme Court in France. Prior to the establishment of the Fifth Republic, this meant that there was no way a law passed by parliament could be declared unconstitutional—regardless of how flagrantly unconstitutional it might be. This situation was somewhat ameliorated by the constitution of 1958, which created a Constitutional Council to be convened to review certain laws passed by parliament to be sure they were in accord with the constitution. This council was not intended to be a court; no litigants appeared before it. Its jurisdiction could be invoked only by certain officers mentioned explicitly in the constitution. An examination of the development of the text of the constitution of 1958 makes it abundantly clear that the main purpose of the Council was to give the executive a means to challenge parliamentary enactments that might impinge upon its own constitutional powers. As one observer put it, the Constitutional Council was originally intended to be "a cannon aimed at parliament" (Stone, 1992, p. 61).

Throughout the 35-year history of the Fifth Republic, the Constitutional Council has played an increasingly important role and has come to be looked upon with considerable justification as a bastion of civil liberties. It frequently strikes down laws passed by parliament that the government itself has supported. It may still be a cannon aimed at parliament; but if so, the government no longer fires it. Indeed, the government itself is now well within its range. Most French legal scholars welcome these developments and see in the Constitutional Council the institutional means, at long last, to endow France with "a legal State" (*Etat de droit*)—that is, a state effectively subjected to the rule of constitutional law.

These events are of enormous importance in the development of French constitutional history, but, for our narrower purposes, their significance lies in the fact that the Constitutional Council relied heavily on the principles of *administrative law* developed by the Council of State to formulate its own constitutional jurisprudence.[15] Thus the impressive constitutional principles that safeguard individual liberties in contemporary France have been developed by an institution in tutelage to administrative law. As noted above, prior to the establishment of the Fifth Republic, laws passed by parliament could not be declared unconstitutional. Administrative decrees could be, however, and were overturned by the Council of State if they were found to violate either a law or the constitution. Thus, prior to the blossoming of the Constitutional Council, there was a well-established jurisprudence in administrative law aimed at controlling *governmental* (as opposed to parliamentary) action— that is, a jurisprudence aimed at decrees rather than at laws. The Constitutional Council mined this jurisprudence to discover legal principles that it applied against laws voted by parliament. This is a complete reversal of the American legal experience wherein administrative law is thoroughly dominated by the constitutional law developed in the ordinary federal courts and, indeed, in the long history of the common law.

I believe the important role of the Council of State in safeguarding civil liberties through its administrative jurisprudence challenges the facile assumption that a powerful administrative state necessarily jeopardizes individual rights.[16]

The role of the prefect in French administration provides a second example of the relationship between administrative action and the strong-state tradition. Since the Revolution, France has been divided into "departments" (*départements*) that are supervised by a prefect. Today, there are 96 departments in metropolitan France. Prior to a decentralization reform in 1982, the prefect was in the anomalous position of being the executive officer of the local (departmental) government even though he was appointed by the national government in Paris. Thus his role required considerable political skills. As a representative of the state, he had to see to it that national programs and standards were enforced in his department, but, as the department's executive officer, he was expected to alert the central government in Paris to local needs and desires. Thus the prefect was traditionally called upon to exercise considerable bureaucratic statesmanship. When this complicated system was at its best, it gave a good example of what F. F. Ridley (1974a) has called "integrated administrative decentralization" (see also Ridley, 1974b).

Needless to say, the system was not always at its best and, consequently, the Socialist government that came to power in 1981 introduced reforms intended to be far-reaching.[17] Just how far-reaching they have in fact been is a matter of some dispute. At first, it seemed the prefect would be a casualty of the reform because the president of the locally elected departmental council (*conseil général*) replaced the prefect as executive officer of the department. As if to add insult to injury, the prefect lost his venerable title as well. Henceforward he was to be known as the *commissaire de la République* ("superintendent of the Republic"), but a few years later his venerable title was restored, thereby confirming the stability of administrative traditions in France.

In recent years there has been a marked growth of "regionalism" in France that has divided the country into 22 regions, each of which includes several departments. Each region has its own prefect who doubles as prefect of one of the departments in the region. The regions, like the departments, have their own elected councils whose presidents serve as executive officers. The prefects are tasked with monitoring the legality—that is, the conformity with the law of the state—of actions taken by the regional and departmental councils. At times this duty can create stressful relations between a prefect and a council president. Because neither officer is the hierarchical superior of the other, personal relationships and political skills assume considerable importance in the mutual effort to avoid serious public embarrassment. Although the formal powers of the prefect have been diminished by the decentralization reform of 1982, he or she retains considerable informal influence both over the workings of local governments and, perhaps more importantly, as an advocate for local causes with officers of the central state in Paris.

The resilience of the prefect's office was cleverly summarized by a civil servant in an article written for *Le Monde* at the time of the decentralization reform. Noting that the "prefect" would disappear only to be reincarnated as "superintendent of the Republic" and that his diminished duties would require each department to replace him with a new "head of departmental services" (*chef des services départementaux*), the author formulated the *théorème de Deferre* ("Deferre's theorem")—so named after Gaston Deferre, the Minister of the Interior who championed the decentralization reform. The theorem was *moins un égale deux* ("minus one equals two": $-1 = 2$). That is, the loss of one prefect leads to the creation of two officers in his stead (Kessler, 1986, p. 212, citing article from *Le Monde* of April 20, 1982).

For a third example of administrative practice within a strong-state tradition, let us consider the way in which private associations in France participate in the policy-making process. Here we find a sharp contrast with policy making in the United States, where notice of proposed rules appears in the

Federal Register along with an address to which all interested parties should send their comments. In France, policy making includes a procedure called *concertation* ("dialogue" or "consultation"), in which high-ranking ministry officials contact certain groups they think might be interested in a forthcoming policy initiative. Civil servants and representatives of these associations then discuss the proposed policy and how it might be strengthened. The difference between the two countries is that in France the state selects the private groups to which it will listen. The idea behind *concertation* is that the state and private groups embark together on a quest for the common good with the very important proviso that only those groups invited by the state may participate. The French procedure has the decided advantage of expediting the rule-making process that in the United States has been known to drag on for years. The price the French pay, however, is that excluded groups challenge the legitimacy of the outcome and readily take to the streets to register their displeasure in ways that are never pleasant and sometimes become violent. There seems to be a direct relationship between the exclusionary character of *concertation* and the readiness of Frenchmen to resort to "direct action" to manifest their displeasure.[18]

My fourth and final example of administrative action comes from the way in which the conservative government, which was in power from 1986 to 1988, privatized some industries that had been nationalized by its Socialist predecessors. As we have already seen, President Mitterrand, a Socialist, was elected in 1981. Shortly after assuming office, he dissolved parliament and called for new elections—in which his Socialist Party prevailed. French parliamentary sessions ordinarily last 5 years, whereas the presidential term is 7 years. The 1986 parliamentary elections returned a conservative majority, which led to the formation of a new government headed by Jacques Chirac, a conservative, as prime minister. Mitterrand continued to serve as President of the Republic, thereby initiating what came to be known as the period of *cohabitation*.

To redeem his campaign pledges, Chirac proceeded to privatize several industries nationalized by the Socialists. Because the French president has no veto power, Mitterrand could not formally block the conservative privatization program. As head of state, however, he had sufficient influence to have his complaints taken seriously by the media and the public. The president based his attack on the patriotic grounds that privatization would lead to foreign control of key elements of French industry.

To meet this objection, the Chirac government saw to it that control of the privatized industries would remain in French hands. They did this by taking several measures that underscored the role of the French state in the nation's economy even while executing a seemingly free-market policy of privatization. First, the privatization law of 1986 forbade any foreign investor to own more than 20% of a newly privatized firm. Second, the Minister of Finance received discretionary authority to reduce this limit to 10% should such need arise. Third, and most important, the Chirac government discouraged foreign takeovers by selecting several privately owned French firms that were authorized by the state to buy controlling blocks of stock in the companies that were to be privatized at a considerable discount below market value. As a trade-off for this windfall, the favored companies were obliged to hold the stock for at least 2 years.[19] These peculiar details of the 1986 privatization plan made little economic sense, but they responded shrewdly to the political imperatives of French economic nationalism. The plan had the fingerprints of the strong-state tradition all over it.[20]

▬ Rights

The final section of this chapter will consider the treatment of individual rights under the French strong-state tradition. Here, the focus of our inquiry moves from questions of public administration to broader questions of governance.

Commentators have often noted that in the United States rights are established negatively—that is, by prohibiting the state from doing something, whereas in France (and throughout most of Europe) they are positive grants from the state.[21] Compare and contrast, for example, the First Amendment to the Constitution of the United States with the 10th article of the Declaration of the Rights of Man and of the Citizen of 1789:

> Congress shall make no law respecting an establishment of religion, or prohibiting the free exercise thereof; or abridging the freedom of speech or of the press, or the right of the people peaceably to assemble, and to petition the Government for a redress of grievances.

> Free communication of thought and opinion is one of the most valuable rights of man; thus, every citizen may speak, write and print his views freely, provided only that he accepts the bounds of this freedom established by law.

To focus only on freedom of the press, one sees that—at least in principle—the American text renders Congress simply incapable of acting in this matter at all, whereas the French text demands that this freedom yield to duly enacted laws. Both texts recognize the value of a free press, but they support this value in different ways—one by declaring it off limits to the legislature and the other by affirming the need for laws to ensure its proper exercise. Not surprisingly, then, the press in France is a regulated industry.

The underlying rationale for the regulations is the duty of the state to protect the interests not only of those who publish newspapers but of those who read them as well. Indeed, the Constitutional Council has interpreted freedom of the press to be primarily a right of the reader.[22] A free press flows from the logic of democracy wherein the principle of universal suffrage requires that the people have precise information on important events and this, in turn, justifies state intervention in the way the press conducts its affairs (Rivero, 1989, p. 204). For example, to establish a newspaper, the publisher must leave with the public prosecutor's office the names of his editor and his printer in case the newspaper should be the target of future litigation. No money can be accepted from foreign governments, and the degree to which foreigners may participate in the ownership of the enterprise is strictly regulated. The publisher must agree to distribute copies of his newspaper to public libraries so that there will be a record of all that is printed in France. A statute specifically for journalists states the characteristics one must have to be considered a member of that profession and the state issues a card identifying them as such. Newspaper publishers benefit from a number of laws and regulations granting favorable postal and rail rates. Journalists receive special tax considerations to encourage them in their work and even benefit from a "conscience clause" providing several weeks' pay for reporters who feel morally obliged to leave a newspaper that has changed its political orientation (Rivero, 1989, pp. 221-226).[23]

One of the most interesting aspects of the French effort to support freedom of the press by law and regulation is the *droit de réponse* ("the right to reply")—a right that does not exist in the United States. In 1974, the Supreme Court of the United States declared unconstitutional a Florida statute that, as applied, would have required the *Miami Herald* to provide free column space to a candidate for public office whose character had been impugned by the newspaper.[24] The court justified its decision by underscoring the paramount importance of "editorial control and judgment" unfettered by state regulation.

The French approach to this issue is precisely the opposite. Newspapers are required by law to publish replies from anyone mentioned in their columns. Minute regulations govern this obligation. For example, the person has 1 year in which to submit his or her reply, but the paper has only 3 days in which to print it. The reply may be as long as the article, provided it does not exceed 200 lines, and it must not attack the honor of the journalist unless the journalist has attacked the honor of the person writing the reply. The journalist may add a brief rejoinder if he or she wishes.[25] Thus the French defend freedom of the press by mandating access to the columns of a newspaper in order that the public may hear both sides of a story. Americans defend it by prohibiting governmental authorities from interfering with editorial discretion. In a word, Americans rely on individual rights to defend freedom of the press, whereas the French defend it by law.

The intractable American problem of gun control can be explained at least in part by the weak-state tradition reflected in the Second Amendment to the Constitution: "A well regulated Militia, being necessary to the security of a free State, the right of the people to keep and bear Arms, shall not be infringed." This constitutional provision is utterly at odds with Max Weber's famous description of the state as the institution that claims a monopoly on the legitimate use of violence. A fair reading of the Second Amendment would seem to suggest that "the right of the people to keep and bear Arms" is intended precisely to deny this monopoly to the state (Levinson, 1989, p. 650). Advocates of gun control would do well to enlarge their target to include not only the National Rifle Association but our weak-state tradition as well.

Many of the complaints about the low quality of the public debate over abortion can be traced to the American penchant to frame issues in terms of rights—in this case the fetus' right to life versus a woman's rights over her own body. Abortion is readily available in France, even though there is no *right* to have one there. Abortions are permitted as an *exception* to the legal principle that "guarantees the respect of every human being from the commencement of life" (Glendon, 1987, p. 16, citing Law # 75-17 of January 17, 1975).[26] There is an explicit exception from this principle for any pregnant woman "whose condition places her in a situation of distress" (Glendon, 1987, p. 15). *Distress* is not defined in the statute, which "makes the woman herself the sole judge of whether she is in it" (p. 15). The pregnant woman can make use of this exception for the first 10 weeks of her pregnancy. Thus, in effect, France has a policy of abortion-on-demand for a 10-week period. The state pays 70% of the cost of abortions for women in distress and the entire cost of abortions medically certified as therapeutic.

The French abortion statute reveals the character of the strong-state tradition by the way it regulates the conditions under which the abortion takes place. There are a series of complex regulations clearly intended to discourage the woman from going through with the abortion unless she has a very serious reason for doing so. Thus 1 full week must elapse between the initial contact with the physician and the abortion itself, but this requirement can be waived if the physician believes it would carry the pregnancy beyond 10 weeks. To prevent the establishment of "abortion mills," the statute "provides that all abortions must be performed by physicians in approved facilities, and that the annual number of abortions in such establishments may not exceed twenty-five per cent of all the surgical and obstetrical operations carried out there"

(Glendon, 1987, p. 17). After the 10-week period, abortions can be performed only for "therapeutic reasons" that must be certified by two physicians.

The purpose of the statute seems to be to teach as well as to regulate. A close examination of the text reveals first a pattern of seemingly stringent conditions confining the practice of abortion and then a pattern of generous exceptions for those who really want to abort. The statute teaches the lesson that abortion is a terribly serious matter that should take place only for the most serious reasons. A good illustration of the statute's pedagogical nature is its provision that abortion should not be treated as a means of birth control. Instead of trying to punish those who might treat it that way, the law merely imposes upon the *state* the duty "to take all measures necessary to provide information on birth control on as wide a scale as possible." Thus, the prohibition against abortion as birth control imposes no legal obligations on pregnant women but only on the state.

Mary Ann Glendon (1987) captures nicely the tone of the French law when she describes it as "pervaded by compassion for pregnant women, by concern for fetal life, and by expression of the commitment of society as a whole to help minimize occasions for tragic choices between them" (p. 18).

The French approach to abortion seems quite consistent with pollsters' findings on American public opinion on this issue. Few Americans support a total ban on abortions, but the vast majority favor *some* regulations[27]—a finding that will bring little comfort to hard-core adherents to either pro-life or pro-choice orthodoxies. The attitude suggested by this finding contrasts sharply with the legal basis for abortion in the United States and, especially, with its foundation in the right to privacy and the principle of freedom of choice. Such a position makes serious moral argument difficult because it bypasses the fundamental question of under what circumstances a woman *should* choose to abort. If the basis of the argument is a woman's right over her own body, then the short answer to the question I characterize as "fundamental" is that it is no one's business other than that of the woman herself.

Not only does such a response put an end to dialogue, but it also proves far too much, and this for three reasons. First, if the case for abortion rights rests on a woman's rights over her own body, she can then abort for *any* reason—for example, sex selection or because she wants her child to be an Aries rather than a Leo. To ground the abortion debate in a woman's rights over her own body trivializes the issue by leveling all the possible reasons for which a woman might choose to abort. A woman choosing to abort because an unplanned pregnancy interferes with a summer vacation has no less rights over her body than the woman whose abortion was based on solid medical advice that her pregnancy posed a serious threat to her health.

Second, it proves too much because its logic weakens the serious and the thoroughly admirable reform effort to strengthen the laws making wayward fathers contribute to the support of their children. If the choice to abort is simply a matter of the mother's rights over her own body, then it follows that every pregnancy that comes to term does so only because the mother has chosen not to abort. Why then should the father have any responsibility to support a child whose existence is due to its mother's choice not to exercise her right to abort? To be sure, the father and mother together caused the fetus to come into existence, but its continued existence is due to the mother's choice to give birth to a child—a choice with which the father has no legal right to interfere regardless of whether he is for or against abortion. A case for abortion grounded in the individual rights of a woman over her own body has the perverse effect of bringing aid and comfort to irresponsible fathers.

Third, it proves too much because, if taken seriously, it introduces a wholly new and very unsettling logic into the troublesome issue of using fetal tissue for medical research. If a woman's right to abort is grounded in her rights over her own body, why can't she undergo multiple abortions and then *sell* the fetal tissue to interested researchers? Why don't we condemn the policy forbidding such commercial transactions as an unconscionable interference with a woman's right over her body?

Clearly, no proponent of abortion rights advocates so outrageous a position. And why not? I believe it is because they do not really believe their own rhetoric about a woman's rights over her body. I believe the proponents of relaxed abortion laws are trying to accomplish something more profoundly and more tragically human than the individual rights language of their position suggests. Part of that "something" may well be found in the French statute that seems to embody such a sensible compromise. Perhaps the French strong-state tradition could illuminate the sterile shouting match about rights that has deprived us of the serious debate we need over the dreadfully divisive issue of abortion.

To conclude our discussion of rights, let us leave French governance in order to consider an exclusively American issue wherein our preoccupation with rights together with our neglect of the state may have obscured our moral vision. I refer to the timely issue of affirmative action for African Americans. To be sure, affirmative action programs concern groups other than African Americans, but I want to focus on this group alone to simplify my argument.[28]

The main reason affirmative action programs for African Americans are so controversial is that they are not the only group that can point to historic injustices perpetrated against their ancestors. Italians, Poles, Jews, the Irish, Germans, Greeks, and just about every other ethnic group in this country can call on a rich folklore about outrages their newly arrived ancestors once endured. The argument for special treatment for blacks founders on the shoals of individual rights. A third-generation Polish American is fully justified in resenting the exhortations he hears from *state officials* about the need to show special "sensitivity" to the needs of African Americans because of historic injustices that were not of his doing. The idea that history confers a privileged position upon some groups but not others defies the fundamental American principle of equal rights for every individual. This explains in part why affirmative action programs create such resentment among people who earlier in their lives might well have applauded the collapse of segregation, the Voting Rights Act of 1965, and the public accommodations provisions of the Civil Rights Act of 1964. These were questions of individual rights and therefore their advocates swam with the current of American values. Affirmative action swims against it and therefore produces resentment, backlash, and the reinforcement of the racist sentiment that "blacks can't make it on their own."

Clearly, the history of African Americans *is* different from that of all other groups because of the unspeakable evil of slavery. Thus one can argue plausibly that even though nearly all ethnic groups have suffered *some* historic injustices, blacks have suffered the most and therefore deserve some special consideration. The flaw in this argument lies in its "more or less" character. That is, it presents slavery as an injustice that differs from other injustices only in degree and not in kind. If we say that blacks deserve special treatment because they suffered more than anyone else, then what about those whose ancestors have suffered *less* than blacks but *more* than every other ethnic group? And what about those in third and fourth place? Did Irish immigrants suffer *less* than Germans because they spoke English or *more* because they were Catholics? Such a discussion leads to a destructive wallowing in self-pity as participants seek to reconstruct a comparative misery index.

If, however, we set aside questions of individual rights and look instead to the *duties of the state,* the issue is entirely transformed. The institution of slavery was encouraged by the state—both at the national level and in a good number of the states as well. This makes it *qualitatively* different—that is, different in kind and not merely in degree—from the *societal* discrimination visited upon the other ethnic groups. When the Irish were told they "need not apply," the message ordinarily did not come from state officials but from private citizens. This is what I mean by societal as opposed to state-based injustice. Now, the state is a legal person with rights and duties and through its legal personality achieves a longevity—if not an immortality—denied to all natural persons. There is no way—at least in this world—that the slave-trader, the master, and the overseer of yesteryear can make amends for the wrongs they perpetrated against an enslaved people. They are dead; but the state lives. The same state—the United States of America—that encouraged these historic wrongs lives the life the law breathed into it long ago. This state *today* has a duty to right the wrongs *it* committed. The duty is not historical but *personal* because the wrongs were perpetrated by a legal person who is still alive.

My point is to reframe the issue of affirmative action by substituting *state duty* for the rights of African Americans. The state, like any person, has a right to carry out its duties—just as I have a right to acquire property because I have a duty to care for my family. Affirmative action programs, duly enacted by law, should be looked upon as the way in which the state chooses to exercise its right to fulfill its historic duty in order to make amends for its past transgressions. Today's African American has no more *rights* to these programs than any other ethnic group. Each African American is an individual citizen of the Republic—nothing more and nothing less—with no special claims upon the state. If the state chooses to confer a benefit upon African Americans, it is only because it has a right to fulfill its duties. It cannot confer a similar benefit upon Italians, Poles, Germans, et al., because it has done them no wrong. It has no duty toward them and therefore it has no right to favor them at the expense of others. To do so would be sheer favoritism, which would violate the state's duty of neutrality. The ancestors of these people were wronged but the wrongdoers are all dead. Nothing can or should be done about it today. Only the living can right their own wrongs. The state lives and should right its wrongs but not the wrongs of others.

This chapter has been an exercise in political imagination. I do not really believe that my countrymen are about to look favorably on the strong-state tradition of the French. To do so would probably do us more harm than good. We would no longer be ourselves. Nevertheless, in leading the reader through these questions of language, practice, and rights, I have tried to share some of my concerns over the limitation of our own way of thinking. By reflecting on the strong-state tradition, minds more creative than my own may see ways to improve our governance.

▬ Notes

1. Discussions and definitions of the state are many and varied. Virtually all social science and general encyclopedias have articles on "the state." Those that I have found the most helpful appeared in Edwards (1972), and *The New Encyclopedia Britannica* (1978). An extended analysis of the meaning of the state will be found in Dyson (1980). The best discussion of the state in relation to other terms such as *society, community, nation,* and so on, is in the first chapter of Maritain (1951). A good discussion of the state in its relation to the French constitutional tradition appears in Duhamel & Mény (1993, pp. 412-415). A brief but workable definition will be found in Smith & Zurcher (1955). Periodically, we are told that political scientists have rediscovered

"the state." For a representative discussion of the most recent rediscovery, see Almond (1988, pp. 855-901). Almond's article is followed by substantial rejoinders from Lowi, Nordlinger, and Fabrini. For a discussion of the state as a moral person in French law, see Braibant (1988, pp. 39-47). The classic definition for Anglo-American law appears in *Black's Law Dictionary* (1968).

2. Depending on the context, the English *administration* can also be turned by *gouvernement* or by *direction*.

3. In 1991, Prime Minister Edith Cresson decided to move ENA to Strasbourg, much to the dismay of the school's alumni, students, and administration. The new facility is presently under construction. The fact that the relocation of ENA received considerable attention in the mass media is a good indication of the importance of public administration in France. See, for example, Grosrichard (1991), Passeron (1991a, 1991b, 1992), and Stasi (1991).

4. One senses that many Frenchmen today are somewhat uneasy about the term *administré*. I recall the delightful cynicism of a French lawyer who told me that the real difference between *citoyen* and *administré* is that the former is essential and the latter existential! When one speaks of persons who make use of nationalized services such as the Paris metro, the most common term is *usagers* (users). See, for example, the five-volume report titled *La Relation de service dans le secteur public* published in 1992 under the general editorship of Isaac Joseph. Volumes 3, 4, and 5 of this report contain papers presented at a conference in Paris in January 1991. The conference, which dealt with the theme of integrating the principles of coproduction into French administration, had the provocative title: "*A quoi servent les usagers?*"

5. General de Gaulle wrote two memoirs. The first was his war memoir, which was published in three volumes titled: *The Call to Honor, Unity,* and *Salvation.* The second memoir was intended to cover the period from his return to power in 1958 until his resignation as president of the Fifth Republic in 1969. The general died before the second memoir could be completed. He had envisioned another three-volume work with the titles: *Renewal, Endeavor,* and *Completion.* At the time of his death, he had completed the first volume and two chapters of the second. Hence the subtitle of the English translation is *Renewal and Endeavor.* For another eloquent celebration of the state, see General de Gaulle's famous Bayeux address of June 16, 1946, in which he laid out many of the constitutional principles that would be realized at the creation of the Fifth Republic in 1958. The second paragraph of this speech has been called de Gaulle's "hymn to the state." The full text will be found in Decaumont (1991, pp. 217-221).

6. (1990, March 3). *Le Monde,* p. 12.

7. (1991, January 17). *Le Monde,* p. 8.

8. (1990, November 28). *Le Monde,* p. 6.

9. Like the *grands corps,* the expression *hauts fonctionnaires* is not as clear as it is common. Just which *fonctionnaires* are really *hauts* is a matter of some dispute. See Boudigel & Quermonne (1983, pp. 11-81).

10. There are other *grandes écoles* in France but I would have considerable trouble naming them. In questioning knowledgeable Frenchmen on this topic, I received so many different answers that I finally decided no one really knows which schools are truly *grandes.* The one consistency I observed, however, was that nearly everyone I asked assured me that his or her school was among *les grandes écoles.* Following the example of my French mentors, I can assure the reader that the school with which I was affiliated, *l'Institut d'Etudes Politiques de Paris* or "*Sciences Po,*" as it is affectionately known, is one of the *grandes écoles.*

11. To put into proper perspective the extraordinarily high number of civil servants who serve in parliament, one should recall that in France teachers are civil servants. Because teachers are very heavily represented in the Socialist Party, a good number of them held parliamentary seats when the Socialists came to power.

12. The civil servant in question was Bernard Tricot. The story is told by Bornstein (1988). For a more recent example, see accounts of the weighty responsibilities given to Hubert Prévot in the extremely important question of immigration: Solé (1990, p. 44) and Malaurie & Stein (1990, p. 55).

13. (1990, January 25). *Le Monde,* p. 9.

14. Canal, Robin, & Godot; C. E. Ass. 19 Oct. 1962; Rec. 552; In M. Long et al. (1990, pp. 608-614).

15. For the relationship between the Council of State and the Constitutional Council, see Costa (1993, pp. 117-123); see also Stone (1992), passim.

16. I develop this point in some detail in a forthcoming book, *Founding Republics in France and America: A Study in Constitutional Governance* (Rohr, in press).

17. There is an extensive literature both in French and in English on decentralization in France. See Aubry (1988, 1992) and Schmidt (1990).

18. For a good discussion of *concertation,* see Wilsford (1991b). Wilsford (1991a) explores this question in greater depth with regard to the medical profession in his *Doctors and the State: The Politics of Health Care in France and the United States.*

19. The privatization program is discussed in some detail by Feigenbaum (1993).

20. In presenting various French administrative practices, I realize I may have given an idealized version of French administration as a whole. My purpose has been to give concrete illustrations of how the strong-state tradition expresses itself in administrative actions and institutions. This chapter would lose its focus if I were to essay a nicely balanced *evaluation* of each of these actions and institutions. To introduce a modicum of balance, however, I will list a few of the most common criticisms of those aspects of French administration I have described above.

    a. The *grands corps* are prone to use the interest of the state as rhetorical cover for promoting their own interests. They "colonize" the ministries of the state and French industry, using their positions of influence to further the interests of their corps.

    b. ENA does not really teach its brilliant students; it simply ranks them.

    c. The extraordinary power of the *grands corps* makes French administration top-heavy. That is, the strongly conceptual orientation of the highest civil servants favors the decision-making aspect of administration at the expense of implementation and evaluation.

    d. The "sense of the state" goes awry too easily as was seen recently in the dreadful scandal of the "contaminated blood," wherein officials in the ministry of health knowingly distributed blood that was HIV positive to unsuspecting hemophiliacs.

    e. The Constitutional Council functions more as a third chamber of the legislature than as an authentic judicial body.

    f. The tendency of the civil service to bring stability to France has been excessive at times. Too many civil servants were too willing to cooperate with the Vichy regime.

21. Interestingly, Publius opposes the addition of a Bill of Rights to the Constitution because it would be redolent of monarchy. Kings grant rights. Such a grant would be incompatible with republicanism, he maintains. *Federalist # 84.*

22. See the commentary on the Constitutional Council's decision on *Conseil Supérieur de l'Audiovisuel* of January 17, 1989 (248 DC) in Favoreu & Philip (1989, p. 733). See also the decision of the Constitutional Council on *Entreprises de Presse* of October 10-11, 1984 (181 DC) in the same volume, pp. 596-604. See especially paragraph 38 of this decision.

23. My comments are based on the text cited and on an interview with a reporter for *Le Monde* in Paris on June 22, 1990.

24. *Miami Herald Publishing Company v. Tornillo* 418 U.S. 241 (1974). The Court's decision in this case is difficult to reconcile with *Red Lion Broadcasting Co. v. FCC* 395 U.S. 367 (1969). Taken together, they seem to emphasize the character of American television and radio as a regulated industry.

25. My remarks are based upon an interview with an attorney for *Le Monde* at Ivry-sur-Seine on August 22, 1990. For examples of the *droit de réponse,* see the comment by Jean-Marie Le Pen in *Le Monde* on August 21, 1990 (p. 7) or that of Pierre Silvestri in *L'Express* of December 9, 1993 (p. 21).

26. Glendon (1987) provides generous excerpts from this law in an appendix to her book.

27. For a full and eminently sensible discussion of what the opinion polls report on abortion, see Craig & O'Brien (1993, chap. 7, titled "Public Opinion and Abortion").

28. I have discussed affirmative action for other groups elsewhere. See my review essay (Rohr, 1992) of Dinesh D'Souza's *Illiberal Education: The Politics of Race and Sex on Campus*.

▬ References

Almond, G. (1988). The return to the state. *American Political Science Review, 82,* 855-901.

Aubry, F.-X. (1988). *Essai sur la Décentralisation*. Paris: Groupe des Publications Périodiques Paul Dupont.

Aubry, F.-X. (1992). *La Décentralisation contre l'Etat: l'Etat semi-centralisé*. Paris: Librairie générale de droit et de jurisprudence.

Barsoux, J.-L., & Lawrence, P. (1991, July-August). The making of a French manager. *Harvard Business Review,* p. 64.

Black's Law Dictionary. (1968). (4th ed.). St. Paul: West.

Bornstein, S. H. (1988). The Greenpeace affair and the peculiarities of French politics. In A. S. Markovits & M. Silverstein (Eds.), *The politics of scandal* (pp. 91-121). New York: Holmes & Meier.

Boudigel, J.-L. (1990). Political and administrative traditions and the French senior civil service. *International Journal of Public Administration, 13,* 711-713.

Boudigel, J.-L., & Quermonne, J.-L. (1983). *La Haute fonction publique sous la Ve République*. Paris: Presses Universitaires de France.

Braibant, G. (1988). *Le Droit administratif français* (2d ed.). Paris: Presses de la Fondation Nationale des Sciences Politiques & Dalloz.

Bréhier, T. (1991, November 17-18). Michel Rocard: inspecteur général des finances. *Le Monde,* p. 9.

Brown, L. N., & Bell, J. (1989). Recent reforms of French administrative justice. *Civil Justice Quarterly, 8,* 71.

Cook, D. (1983). *Charles de Gaulle: A biography*. New York: G. P. Putnam.

Costa, J.-P. (1993). *Le Conseil d'Etat dans la société contemporaine*. Paris: Economica.

Craig, B. H., & O'Brien, D. M. (1993). *Abortion and American politics*. Chatham, NJ: Chatham House.

de Baecque, F. (1987). Les Fontionnaires à l'assaut du pouvoir politique? *Pouvoirs, 40,* 61-80.

Debré, M. (1957). *Les Princes Qui Nous Gouverment*. Paris: Plan.

Decaumont, F. (Ed.) (1991). *Le Discours de Bayeux*. Paris: Economica.

de Gaulle, C. (1971). *Memoirs of hope: Renewal and endeavor* (T. Kilmartin, Trans.). New York: Simon & Schuster.

Duhamel, O., & Mény, Y. (1993). *Dictionnaire Constitutionnel*. Paris: Presses Universitaires de France.

Dyson, K. (1980). *The state tradition in Western Europe: The study of an idea and institution*. Oxford, UK: Martin Robertson.

Edwards, P. (Ed.). (1972). *The encyclopedia of philosophy*. New York: Macmillan.

Favoreu, L., & Philip, L. (1989). *Les Grandes décisions du conseil constitutionnel* (5th ed.). Paris: Sirey.

Feigenbaum, H. B. (1993). France: From pragmatic to tactical privatization. *Business and the Contemporary World, 5,* 67-85.

Glendon, M. A. (1987). *Abortion and divorce in Western law*. Cambridge, MA: Harvard University Press.

Grosrichard, F. (1991, November 8). L'ENA sera transférée à Strasbourg. *Le Monde,* p. 1.

Joseph, I. (Ed.). (1992). *La Relation de service dans le secteur public* (Report, 5 vols.) Paris: Plan Urbain, Régie Autonome des Transports Parisiens (RATP,) and Délégation à la Recherche et à l'Innovation (DRI).

Kessler, M.-C. (1986). *Les Grands corps de l'Etat.* Paris: Presses de la Fondation Nationale des Sciences Politiques.

Levinson, S. (1989). The embarrassing Second Amendment. *The Yale Law Journal, 99,* 637-659.

Long, M., et al. (1990). (Eds.), *Les Grands arrêts de la jurisprudence administrative* (9th ed.) (pp. 608-614). Paris: Sirey.

Malaurie, G., & Stein, S. (1990, February 23). Hubert Prévot: un vrai-faux ministre. *L'Express,* p. 55.

Malraux, A. (1971). *Felled oaks: Conversations with de Gaulle.* New York: Holt, Rinehart & Winston.

Maritain, J. (1951). *Man and the state.* Chicago: University of Chicago Press.

Mauriac, F. (1966). *De Gaulle* (R. Howard, Trans.). Garden City, NY: Doubleday.

The new encyclopedia Britannica. (1978). (15th ed.). Chicago: Encyclopedia Britannica.

Osborne, D., & Gaebler, T. (1993). *Reinventing government: How the entrepreneurial spirit is transforming the public sector.* New York: Penguin.

Passeron, A. (1991a, November 9). Controverse chez les hauts fonctionnaires. *Le Monde,* p. 8.

Passeron, A. (1991b, December 11). L'installation définitive de l'ENA à Strasbourg n'aura lieu qu'en 1993. *Le Monde,* p. 10.

Passeron, A. (1992, January 4). M. René Lenoir estime que le transfert de l'ENA exige le doublement du budget de fontionnement. *Le Monde,* p. 6.

Renault-Volvo: L'Etat repoussoir. (1993, December 16). *L'Express,* p. 14.

Ridley, F. F. (1974a). *The French prefectoral system: An example of integrated administrative decentralization* (Commission on the Constitution, Research Paper 4). London: HMSO.

Ridley, F. F. (1974b). The French prefectoral system revived. *Administration & Society,* pp. 48-72.

Rivero, J. (1989). *Les Libertés Publiques* (4th ed.) (Vol. 2., p. 204). Paris: Presses Universitaires de France.

Rohr, J. A. (1992). [Review of *Illiberal education: The politics of race and sex on campus.*] *Society, 29,* 85-88.

Rohr, J. A. (in press). *Founding republics in France and America: A study in constitutional governance.* Lawrence: University Press of Kansas.

Schmidt, V. A. (1990). *Democratizing France: The political and administrative history of decentralization.* Cambridge, UK: Cambridge University Press.

Smith, E. C., & Zurcher, A. J. (1955). *Dictionary of American politics.* New York: Barnes & Noble.

Solé, R. (1990, February 22). Le Haut Conseil à l'intégration a été constitué. *Le Monde,* p. 44.

Stasi, B. (1991, November 21). Tapie à l'ENA! *Le Monde.*

Stone, A. (1992). *The birth of judicial politics in France.* New York: Oxford University Press.

Suleiman, E. N. (1974). *Politics, power, and bureaucracy: The administrative elite in France.* Princeton, NJ: Princeton University Press.

Wilsford, D. (1991a). *Doctors and the state: The politics of health care in France and the United States.* Durham, NC: Duke University Press.

Wilsford, D. (1991b). Running the bureaucratic state: The administration in France. In A. Farazmand (Ed.), *Handbook of comparative development* (pp. 611-624). New York: Marcel Dekker.

Zeldin, T. (1973). *France: 1848-1945.* London: Oxford University Press.

5

Moving Beyond Prescriptions

*Making Sense of Public
Administration Action Contexts*

JAMES F. WOLF
Virginia Polytechnic Institute and State University

Publication of the Blacksburg Manifesto and *Refounding Public Administration* produced varied reactions. For some readers, the works seemed abstract, and their relevance for public administrators was difficult to visualize. Others interpreted the authors as claiming to have found the answer for fixing public administration's ills, thereby rendering all other approaches either obsolete or inimical to the public interest. Predictably, the authors' ideas had all the makings of the next *fad du jour* to be foisted upon administrators trying to face administrative challenges.

All fads and new prescriptions tug and pull at public administrators, and all urge adoption of new ways to fix problems. Unfortunately, these efforts often result in wasted energy and cynical managers. MBO, PPBS, entrepreneurship, reinventing government, and TQM (total quality management) are but a few examples of the fads that have crossed public managers' horizons during recent decades. The assaults gain momentum with the arrival of books, consultants, acronyms, and training programs, each heralding apparently novel administrative elixirs. Each new prescription becomes a commodity, gains prominence for a period, creates demand for new ways of behaving, and gets pushed aside to make way for yet another new solution. For public administrators, perhaps most disheartening of all is the near-certainty that, by the time a fad gets to the public sector, it has most likely run its course in the business world.

Why do prescriptions for fixing administration become popular and then seem to fade after being initially welcomed as a challenge to an apparently ineffective practice? For example, Simon's decision theory attacked the "principles" of POSDCORB, Human Relations ideas reacted to the narrow prescriptions of Scientific Management, program budgeting challenged the weakness of line-item approaches, and so on. All new perspectives in some way challenge or react to perceived limitations in current theory and practice. These prescriptions may also be seen as reactions to a specific and current concern. *Reinventing government* initiatives, for example, seeks to energize outdated bureaucracies. MBO was promoted as increasing accountability, while others saw opportunities for joint goal setting. Thus each prescription emerges like a new magic formula detached from existing practices and is often served up as an antidote for a prevailing ill.

Many fads seem to come in cycles as newly touted solutions fall into disfavor. For example, managers are urged to centralize to gain more accountability. When that fails, they should decentralize in order to empower workers. When new approaches fade from memory for a period, they reappear in new wrappers; and often trouble follows when they are recognized for what they are—old wine in new bottles. This tendency forces Osborne and others like him to present the ideas as new and dramatic.

New approaches to administrative problems also face tough futures in part because they are too abstract and artificially forced onto specific administrative situations. Even though many prescriptions contain reasonable responses to some parts of an administrative problem, advocates often promote them in simplified ways in order to sell them to busy managers. Leaders, managers, and politicians become impatient and quickly tire of the new ideas. Thus fads have abbreviated lives, caused in large measure by application of simplified approaches to often complex and confounding settings. Because the useful elements of the proposed elixir do not solve all administrative ailments, disappointed followers reject these more limited contributions.

Finally, U.S. political and administrative processes are bound up in very dense systems of accountability, law, procedures, institutions, and interests. These forces serve as a potent barrier to allowing any idea to pass through in a pure form. New prescriptions must be modified to accommodate this terrain, often to such an extent that the integrity of the new idea is lost and these new approaches begin to look more like existing practices than any new initiative.

Even admitting that many prescriptions add little value, there must be more to the problem when so many commonsense ideas come and go so frequently. What causes this inability to take advantage of lessons learned from administration and to stay with valuable ways of acting long enough for them to become stabilized behaviors? More to the point, how can the ideas found in *Refounding Public Administration* and in this book escape such a fate? The sad reality is that they probably will not unless we can propose ways of placing the myriad proposals for improving public administration into some broader framework for making sense of action possibilities.

▬ Placing the Blacksburg Perspective in a Broader Action Context

This chapter places this volume, and its predecessor, *Refounding Public Administration* (Wamsley et al., 1990), within a broader context of everyday administrative action. By doing so, it provides a grounding for the prescriptions implied in this volume and will allow practicing public administrators to imagine the appropriateness of action alternatives in specific settings. The chapter maintains that part of the difficulty stems from administrators' inability to read effectively the multiple administrative contexts in which these prescriptions must be implemented.

The prescriptions called for in the Refounding effort can avoid this problem only if they are located within a broader perspective, and if we recognize that its ideas do not fit all public administrative situations. Public administrators need to understand that situations vary and different responses are appropriate in these situations. This constitutes the core of the argument in this chapter, and it can be summarized as follows:

1. There are enduring and powerful dynamics in public settings that form *contexts* for action. These contexts can also be characterized as structures, patterns, or constellations of social forces developed out of our governance and administrative history. They define administrative situations and can evoke specific responses from public servants enmeshed in these settings.

2. At least six such action contexts exist in the public administrator's everyday world that characterize a large part of current administrative experience. Each of these action contexts suggests particular lines of action for administrators who find themselves working in any one of the contexts.

3. Many current prescriptions for action, including fads, are embedded in one or more of these action contexts. Although many prescriptions do become fads, elements of the prescriptions often contain practical advice and constitute valuable ways for understanding, interpreting, and engaging in action in the public administration.

4. A more balanced repertoire grounded in a broader vocabulary for seeing specific action contexts can lead to more appropriate and effective adminis-

trative action. Currently, both administrators and scholars systematically ignore several of these structures and do so at the expense of effective action.

5. Public administrators can be more effective when they "read" situations and ferret out the operating action context(s).

6. The images and challenges raised by the Blacksburg effort form part of a larger set of diverse and powerful currents that shape the possibilities for administrative action. The perspectives in this effort also find a home in several of these action contexts. The approaches in *Refounding Public Administration* are certainly not appropriate for all public administrative situations; however, they do add an important framework for understanding and acting in the public sector. If applied self-consciously in appropriate situations, there is less danger that the ideas of this book will suffer the unfortunate and traditional fate of fads.

As public agencies face postmodern conditions, public servants must contend with a special kind of incoherence. Though the environment of public agencies displays many of the characteristics of a postmodern condition, the inside world of the agencies may be quite different from those described, for example, by McSwain and White later in this volume (see O.C. McSwite, Chapter 7, this volume). The everyday world of public administrators blends many of the characteristics of the modern and postmodern worlds. Parts of the administrators' world form coherent clusters of meaning and action. People go to work day after day and find a continuity that makes sense to them and makes efforts to understand and sometimes control these worlds perfectly sensible. At other times, the chaotic and unstable worlds that are more appropriately understood as elements of a postmodern condition prevail. To a large extent, an agency's world often seems more like a set of overlapping and dense contexts. The condition is neither modern nor postmodern, but some point between where the world is stable and clear, and where it is much more one of alternating powerful worlds. They are not surface, but deep structures characterized by the action contexts presented below. They each have their own logic and coherence. At any time, managers may find themselves pulled into the vortex of any of these worlds. Most public employees underestimate the variety of worlds in which they must work, and that frequently these contexts operate on a given situation at the same time. So, prescriptions may be appropriate in one moment, but out of order in another.

The Action Contexts: Structural Elements

Although proceeding much farther in this argument may require some extensive ontological statement, I demure from this tedious, difficult, and rigorous task. Rather, I take a looser and more general approach by presenting some elements, textures, and moods that may be characteristic of the six action contexts in the administrative situations described below. These structural types should not be seen as pure types, for each is made up of variations and mixes of the others, and abide in relation with each other. At the same time, the variations are enormously broader than the six presented here. Nevertheless, it is hoped that readers and administrators alike may find them useful for understanding many organizational experiences found in the day-to-day.

These action contexts can be understood in different ways. They form themes that seem to drive the unfolding of events, like a storyline people use to make sense out of events in an organization. To some extent, the idea of an organizational culture or subculture captures important dimensions of the patterns.

They also result from socially constructed realities (Berger & Luckmann, 1966) that contain fundamental beliefs, taken-for-granted views of how the world operates, or how people or organizations work. For example, supporters of David Osborne's ideas would argue that choice mechanisms are preferable to centralized control. Finally, they contain structural or patterned elements that are to some degree like archetypes that organize and evoke energy or a line of action in an individual, group, or organization.

Consider the metaphor of weather maps. They show different high- and low-pressure systems, cold and warm fronts, tropical disturbances, and other meteorological forces that determine weather in a particular area. Similarly, administrative action contexts also create patterns that affect wide areas for given periods of time. Some become powerful, while others wait "in the wings" for the right combination of events to trigger a more sustained pattern. At the same time, these action contexts form in relation to each other. Because of this, one can never know the exact way any one weather pattern will develop. Rain may come, but the exact place, force, and duration remain unclear until it happens.

Action contexts arise out of relationships: relationships of challenges from society, and of government's responses to them. Often these relationships are seen as competing with one another for primacy, each context arising at times when it makes sense, when there is a fit between context and emerging situation. However, they are understandable only in relation to each other. They arise from tensions among them and often compete for public administrators' attention. The specific outcome of working within any one of these contexts is always indefinite. Thus the contexts are fashioned from social and administrative challenges that, in turn, form our approach for acting on the situation.

These administrative situations capture some of the character of the six action contexts. They include bureaucracies, markets, organizations, networks, communities, and institutions. Bureaucracies, markets, and communities seem more like pure types, although each contains elements of the others. The remaining three, organizations, institutions, and networks, more clearly combine elements of the first three. Although the action contexts presented below may help define the situation in which public servants act, they are also simplified versions of a world too rich and too varied to present fully in any chapter or volume. I do not make a detailed case for each. Rather, I try to capture the essential character of the more powerful structural dynamics. From my own administrative experience, reading, research, and listening, however, specific administrative situations do seem to evoke or be embedded in a web of forces that tend to define the situation.

The Familiar Action Contexts—
Bureaucracy, Markets, and Organizations

The bureaucratic, market, and organizational action contexts form the greater part of worlds for most private corporations and public agencies. The language, logic, and power of these first three forces often seem to encompass most of what we know or need to know about the world of the public sector. The first, bureaucracy, is ubiquitous and at the same time everyone's *bête noire*. The market has also been around a long time and appears to be the latest idea in good currency. The third, organization, has evolved during the past half-century and comes primarily from the ascendance of organization theory, management science, and the MBA degree of business schools.

Bureaucracy

Administrative Setting #1. Shortly before becoming a program director of a state highway safety program, Mary Scavio was called to a meeting with the senior administrator in the Transportation Department to discuss the future administrative home for the program. Prior to the meeting, the staff of the program met to discuss the options and how to head off one particular way of reorganizing the program. The staff came up with a range of acceptable options and were ready to make a strong case for various acceptable restructuring options. Unfortunately, the senior department official came with a different understanding of the situation. The program would be moved into a new administrative unit: an option the program staff had failed to consider. The senior official informed the program leader that the move would occur and that she was there to get the word. She quickly realized the way the situation was configured, accepted her program's fate, and pleaded for some time to adjust to the change. *Action Context: Bureaucratic.*

Few public servants live their work worlds outside of bureaucracies, and this has been condemned by many and supported by few. Most of us know when we are in a bureaucratic world: the notice we get for an overdue library book, the traffic fine with its attendant penalties for late payment, and the work and deadlines we receive from superiors all elicit feelings about the bureaucratic world.

Bureaucratic action—grounded in legitimate authority, rationalization of action, and emphasis on procedures—describes a great deal about living in public agencies. Expectations of compliance with deadlines, acquiescence to regulations that seem out of touch with the demands of the situation, and procedures for awarding contracts all capture elements of this bureaucratic world.

At its best, and in its best sense, bureaucratic life involves equal treatment for all employees; reliance on expertise, skills, and experience relevant to a particular position; no extraorganizational prerogatives of the position; specific standards of work output; extensive record keeping dealing with work and output; and rules and regulations that serve the interests of the organization. Bureaucratic norms also bind managers and employees to the same rules and regulations (Perrow, 1986, p. 3). These same kinds of controls also ensure accountability of public organizations to elected officials.

Bureaucratic dynamics in the public sector often combine these more rational aspects with problematic elements: compliance mechanisms that come with systems of political accountability. Blend in the array of political agendas that individuals, groups, and agencies bring to the mixing bowl, and the best and worst dimensions of bureaucratic politics rise to the top.

Mary Scavio, director of the state safety program, understood that she had to accept the proposed reorganization of her program. She accepted the boss's authority and could feel the threat of severe consequences if she fought the proposed reorganization. Her appropriate response was to try to live with it and make the best out of a decision she neither sought nor wanted. One alternative might have been to engage in bureaucratic politics to fight the decision. Sober reflection, however, strongly pointed to a more compliant strategy. Her decision to work on the terms of the merger rather than the formal organizational change itself was very likely a prudent approach.

Although done in the name of efficiency and effectiveness, reorganization constituted by the redrawing of lines of authority has a nearly irresistible attraction for newly elected officials trying to make a quick impact on the political system. Thus reorganization often becomes the fad of choice for new administrations. Most seasoned public servants quickly recognize this period in the political process for what it is and develop an assortment of ways to deal with the challenges and pressures. Some work along with the elected officials, others drag their feet, still others hide, hoping the changes have minimal effect on their lives and programs.

Reorganizations are not the only manifestation of this action context. Efforts to keep certain agendas off the table consume much energy in a bureaucratic world. Getting key political and administrative personnel on board with one special view of the problem takes up a large part of an administrator's attention. Further, successful administrators know that timing constitutes a crucial part of managers' attempts to advance agendas. Moreover, taking advantage of an open critical policy window (Kingdon, 1984) occurs most often when incumbents of key bureaucratic positions move or are replaced by more sympathetic policy makers. When this action context operates, public servants are wise to recognize and adapt to such shifting power constellations.

For a civil servant, the costs of violating procedures, going against policy, or being on the losing side of a bureaucratic political fight can include reprimands, dismissals, ends to career advancement, and even criminal proceedings. Even if one can avoid outcomes that are personally disadvantageous or severe, programs and organizations can lose staff, operating freedom, new opportunities, and many other organizational resources by being on the wrong end of a bureaucratic struggle.

Larry Lane (Chapter 8, this volume) critiques the politicized presidency that has developed since 1968. He characterizes the presidency as a combination of centralized legitimate power in the White House, political appointees in the agencies, and hierarchically driven management processes. Lane goes on to suggest what this kind of bureaucratic compliance system can augur for our democratic constitutional tradition.

At the political level, public servants' compliance with legitimate bureaucratic power does act as a major safeguard for our democratic system. Citizens have more freedom and the political system manifests more democracy when public servants are accountable to legitimate supervisors. Top-down democratic control processes are very much within this compliance structure and are made possible by legitimate authority and routinization. Thus they are all-important safeguards for our political system.

At the same time, these safeguards have a substantial downside for public administrators trying to do effective work. At the national level, for example, Congressional committee and oversight processes; investigative activities of Inspectors General; and an overall fear of being found making mistakes, not being loyal, misinterpreting congressional intent, or not being on the right side of political agendas, all lead to many of the disruptive aspects of an overdeveloped climate of compliance and fear (Lane & Wolf, 1990). Vice President Gore's National Performance Review correctly saw this danger in its recommendations concerning the Inspectors General approach to working with agencies.

Markets

Administrative Setting #2. Increased budget demands and public dissatisfaction with traditional publicly sponsored recreation programs led Peter Evans, Tower City Director of Recreations, to begin viewing summer participants in the recreation program as customers. He was in constant contact with parents and children about their satisfaction with the program. He conducted market studies and discovered that some parents would be willing to pay more because they saw his services as a good buy when compared with the costs of commercially provided child care. Next year he will structure the programs around the normal working hours of parents and offer a cafeteria of camp themes. He will also charge more for the services. *Action Context: Markets.*

At times, the most appropriate attitude that seems to work for managers is one in which they see themselves as business persons in a big shopping mall. Like shopkeepers, managers respond to efficiency considerations; most importantly as regards customers and competitors. This world eschews bureaucratic command and control strategies and prefers to coordinate actions through some automatic mechanism akin to a market. When operating in this context, one assumes that individuals are purposeful agents—that they have a reason for what they do and sort out more effective ways to get what they want. Each party grounds its choice in some utility consideration. Peter Evans, the Tower City head of the recreation program, operated with such a perspective as he tried to identify potential customers for summer camp activities, to sell it as child care, and to set a market rate for the service.

The overarching assumption operating in this context is that public problems can be worked out most effectively when the hidden hand operates; particularly through a balance or a mutuality governed by self-interest. Rather than imposing hierarchically determined rewards and punishments, the incentive mechanisms in the market system do the work in an automatic fashion. One attractive feature of this world is that coordination occurs absent any complex kind of integration of goals, visions, commitments, or effort. In all cases, one seeks simplifying mechanisms over the more apparently cumbersome bureaucratic forms of command and control. Microeconomic and public choice theories come closest to describing the underlying theory of this context. Public servants are urged to take advantage of individual choice models to avoid the cumbersome and undemocratic character of bureaucracy and other similar control structures.

Finally, competition is assumed to produce both more effective and more democratic public action. At its core, the market world values choice and the mechanisms that make choice possible. The trick is to understand the nature of markets and to see organizational environments and public organizations as potential contexts for market behavior. Thus the profit motive and the drive to compete is a powerful force available to policy makers. Smart public administrators take advantage of this force to set up competitive or quasi-market conditions as a vehicle for carrying out public policy. Peter Evans, for example, may be able to take customers away from private child care providers and neighboring local government programs.

Deregulation and use of market mechanisms are often preferable to bureaucratic approaches to achieve public purposes. James Q. Wilson (1989) maintains that "government bureaus are less likely than private agencies to operate efficiently, at least with respect to the main goal of the organization." They are less efficient because government executives have less discretion for making efficient decisions, have less clear direction about agency goals, and have weaker incentives "to *define* an efficient course of action." Further, they are not " 'residual claimants' who can put into their own pockets the savings achieved by greater efficiency" (p. 349).

Individual workers increasingly face a work world that looks more like markets than the stable job worlds they once knew. With the increase of part-time work without job security and benefits, workers must fend for themselves as bundles of competencies. In this world, every person is a market, selling parts of his or her competencies to different organizations. These temporary and partial arrangements between workers and organizations represent a radical departure from the idea that one starts in an organization as a young person, pays dues, works hard, and eventually retires.

Many elements of the most recent fad, Osborne and Gaebler's (1992) *Reinventing Government,* have been embraced by the Clinton administration and contain large parts of a market logic (see Green & Hubbell, Chapter 1, this volume). Osborne and Gaebler call for an "Enterprising Government: Earning Rather Than Spending" strategy. They agonize over the idea that governments "have no incentive to earn money" (Osborne & Gaebler, 1992, p. 274). They believe that if the incentive system were changed, agency behavior would change. Osborne and Gaebler also favor a Non-Tax Revenue Act that would provide agencies with incentives to find new revenues by allowing them to keep a portion of all "new non-tax revenues they generate"

(p. 275). They call for an innovation fund that would allow agencies to borrow and to "make investments that would increase their revenues or cut their costs" (p. 275). They advocate a competitive government and urge more competition in service delivery. They say that competition is more efficient and that it "[fosters] innovation and excellence . . . when service providers are forced to compete, they keep their costs down, respond quickly to changing demands, and strive mightily to satisfy their customers" (p. 283).

Organizations

Administrative Setting #3. As a university department head, Tom Rouse sees the value of funds for travel, special events, and so on. Research contracts produce overhead dollars, a portion of which comes back to the department to be used for travel and other special operating expenses. The university policy for overhead recovery sharing recently changed, and the share of overhead funds accruing to the department was cut in half. Accordingly, Tom's efforts to secure contracts with overhead dollars also dropped. He now seeks alternatives that bring more support to the department. This is good for the department, but unfortunately is less advantageous for the university. *Action Context: Organizations.*

Organizational patterns combine the worlds of bureaucracy and markets to form some special forces. For most public servants who see themselves as managers, the organizational patterns are most familiar and define a good deal of the speech, thought patterns, and technology used to approach administrative problems. Like bureaucracy, this pattern accepts and works within the system of hierarchy and legitimate authority. However, it also accepts the idea that people conform to the psychological and economic assumptions that present individuals as goal seekers and suboptimizers. The democratic project gets advanced when rational action serves politically legitimate decisions.

Decision making is at the core of organizational activity. The beginnings of the organizational and management approaches in the public sector can be traced to late 19th-century municipal reform movements' concern for technical competence, to the Brownlow Commission's emphasis on central executive capacity, and perhaps most directly to Herbert Simon's organization theory, which placed decision-making processes at the center of administrative action.

Simon (1957) introduces this perspective in his *Administrative Behavior.* His view of organizations as decision-making systems maintains many of the control perspectives of a bureaucracy, but suggests a different way to control. That is, efficient goal management is achieved with top-down control of organization decision-making processes. Thus close attention is paid to controlling the premises people use to make decisions. Despite their limited rationality, Simon's workers can nonetheless be rational in terms of organizational goals because structure, routines, decision making, communication, indoctrination, role systems, and reward systems all control decision premises that guide employee behavior. People no longer need to be controlled through overt power and sanctions or rewards. Rather, routines and stable processes maintain the desired behavior. This is similar to the top-down authority and routinization of bureaucracies, but Simon's bywords are "communication and coordination, not imperative control and authority; of work flow and cooperation, not the demarcation of the rights, authority and autonomy of particular structures" (Meyer, 1983, p. 275).

At the same time, the organizational world taps into the market. Organizational members are self-interested. With the appropriate balance of incentives and inducements, their behavior in the organization can be controlled in the organization's interest. Within the organization, the market structure presents individuals as acting in their self-interest. Individuals are neither good nor bad, simply choosers and people who are driven to achieve self-interest. At the most fundamental level, employees respond by measuring the balance between incentives and job expectations. Chester Barnard's (1938) work on managing the balance between these two forces is an early attempt to present this view as a core element of organizing and executive action.

Because people work best when there is an optimal balance of reward and effort, managers must therefore create performance systems that guide, measure, and reward efforts. There is a strong assumption that those at the top of the organization control organizational direction, but that choice is the essential glue for coordinating cooperative processes. Key management processes tie planning and information processing to decision systems. MBO, PPBS, merit pay, and management information systems technologies, for example, all seek to ensure goal attainment.

In the earlier vignette, Tom Rouse, the university department chair, adapted too well to changes in the contract overhead dollars sharing process. Before the change, the system was working as the university contract managers intended. Tom therefore made his decisions about funding based on the criteria embedded in the university's procedures. As a result of the change in those procedures, however, Tom's action in pursuit of his department's needs short-circuited the higher university officials' intended outcome for its process. The procedures did shape Tom's decisions, but the system was sufficiently ambiguous to allow lower-level employees like Tom to respond in selected, self-interested ways. The contract managers will have to fine-tune their administrative processes if they want to reshape the department heads' decision premises.

In the past three decades the organizational action context has been the major innovation for looking at and acting in agencies. The technological improvements of computers, operations research, organizational design, and often organizational culture have become tools for fostering goal attainment. Many of the approaches presented in the *Reinventing Government* (Osborne & Gaebler, 1992) initiatives call for more organizational management techniques that combine management control with greater initiative of workers at lower levels in the organization. Management wisdom has accepted the need to have more autonomy to allow for greater entrepreneurial spirit and behavior throughout the organization. In this sense, downsizing, contracting out, and flat organizational designs are simply more effective approaches for achieving goal attainment. They still operate within a framework of top-down bureaucratic control and market-driven strategies that give employees the wherewithal to respond to special needs at particular levels of the organization.

If we review the three contexts presented above, it would seem that although we live most concretely in a bureaucratic world, we also decry it. It may be that the next orthodoxy to replace organizational management orthodoxy will be the market, propelled by a combination of modern populism, reinventing government programs, and recommendations of the Gore Report. If this happens, managers will have to live more fully in the three worlds and will need to read situations and themes in a broader framework than ever before. However, the three contexts still present a limited set of lenses with which to look at the world. There is more to the world and to administrative situations. The three structures presented below offer a more robust vocabulary for reading these situations.

The Lesser Contexts: Networks, Institutions, and Communities

Although markets and choice seem to be winning the day over rules and bureaucracy, it is not likely that the bureaucratic world will fade any time soon (Perrow, 1986). All three will remain as firmly entrenched structures in the daily life of public servants. At the same time, however, other forces persist as possible options. In the next section, the action contexts of networks, communities, and institutions are presented as alternative structures that surface from time to time and represent potential ways of interpreting and acting in public agencies.

Networks

Administrative Setting #4. A group of local social service program coordinators have worked with each other on various state task forces over the years. At one meeting, several participants suggested coordinating information about how homeless shelter policies affect each jurisdiction. Each designated a staff person to look at their common problems. One result was establishment of a computer network that allowed them to track people who stayed in these shelters, together with treatment for those requiring services. This social service network functions without designated funds, an established hierarchy, or formal roles. Though the members in the network change over time and rarely meet, representatives from each agency continue to participate in the network. *Action Context: Networks.*

Public administrators face constant demands to create, join, and work through networks. Virtually every public service involves a variety of organizations that must work together—or at least try not to get in each others' way. Local governments in metropolitan areas must work with each other and with private providers of services. States are deeply involved in local government service delivery. Federal agencies must work with one another, and depend on state and local agencies for service delivery. Increasingly, they also rely on a bevy of subcontractors for even essential agency activities. The local government social service agencies that coordinated their homeless policies illustrates an effective network organization.

Each of these situations requires extraorganizational sets of relationships to do business and to bring deliberation to a policy problem. The capacity of public servants to operate in network relationships and to work with network processes becomes ever more essential to the carrying out of our public purposes. Managers and professionals in all fields know the value of being tied to networks that ensure career options and success. Communication networks, policy networks, personal networks, and computer networks are only a few of the current manifestations of this idea.

Network ideas include and build on notions of flat organizations, computer communications, and self-organizing. Axelrod, Hayek, Powell, Johanson, Mattsson, and Ouchi (see Thompson, Frances, Levacic, & Mitchell, 1991) all present characterizations of the network world in which managers work. Networks rely on long-run concerns and relationships rather than on short-run exchange calculations about the value of relating to others in a network. The structures are lighter and less permanent than those of bureaucratic organizations or institutions. The norms of these networks are often reciprocal and call for mutually supportive actions. Networks often work off of cooperative pooling of resources for material gain. Expectations for action do not come from prior choosing; rather they evolve through continuous experience, and the life of networks is constituted as they begin to operate and do things (Thompson et al., 1991).

Networks have elements of markets and organizations. Like organizations, their processes and routines are often embedded in sets of mutual role expectations. There is predictability in the relationships and a balance of rewards or satisfactions that come from being a reliable member of the networks. Departure from organizations and closer similarity to markets can be seen in the lightness and self-organizing character of networks. The formal structure and processes of organizations are considerably softened in networks, and they seem to evolve like buyers and sellers in a market square. However, they also differ from markets. The relationships are not those of one-time-only transactions, and network norms go beyond the contract demands of transactions that are present in markets (Thompson et al., 1991). The relationships build over time and take into consideration the quality of the individuals and relationships. Lorenz's (1991) study of subcontracting in French industry that focuses on networks captures the quality of relationships in networks. He characterizes networks as "neither friends nor strangers" (p. 182). He sees trust as an essential element for making networks function. It is a trust that comes from experience with others in a network, one that comes from an assessment of costs of cooperating versus not cooperating, as well as understanding the kind of persons who are part of the network. He finds Williamson's (1985) transaction cost research helpful in understanding the calculated behaviors that support trust relationships.

Most public administrators are part of several networks. One such example is the local social service managers who established a network for compiling information about how homeless services were handled by each of the local jurisdictions. Types of networks in which public managers and policy makers may find themselves include policy communities nested in functional interests of government; issue networks that span organizations and narrow, functionally related organizations; professional networks; and intergovernmental networks consisting of more general policy and administrative types (Rhodes, 1991, pp. 204-205).

The democratic element of networks becomes somewhat problematic if democratic values come only from public servants operating within a system of overhead democratic control. Networks have the openness of markets and resist attempts at overhead control. Democratic processes within networks can only result from the extent of openness to many participants and the norms of participation. Networks can easily ignore both the democratic controls of overhead democracy that bureaucracy produces as well as the norms of open processes that the community provides. Impenetrable elite networks of any kind pose a challenge for democratic public administration that operates within dense network contexts.

Communities

Administrative Setting #5. Over several years, the heads of four regulatory agencies concerned with the protection of workplace environments met each month at one or another's home to discuss common concerns. The host cooked breakfast. Each time, the host also invited a staff person to record anything they might agree to during these meetings. No agendas were made, no minutes kept. Agreements were turned over to coordinating staffs in each office for further development. The process led to remarkable agreements for cooperative efforts. Once a new presidential administration took over control of the agencies, the meetings stopped. *Action Context: Community.*

These four agency heads who met every month for breakfast at each other's homes developed relationships that were fuller than most of us experience in organizational life. By meeting in a different setting, they grew to understand each other as more complete individuals. They grew to appreciate one another's homes, hobbies, and other elements of their personal histories. Most importantly, they created more authentic processes for talking about problems and about both shared and separate interests. The processes they used, described by Walt Kovalik (1988) as "contactful negotiation," did not ignore agencies, special interests, and responsibilities. However, the participants could discuss problems without the heavy overlay of bureaucratic politics, strategic positioning, or bargaining. The process also increased interpersonal authenticity because the rituals of cooking for each other, eating together, and generally relating to each other cut through much of the ego-protective behaviors that often go along with organizational life. Their discussion was not burdened by layers of meanings. At the core of the discussion was agreement to pursue a safer workplace and to use their agencies as vehicles of cooperation rather than competition. This is an example of an administrative setting that incorporates many elements that describe the action context of a community.

The primary settings for a community context are places where face-to-face encounters occur. These include working relationships among co-workers, work groups, associations among the policy and program networks that surround agencies, and also public organizations that deal in face-to-face relationships with citizens in service-delivery settings.

Relationships and processes form the essential element of community. Within community, relationships are complex. For Philip Selznick (1987), the "to whom" and "for what" of personal responsibility depends "largely on personal history and how we directly affect lives and situations of others." Though relationship in community may begin with some choice, the details of responsibilities are defined by subsequent actions of people in relationship with other individuals (p. 451). Responsibilities extend beyond contract and build "on understanding that our deepest and most important obligations flow from identity and relatedness, rather than from consent" (p. 451).

Following this line of argument, relationships and responsibilities in a community context would be reciprocal from agency to employees and back to agency. Both do more than weigh the calculus of incentives and expectations before committing to effort and action. When an agency tries to live as a community, its concerns and responsibilities take into account the whole person, not simply the person as a labor slot. It accepts employees' developmental needs and security requirements as legitimate concerns. It maintains flexibility in dealing with individual successes, mistakes, and requests in a way that may have to go beyond the specifics of personnel policies. At the same time, employees understand that their responsibilities emerge as much from the special concerns and demands of situations as from the job description. Such a view is not a license for extortion and unreasonable demands, because this would deny the full dimension of the individual's life. Rather, it acknowledges that appropriate lines of action and commitment to action come as much out of the situation as out of the formal expectations.

Openness to the fullness of situations and anchoring discussion and action in the physical world characterize community. Thus, the situation and the physical world are crucial elements within community, where attitudes, behaviors, and processes encourage acceptance and inclusion of others. Participants in agencies search for ways to ground visions, policies, programs, and decisions in the specific circumstances of the agencies' action arena (Selznick, 1987, pp. 457-462). Acceptance requires processes that anchor its members to those affected by the agency's actions. They are not simply customers to be pleased, but rather are members of the community who have to be included as an agency's line of action emerges.

Such anchoring can only occur in settings where people can be in contact with others; when people are aware of and can discuss what they feel is real. Mary Parker Follett's focus on the necessity to be in touch with the concrete realities of the situation is essential for effective community. In communities, effective action means moving beyond the current situation by facing the facts of that situation. Participants seek development, improvement, and understanding from those in the current situation and action flows from the situation.

In organizational settings, such relationships are very difficult to achieve because strategic posturing, bureaucratic politics, premise controls, and calculating behaviors all require public servants to figure out the agendas of the other before acting. The four agency heads who met over breakfast may be remarkable because their process existed as long as it did. Processes then become an essential focus in community. Processes that allow people to gain access to the facts of the situation must be developed. These processes are essentially cooperative processes; processes that allow people to be in relationship with each other to support each other's development, that allow those in a particular setting to get to the facts of the situation, and that increase the capacity of community members to cooperate in a way that addresses the issues of the situation and fosters the move to a creative outcome.

Willingness to live processes of the community are essential in order to achieve effective action. Such processes are often difficult in agencies because the predominant action contexts emphasize competition and strategy rather than open authentic relationships in order to work through conflict and achieve new creative and integrative situations. Community, then, provides a context for dialogue and conversation—a context within which to communicate with one another. Such dialogue allows participation in discussion and decision making, and in sharing priorities that define community. Lisa Weinberg (Chapter 10, this volume) discusses how such relating becomes possible for people working inside organizations.

The perspectives offered by Weinberg, by Stivers, by Dennard, and by McSwain and White (Chapters 10, 9, 11, & 7, respectively, this volume) each in some way extends our understanding of this community context. Each emphasizes the importance of bringing public administration within democratic processes. Stivers focuses on the needs to broaden our ideas of who need to be included in the democratic dialogue.

Dennard (Chapter 11, this volume) enriches this understanding in public organizations by her discussions of the need for democratic relationships, the inclusion of human aspirations, empowering citizens to have control over what happens in communities, and for public administrators to understand the importance of the democratic character of each action.

McSwain and White (Chapter 7, this volume) place the role of public agencies in community within a postmodern perspective. For them, public agencies can work toward community only through democratic and authentic processes rather than through an appeal to some superordinate set of values. They place agencies within governance. Agencies would involve the citizens they serve. These agencies would be surrounded with a process of dialogue that would be characterized by common sense, a community of meaning, and discourse.

W. Edwards Deming's (Neave, 1990) work also incorporates many important elements of a community and process approach. He emphasized the importance of staying very close to the processes of organizations. He emphasized systems and processes and scientific methods that allow people to get to knowledge of these systems. External and hierarchial systems of control only keep workers from being able to work in the processes. Deming's approach was ever watchful for barriers that keep workers from being connected to processes. He rejected many management control systems because they did not stay close to process.

Deming focused on variation and demanded the use of scientific methods that lead to knowledge about the work processes. Rather than an organizational science that focuses on outcomes, rational decision making, goals, MBO, and other management control processes, Deming advocated techniques that encourage authentic relationships with members of the organization—a prerequisite of community. He also recognized the connectedness of people in communities. He argued that people need relationships with others, and need to be loved and esteemed by others. Organizational processes should facilitate individual growth and joy (Neave, 1990, p. 198).

Deming's ideas have formed with other forces to become an action context in many public agencies. Bits and pieces have been picked up by the National Performance Review of the Clinton administration, and total quality management programs have also built heavily on these processes. The problem is that many of these efforts are grounded more in an organizational than in a community and process world. The kind of process that Deming called for can be evoked in organizations, but applications have been spotty.

Institutions

Administrative Setting #6. Forest Taylor, planning director for a state fish and game commission, faced an upcoming revision of the commission's policy for fishing on state lakes. He now confronted new demands by environmental groups to eliminate certain practices for stocking fish in state lakes. Though sympathetic with the environmentalist proposals, he also recognized the long-term commitment of the agency to the sporting community. He decided to schedule some work sessions throughout the state. These meetings would involve the sporting and ecological groups in hopes of arriving at some outcome that incorporated environmental safeguards but did not destroy the agency's long-term support for fishing on state lakes. *Action Context: Institutional.*

Institutions are not wholly bureaucracies, organizations, or communities. They contain elements of each and something more. In many ways, the institutions form the core of public administration life. Institutions provide a context for developing individual and social identity. Second, and at the same time, institutional capacity makes them instruments of social action. Institutional dynamics include

> patterns of social activity that give shape to collective and individual experience. An institution is a complex whole that guides and sustains individual identity . . . enabling individuals to realize themselves in particular relationships such as parents, employees, consumers and citizens . . . by making possible or impossible certain ways of behaving and relating to others. . . . Institutions are essential bearers of ideals and meanings. (Bellah et al., 1985, p. 40)

In addition to this role of institutions as shapers of identity and meaning, public institutions can also engage in instrumental social action because of their bureaucratic capability. They have stable routines and hierarchical authority based on political legitimacy. Our governance processes rely on the design of political institutions in addition to broader societal and economic conditions (March & Olsen, 1989). Institutions have both coherence and autonomy. This means that institutions do at times act as coherent entities that are capable of decisions. They are also to some degree autonomous, or more than "simple echoes of social forces" (March & Olsen, 1989, p. 159).

Consequently, institutions make a difference. They provide a context for understanding action; they provide a vehicle for appreciating problems, actions, and solutions, and for forming conclusions about the appropriateness of interpretation, problem definitions, and decisions. At the same time, they possess capabilities for action through their routines and resources. Actions are "institutionalized through structures of rules and routines" (March & Olsen, 1989, p. 38). Within an organizational context, organizational roles help create premises for decisions and facilitate rational specialization of labor. However, these same roles have a richer dimension within an institutional world. Roles do provide the rational benefits of the organizational design; within institutions, however, they enable a person to define action in the context of the meanings developed within the institution.

Joy Clay (Chapter 3, this volume) argues that public administrative institutions are not manifested only through agency structures. Public servants also encounter institutional contexts through public administrative processes. While public servants may experience budgeting, personnel, contracting, and regulatory processes as instrumental bureaucratic routines or instrumental management processes, there are often institutional dimensions to these as well. Clay maintains that public administrative processes are not only important for the end products they produce (e.g., a budget document), but also for enabling agencies to interact with their interested publics, make sense of institutional environmental forces, marshal resources, and serve the public interest. She goes on to show how these institutional processes offer a sense of stability for those people involved by allowing for the development of shared understandings.

The experience of Forest Taylor, the planning director in the state fish and game commission, illustrates how an institutional perspective can influence a public administrator's action. This planning director acknowledged the significance of prior commitments and of history in the work of the agency. Taylor saw the need to retain the institutional commitment to fishermen and at the same time be open to newer voices as the agency reviewed its policies. The planning processes provide the context for keeping institutions faithful to prior commitments and also open to newer concerns. In this way the agency and the planning processes provide concrete ways to maintain democratic governance within agencies.

Because institutions do provide stability, many see them as rigid and fixed. March and Olsen (1989), however, argue that institutions are open to change. Identity, meaning, and action are not necessarily fixed by a previously developed order. As a consequence, there is an emergent character to institutions. Even though rules bring stability and order, sets of rules are potentially "rich in conflict, contradiction, and ambiguity, and thus as producing deviation as well as conformity, variability as well as standardization" (pp. 60-64). The areas of ambiguity and conflict provide ample territory for elaborating on existing routines and changing the character of the institution (March & Olsen, 1989, chap. 4). Institutions contain other emergent possibilities as they take on more of the character of community. They become open to change to the degree that they ground or anchor their interpretations and actions in the situation and the people who constitute the institutional world. All situations and people have a developmental dynamic and grounding that necessarily produce an openness to change.

We saw earlier that reorganizations are often part of a power-driven bureaucratic world. Though this often is the case, an institutional perspective casts a somewhat different light on such efforts. Organization types have embedded in them both the institutional life of the agency and of the larger political system. The structure acts as a symbol of prior public commitments, and to certain approaches for addressing public issues (Seidman & Gilmour, 1986). The specific structures incorporate ways for understanding appropriate approaches for doing business around particular problems, ways for people to understand how to address given issues beyond the specific personal self-interest of employees.

The boxes and lines along with specific organization of roles signify ways to act and offer some assurance that people outside can trust the way public servants will take on particular tasks and processes (Kass, 1994). When public servants can move beyond bureaucratic and organizational action contexts and invoke an institutional one, a richer public process becomes possible. It calls for an agency perspective as envisioned in the Refounding Public Administration project.

The perspective of *Refounding Public Administration* (Wamsley et al., 1990) is most directly tied to the world of administrative action grounded in an institutionally based constitutional order. This perspective joins community with bureaucracy and is thereby able to take the public servant beyond the rather rigid confines of implementing someone else's policy. An institutional context enables public servants to invoke an agency perspective; a legitimate and important one for democratic governance.

Public administrative institutions are anchored in political life. At this general level, American public administrative institutions derive their meaning from constitutional and governance contexts. An important source of meaning for public administrative agency action is formed by the regime values and processes that have emerged from our political community over the past two-plus centuries (Rohr, 1986). Agencies gain meaning from this broader constitutional order and the character of our governance community continues to emerge, partially through the actions of public agencies and processes.

Larry Terry's (1990) stewardship emphasis for the public administrator captures one dimension of a public administrative institutional world. Rather than being concerned only about responsiveness to political superiors or customers, the conservator also incorporates previous agency commitments and its own sense of mission developed during prior efforts to work in a specific policy context of our broader constitutional system. For example, Terry would have preferred that the local government day care coordinator place greater emphasis on the local agency's historical reason for providing day care for children of the working poor before turning to a market-oriented summer camp. This focus on past missions is not because of rigidity and self-protection, but rather because the agency, as it acted appropriately within the governance process, developed a positive meaning of acting in the public interest in very specific institutional ways. As a bureaucracy, organization, or market, it would have no problem shifting to new entrepreneurial opportunities. However, because of its institutional character, the recreation department's summer camp is something that merits appreciation (Terry, 1990).

The public administrative institution, then, becomes more than a tool in the hands of politicians. It is more than an organization choosing efficient approaches to a goal. It is more than a cluster of people, groups, and customers acting as market-driven optimizers. By taking in elements of bureaucracy, organizations, and communities, administrative institutions have the capacity to be very important in the development of democratic policy and program communities, of values and language for looking at and finding the meaning of actions and fitting actions to appropriate responses.

▬ What to Make of This Discussion

This chapter began with a lament. *Refounding Public Administration* (Wamsley et al., 1990) seemed to come across to many readers as another fad for how to fix public administration—one more in a line of fads from the executive budget, scientific management, POSDCORB, BBPS, ZZB, MBO, and TQM. Wamsley's idea of Agency Perspective, for example, was particularly tarred with this problem. In an effort to save our project from the fate of management fads, the *Refounding Public Administration* project was placed within a broader framework for understanding the world in which public servants live.

Public servants find themselves deep in different contexts that evoke different kinds of actions. These action contexts are enduring and powerful dynamics in public settings. They also have a structural quality, developed over time and out of the experiences of administrative action. They define specific situations and evoke particular kinds of responses from public servants. I went on to describe six such action contexts that seem present in administrative settings and argued that each setting suggests a line of action for new situations.

Many of the fads and prescriptions for fixing the public administration come out of, and are in response to, one or more of these embedded contexts. These responses often make sense, often offer practical advice and constitute valuable ways for understanding, interpreting, and engaging in action in service to the public.

Reading Administrative Situations in a Multiple, Diverse, and Often Incoherent World

The world of the public administrator is a diverse one. Personal and agency effectiveness demand an ability, and willingness, to connect appropriately with this diversity. This framework of action contexts offers one way for the administrator to engage this diversity. First, each context constitutes a way of seeing and reading administrative situations. The six action contexts provide a richer vocabulary or set of lenses with which to help public administrators read the structures of different situations.

Second, for the public servant facing administrative problems and pressures, the ability to read situations, to identify operating action contexts, and to take cues for subsequent action offers enhanced capacity for effective action. Effective action becomes possible because the public administrator can seek solutions that are appropriate for given contexts. This does not mean that administrators know the specific bag of tricks to employ in each situation. Even though the contexts can be identified, the specific direction of any situation emerges out of the particular constellation of forces of the moment. Like weather patterns, the probability for a particular kind of storm may be present, but the specifics of the weather emerge as dynamic patterns develop from particular random events. However, the ability to recognize operating contexts, emerging problems and dynamics, and to experiment with potential actions appropriate in this context does increase the potential for effective action.

A Commitment to Specific Contexts?

In addition to reading situations correctly, the six contexts provide an opportunity for commitment to a particular one. Clearly, many in the current national administration have rather strong commitments to the market and organizational contexts. Their energy and commitment to the ideas of reinventing government and the Contract With America may perforce become the dominant context within public administration for the foreseeable future. At the same time, networks, communities, and institutions are present, albeit less powerful, in many of the same situations. Again, personal and organizational commitments to these three contexts can also evoke lines of action. Within the public administration there seems to be some reason to hope for commitment to the institutional view evoked in the Blacksburg perspective. The Blacksburg perspective most immediately seeks to evoke the institutional world, but it is also open to the worlds of community and networks in ways that the other three more conventional patterns are not.

The Possibility of a Democratic Public Administration

Does the possibility for a democratic public administration exist in such dense and diverse action contexts? Each context contributes elements that are both supportive and problematic for democratic governance. No one context offers enough to ensure democratic administration in the contemporary political and social setting. No one solution will suffice, and a tension among these contexts is perhaps our best hope for the foreseeable future.

As we saw, each context does produce a kind of democratic solution. Examples of how they do provide such a democratic character can easily be described. The bureaucratic context solves the problem through overhead democracy: political accountability and bureaucratic controls. Markets allow for openness and choice, as long as entry into and ability to participate in the market are equitably available. Organization contexts produce democratic governance as long as rational controls, processes, and analyses serve the interests of political leadership. Networks permit access outside of formal lines in the hierarchy. Communities preserve democracy with processes that have authentic and open relationships as well as accept the tentativeness of outcomes. Finally, institutions produce a democratic character through the grounding in constitutional traditions, agency perspectives, and stable yet emergent administrative processes.

At the same time, the current context tends to see a predominance of the bureaucratic, organizational, and market contexts. Consequently, the obstacles for democratic governance within each grow more acute. The constraints to administrative action provided by overhead democracy, bureaucratic authority, and rational decision premise controls grow increasingly more rigid and muscle-bound. Markets provide satisfaction of wants, but offer no anchor or stable set of relationships. In the incoherence and fragmentation of the postmodern condition, these contexts create situations that are unworkable even if "appropriate" lines of action can be determined. They aren't up to the job of sustaining effective action or democratic governance. Other chapters in this volume, particularly those of Green and Hubbell, Lane, Dennard, and Stivers (Chapters 1, 8, 9, & 11, respectively) present many of the constraints on the current dominant contexts for effective democratic action. The possibility of an increasing presence of the other three contexts provides administrative organizations with a richer blend of options and enhances their opportunities for more democratic action. Networking frees up systems to adapt and self-organize, but we must recognize the danger inherent in permitting elites to work without any kind of sustained grounding in ideas or processes related to the public interest, on the one hand, or without overhead democratic control, on the other. Perhaps the greatest promise comes with the addition of the community and institutional worlds. Through grounding in constitutional, agency traditions, and democratic institutional processes of the institutional world along with the processes and relationships of the community, the chance for more effective democratic governance increases.

Unfortunately, this leaves us with a very messy and unsatisfying situation. If the world is incoherent and full of mixed contexts, the possibility for both effective and democratic action within public organizations is, at best, difficult. Sadly, complex organizations are the only worlds we have at this time. Seeking ways of acting that draw us into any one of these alternative worlds to the exclusion of the others cannot suffice at this moment in history. We are at the cusp of very important changes, but can not know how they will play out. Perhaps we stand between the modern and some kind of postmodern era, or perhaps we will seek some romantic return to the control envisioned by bureaucratic and organizational worlds. Or, we may seek the self-organizing of the market and networks. Others of us find greater comfort in the institutional and/or community contexts as a way to face the coming postmodern world. Whatever lines of action we choose, we will probably have to be able work within all six. An awareness of the democratic and undemocratic elements of each at least alerts us to the problems we face in creating effective democratic governance in public organizations.

▰ References

Barnard, C. (1938). *The functions of the executive*. Cambridge, MA: Harvard University Press.

Bellah, R. N., Madsen, R., Sullivan, W. M., Swidler, A., & Tipton, S. M. (1985). *Habits of the heart: Individualism and commitment in American life*. Berkeley: University of California Press.

Berger, P. L., & Luckmann, T. (1966). *The social construction of reality: A treatise in the sociology of knowledge*. Garden City, NY: Doubleday.

Kass, H. D. (1994). Trust, agency, and institution building in contemporary American democracy, *Administration Theory and Praxis, 16*(1), 15-30.

Kingdon, J. (1984). *Agendas, alternatives, and public policies*. Toronto: Little, Brown.

Kovalik, W. (1988). *Improving federal inter-agency coordination: A model based on micro-level interaction*. Unpublished doctoral dissertation, Virginia Polytechnic Institute and State University, Blacksburg.

Lane, L., & Wolf, J. F. (1990). *The human resource crises in the public sector: Rebuilding the capacity to govern.* Westport, CT: Quorum.

Lorenz, E. (1991). Neither friends nor strangers: Informal networks of subcontracting in French industry. In G. Thompson, J. Frances, S. Levačič, & J. Mitchell (Eds.), *Markets, hierarchies and networks: The coordination of social life* (pp. 183-192). London: Sage.

March, J. G., & Olsen, J. P. (1989). *Rediscovering institutions: The organizational basis of politics.* New York: Free Press.

Meyer, J. W. (1983). Conclusion: Institutionalization and the rationality of formal organizational structure. In J. W. Meyer & W. R. Scott (Eds.), *Organizational environments: Ritual and rationality* (pp. 261-282). Beverly Hills, CA: Sage.

Neave, H. R. (1990). *The Deming dimension.* Knoxville, TN: SPC Press.

Osborne, D., & Gaebler, T. (1992). *Reinventing government: How the entrepreneurial spirit is transforming the public sector.* Reading, MA: Addison-Wesley.

Perrow, C. (1986). *Complex organizations: A critical essay* (3rd ed.). New York: Random House.

Rhodes, R. A. W. (1991). Policy networks and sub-central government. In G. Thompson, J. Frances, S. Levačič, & J. Mitchell (Eds.), *Markets, hierarchies and networks: The coordination of social life* (pp. 203-215). London: Sage.

Rohr, J. A. (1986). *To run a constitution: The legitimacy of the administrative state.* Lawrence: University Press of Kansas.

Selznick, P. (1987). The idea of a communitarian morality. *California Law Review, 75,* 445-463.

Seidman, H., & Gilmour, R. (1986). *Politics, position, and power* (4th ed.). New York: Oxford University Press.

Simon, H. (1957). *Administrative behavior: A study of decision-making processes in administrative organizations* (2nd ed.). New York: Free Press.

Terry, L. D. (1990). Leadership in the administrative state: The concept of administrative conservatorship. *Administration and Society, 21,* 395-412.

Thompson, G., Frances, J., Levačič, R., & Mitchell, J. (Eds.). (1991). *Markets, hierarchies and networks: The coordination of social life.* London: Sage.

Wamsley, G. L., Bacher, R. N., Goodsell, C. T., Kronenberg, P. S., Rohr, J. A., Stivers, C. M., White, O. F., & Wolf, J. F. (1990). *Refounding public administration.* Newbury Park, CA: Sage.

Williamson, O. E. (1985). *The economic institutions of capitalism.* New York: Free Press.

Wilson, J. Q. (1989). *Bureaucracy: What government agencies do and why they do it.* New York: Basič Books.

Administering
in the Public Interest

The Facilitative Role for Public Administrators

THOMAS J. BARTH
The University of Memphis

> Our government is in trouble. It has lost its sense of mission; it has lost its ethic of
> public service; and, most importantly, it has lost the faith of the American people.
>
> Report of the National Performance Review
> (Office of the Vice President, 1993)

As we continue this worthy dialogue over how to "refound" a public administration that is responsive to the challenges of what other authors in this volume eloquently describe as the postmodern age, it is useful to recall that there is a rich tradition of such responsiveness by public administrators to larger problems in the polity. When the nation faced incompetence and corruption in government, the field of public administration was "founded" in response; when the nation was faced with economic collapse in the 1930s and waging World War II, public administrators were there struggling to create new agencies performing functions never before carried out by American government; when the nation tackled social inequity in the 1960s with sweeping civil rights legislation and the Great Society programs, public administrators were there, again leading the way by administering the new programs that were necessary to that effort and through example by hiring and promoting women and minorities at a greater rate than private industry.

We are at another point in our history that demands a courageous response by public administrators: the fragmentation, polarization, and disillusionment of our citizenry with government and the growing interconnectedness of public policy issues. The growing sense that something must be done to change how government is conducted can be seen in the enormous popularity of the book *Reinventing Government* (Osborne & Gaebler, 1992). The authors suggest some new (and some simply forgotten) ways of rethinking the way government bureaucracies manage their money and programs. The much publicized *Report of the National Performance Review* under the direction of Vice President Albert Gore (Office of the Vice President, 1993) borrows heavily from Osborne and Gaebler, citing four key principles underlying a plan "to redesign, to reinvent, and to reinvigorate the entire national government": cutting red tape, putting customers first, empowering employees to get results, and cutting back to basics: producing better government for less.

Moving the Discussion Beyond Innovative Management Techniques

Although worthy, these efforts are far less than sufficient steps toward truly reforming government in at least two ways. First, by focusing so heavily on managerial procedures and service delivery, the authors underplay the more important implications of their work—the need for public administrators to think of their fundamental role in the governance process differently. Second, by focusing on infusing competition, entrepreneurship, and decentralization, they miss the equally fundamental importance of cooperation and working across organizations and sectors that is critical to success in the increasingly complex and interconnected world of American government.

This chapter argues that these phenomena require broadening the way public administrators think about their role and the way public policies and programs are approached. Public administrators need to see themselves not only as innovative managers or entrepreneurs, as Osborne and Gaebler (1992) urge them to do, or as experts and enforcers, as they have traditionally been trained, but also as educators and facilitators. Furthermore, problems and issues must be approached through a truly "transorganizational" frame of reference, not merely more teamwork and cooperative rhetoric that remains rooted within traditional narrow perspectives and preoccupation with "turf." The remainder of this chapter will discuss why these changes are necessary and the implications for public administration.

▰ Changing Self-Concepts

The Public Administrator as Educator and Facilitator

Building on the normative base established in *Refounding Public Administration* (Wamsley et al., 1990), the role of educator and facilitator becomes inescapable when one considers what it means to administer in the public interest as we approach the next millennium. Goodsell (1990), for example, cites several process-oriented "constitutive values or standards" necessary to administer in the public interest. These include: political responsiveness, political consensus, and agenda awareness. These guiding values speak to the need for balance, compromise, and integration. They also imply that for a democracy to survive, there must be an appreciation for the need to find common ground, to respect the concerns and opinions of those who are different, and to hear the needs of the powerless as well as the powerful. Yet the United States of the 1990s is a country increasingly dominated by polarizing forces that are fragmenting the citizenry and political discourse. The causes of this "postmodern" condition are discussed by White and McSwain and by Dennard (Chapters 7 and 11, respectively, in this volume); this chapter focuses on several of the most critical symptoms of this condition and the response needed by public administrations.

Polarizing Forces

Polarization in our political culture is evident at several distinct yet overlapping levels.

Morality. In *Culture Wars,* Hunter (1991) describes the polarizing impulses of orthodoxy and the progressivist worldviews evident in contemporary America. Orthodoxy "is the commitment on the part of adherents to an external, definable, and transcendent authority" (p. 44). The progressivist worldviews share with one another "the tendency to resymbolize historic faiths according to the prevailing assumptions of contemporary life" (p. 45). These competing views capture the tone of contemporary political debates over such divisive issues as abortion, treatment of homosexuals, and sex education—a standoff between those who believe in an unchanging natural law versus those more accepting of the evolving nature of morals and cultural values. Hunter notes that these attitudes reflect passionately held commitments and beliefs. Thus conflict between those espousing orthodoxy versus those adhering to a progressivist worldview is inevitably expressed as a "clash over national life itself"—a struggle over national identity, over the meaning of America (p. 50). Etzioni ("Interview with Amitai Etzioni," 1992) suggests a similar conflict with a slightly different spin, by arguing the country is split into authoritarians who want to impose their moral solution on everyone, and libertarians who oppose any voice other than that of the individual. The implications of the work of Hunter and of Etzioni are the same: Americans are finding it increasingly difficult to discover common ground.

Ethnicity. In *The Disuniting of America,* Schlesinger (1991) describes the current "cult of ethnicity" that is fragmenting Americans. He suggests that instead of a "transformative nation all its own, America increasingly sees itself as a preservative of old identities" (p.2). He laments, "The national ideal had once been *e pluribus unum.* Are we now to belittle *unum* and glorify *pluribus?* Will the center hold? or will the melting pot yield to the Tower of Babel?" (p. 2).

The concept of assimilation that underlies the traditional melting-pot metaphor relies on the acceptance by all groups of certain universal values, attitudes, and behaviors that make effective collective action possible. However, the acceptability of the assimilation model is breaking down, largely because ethnic groups and women are achieving more voice and challenging what they recognize as standards set by and for white men. Nonetheless, the pervasiveness of the assimilation model has fostered the denial of emerging diversity in the workplace and society in general. Thomas (1990) notes that although there has always been diversity in terms of numbers in the United States, only recently have people begun to think about how to "manage" that diversity and capitalize on it. He suggests the melting-pot metaphor needs to be replaced by the image of a rich mulligan stew, where multiple ingredients keep their identity while at the same time coming together to create something greater than themselves.

As Schlesinger (1991) points out, however, there is a delicate balance to be struck here. As one witnesses the growing cultural separateness between black and/or Hispanic inner cities and white suburbs in many American cities, "angry white males" rebelling against the principle of affirmative action, religious fundamentalism, bilingualism, and "political correctness" movements on college campuses it is easy to understand how Schlesinger sees a potential Tower of Babel rather than a rich stew.

Economic Self-Interest/Careerism. As a final example of this polarization and the resulting disconnectedness in society, Bellah, Swidler, Madsen, Tipton, and Sullivan (1991) cite the current prevailing "economic ideology" that turns human beings into relentless market maximizers, thereby undermining "commitments to family, to church, to neighborhood, to school, and to the larger national and global societies" (p. 31). They cite modern city growth as the ultimate example of market maximization, where pursuit of careers and jobs has resulted in lifestyles that lead to a lack of social coherence.

In essence, if public administrators are to further the public interest, these polarizing forces must not be ignored for they make it increasingly difficult to move beyond self-interest toward common ground.

Disillusionment With Government

Coinciding with these polarizing forces is a pervasive disillusionment with government among the citizenry. This disillusionment has at least two sources. In terms of the polarizing forces discussed above, it follows that if you have an extreme position on an issue, or if you are driven by economic self-interest, your faith in government will depend on the degree to which your position or personal well-being is furthered by a particular policy. Because there is thus little concern with compromise or the common good, governance becomes a zero-sum game with only winners and losers. The other source of disillusionment is a group in the middle, probably a very large group, that is typically on the fence over many societal issues and is looking seemingly in vain to our institutions to provide guidance and "do the right thing."

The common thread in all of these groups, whether they be zealots or moderates, is that they are looking to our government institutions to act, and there is a sense that our government institutions have lost the capacity to act (Office of the Vice President, 1993). Greider (1992) cites the usual statistics that reflect citizen disillusionment with government. For example, roughly half of adult America stays home in presidential elections; three in four Americans express dissatisfaction with the outcome of congressional contests, and two thirds of those surveyed are convinced that "the government is pretty much run by a few big interests looking out for themselves" (p. 23). Finally, a recent survey shows that the percentage of Americans who said they trust the U.S. government to "do what is right most of the time" has declined from about 60% in 1964 to 12% in 1993.[1]

Reconnecting With Citizens

Greider (1992) suggests that the cause of this disillusionment is that citizens have been pushed into two unsatisfying roles in politics. In one role, citizens are the mindless, faceless mass audience that speaks in politics mainly through opinion polls. The other narrow role open to citizens is as special pleaders, defending their own personal concerns against other aspirants. Although such self-interested pleas are the "warp of democratic politics and always will be, . . . the contours of modern government make it very difficult for citizens to accomplish anything else" (p. 19). Greider suggests that attention must be brought to rediscovering the middle ground between these two extremes, where citizens' self-interest is harmonized with their broader expectations for the society. He concludes, "That political space is now empty on most important subjects—the vast middle ground where democracy has shrunk and citizens have lost their voice" (p. 19).

As with polarizing forces, pervasive disillusionment with government among the citizenry can have a crippling effect on a democracy. The most obvious symptom is lack of participation in elections, but the more insidious and devastating result is the loss of faith or hope in the possibility of solving problems and building a better life for all through collective action. A government where citizens have effectively abdicated responsibility to elected officials, their appointees, or career bureaucrats is a democracy in name only.

Although heralded as yet another saving revolution, the new Republican Congress and its "Contract with America" represent little beyond the tired rhetoric of the Reagan administration; that is, Washington and the federal bureaucracy are the enemy, cut taxes, put welfare moms to work, replace entitlement programs with block grants (and less funding) to the states, and so on. These ideas may ignite the ire of voters and help win elections, but they do not speak to the fragmentation and disillusionment of the citizenry. As Follett (1965) notes in her discussion of the truly democratic state, "democracy is not worked out at the polling booths; it is the bringing forth of a genuine collective will, one to which every single being must contribute the whole of his complex life" (p. 7).

The question is, what role do public administrators have in reconnecting citizens with the political process in the manner described by Follett?

The Public Administrator as Educator

In essence, for governance both to work *and* to regain legitimacy, we must reforge the links between the political process and the citizenry at every level. One way this must be done is by educating the citizenry. The role of educator is evident in public administration literature. Wamsley (1990) speaks of the need for agential leaders who "create institutions that can produce deliberation, that can educate us to what we can and cannot have, and enlighten citizens concerning the trade-offs" (p. 149). Ventriss (1987) suggests that what distinguishes public administration from other social sciences is that it should be committed to being a "public social science"; that is, dedicated to "employing a critical intellect to those social science approaches so that the public can better understand, debate, and discuss important policy issues" (p. 38). Ventriss talks of using this critical intellect for sorting out misinformation and the distortion of data, analyzing trade-offs implied for each policy choice, and examining the impact of past policy decisions. Finally, Green, Keller, and Wamsley (1993), in arguing that the polity is founded and sustained in public rhetoric or argument, call for public administrators to "look for opportunities to make people aware of governance concerns in public life. Their participation in government action should be cause for their education and formation" (p. 521).

If one considers the quality of the political discourse today, the need for someone to take on this educational role becomes obvious. Political candidates appeal to the public through "sound bites" that are designed to manipulate the electorate instead of educate it, whereas policies and programs are promoted because of their political appeal even though their effectiveness is questionable at best. For example, a politically popular aspect of the omnibus crime bill is the "three-strikes-you're-out" measure that establishes a mandatory life sentence for a third serious felony. Although this measure is intuitively appealing, the number of felons convicted a third time is relatively small (about 70 per year in the state of Washington, 300 in New York). Furthermore, most felons are not convicted a third time until late in their crime careers, when research shows they are least dangerous. When told it will cost $460,000 to keep such a prisoner behind bars from age 50 to 70 (taking up space that could be used for younger, more dangerous criminals), an aid to Texas Senator Phil Gramm said, "This is what the public wants."[2]

It has reached the point where politicians are afraid even to mention publicly, let alone discuss intelligently, reasonable ideas regarding contentious issues for fear of potential damage at the polls. For example, a bipartisan commission on entitlement reform, appointed by President Clinton and headed by Senators Bob Kerrey and John Danforth, discussed reforming social security by raising the retirement age to 70, cutting the benefits of upper-income retirees, and recalculating the Consumer Price Index. Due to the perceived sensitivity of the electorate to any change in the social security system, Kerrey and Danforth could not even get the backing of their own commission. They then submitted the plan to the White House on their own, and Clinton has ignored it.[3]

Seeking Understanding Versus "The Truth"

This combination of political partisanship, demagoguery, and cowardice points to the need for someone concerned with educating the citizenry on the nature of positions or policies that are often masquerading as "the truth" when in reality they are a mixture of facts, values, subjective interpretations, and more. In the highly ideological debates that are particularly divisive among the citizenry, unbiased information is becoming increasingly difficult to find—information is shaded by political influences, ideology, and personal agendas. As discussed by White and McSwain and by Dennard (Chapters 7 and 11, respectively, this volume), the public's susceptibility to this jaded discourse is the product of modernism's obsession with technicism; in other words, that there is an ultimate answer and rational solution to every problem. The false promise of technicism is that someone has "the answer" to complex social problems like crime and poverty, so the public desperately flocks to the sound bites of the latest messiah.

As White and McSwain argue, the reality is that all the parties to a situation hold only partial or momentary answers. Once this epistemological stance is accepted, it opens the parties up to constructive discourse rather than unresolvable ideological debates. Education in this context, therefore, means helping citizens understand the difficulties and trade-offs inherent in the complex challenges facing our society—what White and McSwain would call "glimpses of the truth."

Consistent with this theme, Evans (1993) suggests that we need public administrators dedicated to promoting understanding rather than "truth." In other words, citizens need to understand more than they need to be "convinced" or "sold" something.

In a democracy, who has the responsibility to promote such understanding—politicians, the press, public interest groups? They all have this duty, but public administrators, due to the nature of their expertise, proximity to the data, and relatively secure career status (i.e., agency perspective), have a special responsibility. Such an educative role is sorely needed in our political culture today.

Implications of Educator Role

Yet the public administrator as educator (i.e., purveyor of unbiased information) is elusive in practice because of the traditional emphasis on subordination of career civil servants in our system of governance. Consider the case of the state of Wisconsin's experience with "Learnfare," a controversial policy enacted in 1987 that ties welfare payments to school attendance of children in recipient families. Ethridge and Percy (1993) state that although there is little evidence to indicate that Learnfare is substantially increasing the school attendance of its target population, the policy is likely to continue: "Manipulating participation requirements [for welfare programs] can be politically profitable even if implementation is problematic and results are dismal. Voters generally respond positively to the concept for protracted periods without regard for program success" (p. 345).

In other words, because the coupling of welfare benefits with behavioral responsibilities such as seeking employment or attending job-training programs "play well in Peoria," the programs will continue to be promoted by politicians even though they are ineffective. The result: Unless educated, citizens will continue to support such programs and become frustrated with the government's inability to "solve" the welfare problem.

The dilemma for either local, state, or federal public administrators charged with the role of educating the citizenry on complex and contentious issues, as Ventriss (1987) and others suggest, is that they may have to work for the elected officials or their appointees who may favor the policies or programs for political reasons. Is it realistic, for example, to suggest that the director of the state welfare department should issue a press release on the ineffectiveness of a welfare policy initiative if the governor sees the policy as politically popular?

For those who argue that a key to addressing the polarization and disillusionment of the citizenry is education, the basic dilemma is who will ultimately provide the citizenry with unbiased information? Because of the civil servant's subordinate role to elected officials in our form of government, this is an unresolved dilemma for the field of public administration. Indeed, it raises once again the classic question of who does the public administrator serve: the needs of the elected officials (in the executive branch and Congress) or their appointees, for whom they work in an organizational sense; or the needs of the citizenry, which is ultimately sovereign? As Ventriss notes, their needs are not always the same. The response to this dilemma lies at the heart of what makes government different from the private sector, and it has two implications for the role of public administrators.

Serving Multiple Masters. The responsibility to educate the citizenry implies a degree of autonomy for public administrators when elected officials and their appointees allow the pressure of partisan politics to manipulate or obscure information. What is the source of legitimacy for such autonomy? Rohr

(1990) argues that as constitutional officers in a government of separate but shared powers, public administrators serve all three branches of government: executive, legislative, and judicial. For example, although public administrators at the federal level typically work most directly under the president through political appointees in the agencies, they also are simultaneously answerable to legislative committees and court orders as well.

Applied to the Learnfare example, subordinate autonomy means the public administrator first has a duty to consider educating the governor and suggesting alternative programs that may be more effective, even though the governor may profit politically from the program. This is the essence of neutral competence, or "loyalty that argues back," and is generally accepted as a legitimate role for a responsible public administrator. However, subordinate autonomy may imply the possibility of going further than merely arguing back. If ignored by the governor, it may be necessary for the public administrator to exercise subordinate autonomy and make key legislators aware of the failure of the program, or even go as far as leaking the facts to the press. Although not uncommon, such actions are extreme and could possibly cost the public administrator his or her job. Indeed, some argue that attempts to legitimize such administrative autonomy is "frightening" (Lowi, 1993).

However, to focus on those extreme or rare cases where public administrators must directly confront presidential or congressional initiatives is to miss the point. As Rohr (1990) suggests, subordinate autonomy is about attitude as much as it is about behavior. The point is not to have career administrators in the agencies running amok, sabotaging initiatives they personally oppose; the point is for public administrators to see themselves as more than subordinate technicians carrying out orders as in a private corporation. As constitutional officers, they have a responsibility to continually examine the work they do and the directives they are given in the context of law, statute, and mission of the agency, and to inform executive superiors of the implications even when the information will not be welcomed. Civil service protection, though far from perfect, does mitigate the risks of such action.

In the information age in which the citizenry is inundated with conflicting arguments around complex issues, policies, and programs, public administrators must be vigilant to apply this questioning attitude to the quality of information on which agency decisions are based and on the messages (or lack thereof) sent to the citizenry. For example, the Winter Commission report calls for the creation of citizen liaison offices that would help "assure that accurate and timely information about government policies, programs and pending issues is provided to citizens" (Winter, 1993, p. 55). This is a wonderful concept on paper, but make no mistake about it—the integrity and the quality of the information provided citizens through such "liaison" offices will rely on the public administrators staffing these offices being imbued with the reflective attitude suggested by autonomy grounded in subordination.

Responsible Use of Expertise in a Democracy. A second implication of the role of educator is the responsible or ethical use of expertise by public administrators. Constitutional arguments aside, the Code of Ethics for the American Society of Public Administration (ASPA)[4] states: "Demonstrate the highest standards of personal integrity, truthfulness, honesty and fortitude in all our public activities in order to inspire public confidence and trust in public institutions."

As government policies and programs become increasingly complex, the trust issue will become even more critical for the average citizen who has neither the time nor expertise to sort out all the facts on every issue. If politicians are loose with the facts in order to support their particular interests, then public administrators must think long and hard about what they can do to educate citizens so that they can be more informed. Again, the ethical dilemmas posed by this argument are enormous, but citizens must believe there is a source they can go to for unbiased information. As Tong (1986) suggests, there is no greater threat to democracy than the presence of expertise in the hands of an elite group. Although the concept of unelected public administrators challenging the statements of elected officials and their appointees may strike some political theorists as an unholy threat to democracy, what other more legitimate institution represents a more reasonable means of stemming the unchecked demagoguery that characterizes our current political culture? Public administrators cannot hide their heads in the sand—polarization and disillusionment of citizens will continue unless the public is better educated. Greater understanding of the complexity and difficulties of public policy and management issues will help dispel both superficial ideological stands and increase citizens' appreciation for the difficulty of these issues. Indeed, Wamsley and Wolf (Introduction, this volume) suggest that citizens must realize that part of the perception of why government doesn't work anymore is because we have solved the "tame" problems—paving streets, building interstate systems, laying sewers, and so on. The public sector has left only what Harmon and Mayer (1986) call the "wicked" problems—health care, homelessness, illegal drug traffic, crime and violence, and more. These problems are not merely a product of inefficient bureaucracy or uncommitted public officials; they are intractable because solutions are not known or they involve serious costs, trade-offs, or value conflicts. Public administrators must gently but persistently get this point across to citizens and stop silently assenting to glib promises that more can be delivered.

The Public Administrator as Facilitator

Perhaps a more fruitful approach to addressing the dilemma of how to educate the citizenry is to provide the opportunity for self-education through participation in the governance process. Although there is nothing new about the concept of citizen participation, what may be different is public administrators thinking of their role as that of a facilitator in the process. Bellah et al. (1991) hint at the notion of facilitation by calling on our public institutions to take on a "cultivation" role by providing more "focal structures" or places "where people can meet to focus their attention and gain a sense of the whole of life through the cultivation of memory and orientation" (p. 90). As with the role of educator, the image of a facilitator suggests a fundamentally different orientation than the more traditional roles associated with public servants, such as manager, enforcer, or regulator—roles that emphasize the exercise of power and technical expertise.

A Process Perspective: Facilitating Authentic Contact and Integration Between Government and the Citizenry

The concept of facilitation in this context goes beyond that of education—it speaks to actively fostering processes that engage citizens in governance as a way of bringing them closer to the politicians and politics. Consistent with Bellah et al.'s (1991) calls for more "focal structures" for citizens, Ventriss (1987) suggests that "public administration must expand its activities to those civic and voluntary associations that mediate between individuals and the state" (p. 39).

This facilitation role connotes more than just bringing people together, however, or brokering win-lose confrontations and least common denominator compromises among interest groups. Facilitation here suggests a focus on the nature or quality of the interaction with citizens; that is, the relationship as well as the outcome. For example, in an analysis of the implications of *Refounding Public Administration,* Gaukel (1993) notes White and Stivers's call for public agencies to encourage the building of agency-public dialogue and interaction. Their focus on the use of dialogue to build communities of shared meaning is also seen in what Marshall and White (1990) see as the public agency's role in creating a common language, a lingua franca, that provides a way of talking about things sensibly. The creation of a shared meaning is part of achieving what should be the ultimate goal of facilitation: authentic contact and integration among groups.

Authentic Contact. Absent skilled facilitation, groups may come together but never achieve true contact. The concept of authentic contact goes beyond the typical superficial interactions that occur between individuals and groups; it means people becoming more clearly aware of what they want from others and from themselves. Drawing on Gestalt theory, Herman and Korenich (1986) elaborate that genuine interaction focuses on what really matters between parties, a far cry from the role playing, "tact" and "avoidance" games that frequently go on in the day-to-day work of organizations. The important point here is the focus on the quality of the process as opposed to a preoccupation with positions and outcomes. If the process is legitimate in that it fosters authentic dialogue between the agency and the citizens, not only is resolution more probable but the participants are more likely to walk away feeling positive about the experience.

Integration. The other goal of facilitation is captured by the concept of integration as conceived by Mary Parker Follett. Cooper (1980) describes Follett's concept of integration as the process of taking different ways of knowing the world; understanding what each part symbolizes in terms of interests, desires, and needs; and analyzing their accuracy. Ideally this process leads to a new way of seeing reality, in which "all needs may be accommodated without suppressing any perceptions or desires expressed by any of the participants" (p. 56).

Although difficult to realize in practice, the goal of integration, like authentic contact, is to break through superficial talk and positioning and ultimately come to a more complete understanding of each other. Absent such integration of the needs of all parties involved in a conflict situation, Follett was convinced that at some point one of the parties would work to undermine whatever tenuous resolution was obtained. Some examples from the local government level demonstrate the various ways citizens can be engaged (or alienated) and how public administrators can either help or hinder the contact and integration in their facilitating role.

Facilitating Authentic Dialogue. In the City of Germantown, a suburb of approximately 30,000 on the outskirts of Memphis, there is a strong tradition of citizen involvement through formal Citizen Advisory Committees ranging from personnel to finance to planning. All major city decisions on issues such as pay increases for employees, zoning, and development are discussed with these committees. Each committee is empowered to make recommendations to the Mayor and Board of Alderman. These committees not only enable the city to tap the expertise of its citizens, but they provide a vehicle for education and consensus building. Another major vehicle is the neighborhood association, where citizens get involved in working with the local government to serve the interests of their neighborhood. This, in fact, is the way many aldermen traditionally enter political life.

Citizen participation through advisory commissions and neighborhood associations is certainly not new or innovative. What is interesting, however, is the Germantown city manager's description of how interactions with these groups have forced the city's professional administrators to rethink their role and the way they make decisions. Decisions affecting the community are not merely technical in nature—they have a social or community dimension that may not be apparent or seem important to professional public administrators. The city manager noted this process has been especially difficult for the planners and engineers, who are socialized in their professional educations to believe they can determine "what is best" based on their technical expertise. These committees force the public administrators to "come out of their cubicles" and explain to citizens what they are doing, how they arrive at their data, and so on. In other words, such interactions with citizens can result in authentic contact between the planners and the citizens, where each side expresses what it truly wants and has an opportunity to understand the other.

Even though citizen participation models have been in operation for years, it is striking that professional administrators are still struggling with how to synthesize citizen input with their technical expertise. One explanation is that absent skilled facilitation, citizen participation efforts may be unauthentic, as when the public administrators involved are simply going through the motions of a public meeting with no intention to use the information (a commonly heard criticism of Hillary Clinton's health reform task force hearings). Likewise, citizens may have no real interest in listening to what the public administrators (or other citizens) want—they simply want to coerce a decision that favors their narrow interests. In the Winter Commission report, David Matthews of the Kettering Foundation reflects this view in his assessment of the public hearing: "It is counterproductive because it is neither public nor a hearing. That is to say, it has people there, but it is the showcase of those who would have a particular special interest. It is not a hearing; nobody hears anything because nobody is listening" (Winter, 1993, p. 55).

The significant point here is that the quality of these experiences for citizens and the amount of input they have in the analysis that goes to the politicians is heavily determined by the public administrators. In other words, public administrators must not only redefine how they apply their technical expertise, but they must also see every interaction with citizens as an opportunity to facilitate constructive relationships between the citizens and the political process in a positive or constructive manner. Clearly the opportunities for such interaction are much greater at the state and especially local levels of government. However, advances in telecommunication technology, as demonstrated by the national "town hall" meetings popularized by the Clinton administration, may present unprecedented opportunities for more citizen involvement at the federal and state level as well as the local level.

Sharing Power. A very different kind of citizen involvement occurs when the citizens' goal is to not only listen and comment, but to obtain the power to influence decisions. An example is the Industrial Area Foundations (IAF), founded by the renowned community organizer Saul Alinsky in the 1940s. Although community organizing movements went through a period of decline after flourishing in the 1960s, there has been a resurgence to the point where there are now 24 organizations in seven states, encompassing 1,200 congregations and associations with nearly two million members (Greider, 1992, pp. 224-225). They are based on the premise that ignored and powerless citizens are fully capable of assembling their own power and leading their own politics. IAFs typically begin by establishing relationships with enduring community institutions such as church congregations and civic associations (Greider, 1992). These groups obviously are not a part of the government establishment—they are there to change the structure of power in the political process itself.

The IAF established in the Memphis area is called Shelby County Interfaith (SCI). The lead organizer states that although their target is normally elected officials, they often work through public administrators, such as the director of public works, housing, transportation, or a city manager. An example is a survey of poor neighborhoods conducted by SCI that produced a list of items that they released to the media and presented to the head of housing and public works to address. Because of the fear of negative publicity, the departments addressed many of the items, but the top appointed officials from the relevant departments refused to appear at a public meeting with SCI to discuss progress. The message to the citizens affiliated with SCI was clear: As public administrators we will work with you because we fear you, but we will not give the public appearance that we are in partnership with you, or see that you get any credit for forcing the bureaucracy to respond.

This is an example of public administrators failing to seize an opportunity to facilitate contact between citizens and a fractured governance process. If community activist groups like SCI appear rude and intolerant to public administrators, perhaps that is the only way they know how to act in the face of a faceless, unresponsive bureaucracy that they have learned to mistrust. The confrontational tactics of such citizen groups then foster even more unresponsiveness and paranoia on the part of the public administrators, and the destructive cycle escalates.

To reestablish constructive relationships, public administrators must see such citizens as partners, where the issue is not "power-over" but "power-with"—working together to solve problems. Follett's concept of integration speaks directly to the issue of power. Absent an understanding of integration, groups in conflict resort to a power-over mode, an attempt to gain control of a situation or conflict through coercion. According to Follett, however, this need to achieve control through coercion is because people do not know any other way of gaining control. Cooper (1980) explains that for Follett "genuine power is the process of creating wholes, of integrating new material into an existing gestalt, or of creating an entirely new gestalt or pattern from two different ways of seeing and experiencing a situation" (p. 41). Absent individuals who are trained in facilitating such creative approaches to conflict resolution, groups will tend to fall into the more familiar and comfortable modes of coercion or compromise that leave one or both sides dissatisfied.

Implications of Facilitator Role

As with the role of educator, the role of facilitator implies several challenges for the field of public administration as it is currently constituted. Chief among these are how we currently train public administrators, the way public employees are managed, and attitudes toward citizens.

Training of Public Administrators. Despite the need for public administrators to be more than technical experts, the current curricula of graduate programs in public administration tend to center around technical preparation in such areas as, for example, personnel, administrative law, finance/budgeting, or program evaluation. That these skills are necessary but not sufficient for effective public administration in the modern world is demonstrated by the language found in the report, *NASPAA's Task in Encouraging Reform in State and Local Governments* (National Association of Schools of Public Affairs and Administration [NASPAA], 1993). The report recommends the development of new skills for graduates, such as team building, negotiation, communication, employee and citizen involvement, cultural awareness, quality, and an understanding of how the media work. In general, the focus should be on developing the capacity of managers to act as coaches and facilitators rather than as supervisors and controllers.

An excellent example of this change for a particular group of public administrators is the community policing movement. Police officers are traditionally trained primarily in law enforcement, and this is how they view their role—making arrests, rescuing innocent citizens from criminals, solving crimes (Webber, 1991). This role is fundamentally different from what one Memphis police officer describes as the "social work" orientation of community policing, where the police officer is transformed from "an investigator into a catalyst in a process of community self-help" (Osborne & Gaebler, 1992, p. 50). Given the ethnic tensions in our society described earlier and the daily involvement of police officers with diversity of all kinds, to what degree are police trained and socialized to be culturally sensitive? Pioneers in the community policing movement, such as New York City Police Commissioner Lee Brown, recognize the implications of such a fundamental culture change. He states,

> like any change program in any company, you can't keep the same training system, evaluation system, reward system, and expect to change the way you police the city. My goal is to change all those systems to be supportive of community policing and not supportive of traditional ways of doing business. (Webber, 1991, p. 117)

The other skills mentioned in the NASPAA task force recommendations imply a similar reorientation for many of the subfields of public administration.

Management of Public Employees. One argument as to why citizen participation models have not taken hold is that the public administrators who manage such so-called participation efforts are themselves the products of autocratic organizations. Put another way, is it any surprise that public employees who are not treated as citizens in their own workplaces would not be very effective at facilitating such processes with other citizens outside the agency? In his classic work on ethics for public administrators, Cooper (1990) cites David Ewing's statement that "for all practical purposes, employees are required to be as obedient to their superiors, regardless of ethical and legal considerations, as are workers in totalitarian countries" (p. 214). If public administrators are to facilitate citizen participation processes effectively, the public agencies in which they work must change from the command-and-control style of management to a more participative, bottom-up style that has been discussed widely in both private and public sector management literature.

In the same vein, calls for public administrators to be sensitive to managing diversity in the community are unlikely to be heeded if diversity is addressed poorly in their own agencies. In other words, is diversity merely tolerated as a grudging concession to pressures from affirmative action policies, or is there an agency culture that truly embraces diversity and sees difference as a strength?

View of Citizens. Nowhere is the need to broaden the self-concept of public administrators more evident than in the ongoing debate over the proper way to view citizens. Osborne and Gaebler (1992) argue that public administrators viewing themselves as professionals and citizens as clients has contributed to the current state in which citizens feel helpless and everyone looks to the bureaucrats to solve problems by applying their professional expertise.

The professional-client model is indeed dangerous if it is used inappropriately, for it can create isolated, arrogant professional administrators and passive, unreflective clients. Yet at times the knowledge gap implied by the professional-client model is appropriate, for public administrators do have expertise that citizens may lack and they should not be reticent about using that expertise even though citizens do not like what they hear.

The total quality management movement implies that the problem with government lies in the failure of public administrators to view citizens as customers, a theme also emphasized by Osborne and Gaebler. The customer metaphor is not without value, because it connotes service and understanding the customer's wants and perceived needs.

However, a narrow use of the customer image has serious pitfalls for public administrators, as is argued by Stivers (Chapter 9), Dennard (Chapter 11), and other authors in this volume. For example, thinking of yourself as a customer demanding service does not foster concern with the public interest or common good, only with whether you are getting what you want or need out of the government. Similarly, if public administrators think of citizens primarily as customers, the tendency to focus on the needs and wants of the loudest or wealthiest is strong. The customer image also easily translates to "selling" rather than "educating," precisely the phenomenon exhibited by politicians and the media today.

Although the Gore Report (Office of the Vice President, 1993) is perceptive in seeing the dangers inherent in a narrow view of citizens as voters only, the answer is not creating another image like "customer" with the potential to be equally narrow. The reality is that there is no "one best way" to view citizens, just as there is no one role that adequately captures the responsibilities of public administrators. Rather, what is needed is an enriched view of active citizenship as argued by Stivers, which involves meaningful participation in governmental affairs, concern for the public interest, development of personal capacities for governance, and the building of community.

Such an enriched view of citizenship reinforces the broadened role for public administrators suggested in this chapter. Images like educator and facilitator—in addition to the traditional images of analyst, manager, administrator—are consistent and appropriate ways of approaching both enlightened citizens and fellow citizen-administrators within public agencies. However, broadening self-concepts is not enough for public administrators in the modern world: The following section addresses the need to also turn outward and examine the adequacy of traditional ways of approaching public policies and programs.

Changing How Policies and Programs Are Approached

A "Transorganizational" Frame of Reference

Just as public administrators must redefine self-concepts to respond to an increasingly polarized and disenchanted citizenry, we must respond to the fact that in an increasingly interconnected world, the tendency of our institutions to fragment or disaggregate knowledge is becoming increasingly dysfunctional. If we are truly to "reinvent government," addressing this issue is at least, if not more, important than calls for more competition and entrepreneurialism.

Luke (1992), in arguing that interconnectedness is the essential feature in the environmental context of public administration today, concludes that public action "occurs in expanding and crowded policy environments in which everything depends on everything else and power is dispersed and shared by a multiplicity of public and private actors" (p. 15). This theme of interconnectedness is anything but new in public administration literature. Wamsley and Zald (1973) speak of the web of policy subsystems that define a public organization's political economy; Hanf and Scharpf (1978) focus on the interorganizational characteristics of government problem solving; and many scholars are producing research on the cross-sectoral linkages among the public, private, and nonprofit sectors (Kettl, 1993; Milward, 1994). Although the interconnectedness of policies and programs has been well established, public administrators will not operate effectively in this increasingly interconnected world until they undergo a shift from a frame of reference based on differentiation and boundary maintenance to a "transorganizational" frame of reference. The term *frame of reference* is used to convey the basic orientation or lens through which individuals view the world. The concept is similar to the use of organizational metaphors used by Morgan (1986), who suggests how a metaphor "implies a way of thinking and a way of seeing that pervade how we understand our world generally" (p. 12). The following describes the current and needed frames of reference that can be used to approach public programs and policies.

The Current Frame of Reference: Differentiation and Boundary Maintenance

Although we give lip service to the issue of interconnectedness and the need to coordinate, traditional ways of organizing based on bureaucracy and the rational model have created individuals who see the world as fragmented or segmented. Although it is not possible in the space of this chapter to review the massive literature on the limitations of bureaucracy and the rational model, some illustrative citations are instructive.

Weick (1979) argues that the one metaphor that dominates the business world is the military. One reason for the power of this metaphor is that "People don't like to deal with uncertainty or disorder, so they impose military trappings like hierarchies and they impose spans of control to conceal the disorder" (p. 50). Military hierarchies, for example, are obsessed with boundaries and turf. Schmidt (1992) builds on this point by arguing that the contemporary institutions of science, engineering, and bureaucracy "rationally structure and suppress information and disaggregate knowledge of the whole" (p. 81). In order to control and make things orderly at the bottom of the hierarchy and predictable over time, designs and policies become increasingly specialized and fragmented.

Bailey (1992) is representative of the "antirationality" sentiment by noting how public administration has long been organized around the rational model of decision making. The implications of this model are that human beings, agencies, nations, and the like "are all seen . . . as separate units whose actions and policies can be individually developed in isolation from other considerations" (p. 33).

This bureaucratic/rational frame of reference is pervasive because it operates at both conscious and unconscious levels. Morgan (1986) notes how organizations can be partially understood through the metaphor of a "psychic prison" in which they are "ultimately created and sustained by conscious and unconscious processes, with the notion that people can actually become imprisoned or confined by the images, ideas, thoughts, and actions to which these processes give rise" (p. 199). Milward (1994) sees the impact of this frame of reference in the interactions between nonprofit agencies and government. He notes, "When bureaus interact, the assumption of boundary maintenance still exists. Bureaus conflict over turf and money. Even when scholars speak of policy subsystems, bureaus, together with interest groups and congressional committees, are the actors" (p. 76). In other words, although we may *talk* about the importance of relationships between subsystems, we still *think* in terms of boundaries and turf. He argues that such a basic assumption is inappropriate in a privatized system such as exists today, where the central task of government is to arrange networks, not manage a hierarchy. Another example is cited by Perrow (1986) with the Model Cities programs of the 1960s. He notes how despite the existence of a dense network of closely related agencies operating in a community, a common "institutionalized thought structure" among agency administrators produced surprisingly little contact or interdependence.

The Needed Frame of Reference: Transorganizational Management

Agranoff (1991) reflects an understanding of this frame of reference issue in his analysis of the enduring problem of human services integration in such areas as welfare, homelessness, and AIDS. He suggests that the standard attempts to coordinate services for the past two decades have fallen short because they have been rooted in the operation of single and separate organizational structures.

In other words, as long as public administrators see and define their world in terms of separate and distinct organizations, attempts to overlay coordination and integration strategies will be superficial and ineffective. He suggests that public administrators must begin to think in terms of a "transorganizational management" perspective that places emphasis on the development and operation of interactive and collective systems.

Schmidt (1992) provides a wonderful image of a transorganizational frame of reference by describing the knowledge of workers who fill cracks and holes in damaged dams. She describes how through direct observation of the details of each individual fissure and the area around it, they acquire a more complete knowledge of the heterogenous surface than anyone had had before, or had then, or would ever have again. She terms this a "feel for the whole," and then argues how this kind of knowledge is disaggregated by the formal bureaucratic organization and conditions at the site.

For public administrators today, this new way of thinking pertains not only to working across organizations within the public sphere, but rethinking the nature of relationships with the private sector. The following story from the *Wall Street Journal* involving the U.S. Environmental Protection Agency (EPA) and the Amoco Oil Corporation is illustrative.[5]

The Case of Pollution Control. This case describes a refinery study, called the Yorktown Project, that began with a chance meeting on a plane between two officials who once worked together in the energy industry but now are at

EPA and Amoco. After exchanging stories about the old days, the tenor of their conversation turned to, "If we could be king and queen for a day, wouldn't it be nice if we could restructure the world of environmental analysis." They wondered if something might come of a joint look by regulator and regulatee at a particular pollution site.

The two officials were not sure how to pursue the project at their respective organizations. For the EPA official, the notion of working with an oil company was dangerous heresy. For the Amoco official, "lots of people thought that opening the gates was stupid," because the EPA regulators would end up crawling around a plant and find problems. Nonetheless, they were able to proceed cautiously and began to meet, with Amoco offering its Yorktown, Virginia, oil refinery as a study site.

The lessons learned from this joint venture are fascinating examples of what it means to gain a "feel for the whole" and the resulting benefits. The first lesson is the language barrier between the two organizations. Amoco executives kept referring to *RVs,* Amoco-ese for relief valves. An EPA staffer thought they meant recreational vehicles. The industry types also spoke of "pigging out the line." It turned out to mean cleaning a pipeline by pushing a scrubber called a pig through it. Amoco was equally stumped by EPA jargon like "red border review." It means the final review of an EPA rule before it is published in the *Federal Register.*

Besides the language barrier, working and socializing together (even sharing hotel rooms) changed each project team member's views of the others. By the final night of one conference, an EPA official noted the EPA attitude seemed to be, "Gee, you don't all have horns." The Amoco consensus was, "Wow, not everybody at EPA was walking around with a pair of handcuffs." One EPA employee stated, "What was so exciting was not just the camaraderie . . . but it was like we were all on the same team."

A second lesson is that both sides realized they did not know precisely how to measure emissions from the refinery. Surprisingly, this was new ground for both. Even though air pollution control is a central mission, EPA doesn't often measure emissions from industrial plants. Once regulations are in place, inspectors from each of the pollution-control divisions—air, water, and solid waste—visit plants periodically with long checklists. Too many missed checks may result in an order to modify the plant or in a fine. But to what extent the rules are actually reducing pollution at a given site—and whether they are doing so in the most proficient or efficient way—is normally not at issue. The regulated company also does not measure actual pollution— it, too, focuses on meeting the regulations.

The project team realized that if it was going to examine the efficiency of current pollution control efforts, it would have to devise ways to measure the pollutants given off by the refinery as a whole—fumes, fluids, and solid wastes. Only then could it consider the best ways to keep them out of the air and water and soil. Using this approach, the project discovered that the refinery could achieve greater pollution reduction for about $11 million than it is getting for a $41 million expenditure required by current EPA regulations. An equally startling finding was that although that $41 million was spent to trap air pollution from the refinery's waste-water system, no controls at all were required—or yet existed—on a part of the plant that the study showed to emit 5 times as much pollution—which could be dealt with for a mere $6 million.

A third lesson is the surprising fact that the EPA officials regulating different kinds of pollution seldom speak to one another. They operate from different offices, enforcing separate pollution laws and maintaining their own regulatory staffs. In fact, EPA had to organize the project very carefully to avoid conflicts with turf-conscious division regulators. It should be noted that this structure is reinforced by the way the environmental statutes are written and the composition of congressional oversight committees.

Consistent with the results of this project, EPA Administrator Carol Browner has stated that "the adversarial relationship that now exists [between the regulator and regulated] ignores the real complexities of environmental and business problems," and further that "the idea that one solution works in every situation is something we've probably passed beyond, and we need . . . to become more flexible."

The point here is to illustrate that administering in an interconnected world will take shifting to a different frame of reference, as Agranoff (1991) suggests. It is one thing to recognize on an intellectual level that it is necessary to begin thinking in terms of interconnected systems and collective action; it is quite another to approach and see the world from that perspective. In reacting to the findings of the Yorktown Project, it is interesting that an Amoco official stated, "It was like 'My God, a blind person could see this.' " It would be appropriate to add that a blind person could indeed have seen what was obvious if he or she thought of pollution in holistic terms or saw the other side (whether it be the regulator or regulatee) as part of the solution instead of the problem.

Implications of a Transorganizational Frame of Reference

As the EPA example demonstrates, the shift to a transorganizational frame of reference is slowly occurring out of necessity as societal programs grow more and more intractable. We are discovering that addressing problems like crime and poverty takes more than simply increasing arrest rates or income transfers; rather, a comprehensive approach is required that includes education reform, job training, sex education, drug treatment, and more. Because government agencies and their employees are critical actors in the development and implementation of policies and programs to address such societal ills, the structure and culture of public agencies must change if a transorganizational or holistic frame of reference is to occur.

Changing Structures and Culture. A clear implication of this chapter is that public agencies must be restructured to operate effectively in an interconnected world. Bailey (1992) is representative of a large body of literature calling for public sector organizations to be more open and fluid (using interlocking teams with floating membership), participative, interdisciplinary, and more open to the expertise of citizens and other publics. The Gore Report (Office of the Vice President, 1993) on reforming the federal government and the Winter Commission (Winter, 1993) on reforming the state and local public service recommend flattening organizational hierarchies, forming cross-agency teams, and consolidating overlapping units.

Certainly there is nothing new about such a call for an end to hierarchy, for more participation, and for more interdisciplinary teams, but what is needed is greater understanding of the fact that we must also address the organizational cultures that have developed over years of operating in hierarchical structures. In echoing the need for information-based organizations, with flatter structures and the work largely done by task-focused, interdisciplinary teams, Drucker (1989) emphasizes how difficult the change will be for government organizations. We are very experienced and comfortable running command-and-control organizations, but do not yet know nearly as much about how to create a unified vision in an organization where knowledge resides in specialists on the line or how to devise an appropriate management structure for an organization of task forces, where boundaries, roles, and lines of authority are more fluid (p. 216).

The point is that simply imposing a transorganizational structure over a hierarchical culture will likely be ineffective. Thomas (1990) provides a useful image for conveying this point by describing organizational culture as a kind of tree:

> Its roots are assumptions about the company and about the world. Its branches, leaves, and seeds are behavior. You can't change the leaves without changing the roots, and you can't grow peaches on an oak. . . . So if you want to grow peaches, you have to make sure the tree's roots are peach friendly. (p. 114)

For a transorganizational frame of reference to take hold, public agencies must do more than talk about looking at the big picture and working in multidisciplinary teams; they must start by examining their "roots." In the case of EPA, this means understanding and altering what fosters and reinforces competitive fiefdoms and communication barriers—only then can the agency begin to bear new fruit like the Yorktown Project previously discussed. Another good example is the U.S. Fish and Wildlife Service, which is shifting to an ecosystem management approach. This is a shift from what has historically been a focus on individual species management to the holistic concept of biodiversity or ecosystem management. In discussing the implications of this shift in a memorandum to all employees, Director Mollie Beattie states that "adopting an ecosystem approach to fish and wildlife conservation as an underlying foundation for our operational activities will mean significantly changing the way we think, act, and solve problems" (cited in Sparrow & Stewart, 1994, p. 4).

Interdisciplinary Training of Public Administrators. If public administrators need to start thinking in transorganizational terms, an obvious place to foster such a change is in the content of academic and in-service training programs. For example, Delmer D. Dunn, Chair of the NASPAA Task Force on Education for the State and Local Public Service, suggests that the Winter Commission's recommendations require the development of education and training programs that "truly take advantage of interdisciplinary expertise and perspectives" (NASPAA, 1993, p. 110). What better way to foster transorganizational thinking than to expose students in schools of public administration to appropriate coursework from other disciplines—such as business, psychology, sociology, and others?

Furthermore, as discussed earlier, public administration programs must examine the degree to which they are preparing students to work effectively and cooperatively in teams and encouraging critical thinking, rather than focusing solely on the development of traditional technical skills such as budgeting and personnel.

Finally, administrators must examine the degree to which government in-service training programs offer courses cooperatively with other agencies they work closely with, or send employees to centralized training that is open to all agencies in a geographic area versus courses that are primarily in-house. Although these ideas might appear trivial, they are examples of how an organization can begin to foster transorganizational thinking by incrementally changing routine practices. One thing is certain—the oft-seen response to interconnectedness today of throwing employees together on cross-agency task forces without any experience in such an environment and expecting productive outcomes is unrealistic.

Role of the Legislative Branch. A holistic approach to the administration of public policies and programs will not be possible without changes on the legislative side. The Winter Commission Report notes that "State legislative processes sift statutes through a confusing committee structure, splitting what should be comprehensive bills into hundreds of pieces" (Winter, 1993, p. 19). Moe (1994), however, reflects the legislative point of view that although Congress may be accused of exacerbating fragmentation through the organiza- tion of its committee systems, it safeguards accountability. He is concerned, for example, that calls for more interagency committees in the Gore Report are dangerous because "accountability is necessarily dispersed and there emerges a disconnect between statutory authority and institutional capacity. Interagency committees, by making all participants responsible, make no single participant accountable" (p. 118). Perhaps, in the words of Osborne and Gaebler (1992), this committee structure has become so focused on accountability that it has made it impossible to manage or govern. It is a question of balance.

Although resolution of the tension between legislative committee struc- ture and transorganizational management approaches in the agencies cannot be resolved here, it is obviously a significant issue that cannot be ignored (as Moe accuses the Gore Report of doing.)

Entrepreneurialism and Competition. Finally, this need for an organization culture that fosters better communication and cooperation across traditional barriers may conflict directly with calls to inject more entrepreneurialism and competition found in *Reinventing Government* and the *National Performance Review,* as argued by Green and Hubbell (Chapter 1, this volume). For example, can a culture of competition coexist with a culture of cooperation? Perhaps, depending on how success is measured and how reward systems are structured (e.g., team awards). The point is that whatever changes are considered should be viewed from the perspective of whether a "feel for the whole" is enhanced or inhibited.

▬ **Conclusion**

This chapter argues that the polarization and disillusionment of our citizenry with government and the growing interconnectedness of public policy issues demands a different response by the field of public administration if the public interest is to be served.

The need to involve and educate citizens in order to reduce polarization and to restore faith in our government institutions will require public administrators to go beyond the role of technical or management expert and become educators and facilitators. Furthermore, a transorganizational frame of reference must supplant the deeply rooted orientation toward differentiation and boundary maintenance in order to administer effectively in an interconnected world.

Both of these perspectives point to the need for a greater connection between citizens and communities, and they reinforce the need to break down traditional ways of structuring and organizing our public bureaucracies. These ideas are not new, but the interest stimulated by such recent works as *Reinventing Government* (Osborne & Gaebler, 1992) demonstrates that they have yet to be realized. This chapter suggests that these ideas will remain unrealized as long as public administrators are imprisoned by the impoverished self-concept of technical or management expert and the tendency for our institutions to fragment or disaggregate knowledge.

However, these broadened self-concepts and ways of organizing raise several dilemmas for the field of public administration. First, there is the issue of the relationship of the public administrator to the three branches of government. The role of educator may conflict with the subordinate position of public administrators to their elected superiors, particularly when the truth about policies and programs does not serve political interests. The reality and legitimacy of public administrators exercising autonomy grounded in subordination must be understood and embraced by scholars and practitioners if this critical role of public educator is to be realized. The current political discourse characterized by demagoguery and sound bites indicates the failure of elected officials to provide a voice the citizens can "look" to for an understanding of the issues. Public administrators can and must be a lone voice in the wilderness.

The second issue is the self-concept of technical expert reinforced by the professional schools that feed public agencies. The majority of public administration degree programs, let alone those of law, planning, criminal justice, and other relevant schools, place precious little emphasis on the types of skills implied by this chapter: leadership, negotiation/conflict resolution, managing diversity, intergovernmental relations, working in teams, and so on. The focus remains on traditional technical skills such as budgeting, personnel, quantitative methods, administrative law. These skills are necessary but no longer sufficient. One promising sign, however, is the growing number of MPA programs that are incorporating administrative ethics into their curricula.

Third is the current focus on entrepreneurialism and interjecting more competition into government. Entrepreneurialism has something to offer in terms of looking for new solutions, taking risks, being flexible, and so on. However, the notion of competition that is stimulated by entrepreneurialism can be problematic. The implication of living in an interconnected world is the need for more teamwork and communication, not competition.

In ending, Goodsell (1990) notes that the public interest has constitutive rules or standards. This means rules or standards that require one to re-create and redefine oneself. Thinking of oneself as an educator and facilitator is quite different from seeing oneself as a technical expert; likewise, thinking in terms of interconnectedness is very different from protecting turf or being preoccupied with single issues. This chapter suggests that such redefinitions will not only further the public interest, but will help reduce what Al Gore (Office of the Vice President, 1993) terms the "trust deficit" the American government is experiencing with its citizens.

Notes

1. Cited in the July 19, 1993, issue of *Time* magazine. Sources: Center for Political Studies, University of Michigan (1964-1992); Los Angeles Times Poll (1993).
2. Data from February 7, 1994, issue of *Time* magazine, p. 52.
3. *Time* magazine, March 20, 1995, p. 32.
4. The ASPA Code of Ethics appears on the back cover of every edition of the *Public Administration Review.*
5. The case described here, including all quotes, closely follows the story that appeared in the *Wall Street Journal* titled "What Really Pollutes? Study of a Refinery Proves an Eye-Opener," March 29, 1993, p. A1 (Staff, 1993).

References

Agranoff, R. (1991). Human services integration: Past and present challenges in public administration. *Public Administration Review, 51*(6), 533-542.

Bailey, M. T. (1992). Beyond rationality: Decisionmaking in an interconnected world. In M. T. Bailey & R. T. Mayer (Eds.), *Public management in an interconnected world* (pp. 33-52). New York: Greenwood.

Bellah, R. N., Swidler, A., Madsen, R., Tipton, S. M., & Sullivan, W. M. (1991). Breaking the tyranny of the market. *TIKKUN, 6*(4), 30-32, 89-91.

Cooper, F. A. (1980). *Mary Parker Follett.* Unpublished doctoral dissertation, School of Public Administration, University of Southern California.

Cooper, T. L. (1990). *The responsible administrator.* San Francisco: Jossey-Bass.

Drucker, P. (1989). *The new realities.* New York: Harper & Row.

Ethridge, M. E., & Percy, S. L. (1993). A new kind of public policy encounters disappointing results: Implementing Learnfare in Wisconsin. *Public Administration Review, 53*(4), 340-347.

Evans, K. G. (1993). *The paradigmatic roots of the "Blacksburg Manifesto" and Refounding public administration.* Unpublished manuscript, Virginia Polytechnic Institute and State University, Center for Public Administration and Policy, Blacksburg.

Follett, M. P. (1965). *The new state.* Gloucester, MA: Peter Smith.

Gaukel, C. R. (1993). *Entrepreneurial government, the Blacksburg Manifesto, and bureaucratic accountability.* Unpublished manuscript, Virginia Polytechnic and State University, Center for Public Administration and Policy, Blacksburg.

Goodsell, C. T. (1990). Public administration and the public interest. In G. L. Wamsley, R. N. Bacher, C. T. Goodsell, P. S. Kronenberg, J. A. Rohr, C. M. Stivers, O. F. White, & J. F. Wolf (Eds.), *Refounding public administration* (pp. 96-113). Newbury Park, CA: Sage.

Green, R. T., Keller, L. F., & Wamsley, G. L. (1993). Reconstituting a profession for American public administration. *Public Administration Review, 53*(6), 516-524.

Greider, W. (1992). *Who will tell the people?* New York: Simon & Schuster.

Hanf, K., & Scharpf, F. W. (Eds.). (1978). *Interorganizational policy making.* London: Sage.

Harmon, M. M., & Mayer, R. T. (1986). *Organization theory for public administration.* Boston: Little, Brown.

Herman, S. M., & Korenich, M. (1986). *Authentic management: A gestalt orientation to organizations and their development.* Reading, MA: Addison-Wesley.

Hunter, J. D. (1991). *Culture wars.* New York: Basic Books.

Interview with Amitai Etzioni. (1992, April 23). *USA Today,* p. 13A.

Kettl, D. F. (1993). *Public governance and private markets.* Washington, DC: Brookings Institution.

Lowi, T. J. (1993). Legitimizing public administration: A disturbed dissent. *Public Administration Review, 53*(3), 261-264.

Luke, J. S. (1992). Managing interconnectedness: The new challenge for public administration. In M. T. Bailey & R. T. Mayer (Eds.), *Public management in an interconnected world* (pp. 15-32). New York: Greenwood.

Marshall, G. S., & White, O. F. (1990). The Blacksburg Manifesto and the postmodern debate. *American Review of Public Administration, 20,* 61-76.

Milward, H. B. (1994). [Book review of *Nonprofit contracting and the hollow state.*] *Public Administration Review, 54*(1), 73-77.

Moe, R. C. (1994). The reinventing government exercise: Misinterpreting the problem, misjudging the consequences. *Public Administration Review, 54*(2), 111-122.

Morgan, G. (1986). *Images of organization.* Beverly Hills, CA: Sage.

National Association of Schools of Public Affairs and Administration. (1993). *NASPAA's task in encouraging reform in state and local governments.* Washington, DC: Author.

Office of the Vice President, National Performance Review. (1993). *From red tape to results: Creating a government that works better and costs less* (Report of the National Performance Review). Washington, DC: Government Printing Office.

Osborne, D., & Gaebler, T. (1992). *Reinventing government.* Reading, MA: Addison-Wesley.

Perrow, C. (1986). *Complex organizations.* New York: Random House.

Rohr, J. A. (1990). The constitutional case for public administration. In G. L. Wamsley, R. N. Bacher, C. T. Goodsell, P. S. Kronenberg, J. A. Rohr, C. M. Stivers, O. F. White, & J. F. Wolf, *Refounding public administration* (pp. 52-95). Newbury Park, CA: Sage.

Schlesinger, A. M., Jr. (1991). *The disuniting of America.* Knoxville, TN: Whittle.

Schmidt, M. R. (1992, March). *Alternative kinds of knowledge and why they are ignored.* Paper presented at the PA Theory Network Conference, Chicago.

Sparrow, E. S., & Stewart, M. G. (1994). *Downsizing, reorganization, and potential effects on the U.S. Fish and Wildlife Service: A case study.* Unpublished manuscript, Graduate Program in Public Administration, University of Memphis.

Staff. (1993, March 29). What really pollutes? Study of refinery proves an eye-opener. *Wall Street Journal,* p. A1.

Thomas, R. R., Jr. (1990, March-April). From affirmative action to affirming diversity. *Harvard Business Review,* pp. 107-117.

Tong, R. (1986). *Ethics in policy analysis.* Englewood Cliffs, NJ: Prentice Hall.

Ventriss, C. (1987). Two critical issues of American public administration. *Administration & Society, 19*(1), 25-47.

Wamsley, G. L. (1990). The agency perspective: Public administrators as agential leaders. In G. L. Wamsley, R. N. Bacher, C. T. Goodsell, P. S. Kronenberg, J. A. Rohr, C. M. Stivers, O. F. White, & J. F. Wolf, *Refounding public administration* (pp. 114-162). Newbury Park, CA: Sage.

Wamsley, G. L., & Zald, M. N. (1973). *The political economy of public organizations.* Lexington, MA: Lexington Books.

Webber, A. M. (1991, May-June). Crime and management: An interview with New York City police commissioner Lee P. Brown. *Harvard Business Review,* pp. 111-126.

Weick, K. E. (1979). *The social psychology of organizing.* Reading, MA: Addison-Wesley.

Winter, W. F. (1993). *Hard truths/tough choices: An agenda for state and local reform* (First Report of the National Commission on the State and Local Public Service). Albany: SUNY, Nelson A. Rockefeller Institute of Government.

7

Postmodernism, Public Administration, and the Public Interest

O. C. MCSWITE
Virginia Polytechnic Institute and State University
George Washington University

Declaring a condition of crisis has become one of the more venerable intellectual traditions, if not clichés, of both theoretical and practical writing in the field of public administration in the United States. As is the case with all clichés, which gain their popularity usually because they offer genuine insight, this tendency in public administration is more than simply a matter of rhetorical style. The overriding crisis in the field of public administration is hardly new; it has persisted since the founding of the field and, given its lack of resolution, has become increasingly significant to the question of public administration's continuing success both as a professional practice and as an intellectual-academic endeavor (Rosenbloom, 1993). The source of the crisis resides in the field's conception of its very identity and role: *Public administration has never adequately come to grips with the problem of finding a legitimate place for itself in the American scheme of democratic government.* Indeed the issue of legitimacy has generally been avoided, initially by early practitioners and scholars who chose to define the founding myth in such a way as to eliminate the question itself and subsequently by generations of public administrators who have ignored the issue's significance as a means of placating both critics and clients. The major exception to this pattern has been the "Blacksburg Manifesto" and the writings that have flowed from it

(Wamsley et al., 1990). We wish to place our chapter within the tradition of the legitimacy literature of public administration and the Blacksburg response to it. Our specific purpose here is to offer a way of thinking about the overarching symbol of the field—the idea and ideal of the public interest— that we hope will mark a step forward in resolving the crisis of legitimacy that has plagued the discourse on the meaning of public administration in American government.

The theory of the public interest has served paradoxically as both the strongest and the weakest point in public administration's attack on the problem of finding a place for itself in democratic governance. It is an idea of great appeal and rhetorical power that has traditionally been the cornerstone of the administrative enterprise, functioning as a symbolic litmus test for appropriate action. At the same time, however, the very strength of the public interest as a legitimating symbol has proven to be a weakness as a defensible justification for action. The public interest became vulnerable to what was seen as the rigorous analytical scrutiny of public administration critics in the late 1960s, and its advocates were unable to mount an effective response (Schubert, 1960; White & McSwain, 1990). Hence, for at least two decades, this supremely important symbol and theoretical anchor point has not been available to either the academics or the practitioners of the field.

Our argument begins with locating the issue of the public interest within the social and intellectual deterioration that many see the United States undergoing at present. This phase of supposed deterioration to which we refer has been named *postmodernism* (the name seems to be generally accepted, so it is probably appropriate). We see this condition both as a set of broadly interrelated social phenomena and as a radically different condition of mind, that is, it is more than simply a change in paradigm. From our vantage point as strong advocates of a positive role for governance in society, the conditions of postmodernism create an opportunity for revitalizing the idea of the public interest and for defining clearly a role for public administration in the structure and process of American governance.

We say this with not a little ambivalence, in that many of the social conditions that characterize postmodernism grate acutely on our humanistic sensibilities. At the same time, however, we see in postmodernism the possibility for escaping the theoretical trap in which the field of public administration has found itself, we believe, since its founding at the beginning of the 20th century. It is fortuitous that such possibilities are arising now, in that there is more at stake at the end of the 20th century in solving this issue than there ever has been before.

As we read the future, the developed world (and inevitably, and in some respects more profoundly, the *developing* world) is moving rapidly to a fork in the road. One route leads to major positive changes in both social and political life. These changes would entail creating new communities of *meaning* (not values) around public agencies, meanings that would keep agencies turned to purposes emerging from and grounded in the public interest. The other route leads to a different future, a future that is already partly upon us, coming about in small, barely noticeable increments. This is technicism, a condition that when fully realized will eliminate human purpose as a guide to social action. In this future, agencies, lacking a sense of direction from any social base, will have available to them only the technical direction of a political process disconnected from human relationship. As is already happening, when social problems escalate to the point where they seem out of control, political pressure builds for the implementation of technical, certain, efficient, mechanical, brute force solutions. The political process of *fin de siècle* America, for example, already has little capacity for sensitivity or nuance. Increasingly as the process of pluralist, interest-based politics directs agencies to establish technical controls, they will do so. Eventually, the systems of stable control that are established, because their rationale has now been defined as the essence of necessity itself—that is, the survival of the social system—will become pervasive, eliminating even the reduced idea of politics that remains, finally operating apart from human agency or the possibility for it. To us, visions such as that contained in the recently voguish book *Reinventing Government* (Osborne & Gaebler, 1992) are chillingly congruent with this dire portent, as such thinking offers the suggestion of cutting agencies loose to respond to the public as customer. There seems to be no sensitivity here to what commercialism has taught us about how malleable and weak people are when confined to the role of customer. A public administration cast from such a mold in our view combines the worst evils of the laissez-faire corporate and the authoritarian state (Osborne & Gaebler, 1992).

We place our hope for finding the first path in a vision that sees the agency within a broader context of governance, of stable institutions with authoritative mandates. Such an agency would serve *citizens* who would control the agency by surrounding it with a process of dialogue that would yield a *common sense,* a community of meaning and discourse. A living and vital idea of the public interest is essential to this vision, thus our project of revitalizing it has the urgency of necessity.

It is our project here to explore the particular opportunities that the current social and intellectual conditions of postmodernism offer us for such a revitalization of the public interest and hence for a reconsideration of, or at least a contribution to, the legitimacy debate in public administration. As we noted above, these issues have important contemporary social consequences because we see public agencies as potentially central to future social development.

Before moving into our consideration of postmodernism, we would like to sketch briefly the history of the public interest under modernism. We hope to indicate that modernism and its intellectual devices are failing across a broad front to sustain a meaningful social process. We see the source of this problem to be that as modernism has reached the limits of its power to sustain meaning it has turned on itself. In this section we wish to consider directly the Blacksburg response to the modernist characterization of the public interest and to set the stage for moving beyond what we see to be the ultimate limitation of this and any line of discourse that remains constrained by modernism.

Next we want to discuss postmodernism in two related aspects—as a set of social conditions and as an intellectual movement. Our idea in doing this is to indicate how postmodernism is arising as a result of the failure of modernism and how, consequently, it affords a response to the intellectual crisis of modernity. We also offer a third set of comments in this section, endeavoring to place postmodernism in perspective and render it somewhat less esoteric as we explore its connections to the singularly American philosophy of pragmatism.

Finally, we take up directly the opportunities for newly appreciating the public interest under conditions of postmodernism. We attempt to respond to the negative sentiment surrounding postmodernism and, using its deconstructive epistemology, find the pernicious bias of gender that has rendered the idea of the public interest impotent as a guiding symbol within modernism. It is in letting go of the traditional modernist and masculine project that we find a potential for seeing the public interest anew.

▬ The Idea of the Public Interest Within the Perspective of Modernism

The concept of the public interest has a long and venerable history in the fields of public administration and political science. The debate over what it means and how it is found in specific circumstances of administrative action has entailed the fundamental question of how to achieve responsible governance itself. Though this debate has a rich history, our present interest is in where the debate stands now and how can it be moved forward.

In our view, the latest and best statement on the question of the public interest was made by Charles Goodsell in the widely noticed, multiauthored book, *Refounding Public Administration* (Wamsley et al., 1990). An entire chapter, written by Goodsell, is devoted to the task of revitalizing the concept of the public interest as a workable guide for practicing administrators. In his essay, Goodsell first reviews the history of the idea, concluding that it has been in a state of virtual eclipse since the publication of Glendon Schubert's (1960) critique of it in his book, *The Public Interest.* Schubert found in his analysis three major schools of public interest thought: rationalism, idealism, and realism. Rationalism holds that the public interest is defined through a form of reasoned political discourse in the legislative process; idealism sees it as a transcendent moral good discovered by the mind-work of a modern-day approximation of Platonic philosopher kings; realists see the public interest as the result of the interplay of power-wielding interest groups in the policy-making process. Schubert's unqualified conclusion is that none of these schools of thought produces a viable public interest theory and that those interested in effective government should abandon the whole project of philosophizing about this hopelessly vacuous idea and devote their efforts instead to "nurturing concepts that offer greater promise of becoming useful tools in the scientific study of political responsibility" (Schubert, 1960, p. 244). Goodsell is not alone in concluding that Schubert's critical analysis of the idea of the public interest rather thoroughly crippled its credibility in the dialogue of public administration and policy. Although it is problematic to assign unitary causality to anything, it is worth noting that the publication of Schubert's book was concomitant with the nearly complete disappearance of the idea of the public interest in scholarly and practitioner arenas.

What this rather striking evaporation of the concept seems to teach us is how profoundly the theory of the public interest was grounded in and given credibility by a distinctive set of social-existential underpinnings. The acceptance and use of the idea of a public interest was made possible by a certain ethos that began to take hold in the United States probably at about the same time that public administration began to emerge as the main venue for governance, the period at the end of the 19th century and the early part of the 20th century. During this period the nation went through enormous social, cultural, and political changes. These changes, which produced the Populist and subsequently the Progressive movements, constituted a period of crisis for America. The 19th-century worldview disintegrated; the population underwent a quantum leap in diversification as a result of immigration; and democratic politics, for all intents and purposes, failed. The American populace, whose central value has always been stability, was eager to accept the new reform proposals of Progressivism for good government through collaborative, scientifically informed administration. They were equally receptive to the metaphysical idea that there was a basis of common interest for the multiple groups in society and that this interest could serve as a moral guiding light for a new system of administrative governance. Faith in the symbol of the public interest was strengthened as its role became all the more important in coping with the bewildering complexity of government programs required to respond to the depressions of the 1930s and World War II. The idea that people share a common stake in their collective weal makes most sense, it would seem, under conditions such as depression and war.

After the war, circumstances became quite the opposite. In mobilizing to fight the war, America had reached its highest degree of systemization. This fact, coupled with the success of the war effort and the resultant burgeoning of the economy, produced a new, more rationalist mood. As one systems theorist puts it in describing the work of Talcott Parsons, a social systems theorist whose work grew in influence through the postwar period and reached its zenith in the social sciences in the mid-1960s,

> Parsons' work represents an early "optimistic" phase of systemic modernism, reflecting the managed resurgence of capitalist economies after the Second World War and their stabilization [*sic*] using, particularly, the mechanism of the modern welfare state. . . . In this, instrumental reason is completely triumphant as everything is subject to the rational requirements of the societal system. It is the system which is the vanguard of history and progress, as it follows its own logic to increase "performativity" (in terms of input-output measures) and handle environmental uncertainty. Individual hopes and aspirations simply respond to the system's needs and consensus is engineered to improve the system's functioning. Even internal dissension, strikes, and conflict represent the system readjusting to increase its viability and effectiveness. (Black, 1961, p. 14)

Within this overall context, it is easy to see how the idea of the public interest came to seem useless and unnecessary. The image of life that obtained was one of rationally motivated individuals maximizing their well-being according to their own personal calculus within an increasingly structured and rationally operated social system. There is little grounding in such an image for an idea that appeals to metaphysical symbols like the "collective weal" and the "general good" for its sense of meaning. What makes more sense is to respond to Schubert's (1960) call for scientifically studying the dynamics of social processes like politics so that they can be adjusted, improved, and made more predictable by the engineering-like methods that result.

In our view, contemporary social conditions, like those at the turn of the 20th century, have once more become compatible with the idea of the public interest. It is the emergence of these conditions that perhaps accounts for the renewed attention given to the task of defining the term. Goodsell goes about his work of rejuvenating the concept by seeking contemporary conceptual grounding for the symbol, specifically in the work of the philosopher, John Searles. Somewhat in the vein of Kant's reasoning in deriving "categorical imperatives" by determining the minimal, logically necessary rules that must be in place if stable social order is to exist, Goodsell reads Searles as arguing that any term that people use necessarily indicates a commitment to a set of underlying values to which the term (again, necessarily) refers. Drawing from Searles, Goodsell posits that the presence of a term like *the public interest* in public discourse indicates that administrators, citizens, and politicians are committing themselves to at least six "constitutive rules" or values that the term reinforces. These rules or values together constitute an operational definition of the term "public interest" and reveal how the term structures, limits, and thereby gives guidance to the work of those involved in the process of governance.

Goodsell's essay is an important adjunct to the argument made by Gary Wamsley in the *Refounding* volume, which is in many ways the keystone of the "Blacksburg Manifesto" perspective (Wamsley, 1990). Wamsley describes what he terms an "agency perspective," an image of the public administrative agency as the hub of a community of dialogue that can produce legitimate and workable policies and implementation strategies. Critical to the successful creation of this dialogue is "agential leadership," a form of administrative leadership that is primarily oriented toward creating and guiding policy dialogue. These agential leaders are different from traditional administrative leaders because they are *normatively grounded,* which is to say, guided and even controlled by values that are generally shared because they reflect a common interest. The presence of this value framework and its embodiment in the agential leader forms a context for policy dialogue that—it is prom- ised—will render that dialogue *nonideological.* This means that the dialogue will be able to transcend the expressions of specific interests that will arise and produce a neutral synthesis of them, a synthesis that reflects the genuine common interest of all the parties touched by the policy or the line of administrative action. In this context, it is clear how essential is something like Goodsell's idea of the public interest, as a symbol that automatically invokes a set of guiding values just through its use in discourse, to the argument Wamsley wants to make. In order to depict the agential leader as the legitimate guide of the policy/administrative dialogue, Wamsley must show this leader to be bound by a set of generally agreed-upon values. Goodsell's understanding of the public interest supports this idea. Simply by using the term *public interest,* the agential leader comes under the control of the set of binding, commonly acceptable values that are necessarily evoked by the term itself.

The rhetorical power of Wamsley's (1990) essay is considerable, and it is nicely complemented by Goodsell's (1990) tightly constructed definition of the public interest. Nonetheless, the operational conceptualization of the public interest that the agential perspective produces must, in the end, be judged as neotraditional and unsatisfactory. The agential perspective ultimately amounts to the same exhortation to "Be Good!" that Schubert (1960) found in the school of public interest thought he dubbed idealist. The implicit presumption that the idealist position must make to justify its central premise that values can guide or control the administrator is: *Values can carry meanings that will be clear and unambiguous to all the parties that wish to apply them and in all the possible situations that they will encounter.* Testimony that this premise is not convincing can be found not only in philosophy, but in the skepticism that the average citizen manifests when exhorted by those in positions of power to "Trust us, we're professionals who have your interests at heart, and are just trying to do a good job, and work on the basis of an ethical code," and so on. Long and well-documented experience with all types of professions and leaders has disabused even the most naive of the belief that they can rely on such assurances.

Nonetheless, in both the rarefied circles of professional philosophy as well as in society generally, a search for workable, that is, clear, definite, unambiguous, controlling, values continues. This search is expressed in the resurgence of interest in ethics and in the continuing issuance of codes of ethics for professional groups, occupational categories, and others. Curiously, modern society embraces an obvious and widely acknowledged contradiction: There are or can be unambiguous values that are applicable to all contexts, and it is impossible ever to find or to frame value statements that can function in this fashion. When we reflect further, however, we begin to see the reason why this contradiction is so powerful and why we continue to operate our institutions by it. The contradiction works as a powerful conservative force, the effect of which is to provide a stable, neutral, reasonable institutional structure within which social dynamics can occur without causing serious disruption. The inexorable forces of social change can thus be given vent without their creating the disasters that they have been known to create in situations lacking such stable institutional containers.

This is accomplished fairly simply. Once a firm belief in operative ethical values has been instilled, experience will quickly demonstrate that value systems do not operate unambiguously even within themselves, that is, ethical codes contradict themselves in application. It is also obvious that various codes cannot be integrated under some broader umbrella principle(s) that render them consistent. One person's ethical act is another's evil deed. Hence, the need for arbiters of ethical codes arises, and the tension generated by the contradiction creates a disposition to defer to these arbiters. The institutionalization of such a system of reasoned arbitration—as for example in the establishment of a system of law courts—is, of course, not a completely satisfactory answer to the problem the contradiction creates, in that arbiters present society with the same problem of control that was the impetus for initially setting up the ethical codes. However, such systems have worked, for the most part, especially in the United States. Though we may be suspicious of the ability of our Supreme Court Justices to be nonpolitical and neutral in their adjudication of constitutional law cases, we have, nonetheless, accepted them. The same could also be said for arbiters in our other institutions.

However, such acceptance remains contingent on the continuance of a general embracing of the contradiction of ethics. As soon as society begins to refuse to continue to hold and struggle with this contradiction, the disposition to accept the illusion that conflict can be resolved through fair arbitration will begin to evaporate. What might bring about a refusal of the contradiction? In our view such a refusal has begun. This period of incipient refusal is being called postmodernism, and it has arisen because the underlying social conditions that have supported acceptance of the contradiction have changed. As long as modernism seemed to work, to be producing what it promised, it had legitimacy even though it appeared to be grounded in ambiguity and contradiction. What seems to be happening now, however, is that modernism, especially in the form of the aspirations of the liberal welfare state grounded in advanced capitalism, is grinding to a halt and, more importantly, seems to have given up its own project.

The legitimacy of modernization was dependent upon the acknowledgment of an unspecified Good (with a capital G) toward which modern society was struggling to move. That was to be attained through discovery and application of an unspecified Truth (with a capital T). Because we do not seem to be getting there (after great effort and the expenditure of much treasure), and in addition because many appear to be giving up on trying to get there at all, questions are being raised generally about the arbiters who hold the privileged positions through which society, at least in principle, was to be guided toward this promised end state.

The condition of failing and/or giving up on the modernist project of building a way of social life that reflects the Good can serve as an operational definition of the crisis of representation that has given postmodernism its central reference point. Modernism's failure to produce the metaphoric "heavenly city," the city that represents heaven on earth, has brought its central principle, the principle of representation, into fundamental question. Indeed, representation seems to have turned in upon itself. Facts constantly change, shift, mutate rather than move toward a central focus. Art produces simulacra rather than new, more evolved images of the divine in the human spirit. Values proliferate into sectarian diversity rather than coalescing into a generally held sense of the common weal. It is no surprise that writers like Derrida have arisen concomitantly with such social conditions, that books are becoming "hypertexts," and that art is constituting the viewing subject as a "floating point" or "punctum"—the sort of subject that is comfortable spending long hours viewing the constantly shifting surfaces presented on MTV.

It is no surprise either that representatives of modernism, responding to these developments, are beginning to scream out somewhat hysterically that the central premise of modernism—that there are fixed scientific truths and undeniable moral values, and that we can represent these—is TRUE (McCoullough, 1991). The great irony of the present is that it appears we need the idea of a truly public interest more than at any time in the past, but the intellectual ethos within which such an idea must be produced seems more incompatible, if not hostile, to such a notion than ever.

We, of course, want to challenge this conclusion and argue that the circumstances of postmodernism, though seemingly hostile to the idea of the public interest, actually afford a rich opportunity for its revitalization. In fact, that opportunity has existed for some time in our history in the works of the American pragmatists and only now, with the failure of the modernist project and the resulting conditions of postmodernism, has its true potential to reinvigorate the public interest become visible. In order to explore this, we turn now to a more detailed discussion of postmodernism as a set of social conditions and then as an intellectual movement, closing the following section with a discussion of pragmatism.

▬ Postmodernism Characterized

Describing postmodernism as a pattern of social life is relevant to our purpose in this chapter, but it does not serve our objectives directly enough to warrant a full-scale treatment. In general, all we want to describe is the epistemic logic of postmodern social life. The beginning place for such a description must be the *rejection of the possibility of representation.* The denial that representations actually represent phenomena that exist objectively apart from the system of representation is the paradigmatic crux of postmodernism's opposition to modernism. The hallmark of modernism as an historical episode is its commitment to progress. Progress as an image, in turn, is grounded in the faith that human consciousness can produce valid, that is, to some extent *accurate,* descriptions of the Good and from these can create designs for social life that to one degree or another approximate utopia or move us toward it. This logic entails a prior belief in the possibility that consciousness can or has the potential to apprehend and represent the divine or the utopian. Such large faith in itself is what modern consciousness inherits as a child of the Enlightenment.

The postmodern sense of social life begins with the failure or the rejection of this modernist faith. The designs for life that are emerging from postmodernism communicate that progress is over. Contemporary cities are fascinating instances of this. Postmodern urban architecture is breaking cities into separate, closed environments that themselves, even in their self-containment, confuse and disorient the modern sense of space as coherent pattern. This architecture rejects the modern sense of urban life as a venue for civic possibility, where the city's design attempted to bring urban dwellers together into common, shared experiences, the intention of which was to produce coherent contexts for social and political conversation that could regulate social life and inform the further evolution of the city.

What this amounts to is that cities are losing their *meaning* as the locus of civilization. The message signified by urban and suburban areas that are simply collections of self-contained spaces is that civilized, public life, the life of citizens in common relation and discourse, exists only in appearance, at the surface, and is no longer real. It is this characteristic that is probably most widely associated with postmodernism, that signification has moved to the surface such that social process has become little more than an interplay of shifting images. The traditional, modern, sense of meaning, of a real connection between the realm of signification and the inner life of the person, is evaporating. The artifacts of the city make no pretense toward symbolic power; they simply send a message: Stay in your place and keep to your business (Ritzer, 1993).

Emblematic of the movement of meanings to the surface is what has happened to commercial process, or more specifically, its main signifier, money. Money has undergone a transformation from *being* valuable (the gold coin), to various degrees of representing value (not gold itself, backed by gold, then, not backed by gold but floating and standing for the viability and the economic vitality of the issuing nation state, so that it truly becomes "paper" money). In the present situation, money is increasingly being transferred through electronic media. It has become simply an electronic blip on a computer screen, more and more frequently not even backed by paper money (Rotman, 1987).

The same pattern is found in the media, the central venue of postmodern culture. MTV provides such a cogent example of how meaning has been reduced to the interplay of surfaces that it seems redundant to do more than mention it. That the music video style has penetrated to the level of conscious-ness itself is given evidence in the widespread practice of "channel flipping" or "surfing." This alteration of consciousness has become institutionalized in channels that transmit four stations at once on a split screen, with the sound rotating from one to the other every few seconds. Watching such channels for protracted periods is a good first step toward developing a postmodern consciousness. (The next step is to practice channel flipping up to the point where one can routinely flip away from climactic scenes without feeling regret or vestigial curiosity!)

What such changes mark is *the renunciation of narrative as the locus of meaning*. The coherence, connectedness, linearity, and closure of a story-like explanation no longer matter. As one postmodern television critic put it when reviewing a new dramatic series: "The plot ultimately makes no difference, these things just go on and on until they're over." As, the postmodernist would say, this is the case with life itself: It just goes on and on until it's over. The idea that life must "make sense," that is, be "the story of one's life," is only a limiting construction. The rejection of narrative has implications that go beyond art, of course. Science is seen by many as the religion of modernism; science is also a form of narrative. It is a certain kind of story we tell each other. In a postmodern world, then, science is only a narrative, and explanation loses its appeal as the central form of meaning. Nothing seems to be changing faster or more pervasively than facts and the understanding generated from them. The postmodern mind says, "What counts is what is; who cares (and who knows) why?"

What has replaced narrative as the basis for meaning in the postmodern condition is consumption, specifically consumption of surfaces. Any con-sumption that takes place outside a narrative context is surface or superficial consumption, consumption for its own sake. Without narrative to provide the context, there is no identity in the modern sense. Without an identity, the human subject becomes a transient consumer of surfaces, of "looks." Rules, like etiquette, are both unnecessary and are impediments. Because a look is everything, virtually nothing about personal appearance goes unattended, but all possibilities for generating new looks are open. Because all narratives are possible, no narrative carries particularly compelling meaning.

Other narratives of modern identity—personality, career, relationship, even gender—are part of the open-ended, unspecified metaphor of personal development. Through the venue of this infinitely relative metaphor, one can explore one's own personal surfaces. In the case of gender, for example, for men, one can develop in an androgynous, sensitive male direction or seek masculine power in a Robert Bly "wild man" workshop (Bly, 1990). One can round out one's personality type, strategically change one's career identity, alter one's lifestyle, and more; these are endlessly fluid surfaces. Under the metaphor of personal development, one's self becomes a product, a presentation of surfaces intended to please both the possessor and others. The narrative of self thus becomes trivialized, as relative as all other narratives. The humanist vision of what a human being is, what the self is, becomes only one in a cacophony of stories.

In such a context politics tends to become a clash of trivialized narratives. Hence the Newt Gingrich "family values" narrative is pitted against the supposed Hillary Clinton female "career development" narrative. These narratives are trivial in the sense that they do not provide meaningful explanations of the difficult realities of actual family life or of the complexities of womanhood under postmodern conditions. But in a postmodern world such trivialization is acceptable—in fact, it is the point. Narrative reduced to the sound bite creates the possibility of manipulation of opinion through the media, and such manipulation is all that is required in order to move public opinion. Under modern conditions, according to traditional political science research, the media were filtered significantly through stable primary group relationships such as families, unions, communities, and the like, and superficial manipulation was not efficacious. This is no longer so, as a larger and larger sector of the voting population has become unattached and unconnected in any traditional sense and carries an allegiance that simply floats from one news event to the next and aligns with people and opinions according to the superficialities of the moment.

We hope that these few remarks convey a sense of the deeply pervasive and to us troubling nature of the postmodern social condition. Much more could be said by way of describing it, but as we noted above it is only to our purpose here that we suggest in outline the social crisis that is arising as modernism fails. It is the overall failure of modernism to sustain the process of generating meaning that has produced postmodernism. This failure underscores the importance of revitalizing the idea of the public interest as a grounding for a legitimate public administration. Without some such grounding, the endless shifting surfaces of meaning will render public administration incapable of anything other than becoming the handmaid of technicism. As a way of approaching this revitalization, we will now move on to discuss the development of a postmodern sensibility in the world of intellectual discourse, using a brief introduction to several relevant concepts in the work of Jacques Derrida (1976, 1978). We see the intellectual and the social as connected through a mutually operative causality. There appears little possibility for directly mitigating the ravages of postmodernism in the social arena; however, it seems to us—paradoxically perhaps—that postmodernism's intellectual aspect offers an answer to its social consequences.

There are currently a number of well done general descriptions of the academic-intellectual literature of postmodernism available. One of the best is Pauline Marie Rosenau's (1992) recent book, *Post-Modernism and the Social Sciences,* which can be described as a text that documents the full range and variety of the movement. It is not our intention here to survey or even present an overview of the widely ranging intellectual currents that are considered postmodernist; the scope and depth of Rosenau's work is testimony to the impossibility of such a task in a chapter. We want only to sketch out the few aspects of the postmodern perspective that are required for our discussion of the public interest. In fact, we intend only to introduce aspects of the postmodern theories of one of its more prominent writers, Jacques Derrida (1976, 1978; Kamuf, 1991).

We begin with the same issue with which we began our sketch of postmodern social conditions, the rejection of the possibility of representation. The postmodern critique of traditional philosophical discourse, identified typically as "the Western civilization canon," is aimed at exposing what it sees to be the chief and insupportable pretense of this tradition: the axiomatic assumption that its discourse mirrors or re-presents a reality from which the discourse stands apart. By grounding itself in this axiom, discourse inflates itself to something more than it is. It is no longer simply discourse, but carries the authority of the objective intermediary, an authority that is, of course, dependent upon the metaphysic of representation.

In denying that discourses and the texts they produce are able to represent anything outside themselves, postmodernism is asserting that texts can only be *self-referential.* That is, the meanings they create are the products solely of the rhetorical manipulations contained in the text. The summary impact of this critique is that texts are, from the point of view of modernism, rendered relative. They no longer can be seen to carry stable or consistent meaning and can even be taken away from the author by the claim of equal authority for the various responses that the text's rhetorical manipulations can evoke in readers. When the axiom of representation is denied, meaning in the modern sense of the term quickly evaporates.

In a certain general sense, then, postmodernism is mainly a way of reading, not just linguistic texts, but the text of lived experience itself. This way of reading requires that the reader refuse to go along with the romantic manipulations of the text. T. S. Eliot, representing reading in the modernist mode, saw it as a process of submitting to a text, of allowing oneself to be seduced by it, and then recovering from the seduction by gaining, through post hoc reflection, some perspective on it. The postmodern reader refuses the seductive moves of the text and may even use these as the basis for a playful refusal of it (Scholes, 1989).

The postmodern approach to the text might be characterized as an exposé "of the word." As such it is clear that it has strong philosophical grounding in the work of Nietzsche and Heidegger. From Nietzsche, postmodernism inherited the idea of denying to discourse the existence of a superordinate term as an anchor with which it can ground its rhetorical manipulations. Grounding rhetoric in a privileged term allows the transformation of meanings within a text into trans-textual meanings, meanings that can then be credibly carried beyond any specific text. From Heidegger, postmodernism was given precedent for its sense of the inadequacy of the word, the idea that words are incapable of carrying the freight of meaning that is demanded of them by the text.

Perhaps the clearest way of seeing just how this dual heritage of postmodernism is expressed, is through Derrida's "deconstruction" approach to the text. Central to Derrida's philosophy is the starting premise of Saussurean linguistics, namely that meaning in language is *synchronic,* or produced by the system of oppositions that define its constituent words. That is, we know the meaning of a word by knowing other words that are different from it, which is to say that other words tell us the meaning of a given word by telling us what it is not. This idea affronts the commonsense view of language, which sees words as gaining their meanings from the objects or concepts to which they refer. Viewing language in a synchronic way, systematically, reveals that words as signifiers exist on an infinitely sliding scale of meanings. A word actually signifies only another word, the signified, which, at the same time, is the signifier of yet another word, in a kind of infinite process of interlocking, interdependent meaning generation. Simply: Words mean other words that mean other words, and so on, infinitely. The only way to stop this infinite sliding of meaning is to insert into the system a signifier that is regarded as standing outside the system. This signifier is necessarily, by its place and role in the system, put into a superordinate position, but one that can be grounded only metaphysically. The name of this signifier changes through history (God, Scientific Truth, The Good, The Self, etc.). It can be referred to and maintained in its metaphysical place both by calling its name or by invoking its opposite (The Devil, Superstition, Hitler, etc.). What Derrida reveals (1976, 1978), or better, exposes, through his way of reading is the total dependency of the text on the existence of this superordinate signifier and at the same time, the total dependency of the superordinate signifier on the text. The one maintains the other, and, because they both reside in the same system, the text the system produces can be said to be purely (and merely, from a critical standpoint) *self-referential.*

Derrida's deconstructive reading is the ultimate relativization of the text and, thereby, of all meaning in the modern sense. It reduces the text to discourse, to exchanges between text producers. Its implications, from a modern perspective, are radical and profound. In denying the superordinate signifier a privileged place, meaning is unhinged, unanchored. Texts can be read as meaning anything, including and especially the opposite of what the author intends. The only limit is the playful cleverness of the reader. Authors lose their privileged place (i.e., as writing from the domain of the superordinate signifier), and readers are given equal rights with authors to say what the text means.

The reaction to deconstructionism as the salient or at least the most visible aspect of postmodernism has been intense. The amount of vitriol that the reaction to deconstruction has produced is so great that it seems to have configured, at the subtextual level, an issue of religious dimensions, perhaps even pan-religious dimensions. The defenders of modernism sometimes shriek that deconstruction intends to destroy all possibility for meaning of any sort and to leave humankind in a consuming vortex of relativism. It certainly offers no possibility for religion, its critics say, and gainsays even ethics, opening the door wide to evil itself. Derrida's response to such attacks, in our view, is powerful. He retorts that the most important result of deconstruction is that it eliminates the possibility for authoritarian and totalitarian regimes (Wood, 1987). When can evil do more harm than when it has ensconced itself as an ideology through rhetorical trickery (whether it be through the venue of science or of demagoguery) as legitimate authority in the minds of a people?

The reason that deconstruction has produced such an affront is, of course, that it calls into question the most basic aspect of human identity as it is constituted by the intellectual traditions of Western civilization, specifically the Cartesian self produced by the famous *cogito,* the self that is because it is able to experience itself as *thinking,* as being consciously rational. The modern faith in the metaphysic of representation is hinged to this model of self: The integrity of the representational image must be matched by a perceiving entity of equal integrity. It is the de-centering of this image of subjectivity that deconstruction offers. However, given that our traditional sense of ourselves demands a kind of meaning that deconstruction denies and for which it provides no adequate substitute, the resistance to it is enormous.

Before we return to our primary concern, that is, the public interest in public administration, we want to place the postmodern viewpoint in perspective. Because we intend here to suggest how the idea of the public interest can be better vitalized by reconceptualizing it from the postmodern viewpoint, it is necessary to lend postmodernism more plausibility than is readily available in a context such as the present one, which is predominantly modern. Indeed, within the mind-set of modernity, postmodernism often seems quite bizarre.

To the American mind, which has been formed by traditions grounded in a Constitution designed for the purpose of facilitating economic expansion and commercial activity, the aspect of postmodernism that is most offensive is its rejection of the metaphysic of realism. Hardheaded commercialism is most compatible with what might be characterized as commonsense positivism. This is an epistemology that presupposes that human beings are pain-avoiding, pleasure-seeking physiological entities who are seeking to come to terms successfully with a world of objects, external to them and governed by a hostile, or at least an uncaring, nature. In this context words refer to objects and emotional states only or, at the most, to objects, emotional states, and concepts that can be discretely defined by words. Derrida's reading of Saussure's synchronic theory of language, which depicts words as gaining their meaning from their differences from other words such that, to quote a famous postmodern psychologist, Jacques Lacan (1966/1977), "It is the world of words that creates the world of things" (p. 65), seems completely nonsensical. Brief reflection indicates, however, that both science and philosophy have moved far beyond the naive realism of the object on which common sense is based. Indeed, from the point of view of common sense, Saussure's theory of language seems to require considerably less straining to understand than does understanding the view of physical reality provided by contemporary physics or molecular biology. We venture the speculation that if postmodern philosophy were given the publicity in magazines and PBS television that is given new scientific theories and models, it would quickly become accepted in the way that scientific theories are—as strange (but necessary and therefore acceptable) ways that intellectuals look at the world in order to figure it out and come to terms with it. To a large extent this has already happened. The debate that remains over the postmodern perspective in the United States seems to us to be primarily in universities and to draw its energy from the political circumstances that have arisen in American academia over the eclipse of the so-called Western civilization canon. Otherwise, postmodernism is generally dismissed as irrelevant or viewed as a new and hence inevitably controversial development on the intellectual scene. Our assessment is that postmodernism has become either the central focus of intellectual discourse in many areas or has assumed a place alongside other schools of philosophy as one among a number of legitimate paradigms through which discourse is carried forward.

The distinctive problem that postmodern theory has in becoming sensible at the collective level is that it flies in the face of our conventional understanding of language as a referential code and consciousness as prior to and apart from language. This does not square with Saussure's idea of how language in fact is operating as we use it. At issue specifically is the de-centered model of the human self that is given by the linguistic theory on which the postmodern viewpoint is implicitly or explicitly based. The naive realism of the object that postmodernism denies is the essential experience of the self as individual and as rational agent that is so especially strong in America.

In the intellectual realm, curiously enough, there are actually more theories depicting the self as de-centered than those that show it as centered and rational. We judge that it is, in fact, the dominance of economic rationalism inflicting a prejudice on common sense that accounts for the powerful resistance to the idea of the self as de-centered. When psychology was more in vogue in America, during the late 1960s and the 1970s, and was given more popular publicity, the public became quite comfortable with and accustomed to seeing people and human relationships in the textual, de-centered terms of psychological models like Berne's (1964, 1976) transactional analysis and Perls's (Perls, Hefferline, & Goodman, 1951) gestalt theories. Further, we see no reason to abandon the idea of an intrinsic self as a necessary implication of postmodern theory. We would even go so far as to say that at some generic level a postmodern theory of subjectivity can be reconciled with Carl Jung, the psychological theorist perhaps most associated with the idea of a humanistic self. In our view this objection to postmodernism on the point that it denies the human self means only that a really rather narrow concept of the self as ego-centered, rational, and individualistic is denied. Viewed in this light, postmodernism is no different in its critique of the reigning model of subjectivity than are traditional humanistic theories like Jung's.

Perhaps the viewpoint from which postmodernism is rendered most plausible, however, is that of our own common experience. The world as we currently know it and live in it *is* the world of the de-centered self of surfaces, a world in which human activity is marked by an implicit, undiscussed sense of lack, a continuing feeling of deficit that energizes a relentless desire and consequent fruitless pursuit of fulfillment that people recognize as the meaning of their lives. It is a world that emphasizes a sense of scarcity, threat, struggle (against nature, ultimately) and makes this emphasis the core of its cultures.

No matter how plausible the postmodern viewpoint might become, however, what is its relevance to public administration? In our view, postmodernism is opening the door for the reentry of American pragmatism into the discourse of public administration. This door could probably not be opened by any means less radical than an approach like postmodernism. Pragmatism was the original foundation of American public administration, but it was quickly eclipsed by rationalism, the exemplar statement of which is the work of Herbert Simon (1947). In our opinion this was the gravest conceptual error the field of public administration has made. Postmodernism provides the pry bar for cracking the hermetic enclosure that rationalism has constructed around itself and that has made it appear so resistant to effective critique in both the academic and the popular mind. It may seem nothing less than bizarre to link a turn of past-century American philosophy with a contemporary turn of the present-century philosophy that is ostensibly French, but there are such linkages. In the linguistic/semiotic aspect of postmodernism, there is a tie back to the work of Charles Sanders Peirce (Peirce, Hartshorne, & Weiss, 1931). Postmodernism's theory of subjectivity and the image of social process that derives from it are quite congruent with the theories of Mary Parker Follett (1965, 1973) and George Herbert Mead (Scheffler, 1974). We mention these only as rather obvious examples. There are many more such linkages that a fully elaborated analysis would reveal. Richard Rorty (1979, 1982, 1989) and Richard Bernstein (1991), both widely read contemporary philosophers, have described the explicit connections that they see between the pragmatists and the postmodern viewpoint. We see the emergence of postmodern theory as an opportunity to begin reformulating the approaches that public administration is making (mostly ineffectively) to its central theoretical issues and to the problems of practice that these conceptual difficulties create and mark. The one such reformulation we want to address next is the idea of the public interest as a conceptual guidepost for the working administrator.

The Idea of the Public Interest Within the Perspective of Postmodernism

From the point of view of the modernist perspective, there seems to be little hope for a serious reconsideration of the idea of the public interest. Further, at first glance, the social and intellectual conditions of postmodernism also seem to deny the possibility of any such reconsideration. We agree that within the modernist mind-set the public interest is a hollow concept. But we strongly disagree with the apparently pessimistic assessment of postmodernism and argue that there is just as much potential for renewing the idea of the public interest within current postmodern conditions as there is threat to it.

What Derrida's (1976, 1978) work shows is that the crisis of modernism, the failure of the idea of representation, is in its essence located in the dynamics of language. As we described earlier, the central strategy of Derrida's deconstructionism is to refuse the pretense that words are sufficient to meaning apart from their linguistic context. At the first level of this refusal, Derrida, following Heidegger, puts words "under erasure." He discloses that words in a text must, in fact, depend on implicit, undisclosed references to other words if they are to create any sense of meaning. Ultimately, however, the refusal of the deconstructive reader is grounded in a denial of the "first" word, the primary word or the *superordinate term* on which the text, and indeed language itself, depends if it is to generate meaning. As we explained earlier, this superordinate term must remain essentially mysterious, yet must be regarded as the very source of all clarity of meaning, and it must be treated as if everyone respected and deferred to it. When the superordinate term is exposed through deconstructive play, all meaning within all texts begins to shift, slide, and become unstable.

This sort of denial is what Glendon Schubert (1960) did in his critique of the idea of the public interest. The most remarkable and powerful aspect of his analysis is his blunt denial of the term itself. He was able to accomplish this because changing social conditions had moved a new version of the superordinate term, "system equilibrium," into place in the general consciousness. Thus what Schubert actually did was simply to replace one superordinate term with another. What is different about Derrida's version of philosophical critique is that he denies *all* varieties of superordinate terms. Without this denial, deconstruction becomes yet another way, in a long line within the history of philosophy, of refusing to go along with a text.

Throughout its history, the idea of the public interest has been touted as a device for controlling the actions of participants in the process of governance. The argument was that by looking to the public interest, public administrators and others could avoid doing wrong. As such, the public interest represented Truth with a capital T and moral Good with a capital G. As we have sought to orient our institutions to this idea of Truth and Good, factionalism, inevitably, has developed as different interests have sought to push their versions of Truth and Good. We say this is inevitable because the whole Truth of any matter is never accessible; yet because the whole Truth remains the standard, all partial statements of Truth, no matter how incomplete or insufficient, must seek to represent themselves as at least the best available approximation of the entire Truth. Hence dialogue becomes ideological.

We noted earlier that the device that has been used as a response to this problem is the arbiter, fair judge, or as we like to term it, the "Man of Reason." That is, ideological conflict is overcome by establishing arbiters in key institutional positions who can oversee the ideological squabbling and resolve it by considered, objective judgment. This is the way that both the administrator's and the politician's role has been conceptualized traditionally, and the basis on which legitimacy has been claimed for them. The problem, of course, is that setting the Man of Reason in place only relocates the issue rather than resolving it. To what guide does the Man of Reason refer in order to attain the objectivity required for refereeing the battle of ideologies? It can only be the public interest, called by one name or another, and grounded in Truth. The implicit claim is that such Truth is only available to Men of Reason, not to others, who are ideological. The claim that the Man of Reason occupies a disinterested position is unconvincing. Even with respect to the Supreme Court, it is simply not believable that people can put themselves beyond all the varieties of sentiment that inspire ideology. Hence the nomination and confirmation processes for new justices have become increasingly contentious and ideological. Also, no matter how neutralized a role position might be, it must ultimately be tied to a stake of power, the power to take the final decision and to act. Arbiters are always open to the charge that they are, at the very least, invested in maintaining their role positions. Even philosopher kings can be charged with this.

What we have then, is a vicious circle of ideology, and consequent delegitimation, for administrative and policy institutions. It begins with the need for viewing Truth in terms of the Enlightenment model, at least in principle, as singular and enduring, to be written with a capital T. This commitment implies that its corollary, control, is necessary; that is, that those involved in governance must be kept to the path of Truth. A second corollary is that all claims to truth will be disadvantaged unless they claim to be the whole, complete, or objective Truth, or at least as close as anyone can come to it at the moment. This situation implies a need for arbiters, who can distill the real Truth from the ideological struggle. In doing this, however, they must claim a special access to the real Truth, a claim that it seems can be grounded only in tradition. They have special access to the Truth because they are in positions that have always been seen as having such access. There is really no other argument to support this.

What is revealed here is that this vicious circle begins with the capital T idea of Truth. We must then ask the question: What stake or investment produces the need for capital T Truth? It is in answering this key question that the postmodern perspective can be helpful. What it implies, as we have already mentioned, is that it may be possible to have meaningful discourse without anchoring language in capital T Truth. Such a discourse would be, of course, merely relativistic babbling from the point of view of the discourse of Truth. It would be a discourse that denies the possibility of narrative, of heroic stories like the Enlightenment project of progress and all the subplots that have gone with it. It would be a discourse that accepts death and sees it as just an aspect of life, and that sees nature as something of which we are just an aspect and hence need to relate to rather than conquer. Likewise, it would see cooperation rather than competition as the natural basis for social process.

What would such a discourse mean for the world of public administration and policy and the institutions of which it is comprised? Most obviously, there would be no capital T Truth as a central reference point. Instead, all the parties to a situation would be seen as holding multiple, partial, and momentary truths. These truths would have to be put together in a tentative pattern through a group process grounded in authentic communication. The resulting pattern would form the basis for experimental, iterative activities, taken in decentralized settings, that would be judged by their consequences. There would be no accountability in the sense of blame for outcomes, only reassessment and further iterative action. The only protection against error would be the iterative, experimental nature of the process itself.

The postmodern perspective is also helpful here. The modern viewpoint finds it difficult to trust process, which is to say, to trust experimental action that is designed from within an open relationship, as a safeguard against falsehood and evil, because it is essentially rationalist. This is to say that it relies exclusively on the exercise of the *conscious attitude* as the device for finding right lines of action. There is no role for the unconscious in the modern approach; the unconscious is seen as part of the problem, as irrational. The postmodern theory of subjectivity casts the unconscious in a new and different light. The unconscious is the location of the Other, the source of language, a place from which the limited, mundane, and determined doings of the ego can be transcended. Although the philosophies of the rational, conscious mind may have difficulty or find it impossible to set out lines of right action, the voice of the unconscious/Other is free of such difficulties. Rationality finds ambivalence intrinsic because it is spoken from a subjectivity that has not moved fully under the rule of the unconscious, what Jung called the Self. The voice of the Other speaks from the position of Thanatos and is not encumbered with ambivalence. Postmodernists, in denying the possibility for transcendent truth, curiously provide us more hope than do modernists that human beings have a capacity for bringing a transcendent perspective into their actions.

Such an approach to operating administrative and policy institutions would from our present perspective seem conservative, in the classical sense of the term. This is an accurate description because resultant actions would not be designed from principle but rather from experience, and they would be oriented only toward what the group wanted to do next at each action moment. It would be a very concrete approach to governance, one in which ideology would have little or no place. As a consequence, there would be no basis for domination, for ambitious, grand, large-scale programs, and for concomitantly disastrous mistakes. Most important, however, institutions built around such a process would, ipso facto, be legitimate. Ironically this is quite close to a persistent countertheme that resonates throughout American history since the Founding. Originally heard in the Anti-Federalists' perspectives, its tones have echoed and become more prominent in subsequent periods, perhaps most notably in the works of the American pragmatists.

Conclusion

We wish in our conclusion to step back from our chapter and view it as a whole, in suspense from its own rhetoric. From this vantage point, we ask the question: What is the nature of the argument made here for an alternative image of the public interest? Is this simply an importation of an esoteric theory from another field, another country, into the field of public administration and policy, one that provides no more force than the intellectual interest a different perspective might generate? Such importations are a long-standing tradition in the field, and, in the main, they seem to have produced no more than temporary curiosity.

We argue to the contrary, and we base our counterargument in common sense and the plain facts of everyday contemporary life. Postmodernism challenges the axiomatic foundation of our very epoch, the fundamental pattern of the way in which we are living. As such, it affords us a perspective from which to look at this pattern, a pattern that for the most part goes unnoticed because it is so ubiquitous, ingrained, and taken for granted. The starting place for our pattern of social process is gender. We have organized life around gender and created a system in which members of the male gender are in positions of importance, power, control, and privilege. Consequently, social structure and intellectual discourse are ordered by their terms. Although this pattern has begun to change, its existence seems to us undeniable.

In raising this, we hasten to state that we are not questioning the fairness with which women are treated in societies around the world or in the United States. We are certainly concerned about this equity, and we have a very clear position on it—we are for equality in the status of women in all areas. This essentially moral and political matter does not concern us here, however, and indeed, we relate to it only through the aspect of ourselves that plays the role of citizen in a *modern* world.

What we are interested in, rather, is how the issue of gender has led to a bias in discourse that results in limitations on the efficacy of social process. Jacques Lacan (1966/1977) argues that the way language and discourse currently operate is grounded in the male issue of separation from the mother, most importantly, the oedipal event. This may seem esoteric or even weird. However, it seems incontrovertible that men have, rather universally, structured and controlled discourse. How then could discourse *not* reflect the distinctive psychological issues of men? Further, how can anyone deny that a category as powerful, intimate, and comprehensive as gender not produce distinctive psychological issues? Modernism is, clearly to us, a masculine epoch, and it has changed only in degree over time. Social patterns have essentially stayed the same, only developing through different levels as modernism has marched down the road of progress. Testimony to this is that even with the expenditure of huge amounts of resources and tremendous effort, we have not solved the problems we have defined.

Our view is not that this means modernism has failed. Rather it indicates to us that there is a powerful, implicit, if not unconscious, stake in keeping things the same, especially in holding onto our problems. At bottom, a problematic world indicates and legitimates as necessary the heroic stance toward life and nature that comes so naturally to the male psyche. C. P. Carafy's poem is exactly on the mark in this sense: We require our barbarians—they justify us. In such a context, a discourse around the idea of the public interest that never gets anywhere, that continues to pose the question but never answers it, a discourse that produces only mirages and illusory ideals, is to be expected. Were we to define the grail, and then actually find it, the quest would be over, and we would have nothing to do.

Are we are saying that the problem is men? Are we arguing that men should turn the world over to women and that our problems would then be solved? Not at all. The problem is not men themselves, but the idea of capital T Truth that has resulted from their occupying so pervasively the role positions through which discourse, and indeed, the operation of language itself, is structured. Because this idea of Truth may be a substitute for a longing to find the Eden of the womb and as such is more a male quest than a female one does not mean that men alone are the problem. Most people, of both genders, accept Truth and its corollary, Good, as reference points for their actions. The worldview of modernism is pan-gender in our culture. The possible marginality of women to the realm of signification indicates only that there may be the possibility of a workable alternative to Truth and Good: truth and good.

What does this alternative mean, and what sort of call does it make to us? It means accepting truth and good without the binding imperative of abstraction, accepting an idea of truth and good that remains grounded in specific groups and specific situations and that relies on human relationship for its protection from falsehood and evil.

This is an idea that forfeits, of course, the heroic possibility of superordinate judgment and a vision of heaven generated by mortals that can be held out as a collective goal. This is the aspect of postmodernism that creates the most discomfort in its critics. The heroic pose historically seemed to come more naturally to men than to women, but contemporary women seem to be assuming it more and more. There seems to be a general resistance to giving it up.

To give it up, ironically, would not mean anything very radical or strange, in *our* view. It would mean that all those involved in governance—citizens, politicians, and administrators—would engage the process shoulder to shoulder, in groups characterized by valid human relationship. The aim would be to act experimentally in a process oriented toward improving the human condition. There would be no heroes, but the process of governance would attain a de facto legitimacy that it has never had up to now, at least in the United States. It would, in short, mean moving to a process-based communitarian approach to governance, where the connection of people to the community was relationship rather than an ideologically distorted deference to the ideals of Truth and Good and to some inadequate actualizations of them that the members of the community were required to believe.

Not only is such an approach not radical, it is grounded, in America, in some of our most venerable traditions: the revolutionary spirit of the young nation, the government of the Articles of Confederation, and the philosophy of American Pragmatism. It was given specific expression in the work of the American pragmatist Mary Parker Follett. Further, it is an approach that is grounded in the highest tradition of science, the idea of the scientific community as expressed in images of the scientific enterprise such as Thomas Kuhn's (1962). One of the most curious aspects of the history of public administration as well as all academic disciplines in the United States is the persistent resistance that it has shown to incorporating or even seriously considering such images as the starting place for revising the way we define legitimate governance.

We say this resistance has been curious because these images really speak clearly of progress. They are ultimately *progressive,* deeply infused with a spirit that seeks the betterment of the human condition. As Kuhn's idea of progress under science shows, however, the alternative image of progress that they offer involves human actors as *responsible* for the choices that they make as they seek to improve the human lot. The lower-case ideas of truth and good do not allow for the fallback defense of, "We only did what the facts (developed in our rigorous search for Truth) dictated." The terror evoked in the modern mind by taking away this defense is considerable, if not awesome. The irony in this is that Truth and Good, while appearing to be the ultimate justifications for choice and thus the final defenses against personal failure, are also the only grounds for blame and punishment. If there is no notion of Truth, then many truths are possible. What this fear is about is the pain that comes from blame issued in the name of Truth and Good. The alternative image of progress that we sketched above, by substituting truth and good for Truth and Good, obviates the basis for issuing such blame.

We are led at last to a less charitable conclusion about the core reason that the communitarian alternative has been resisted: Those who presently hold the heroic positions of control, who are enabled to speak blame and praise in the name of Truth and Good, simply do not want to move onto the level floor of the community and trust others to the extent that they presently trust only themselves. Like most other holders of high office in history, they want to hold onto their privileged positions, no matter how illegitimate they seem to be becoming.

In all fairness, though, we must conclude that this is an understandable position, and it is no doubt taken unconsciously and overlaid with heroic, self-sacrificing justifications. As the postmodernists would offer it to us, what is at stake here is facing the inevitable truth that people are born to suffer and die. This is not something that human beings are given the strength to do as a matter of choice. It is a gift that comes to us as a consequence of doing what we can do, which is look our own egos in the eye and face the weakness that inevitably resides there. This facing yields the consolation that we become able to move into community with others and find the guidance and support that ultimately resides only there. In our view, this guidance and support is what the public interest is, and it is in finding the public interest that the answer lies to the problem of legitimacy for our institutions of governance.

■ References

Berne, E. (1964). *Games people play: The psychology of human relationships.* New York: Grove.

Berne, E. (1976). *Beyond games and scripts.* New York: Grove.

Bernstein, R. (1991). Pragmatism, pluralism, and the healing wounds. In R. Bernstein (Ed.), *The new constellation* (pp. 323-340). Cambridge: MIT Press.

Black, M. (Ed.). (1961). *The social theories of Talcott Parsons: A critical examination.* Englewood Cliffs, NJ: Prentice Hall.

Bly, R. (1990). *Iron John: A book about men.* Reading, MA: Addison-Wesley.

Derrida, J. (1976). *Of grammatology.* Baltimore, MD: Johns Hopkins University Press.

Derrida, J. (1978). *Spurs: Nietzsche's styles.* Chicago: University of Chicago Press.

Follet, M. P. (1965). *The new state: Group organization, the solution of popular government.* Gloucester, MA: Peter Smith.

Follet, M. P. (1973). *Dynamic administration: The collected papers of Mary Parker Follet.* London: Pitman.

Goodsell, C. T. (1990). Public administration and the public interest. In G. Wamsley et al., *Refounding public administration.* Newbury Park, CA: Sage.

Kamuf, P. (1991). *A Derrida reader.* New York: Columbia University Press.

Kuhn, T. (1962). *The structure of scientific revolutions.* Chicago: University of Chicago Press.

Lacan, J. (1977). *Ecrits: A selection* (A. Sheridan, Trans.). New York: Norton. (Original work published 1966)

McCoullough, T. E. (1991). *The moral imagination and public life.* Chatham, NJ: Chatham House.

Osborne, D. E., & Gaebler, T. (1992). *Reinventing government: How the entrepreneurial spirit is transforming the public sector.* Reading, MA: Addison-Wesley.

Peirce, C. S., Hartshorne, C., & Weiss, P. (1931). *Collected papers of Charles Sanders Peirce (Vols. I-VIII).* Cambridge, MA: Harvard University Press.

Perls, F., Hefferline, R. F., & Goodman, P. (1951). *Gestalt therapy: Excitement and growth in the human personality.* New York: Delta Books.

Ritzer, G. (1993). *The McDonaldization of society: The changing character of contemporary social life.* Newbury Park, CA: Pine Forge.

Rorty, R. (1979). *Philosophy and the mirror of nature.* Princeton, NJ: Princeton University Press.

Rorty, R. (1982). *Consequences of pragmatism.* Minneapolis: University of Minnesota Press.

Rorty, R. (1989). *Contingency, irony, and solidarity.* Cambridge, UK: Cambridge University Press.

Rosenau, P. M. (1992). *Post-modernism and the social sciences: Insights, inroads, and intrusions.* Princeton, NJ: Princeton University Press.

Rosenbloom, D. (1993). Forum: Public administration and the constitution [Special section]. *Public Administration Review, 53*(3).

Rotman, B. (1987). *Signifying nothing: The semiotics of zero.* New York: St. Martin's.

Scheffler, I. (1974). *Four pragmatists: A critical introduction to Peirce, James, Mead, and Dewey.* London: Routledge & Kegan Paul.

Scholes, R. (1989). *Protocols of reading.* New Haven, CT: Yale University Press.

Schubert, G. A. (1960). *The public interest: A critique of the theory of a political concept.* Glencoe, IL: Free Press.

Simon, H. (1947). *Administrative behavior: A study of decision making processes in administrative organizations.* New York: Macmillan.

Wamsley, G. L., Bacher, R. N., Goodsell, C. T., Kronenberg, P. S. Rohr, J. A., Stivers, C. M., White, O. F., & Wolf, J. F. (1990). *Refounding public administration.* Newbury Park, CA: Sage.

White, O., & McSwain, C. (1990). The Phoenix Project: Raising a new image of public administration from the ashes of the past. In H. D. Kass & B. Catron (Eds.), *Images and identities in public administration* (pp. 23-59). Newbury Park, CA: Sage.

Wood, D. (1987). Beyond deconstruction? In A. Philips Griffith (Ed.), *Contemporary French philosophy* (pp. 175-194). Cambridge, UK: Cambridge University Press.

8

The Public Administration
and the Problem of the Presidency

LARRY M. LANE
American University

In earlier years I was an admirer of the Presidency.
I am no longer.

Louis Fisher, 1972, p. 236.

In April 1950 the renowned presidential scholar, Edwin S. Corwin, delivered a lecture at the University of Virginia titled "The Problem of the Presidency." In this lecture, Corwin developed his "Whig interpretation" of the president's proper place in the Constitution, and he also delivered his famous indictment: "Taken by and large, the history of the Presidency has been a history of aggrandizement" (1951, p. 57). Since 1950, Corwin's specter of the superordinate presidency has evolved into Richard Nixon's imperial presidency and then, subsequently, declined into what many critics consider to be the weakened state of today's presidential institution.

The waxing and waning of the presidency is much discussed, but one salient aspect of the relative strength or weakness of the federal executive—the relationship of the president to the administrative establishment of government—is seldom considered and analyzed. That relationship was critical in the ascent of the presidency to dominance in the U.S. political system. Further, and more recently, a remarkable shift in that relationship has created a new "problem" of the presidency and has again significantly altered the political landscape.

The basic position of the refounding of the public administration (Wamsley et al., 1990) is that the genius of American politics can succeed only with responsive and effective administration within the context of democratic governance. Historically, that very formula was pursued and largely achieved from the late 19th century through the 1960s when the presidency and the public administration found common cause together. The recent weakening, if not breaking, of the bond between the two institutions in the latter part of the 20th century has had profound implications for the governance process in the United States. Even more recently, the rapid evolutionary pace of both political development and managerial doctrine raises new issues and questions about the nature of the relationship between presidential politics and public administration.

Alliance

From the latter part of the 19th century until 1969, a close and mutually supportive relationship developed and was maintained between the presidency and the administrative establishment (Arnold, 1986, p. 359; Moe, 1990, p. 130). The alliance was all the more remarkable because constitutional provisions in 1789 had laid the groundwork for conflict between the two institutions (Rohr, 1989, p. 6). As the modern activist presidency developed in scope and strength, the public service became increasingly professionalized. Both institutions were strongly influenced by the movements of progressivism and civil service and budget reforms. Both institutions embraced values of administrative efficiency and governmental effectiveness in a system that required and supported a powerful chief executive who also aspired to be the political embodiment of all the people (Yates, 1982, pp. 20-32). Despite presidential suspicion and frustration with the bureaucracy, both institutions accepted the premise that American democracy required effective public administration, and that their linkage represented a merger of the moral basis of the constitutional system with the powerful methodologies of modern organizational management under strong executive direction.

A merit- and competence-based civil service aided the presidency in breaking free from congressional control and in exerting authority over policy formulation as well as policy execution. In turn, an active, energetic presidency served to protect and expand the civil service and to provide a cloak of political legitimacy for the administrative process. In the 1950s, Herbert Kaufman (1956) noted the strength of the ties between the institutions: "For many years, the proponents of neutral competence and the partisans of executive leadership were able to make common cause, and their alliance became so imbedded in their thinking that the differences between them were hardly recognized" (p. 1067). President Lyndon Johnson was the apotheosis of this relationship—a most energetic, partisan, political president who also strongly supported and appreciated the public service.

The Managerial Presidency and Its Political Payoff

In the early development of modern public administration and the modern presidency, management as a public sector value system merged with the values of neutral competence and executive direction. This merger found its expression in the doctrine of scientific management. Dwight Waldo (1984) asserts that "scientific management was a significant, perhaps a major, input to the sociopolitical realm of the United States" (p. xxi).

This input was rational, scientific, and necessarily nonpartisan. For example, President Herbert Hoover espoused a system that would "be a revolution against politics, committed to the rational, unemotional building of a new, scientific society" (Karl, 1969, p. 408). This legacy of the Progressive movement intended to shift power from corrupt politicians to virtuous, well-educated citizens and "to enhance the capacity of the executive to make and carry out internally consistent, comprehensive plans for implementing the public interest" (Banfield, 1980, p. 5).

For the modern presidency, the model of the chief executive officer (CEO) derived both from Hamiltonian origins and from the private sector. This model represented the forceful implementation of executive direction in the public sector (Cronin, 1975, p. 367; Woll & Jones, 1980, p. 364). The driving force of scientific management was the knowledgeable, energetic, top-down direction and control of activities. This was well suited to presidents who were becoming the preeminent figures of American government, and it resonated favorably with the public. Not only did the CEO concept assure the public that someone was in charge and that the ship of state was being effectively steered, it also provided credibility for the president, who was no longer seen as just another politician. The American people long have been mesmerized by the persona of the private sector CEO and have been willing to grant great latitude to the strong wielders of business power. Transferring that persona to the public sector obviously strengthened the hand of the presidents, who began to be perceived as truly in charge and running the country (King & Ragsdale, 1988, p. 23).

Solving the Responsiveness Problem

A strictly managerial approach to governance is not sufficient in the American political environment. A credible linkage to democratic politics is necessary. In Herbert Storing's (1980) last essay, he identified "the bedrock of principle from which all else derives in American politics" as "popular opinion and scientific management" (p. 91), noting further that the "articulation of these principles and their relation to one another is the whole substance of American politics" (p. 91).

At issue here is some conception of political theory—some theory of the democratic state. Dwight Waldo's seminal *Administrative State* (1984) is primarily concerned with political theory, as evidenced by its subtitle: *A Study of the Political Theory of American Public Administration*. Thus the founding of public administration in scientific management and management science became a vital ingredient in an implicit theory of the state based on positivism and the rationalist paradigm. The linkage to active politics not only required the dichotomies of fact/value and politics/administration, but also required a theory of responsiveness to political institutions.

Responsiveness is an essential tenet of democratic governance. The value premise relies on the fundamental assumption that government is the servant, not the master, of the people. The principal problem of governmental administration in a democratic context is assuring the responsiveness of the administrative process to popular control. This is difficult in a government of separation of powers, webs of interlocking relationships, weakness of hierarchy, and representation of powerful interest groups (Truman, 1951). As Norton Long (1949) observed years ago: "The unanswered question of American government—'who is boss'—constantly plagues administration" (p. 264).

The indispensable theory for answering Long's question is documented by Emmette Redford (1969) in his definition and critique of the concept of overhead democracy (pp. 70-72). This concept has achieved powerful normative status despite its failure to deal adequately with the political and administrative realities of American governance. The doctrine of overhead democracy asserts that democratic control runs from the elective representatives of the people down through a hierarchy of authority and command, reaching from the chief executive down through the units of government "to the fingertips of administration" (Redford, 1969, pp. 70-71).

This traditional doctrine of administration is integrated, hierarchical, legalistic, and it requires obedience to political direction. In this system of administrative responsiveness, the bureaucracy is a monolithic tool that is predictable, reliable, and obedient. It operates in a vertical hierarchy with authority and decisions coming down from the top through delegation and with responsibility moving up the hierarchy from lower to higher official (Thompson, 1965, pp. 206-207).

When merged with the CEO concept of executive direction, this traditional doctrine is a powerful normative theory that satisfies the need for establishing political control over the bureaucratic administrative establishment. Overhead democracy is linked tightly to a dichotomy of politics and administration, together providing a powerful argument for responsiveness. As Pfiffner (1988) notes: "Without this chain of legitimacy, the democratic linkage between the electorate and the government would become unacceptably attenuated" (p. 96). Overhead democracy is also a simplistic myth—a fact that was clear to Redford and many subsequent analysts, but a fact that does not diminish its significance as a component of political and administrative values.

The Modern Presidency

The early formulation of the overhead democracy theory ran, as noted, from people through the congress *and* the executive to the bureaucracy. The rise of the modern presidency, the incumbents of which claimed to be the only representative of all the people, provided a solution to what Mansfield (1981) calls the ambivalence of executive power: "A weak executive resulting from the notion that the people are *represented* in the legislature, a strong executive from the notion that they are *embodied* in the executive" (p. 319). The strong executive linked responsiveness to representativeness within the presidency. In William Morrow's (1984) view, this development originated with Woodrow Wilson, who advocated stronger executive institutions as a means of assuring effective representation of the common interest (pp. 259-260).

This strong executive—the modern president—became central to America's social, economic, political, and administrative consciousness (Moe, 1990, p. 131). Political scientists and other academicians developed a "textbook" presidential model that had as an underlying motif "a quasi-religious awe of the presidency" (Cronin, 1975; Nelson, 1990, p. 5; Neustadt, 1960; Rossiter, 1960). James MacGregor Burns (1965) popularized the image of the heroic presidency, a highly romanticized view of active "Hamiltonian" presidents overcoming the Madisonian checks and balances in order to exert leadership and move the nation. More recently, a writer on presidential leadership could still refer to the president who "bestrides our political world like a contemporary Caesar, reaching into the nooks and crannies of our everyday existence" (Shogan, 1991, p. 4).

A literary figure, E. L. Doctorow (1992), is even more effusive when he comments on presidential character: "The President we get is the country we get. With each new President the nation is conformed spiritually. He is the artificer of our malleable national soul" (p. 534). This artificer—this contemporary Caesar—took on the huge burdens of multiple and often conflicting roles, as identified by Rossiter and others. These burdens were, as Grover (1989) notes, "made more manageable by the vast executive bureaucracy which has flourished in the twentieth century" (p. 27). Thus the modern presidency needed administrative capacity. For its part, the bureaucracy linked its fate to the extraordinarily brilliant presidential star.

The constitutional implications of these institutional developments and literary perceptions are significant. In its evolution over almost a hundred years, the modern presidency has been constitutionally problematic (Tulis, 1990, pp. 85-86; Wamsley, 1990, p. 135). The framers assumed that the people would be primarily represented in the congress and that the president would be principally an executing rather than policy-making officer (Rimmerman, 1993, p. 23). The president would represent the people but be more than merely responsive. He would rise above volatile public opinion and serve the larger public interest (Tulis, 1990, p. 93). The presidency envisioned by the founders derived its authority from the Constitution. The modern presidency of Woodrow Wilson and his successors has its power and authority conferred by the people (Tulis, 1990, p. 107). The personal power of the presidency became "the engine of enlightened administration" (Grover, 1989, p. 37).

Presidential aggrandizement took on the functions of representation and policy determination, as well as execution and administration. In the development of the modern presidency, from Woodrow Wilson through Franklin Roosevelt to Lyndon Johnson, the constitutional problem was ameliorated by the linkage of the presidency to a competent, nonpartisan public service. This was essentially the solution prescribed by the Brownlow Committee in 1937. The report of the Committee made extraordinary claims of broad presidential authority and executive supremacy, buttressed by principles of scientific management (Rohr, 1989, p. 41). The report emphatically proposed executive domination of the budgeting and personnel management processes. However, the Committee also stressed concepts of expertise and competence and the vigorous extension of the career service up to and including the very top posts in federal organizations (President's Committee on Administrative Management, 1937).

Through the Brownlow formula and the continuing symbol and reality of the Civil Service Commission, the president's primary constitutional responsibility for faithful execution of the law (Corwin, 1976, p. 72) was effectively represented, even as modern presidents changed the nature of American government. In this modern governance, credibility adhered to political leadership and to administrative execution. The Congress customarily drafted legislation broadly, charging the executive branch with spelling out the details of implementation (Rimmerman, 1993, p. 29). Similarly, the courts tended to defer to executive branch competence in the administrative issues that came before the bench. Deference and credibility were important aspects of the modern presidency.

There is a certain irony in the need for the extra-constitutional device of a competent, nonpartisan administrative establishment to tie the modern presidency and its anticonstitutional nature into the normative structure of American governance. After 1968, however, the bonds of the modern executive to the Constitution were to be further stretched. As the modern presidency became the lodestar of public administration, academics and practitioners alike tended to share the popular perception of the managerial presidency as the chief executive officer of the nation state. This perception, or illusion, has made subsequent developments of the presidency more difficult to comprehend. Even today, after years of separation and hostility, the administrative establishment still tends to look to the president. But the president now looks elsewhere.

▬ Estrangement

At some point in the middle years of the 20th century, the managerial presidency substantively began to disappear from the American political landscape. Perhaps Dwight Eisenhower was the last managerial president, governing as he did in ways learned in the military bureaucracy and practiced through a rational approach to organizational competence (Burke, 1992, p. 184). After Eisenhower, two intensely political Democratic administrations maintained a respect for and reliance on the administrative capabilities of the bureaucracy and public service. But Lyndon Johnson was followed by the development of a presidency defined by Terry Moe (1985) as the *politicized* presidency.

New Imperatives and Incentives

Prior to the late 1960s, the compatible goals of the modern presidency and the public service—merging executive management, technical competency, and political responsiveness—provided political advantages that masked the divisive factors emerging in American political life in the mid-20th century. In 1956, with uncanny prescience, Kaufman predicted the emerging conflict between the executive and the bureaucracy. He saw that the great growth in the scope of federal governmental action, and of the bureaucracy needed to implement ever-expanding programs, meant that neutral competence could no longer satisfy growing perceptions of a need for increased political control (pp. 1069-1072). Cronin (1980, pp. 224-252) compellingly documents the increasing tension, conflict, and adversarial relationships that developed between the "presidentialists" in the executive office of the presidency and the "departmentalists" in the agencies and bureaus of the federal government.

Ironically, it was big, activist government that created the conditions fostering executive hostility to the administrative capacity and human resources of that very government. The size, complexity, and control-resistant nature of the burgeoning administrative establishment of government led to the ultimate break between the presidency and the public service. In 1968, the election of Richard Nixon to the presidency marked the changed nature of the office and signified the reality of what Heclo (1983) has since called the "institutional estrangement" of American governance (p. 48). In Harold Seidman's (Seidman & Gilmour, 1986) assessment, a system was created "in which the presidency exists wholly apart from other institutions and is at one with the people" (pp. 110-111). Such a presidency no longer seemed to have need of competent administration, and in fact began to regard the bureaucratic establishment as an adversary, much to the bewilderment of many public administrators who continued to look to the president as their leader and chief executive.

From the perspective of the presidency, frustration continued to build over the fact that the administrative establishment was a separate institution within the political system. It was not the president's alone. The presidential reaction to this frustration was, in the context of the separation of powers, a growing suspicion and hostility, followed by specific attempts to manage, control, and subjugate what was perceived to be a threat to presidential rule. Thus, Nixon and his followers became adversaries of the administrative establishment. They abandoned management values in favor of political responsiveness, representing a transition from "technical management" to "political management" (Bower, 1983, pp. 13-45).

Political Administration

The Nixon/Carter/Reagan formula for governance was a model characterized as "administrative presidency" by Richard Nathan (1983) and as "political administration" by Donald Devine (1991). This model is presidentially centered and adversarial to the permanent bureaucracy, viewing the chief executive not only as dominant but as virtually the only legitimate source of political and administrative authority. Nathan argues that in order for the president to achieve his policy objectives, he must extend his political influence throughout the administrative establishment, politicizing administration in order to assure responsiveness to presidential mandates and ultimately to the electorate.

The operative concepts of the administrative presidency and political administration are couched in traditional management terms of authority, command, control, and monitoring, to be accomplished through the agency of a cadre of committed and loyal political appointees of the president, strategically placed at critical places in the bureaucracy. The politicized face of overhead democracy, as described by Robert Rector (1988), envisions political appointees as "the President's eyes and hands stretched throughout an executive branch of 2 million career employees." These appointees act as the president's intermediaries, communicating presidential priorities and transmitting information from the agencies to the White House.

Donald Devine (1991) cites Max Weber to demonstrate the obligation of administrative personnel to follow obediently the moral authority of the charismatic and plebiscitary executive. Devine demands adherence and loyalty to the president as person, and excoriates even the Executive Office of the President for failing to serve Ronald Reagan properly, thus lumping the presidency as an institution with the Congress, the bureaucracy, the press, and a panoply of interest groups that hindered the achievement of presidential policies. A Devine protégé, Michael Sanera (1987), demonstrates the shift from management to politicization when he states that "success in public-sector management is not dependent on good business management of existing government operations, but rather on managing the President's political philosophy and values" (p. 177).

In the political administration model, presidential aggrandizement is complete; however, as Lester Salamon (1981) notes, "presidential government at its best turned out to be constitutional government at its worst" (p. 288). There is no place in the constitutional structure for a president who claims exclusive executive power. This doctrine, as John Rohr (1986) notes, originated not in the Constitution but in Andrew Jackson's presidency. This concept was fulfilled in the Nixon administration, which committed a fundamental error as it attempted to transform "the president from chief executive officer into sole executive officer" (p. 139).

This different type of president began to turn against the administrative institution. The shift occurred definitively with the election of Richard Nixon in 1968. The attacks against the bureaucracy and therefore against the public administration were overt with Nixon, codified with Carter, institutionalized with Reagan, and carried on in a more subdued way by Bush and Clinton.

In the cold light of retrospective reason, the attack on public administration was a strategic error on the part of the presidency. The administrative institution that had been an important resource and support for strengthening the presidency was cast aside in favor of older and less sophisticated notions of political partisanship and unhesitating responsiveness. The net result, as seen in the Carter administration, the last half of the Reagan administration, the Bush administration, and the difficult beginning of the Clinton administration, has been a weakened presidency in terms of its capacity to lead and to act. Politicization of administration may strengthen the immediate political control of the president, but it weakens the capacity for listening to objective advice and taking competent action (Burke, 1992, p. 184). When presidents began to turn against public administration, they lost a source of strength and legitimacy. Similarly, the public administration lost its sense of direction as well as the political legitimacy that had been provided by a supportive presidency.

The Politicized Presidency

President Nixon and his successors have attempted to adopt the centralization of power and the hierarchical management patterns of an administrative efficiency model of government, but at the same time they have denigrated the values of neutral competence, merit, and professionalism of the public service. The result has been a politicized presidency, as characterized by Terry Moe (1985), that valued political support, strategy, and trade-offs above efficiency and effectiveness. What presidents began to demand was a system that responded to their requirements as political leaders—"responsive competence" rather than neutral competence (p. 239).

This development in the presidency requires an expansion of Kaufman's (1956) array of shifting and realigning fundamental values in governmental administration. Responsive competence is different from neutral competence. The control mechanism of the politicized presidency is very different from the concept of executive direction as understood in 1956 when Kaufman presented his theory. Perhaps the term *political administration* is adequate to encapsulate the developments since 1956—developments that Kaufman clearly anticipated as he predicted the dissolution of the executive-administrative alliance.

It seems clear that since the beginning of the Nixon administration the value of political administration (responsive competence) has been in the ascendancy while neutral competence has faded. The executive direction implied in the managerial presidency has been replaced by a political administration that is more interested in ideology than operations. These developments have borne out another of Kaufman's (1956) predictions in which he observed that "the new atmosphere will be a strange and perhaps a bewildering one, fraught with hostilities" (p. 1073).

In the politicized presidency, political and administrative responsiveness is newly defined as responsiveness to the persons of the president and his appointees—not to laws, public interest, Congress, courts, professional standards, or the requirements of technology and natural science. This formula was created in Richard Nixon's "new American Revolution" (Seidman & Gilmour, 1986, pp. 98-111), legitimated in the Carter administration by a new civil service reform, and brought to full flower in the Reagan administration. The concept of political responsiveness solely to the presidency justifies patronage and political affiliation as criteria for membership in the public service. In recent years, the presidential tendency to monopolize the issue of responsiveness has also provided the essential link to the issue of representativeness, although this is a representativeness contained predominantly within the presidency. The president's political agenda is decisively employed to stress the desired representation of a specific array of interests and issues (Light, 1991). Regardless of the parties or interests for whom representation in the governance process is desired, forceful political intervention by the president is essential.

This new concept of the president as a politicized "sole executive officer" has proved to be unworkable, unmanageable, and unsuccessful in terms of effective governmental action. In his critique of the administrative presidency strategy, Waterman (1989) concludes that "the fact that the president shares power over the bureaucracy with Congress means that presidents cannot bully and control the administrative state. . . . The notion that presidents can command the bureaucracy is a sure prescription for failure" (pp. 192-193). Short-term political advantage is purchased at the cost of a long-term decline in the influence and credibility of the presidency (Waterman, 1989, p. 188). In terms of operational governance, the imperatives of a politicized presidency are incompatible with the rational requirements of traditional executive management. Whereas the older concept of the managerial presidency attempted to bridge the gap between efficiency and power (Arnold, 1986, p. 361), the new concept of the politicized presidency concentrates only on power, with little regard for organizational effectiveness, except at the level of campaign rhetoric.

The notion of a single, all powerful, politicized executive at the top of the governmental pyramid relies on concepts of long hierarchy, command and obedience, and top-down control, all of which are clearly impossible, given the size, scope, and complexity of governmental organization. Attempts at political command and control have led to the rapid growth of the immediate Executive Office of the President (EOP), which has become, in itself, a burgeoning and unmanageable bureaucracy, characterized by complexity and tortured decision processes (Helmer, 1981). Heclo (1981) summarizes the evolving condition of the EOP in these words: "The President's own office is an organizational jumble, often generating the illusion of power but the reality of bureaucratic confinement" (p. 15). Thus the institutional presidency has become a bureaucracy that sits atop the regular governmental bureaucracy (Cater, 1964, p. 89), neither of which can be managed effectively.

Of seeming necessity, the politicized president looks for advice solely from those who are personally close. Within the governance system, according to Moe (1985), "The pursuit of responsive competence" has two basic re-sults—"increasing centralization of the institutional presidency in the White House . . . [and] the increasing politicization of the institutional system" (pp. 244-245). Accordingly, the presidency has turned away from its old alliance with the public service in an extraordinary parting of the ways and a striking development in political dynamics. The result is a new configuration—not of politics *and* administration but of politics *against* administration. This con-figuration stretches further the constitutional bonds and understandings of American governance.

The Personal, Plebiscitary, Paranoid, Romantic Presidency

The politicized presidency has also become, in Theodore Lowi's (1985) terms, the personal and plebiscitary presidency: "an office of tremendous personal power drawn from the people . . . and based on the new democratic theory that the presidency with all powers is the necessary condition for governing a large, democratic nation" (p. 20). The plebiscitary presidency attempts to govern without intermediaries (Rimmerman, 1993, p. 24;

Wildavsky, 1991, p. 287), resisting the courts, rejecting the legislature, and denigrating the bureaucracy. The direct relationship of the president to the people requires media command, diversionary entertainment and spectacle, image building, symbolism and myth, manipulation of information, and the management of fantasy (Blumenthal, 1988, p. 260; Lowi, 1985, pp. 112-117; Miroff, 1988, p. 289; Newland, 1987, p. 45).

Since 1968, the presidency has also exhibited marked paranoid tendencies. In his 1965 essay, "The Paranoid Style in American Politics," Richard Hofstadter examines a recurrent tendency running through American history. The paranoid style of politics is characterized by heated exaggeration, suspiciousness, conspiratorial fantasy, systematized delusions of persecution, and self-importance—characteristics that at the national political level are directed against nations, cultures, and ways of life (pp. 3-4). In this context, clearly the political phenomenon of bureaucrat-bashing that became so prevalent (and politically successful) during and after the 1960s, stands as a classic example of carefully directed paranoid expressions that "find and exploit tribal fears and hatreds" (Doctorow, 1992, p. 535).

The presidency of Richard Nixon manifested the paranoid style almost to a clinical level. As described by William Gormley (1989), the hallmarks of the Nixonian approach included: adversaries as mortal enemies; politics as warfare; disagreements as crises; the "denigrative method" of attacking opponents; and bureaucrat bashing (p. 233). Gormley summarizes "Nixonian Democracy" as strident and venomous, converting "distrust into paranoia, disagreement into disloyalty, controversies into crises, critics into enemies. It abjures compromise and coalition-building in favor of combat. . . . And it diminishes the bureaucracy's capacity to respond to policy problems with creativity, flexibility, and imagination" (p. 234). These paranoid tendencies continued unabated throughout the Carter and Reagan administrations, and echoes have reverberated through the Bush years and the beginnings of the Clinton presidency.

The politicized, personal, plebiscitary, and paranoid presidency also has become a locus of romanticism, building on Burns's heroic "great man" interpretation. In this, President Carter was a transition figure, characterized by Beer (1978) as "at once a technocrat and a romantic" (p. 43). When Carter was succeeded by Ronald Reagan, the "marriage of Hollywood and Washington" was consummated (Wills, 1987, p. 202). This romanticism was a conservative adaptation of aspects of the 1960's romanticism of the radical left—specifically, the subjectivity of trusting the heart and not the head as expressed in ideology, and a marked hostility to data, analysis, and professional expertise. As president, Ronald Reagan was a true romantic figure whose disdain of facts and analysis was legendary (Williams, 1990; Wills, 1987, pp. 334-377). President Bush, in his macho campaign mode, also struck romantic poses of the tough fighter, battling against all odds and crushing his opponents. Similarly, President Clinton relishes his role as "the comeback kid."

Since 1968, the presidents have been driven by their personal and political psychology—by their perceived requirements, incentives, and resources—to establish and maintain partisan political control over the governmental establishment (Moe, 1985, p. 237). At the same time, recent presidents have insisted on a new kind of public service, with the subjugation of the values of merit, competence, and professionalization in order to increase responsiveness to a presidency that now exists in the environment of postmodernity.

The Presidency in a Postmodern Time

The American presidency is a quintessentially modern institution. It was designed at the height of the Enlightenment. It was a product as much of the industrial revolution as it was of a political revolution. It grew to preeminence on principles of progressivism and scientific management. It operates through rationalized organizations that function on premises of bureaucratic process and control. Such an institution is by its very nature poorly designed to deal with the striking changes that are occurring throughout the world under the banner of postmodernism.

A study of any aspect of postmodernism needs to begin with a sense of vast, far-reaching, and fundamental societal change, marked by striking intellectual, cultural, economic, and political developments. Borgmann (1992) identifies postmodernism as marking the divide between two epochs, as a watershed when the old fundamental convictions of the modern era weaken and begin to be supplanted by new assumptions, understandings, needs, and imperatives (p. 48). At the level of daily existence, postmodernism is characterized by an ephemeral and ungrounded conception of life. The implications of postmodernism for public administration are discussed in detail by White and McSwain in their chapter (see McSwite, Chapter 7) in this book.

The epistemological face of postmodernism has direct implications for issues of politics and administration. A similar issue is sweeping through American campuses, calling into question the notion that the pursuit of knowledge can be a nonpartisan, apolitical endeavor. The notion that there can be something called "objective truth" is the target of persistent academic attack. As Menand (1993) reports: "The shorthand version of this attack is the slogan 'All knowledge is political' " (p. 12). Similarly, the slogan "All administration is political" has become the rallying cry of advocates of the hegemonic administrative presidency (e.g., Nathan, 1983).

A primary postmodern technique is marketing through image manipulation and advertising. Under conditions of electoral marketing, people don't vote for a president, they vote for an image—"an artificial creature . . . something constructed . . . for public consumption" (Barilleaux, 1988, p. 140). The problem in this for public administration is twofold: (a) public administrators are of necessity "preoccupied by product" or at least by process; and (b) a president dominated by image rather than substance lacks the interest, incentives, and resources to direct and control large-scale enterprise.

Current Approaches to
Defining the Postmodern Presidency

A number of current analysts are beginning to characterize the presidency as postmodern. The two most prominent works in this regard are Rose (1988) and Barilleaux (1988). However, these works do not capture the essence of postmodernity as outlined above and as widely discussed in current literary and social criticism. Rather, both Rose and Barilleaux use *postmodern* primarily in a temporal sense, indicating incremental functional changes over time. These works do not contain a sense of an epochal shift.

Rose (1988) identifies the change in these words: "The difference between the modern and the post-modern Presidency is that a post-modern President can no longer dominate the international system" (p. 3). And, "The defining characteristic of the post-modern President is simply stated: *'The resources of the White House are not sufficient to meet all of the President's international responsibilities'* " (p. 25). Rose does not note, but should, that the resources of the presidency are not sufficient to meet its domestic responsibilities, if those responsibilities are defined in traditional, managerial, chief-executive terms. In fact, no amount of resources would be sufficient. Recommendations to president-elect Clinton in 1992 by the joint Carnegie Endowment and Institute for International Economics Commission on Government Renewal included advice and a trenchant observation and recommendation to the president: "The great domestic departments . . . cannot be run from 1600 Pennsylvania Avenue. Your staff should not cross the fine line between strategy and implementation, between policy formulation and operations" (cited in Williams, 1993, p. 705).

For his part, Barilleaux (1988) identifies six characteristics of the postmodern presidency: "1) the revival of presidential prerogative power; 2) governing through public politics; 3) the president's general secretariat; 4) vicarious policymaking; 5) the president as chief whip in Congress; and, 6) the new vice-presidency" (p. 8). Each of these characteristics is interesting and important, but they are largely evolutionary and functional in nature.

In his critical analysis of Rose and of Barilleaux, Rimmerman (1993) rejects their characterization of a new kind of presidency, rather holding that developments of the 1980s and 1990s are merely a continuation and maturization of the modern presidency, characterized by Rimmerman as "plebiscitary" (pp. 35-38). The critique has merit because, in fact, Rose and Barilleaux have not attempted directly to link developments in the presidency to the intellectual and cultural developments that have characterized postmodernity. However, Rimmerman also avoids such issues, concentrating his analysis on tendencies that seem to demonstrate the continuity of the current presidency with trends and development since the 1930s. Thus neither the postmodern presidencies as depicted by Rose and by Barilleaux, nor the "plebiscitary" presidency as presented by Rimmerman, confront the basic issues of postmodernity and their significance for the American presidency.

Postmodern Characteristics of the Contemporary Presidency

In the postmodern world of politics and administration, the problem of the presidency grows more acute. The institution of the presidency drifts farther and farther away from the premises of the modern age: certainty, progress, meaning, truth, science, prediction, and control. These old premises, of course, are the foundation stones of modern public administration. Consequently, the gulf between the presidency and the public administration widens. The challenge for postmodern presidents is to recognize this development and to adjust to the implications for governance and administrative competence just as effectively as they have already adjusted to the demands of postmodern electoral marketing.

The presidency as it has developed to date—personal, plebiscitary, politicized, paranoid, and romantic—is hostile to the traditional (modern) core values of the public service—impersonal, politically neutral, oriented to law and systems, rationally objective, analytical, and professionally expert. This hostility is attributable to specific postmodern characteristics of the new presidency.

1. The President as Marketing Product. A primary characteristic of postmodernism is, in White and McSwain's (Chapter 7, this volume) words, "the consumption of surfaces." The postmodern presidency reflects this condition in its primary emphasis on marketing technique, primarily through imaginative use of television. The celebrity president is marketed by image manipulation through the medium of television (Barilleaux, 1988, p. 134). This is the "Prime-Time Presidency" as described by Denton (1988), or the "Six O'Clock Presidency" analyzed by Smoller (1990). Of course, the ultimate in the marketing of image was President Reagan, whose role playing and inattention to substance were legendary (Wills, 1991, p. 3).

2. The President as Personality. The media are used by the postmodern presidency not only to market the presidential product but also to strengthen the personal nature of presidential governance. This includes the imaginative use of direct communication with the electorate (e.g., as Clinton has done with the Larry King show), with the effect of merging personality and program. The objective of the postmodern president is to "focus on the person not the issues," and to "project the proper persona" (Denton, 1988, p. 59).

3. The Antianalytical Presidency. A determinedly short-term perspective of the postmodern presidency has sharply reduced the analytical capability, not only of the presidency but also of the governmental establishment (Light, 1991, pp. 250-273). The postmodern intellectual stance on the political nature of "truth" was given form and effect during the 8 years of the Reagan administration: "His unconcern with or distaste for expert policy information, analysis and advice led to the destruction of much of the institutional analytic capacity built up in the executive branch in the postwar period" (Williams, 1990, p. x)

4. The Antiplanning/-implementing/-evaluating/-coordinating Presidency. Reagan's successor, George Bush, pointedly demonstrated his disdain for strategic vision and planning ("the vision thing"). In Williams's (1993) view, Bush "failed to understand that good financial management data, solid performance indicators, and strong analysis . . . are the basic building blocks of organizational prudence" (p. 714). In his discussion of the postmodern presidency, Richard Rose (1988) identifies some of the presidential characteristics that distance the political executive from managerial and administrative imperatives (pp. 179-180). The president lacks incentives and interest in planning. The president and the White House staff are disinterested in program implementation unless it involves a political opportunity or problem. Program evaluation has largely been abandoned by recent presidents, and intergovernmental coordination has been neglected.

5. The Anti-Information Presidency. Rose (1988) also notes the presidential perspective on data and information: "A President does not seek information for its own sake, but information that can be used to his advantage" (p. 180). Political necessity requires presidential ambiguity and vagueness in stating policy objectives (p. 182). In the policy-making process, Rose (1988) contrasts the "organized anarchy" of the presidential approach to the stability, organization, and order of the subgovernments that operate in an environment of shared interests (p. 183).

Implications for the Public Administration

Public administration, as an institution, remains largely mired in the concepts and principles of modernity. The traditional premises of administrative management are founded on principles of objective data and information, clarified objectives, orderly policy processes, analysis, program planning, careful implementation, evaluation, and coordination. As a consequence, public administration shares responsibility with the presidency for the widening gulf between the two institutions. The challenge for public administrators is to recognize the implications of postmodern societal and institutional developments and to revise substantially the fundamental premises of the field.

The presidency as defined by Nixon, Carter, Reagan, Bush, and Clinton has become not the solution to administrative problems, as longed for by the leaders of the administrative establishment (e.g., the Volcker Commission), but rather the problem, standing in the way of traditional modern concepts of competent execution of laws and programs. As a consequence, the problem of the presidency manifests itself in increasingly adversarial relationships with the bureaucracy. Advocates, supporters, and officials of presidential government continue to express contempt for the permanent government, placing unrelenting emphasis on staff and program reductions in the guise of "reinventing" government.

The greatest irony is that the tendencies of recent presidencies have not strengthened the institution but rather have diminished it. The presidency has become a "weakened and trivialized" institution (Denton, 1988, p. 59) in reference to its Constitutional responsibility to carry out the laws of the nation. At the same time, congressional and judicial micromanagement of governmental affairs has further diluted presidential authority and effectiveness in the operational aspects of governance.

The 20th-century presidency reached its nadir in November 1994 when the American voters effectively transferred power away from the presidency by electing Republican majorities in both the House and the Senate. The aggressive beginning of the new Congress in 1995, together with the weak response of President Clinton, perhaps signals the rebirth of congressional government with all of its implications for the further politicization of the administration of public affairs.

▬ Refounding the Presidency

The problem of the presidency and its relationship to the public administration brings into focus a fundamental issue of refounding postmodern politics and administration. Historically, the presidency was critically important in the development of modern public administration, but the presidency as presently constituted cannot be relied on as a foundation for any postmodern refounding effort. Major institutional and societal changes require radical revision of the fundamental premises and theories of management and of democratic politics—of the presidency and the public administration. Just as the combined ideologies of scientific management and overhead democracy characterized the modern period of presidential democratic governance, so now new theories are evolving that will characterize postmodern democratic governance. The loudly proclaimed premises of reinventing government— participative management and empowered employees—are not yet addressing fundamental issues of the management-politics relationship. The logic of postmodern management also requires a postmodern democratic political theory.

Managerial Theory for the Postmodern Presidency

Management guru Tom Peters (1993) has proclaimed, "The industrial revolution came to an end in January 1992" when the stock-market value of Microsoft exceeded that of General Motors (p. 42). Whether that in fact was the precise date or the exact event that ended one epoch and began another, the statement significantly captures the sense of tremendous change in organizational and managerial theory that is now sweeping through the private and public sectors.

The modern managerial ideology of the industrial revolution is clearly described by Bendix (1956): "All economic enterprises have in common a basic social relation between the employers who exercise authority and the workers who obey" (p. 13). Command and obedience, running through hierarchical organizational structures, provided the fundamental dynamic for Weberian bureaucracy and for scientific management and all of its behavioral descendants. In public administration, command and obedience were understood as necessary derivatives of overhead democracy and presidential leadership.

In today's managerial revolution, the "basic social relation" in the workplace is being radically altered as employees are empowered with the discretion to make production and service delivery decisions. The postmodern economic and organizational paradigm is now "characterized by information processing, flexible specialization, and informed cooperation" (Borgmann, 1992, p. 5). Organizational structures are being radically transformed into configurations of clusters, wagon wheels, and most commonly, the inverted pyramid (e.g., Nordstrom, Federal Express, Ritz Carlton Hotels, Cadillac Division of General Motors) (Austin, 1993, pp. 23-26).

The top-down, authoritative, and authoritarian premises of scientific management and of executive direction and control are being replaced by the customer-driven, quality-driven, and employee-centered doctrines of quality management. Prominent government officials such as the Comptroller General step forth, echoing Osborne and Gaebler (1992), and observe that a hierarchical chain of command may have been effective in the past: "But today it is a dinosaur" (U.S. General Accounting Office, 1993, p. 4).

Total quality management (TQM) projects are being instituted at every level of governmental activity. In the federal government, a majority of agencies and activities report implementation of some form of TQM (U.S. General Accounting Office, 1992). The National Performance Review, issued in September 1993, sets forth principles and recommendations that embrace total quality concepts and a new style of management. At the state and local level, the report of the National Commission on the State and Local Public Service (1993) specifically calls for a new type of public manager who will no longer be a director and controller (p. 49). Clearly, major changes in public sector management concepts are emerging.

The basic premises of postmodern organizational management are in many respects at odds with the operational characteristics of the presidency and with the profound suspicion and hostility of the political system to its own administrative establishment. Highly technical, knowledge and communication-based postindustrial organizations, including much of government operations (McGregor, 1988), require patterns of management that feature mutual adjustment and high-commitment work systems, collective instead of individual accountability and performance, shared goals, participation and employee voice, negotiation, employee empowerment, flexibility, and self-directed teams.

New organizational theory requires the flattening of hierarchy, the thinning of managerial ranks, decentralization, delegation of responsibility, reduced overhead, and worker autonomy. The information and communications revolution is radically changing the patterns of authority in postmodern organizations (Taylor & Van Every, 1993). The new manager is very different than the old authoritarian controller and is now thought of as a facilitator, sponsor, coach, mentor, information sharer, team leader, and internal consultant (Dumaine, 1993, pp. 80-84). In the new management patterns, organizational power is being redefined. Standard supervisory duties (scheduling work, assuring quality, administering work schedules, compensation and incentive management) are being delegated to self-managed teams. These are premises that have not penetrated to the presidency except at the level of rhetoric.

The support of top organizational leadership is absolutely essential to the success of total quality programs. In the private sector, this has been a major problem because of the implications of an apparent loss of authority and power for the managers and executives who are required to lead and support the process of change. If this is the case in the private sector, it is even more significant in the public sector where the political system remains committed to old structures of hierarchy, command, and obedience.

These old structures are proving to be managerially inadequate in today's economy and certainly in today's governmental operations. In the public sector, the complex structure and the enormous scope of governmental activity make centralized control impossible. This problem is graphically illustrated by the inability of a president to control even the White House staff. The inability to control is amply documented in Bob Woodward's new book, *The Agenda: Inside the Clinton White House,* which portrays the utter confusion within the White House during the first year of Clinton's presidency. Because the evolved American presidency lacks the resources and capability to manage effectively the nationwide governmental establishment, a new model of leadership is required. Reinventing government demands a reinvented presidency. The point is driven home by Rose (1988): "The President does not have in his own hands the authority to override the preferences of subgovernments in the name of broader national interests" (p. 71). The micromanagement of the Congress and the courts adds to the impossibility of the presidency to manage and control in the conventional managerial sense of those words.

Frustrated by the difficulty of control, recent presidents have attempted to strengthen their position through an emphasis on central authority and political responsiveness. Conventional political wisdom still speaks in terms of controlling the bureaucracy, as epitomized by the advice that the departing vice president, Dan Quayle, gave to the incoming president on the necessity of some method of control "because otherwise the bureaucracy will run all over him and his administration. . . . [H]e has to have something here [in the White House] to ride herd on the unelected bureaucracy, which does not necessarily have his interests at heart" (quoted in Goodsell, 1994, p. 154)

The Reagan administration was noted for its attempt to micromanage the public service by establishing political control over administrative activities and by sharply curtailing the discretion of subordinate public officials (Rockman, 1993, p. 108). The method of choice was political infiltration of the administrative establishment (Rourke, 1992, p. 227). This pattern of political management has left its mark even in academic treatises on the presidency. In an otherwise perceptive treatment, Pfiffner (1988) echoes the conventional wisdom when he advises incoming presidents: "The new president must, after long months (or years) of campaigning, immediately grasp the levers of power and take control of the government" (p. 3). The Clinton administration's much-heralded National Performance Review is silent on the effects of political management and, in fact, has distinct control and anti-public service overtones (Goodsell, 1994, p. 179).

The effect of a central-control mentality has been damage to the program effectiveness of federal governmental units and weakened governmental action. The effect on the presidency has been no less deleterious: "The more presidents attempt to gain control of policy-making initiatives by creating larger staffs and increasing supervision of the bureaucracy, the more they risk losing control" (King & Ragsdale, 1988, p. 25). In the American political system, presidents cannot command compliance even within the executive branch (Seligman & Covington, 1989, p. 127). They must seek other methods of influence.

Obviously, the presidency is critical to successful postmodern governmental management. The two most recent presidents have at least begun to perceive the shape of effective postmodern management. President Bush stated his support for total quality management as early as 1989: "Reasserting our leadership position will require a firm commitment to Total Quality Management and the principles of continuous improvement. . . . Quality improvement principles apply . . . to the public sector as well as private enterprise" (Carr & Littman, 1990, p. 2). For his part, Governor and then President Clinton has expressed his commitment to quality management principles and has reacted enthusiastically to the National Performance Review and its embrace of new management principles. Unfortunately, these expressions of presidential support and commitment have applied only to the lower levels of the public bureaucracy. The structure of the presidency remains deeply layered with a proliferation of political appointees—a pattern that is repeated at the agency level.

The layering problem is, if anything, worse for the Clinton presidency. Although the National Performance Review directs attention to reducing the layers of government, it is silent on the subject of reducing the political layering present at the top of the executive branch and extending deeply into the administrative establishment of government. The extent of the penetration of political appointees has been amply documented over the past 20 years (Light, 1992, pp. 315-317).

The proliferation of layers has accompanied the increasing politicization of the operating agencies of government. Clearly, by the standards of evolving managerial theory, the presidency must change its approach. The focus of presidential activity needs to change from political management and control to a concept of leadership as it is coming to be understood in the postmodern era. The concept of public leadership, as developed by Denhardt and Prelgovisk (1992), is marked by shared vision and by reciprocity and mutuality of interests. This concept regards leadership as less a function of power and control, and more a process of eliciting group action based on shared information and values. In such a model, the "possibility for control is diminished, but the opportunity for leadership, as we define it, is enhanced" (Denhardt & Prelgovisk, 1992, pp. 37-40).

The new managerial theories are as yet imperfectly realized in the federal government, because they are not yet linked to a political theory in the way that scientific management was linked to overhead democracy. Total quality initiatives are still frustrated by their existence within a political system of presidential command and control. The basic issue was framed by Dwight Waldo (1984) when he noted that the inexorable conclusion of the modern concept of politics and administration was that democratic ends could only be achieved through authoritarian means: " 'Autocracy' at work is the unavoidable price for 'Democracy' after hours" (p. 74). That conclusion is now being challenged by the private sector concepts of quality management. The question that still requires an answer is whether the new management theories and practices can be applied to a political system. Specifically, can a new political theory replace the hierarchical and authoritarian concept of overhead democracy?

Political Theory for the Postmodern Presidency

The premises of total quality management and reinventing government are primarily managerial, but there are powerful though as yet unanalyzed political implications. As Milan Dluhy (1992) notes in his review of Osborne and Gaebler, "*Reinventing Government* is fundamentally a prescriptive statement of political philosophy about how government should be operating if it hopes to regain the trust and confidence of the public" (p. 191). The problem is that the "statement of political philosophy" is virtually devoid of any notion of political theory, as are the reports of the National Performance Review (Office of the Vice President, 1993) and the report of the National Commission on the State and Local Public Service (1993).

Conventional political wisdom speaks of control. The managerial presidency insisted on command and control in the conventional sense of the management doctrines of the first half of the 20th century. President Nixon and his successors have insisted on command and control in terms of obedience to political directives and adherence to political ideology. But neither version of the control doctrine is in harmony with the newest developments in management theory and practice.

Bottom-Up Management in a Top-Down Enterprise

The bottom-up premises of reinventing government, and its attendant managerial innovations, present a significant problem of political theory. Governance, democratic or otherwise, is by conventional definition a top-down process of authoritatively enforcing law and policy through the sanctions and rewards available to the sovereign state. How then can the concepts of decentralization, participation, employee empowerment, and other bottom-up aspects of the new managerial concept be made to square with the imperatives of governance as usually understood and practiced, particularly by the presidency? Without a corresponding political theory, reinventing government will be a largely meaningless exercise in futility.

In the United States, the doctrine of overhead democracy has justified hierarchical control through the older managerial mechanisms of executive leadership; scientific management; economy/efficiency/effectiveness; and Weberian bureaucracy with its capacity for transmission of orders, rules, and procedures. In short, the conventional American doctrines of politics and administration have endorsed authoritarian means in a democratic polity. Now, a new political theory is necessary, particularly because, as Rosenbloom (1993) notes, " 'reinventing government' is potentially the ideology of a dominant political movement, it could foster a new administrative orthodoxy" (p. 506).

The old political and administrative orthodoxy, overhead democracy and scientific management, is fundamentally challenged by the premises of total quality management with its emphasis on power flowing into organizations from suppliers and customers and upward in organizations from the working level of the rank-and-file employees. To the extent that a management paradigm is an integral component of a theory of the state, the implications of TQM and the reinvention of government drive toward new theory. The stakes are greater than merely finding a new ideology to justify the managerial premises of reinventing government. The broader point is made forcefully by Chester Newland (1984): "To have a workable separation of powers system, with a reasonable balance of informed continuity and politically responsive change, a model other than the centralized, hierarchical executive is needed" (p. 33).

Process/Procedural Democracy

The model that is beginning to emerge around the concepts of reinventing government and quality management clearly implies the democratization of process and procedure. For example, Donald Kettl (1993) attempts to pull together the strands of the new management developments in an approach that he terms "New Governance." Kettl raises interesting and valid questions regarding the difficulty of maintaining the rule of law, of considering citizens as customers, of measuring results when goals are unclear or conflicting, of encouraging initiative and risk taking in politically charged environments. The answer that Kettl (1993) proposes for these vexing questions is tentative, experimental, process oriented, and radically different from the old hierarchical executive model with its assurance of certainty and command (p. 19).

Some overtly political concepts of a new model of governance may also be found in Robert Dahl's (1977) doctrine of procedural democracy. In bare outline, Dahl establishes five criteria for evaluating political performance in reference to achieving "a society with a political system in which liberty, equality, and justice would jointly prosper" (p. 10). The criteria for collective decision making by the people (demos) are as follows: (a) *political equality* for all members of the demos in the decision process; (b) *effective participation* in the decision process for all members; (c) *enlightened understanding* for all members to discover and validate their preferences; (d) *inclusiveness* of all adult members with an obligation to adhere to decisions; and (e) *final control by the demos* over procedures that are followed when decisions cannot be made through a process of procedural democracy (Dahl, 1977, pp. 11-12).

Dahl identifies two primary impediments to procedural democracy in America. One is the nature of the modern American presidency (to be considered later). The second impediment is the influence of the structure and operating characteristics of the modern corporation and, by extension, governmental civilian and military bureaucracies. The modern corporate model meant that "an increasing proportion of the demos would live out their working lives, and most of their daily existence, not within a democratic system but instead within a hierarchical structure of subordination" (p. 8). This condition leads Dahl (1977) to recommend an openness to new ideas about organizational governance and a belief that "the requisites of procedural democracy hold among the people who work for economic enterprises, and that the criteria of procedural democracy ought therefore to be applied to the government of firms" (p. 16).

Thus does an eminent theorist of democratic politics arrive at one of the fundamental premises of quality management; however, Dahl confined his advocacy to economic enterprises. In later work, Dahl (1990) concludes that rule by the people requires nondemocratic and hierarchical forms of delegated authority (pp. 72-73). In this, Dahl remains caught in the modern concept of overhead democracy, but that concept is being overtaken by the managerial impossibility of the presidency and by the mushrooming application of the premises of reinventing government. Consequently, Dahl's idea of procedural democracy must be appropriated without his permission for application to governmental organizations, for here is the potential for connecting the reinvention of government to the theory of political democracy—the merger of new managerial theory and practice to classical conceptions of democracy. This is an argument that requires overt establishment in theory and demonstration in practice, for it is only in this way that reinventing government can be legitimated politically. This is how a new theory of politics and administration can broaden and deepen the meaning of democracy in America.

Process and procedural democracy provides a compelling basis for replacing the theory of overhead democracy. As John Updike (1992) has President James Buchanan assert: "Power does not flow from the government, in a nation constructed such as ours; it flows upward, from the people" (p. 344). At issue is how this Madisonian truism can be given practical effect. The optimum answer would be a presidency that is redefined in light of contemporary conditions and emergent theories of management and politics.

Redefining the Political Presidency

As noted above, Dahl (1977) identifies a major impediment to democracy in America as "the pseudo-democratization of the presidency," noting that it "was transformed into a kind of plebiscitary principate with despotic tendencies toward arbitrary, ruthless, and self-aggrandizing exploitation of power" (pp. 7, 17). Although this indictment is perhaps overwrought, coming as it did immediately after Nixon and Watergate, it does highlight the problematic characteristic of the late modern and early postmodern presidency.

It is not possible to diminish the significance of the presidency in American political and administrative life (Rimmerman, 1993, p. 125). It is, however, possible to define a new approach to presidential leadership. The presidency can provide a sound basis for governmental administration if it abandons concepts of hierarchical command and political control, and instead focuses on administrative leadership in the sense developed by Selznick (1957): *"The executive becomes a statesman as he makes the transition from administrative management to institutional leadership"* (p. 4).

In this context, leadership is specifically political, involving: defining and redefining the public interest; balancing group interests with the larger public interest; promoting, protecting, and infusing values throughout the polity; defining missions, roles, goals, and ends; defending institutional integrity and the distinctive competencies of agencies; resolving internal conflict; and fostering participation (Selznick, 1957). The presidency is in a strong position to provide the "teleological sense of purpose" that is essential to administration (Gawthrop, 1990, p. 527). The presidency serves as the primary "highlighter" of major national concerns. Administration will be effective if that role is coupled with presidential attention "to the establishment and maintenance of reliable processes through which [other] issues can be handled" (Salamon, 1981, pp. 292-293).

This conception of the presidency is not, in itself, postmodern; however, it may point the direction toward effective presidential governance in a postmodern era. Without such a redefined model of leadership, the manifestation of postmodern characteristics in the presidency is a formula for failure, as attested to by the internal failures of the Clinton White House. The Clinton administration has attempted to adapt to the requirements of postmodern governance. Apparently, Clinton appreciates the new concepts of information-age management and leadership. According to Jack Watson (1993), Clinton's "personal style is exuberant, informal, interactive, non-hierarchical, and indefatigable" (p. 431). Clinton's policy-making process also shows a different approach: "In his use of special task forces, policy councils, and loosely-defined clusters of friends and advisors, he is borrowing the current management technique of 'work teams' from corporate America" (Watson, 1993, p. 431).

The adaptation of new managerial techniques can be effective only if it reaches far beyond the immediate office of the president and looks to the full utilization of the resources and talents of the administrative institution. The president as builder and protector of public sector institutions would be far stronger than recent presidents who have emphasized political control and institutional disinvestment.

The issue of active citizen participation in governmental affairs also must be addressed. One of the problems of the elevation of the modern "textbook" presidency is identified by Grover (1989) as a cheapening or stifling of the quality of citizen participation. An overreliance on the presidency for the solution of social problems inhibits the development and exercise of active citizenship. Any failure of the president fails to meet unrealistically high expectations, as he must inevitably fail, leads to a reaction of cynicism and despair and ultimately a weakening of public institutions (Grover, 1989, p. 53). The logic of the quality management techniques of reinventing government leads to a recognition of the significance of meaningful and effective citizen participation in a model of participatory democracy (Rimmerman, 1993, p. 127). Presidential administrative leadership would find a new strength through a strong commitment to community, citizens, and active citizenship (see Stivers, Chapter 9, this volume). What is needed is not a "strong" presidency as defined in conventional power terms, but rather presidential leadership of a "strong" democracy as advocated by Barber (1984).

Indications for the Public Administration

Should the presidency develop in the direction indicated above, the reinvention of government and the refounding of the public administration would be greatly enhanced. The problem of the presidency would be resolved, and effective, responsive governance would be assured. In this circumstance, the public administration would be responsive to the presidency by creating communities of meaning and discourse in the pursuit of the public interest, as outlined by White and McSwain (McSwite, Chapter 7, this volume).

But what if the pressures of time, events, exigencies, predilections, and electoral imperatives move the presidency back toward the characteristics of the late modern presidency—plebiscitary, personal, paranoid, and antiadministration? If the president does not adapt as a leader and manager to the requirements of the postmodern world, then public administrators must adapt to those requirements in creative ways. The challenge for the public administration, as Dennard states (Chapter 11, this volume), is to develop a democratic ontology—to replace its traditional identity as merely the efficient and effective provider of technical and professional services.

The new emphasis must necessarily shift to citizenship and participation, and to process and procedural democracy. It will not be sufficient to wait passively for orders from above, but rather to work actively in building communities of commitment and participation. Citizen empowerment should accompany public sector employee empowerment. In this way, bottom-up management can be joined by a bottom-up politics. Wilson Carey McWilliams (1980) summarizes the problem in this way: "Democracy requires, I think, an end to the moral dominion of the great modern project that set humankind in pursuit of the mastery of nature. Democracy is for friends and citizens, not masters and slaves" (p. 101).

━ Resolving the Problem of the Presidency

The argument for refounding the public administration, flowing from the Blacksburg Manifesto and subsequent discussions, implies a radical revision of overhead democracy. The emphasis of this perspective is on an agency rather than a presidential perspective and on empowered administrators with discretion for action that is based primarily on the Constitution, rather than on the blind obedience to the authority of political superiors or a slavish devotion to professional and technical expertise.

The refounding argument has been vigorously attacked, most notably by Herbert Kaufman, on the grounds that democratic responsiveness would be lost "if the career officers and employees of governments feel no moral obligation to conscientiously obey elected officials acting through constitutionally prescribed procedures" (Wamsley et al., 1990, p. 314). This criticism is obviously still caught in the ideology of overhead democracy as the only available solution to the problem of administrative responsiveness to democratic politics. Such criticism is specifically oriented to the presidency, following the course laid down years ago by Herman Finer, an emotional believer in the American chief executive, who once characterized the presidency as "the incarnation of the American people in a sacrament resembling that in which the wafer and the wine are seen to be the body and blood of Christ" and also as "belong[ing] rightfully to the offspring of a titan and Minerva husbanded by Mars" (Finer, 1960, quoted in Nelson, 1990, p. 5).

The public administration cannot be founded on such a mythic presidency. Rather, democratic public administration is founded on a combination of technical competence, managerial effectiveness, and most importantly, a democratic ontology. As Rosenbloom (1993) points out, "public administration is an intensely political process that should be responsive to interested publics and legislators" (p. 505). The challenge for the public administration is recognizing and adapting to its political identity in ways that foster process and procedural democracy. Such an arduous task is made easier in the late

20th century by the dramatic changes in managerial theory and ideology that are appearing throughout the American economy, ironically enough coming primarily from the private sector where the concern is not with democracy but with organizational competitiveness. The lesson for the presidency is that it can no longer pose as the chief executive office, or as a plebiscitary leader, but rather as the political leader of process and procedural democracy. The president who successfully defines the politics and management of governance, not as a top-down authoritarian enterprise but as a bottom-up process, becomes the president for the postmodern age.

The lesson for the public administration is drawn by Gawthrop (1990) when he says, "Democracy is meaningless unless administered democratically" (p. 522). At stake is the possibility of democratizing means as well as ends, direction and control as well as policy. Obviously, if the president exerts new leadership and fosters new managerial concepts, the administrative establishment can and will flourish. If not, the public administration will need to establish and develop processes of procedural democracy to connect knowledge and authority, to change policy subsystems into policy communities.

A doctrine of process and procedural democracy offers a constructive response to Kaufman and other critics of the Blacksburg Manifesto who fear the establishment of a nonresponsive, hence arrogant, bureaucracy that escapes the control of the people. However, the critics are attempting to defend an ancien régime as they argue from the obsolete concept of overhead democracy and show their allegiance to the Herman Finer school of unconditional and unquestioning responsiveness to the whims of presidential political direction. The answer to these critics is a democratic answer in a democratic polity. The times demand that the presidency and the public administration abandon Finer; abandon overhead democracy; abandon the false promises of control, hierarchy, and authoritarianism; let go of dependence on direction from the top. As public administrators build alliances with citizens, legislatures, customers, suppliers, and employees, the public administration becomes more than an instrumental function of enforcing the law or operating according to rule. Rather, it becomes a function of carrying out the will of the people as expressed in a complex mix of election results, law and regulation, customer preference, professionalism, and direct interaction with the citizenry.

The public administration then plays an integral role in the true and highest conception of democratic politics—consensus, dialogue, community, and public interest—not merely a function of command and obedience either to elected officials or legal prescriptions. In these postmodern times, both the presidency and the public administration can be legitimated through attachment to a developed concept of process and procedural democracy.

■ References

Arnold, P. E. (1986). *Making the managerial presidency: Comprehensive reorganization planning, 1905-1980*. Princeton, NJ: Princeton University Press.

Austin, N. K. (1993, September). Reorganizing the organization chart. *Working Woman,* pp. 23-26.

Banfield, E. C. (1980). Policy science as metaphysical madness. In R. A. Goldwin (Ed.), *Bureaucrats, policy analysts, statesmen: Who leads?* (pp. 1-19). Washington, DC: American Enterprise Institute for Public Policy Research.

Barber, B. R. (1984). *Strong democracy: Participatory politics for a new age*. Berkeley: University of California Press.

Barilleaux, R. J. (1988). *The post-modern presidency: The office after Ronald Reagan*. New York: Praeger.

Beer, S. H. (1978). In search of a new public philosophy. In A. King (Ed.), *The new American political system* (pp. 5-44). Washington, DC: American Enterprise Institute for Public Policy Research.

Bendix, R. (1956). *Work and authority in industry: Ideologies of management in the course of industrialization*. New York: Harper Torchbooks.

Blumenthal, S. (1988). Reaganism and the neokitsch aesthetic. In S. Blumentahl & T. B. Edsall (Eds.), *The Reagan legacy* (pp. 251-294). New York: Pantheon.

Borgmann, A. (1992). *Crossing the postmodern divide*. Chicago: University of Chicago Press.

Bower, J. L. (1983). *The two faces of management: An American approach to leadership in business and politics*. Boston: Houghton Mifflin.

Burke, J. P. (1992). *The institutional presidency*. Baltimore, MD: Johns Hopkins University Press.

Burns, J. M. (1965). *Presidential government: The crucible of leadership*. Boston: Houghton Mifflin.

Carr, D. K., & Littman, I. D. (1990). *Excellence in government: Total quality management in the 1990s*. Arlington, VA: Coopers & Lybrand.

Cater, D. (1964). *Power in Washington: A critical look at today's struggle to govern in the nation's capital*. New York: Vintage.

Corwin, E. S. (1951). *A constitution of powers in a secular state: Three lectures on the William H. White Foundation at the University of Virginia, April 1950 and an additional chapter*. Charlottesville, VA: Michie Company.

Corwin, E. S. (1976). *Presidential power and the constitution: Essays* (R. Loss, Ed.). Ithaca, NY: Cornell University Press.

Cronin, T. E. (1975). "Everybody believes in democracy until he gets to the White House . . .": An examination of White House-departmental relations. In A. Wildavsky (Ed.), *Perspectives on the presidency* (pp. 362-393). Boston: Little, Brown.

Cronin, T. E. (1980). *The state of the presidency* (2nd ed.). Boston: Little, Brown.

Dahl, R. A. (1977). On removing certain impediments to democracy in the United States. *Political Science Quarterly, 92,* 1-20.

Dahl, R. A. (1990). *After the revolution: Authority in a good society* (rev. ed.). New Haven, CT: Yale University Press.

Denhardt, R. B., & Prelgovisk, K. (1992). Public leadership: A developmental perspective. In R. B. Denhardt & W. H. Stewart (Eds.), *Executive leadership in the public service* (pp. 33-44). Tuscaloosa: University of Alabama Press.

Denton, R. E., Jr. (1988). *The primetime presidency of Ronald Reagan: The era of the television presidency*. New York: Praeger.

Devine, D. J. (1991). *Reagan's terrible swift sword: Reforming & controlling the federal bureaucracy*. Ottawa, IL: Jameson Books.

Doctorow, E. L. (1992). The character of presidents. *The Nation, 255,* 534-536.

Dluhy, M. J. (1992). [Review of the book *Reinventing government: How the entrepreneurial spirit is transforming the public sector*]. *Policy Studies Review,* 189-192.

Dumaine, B. (1993, February 22). The new non-manager manager. *Fortune, 127,* pp. 80-84.

Finer, H. (1960). *The presidency: Crisis and regeneration: An essay in possibilities.* Chicago: University of Chicago Press.

Fisher, L. (1972). *President and congress: Power and policy.* New York: Free Press.

Gawthrop, L. C. (1990). Grail hunting, dragon slaying, and prudent resilience: The quest for ethical maturity in American public administration. *Public Administration Quarterly, 13,* 520-542.

Goodsell, C. T. (1994). *The case for bureaucracy: A public administration polemic* (3rd ed.). Chatham, NJ: Chatham House.

Gormley, W. T., Jr. (1989). *Taming the bureaucracy: Muscles, prayers, and other strategies.* Princeton, NJ: Princeton University Press.

Grover, W. F. (1989). *The president as prisoner: A structural critique of the Carter and Reagan years.* Albany: State University of New York Press.

Heclo, H. (1981). Introduction: The presidential illusion. In H. Heclo & L. M. Salamon (Eds.), *The illusion of presidential government* (pp. 1-17). Boulder, CO: Westview.

Heclo, H. (1983). One executive branch or many? In A. King (Ed.), *Both ends of the avenue: The presidency, the executive branch, and congress in the 1980s* (pp. 26-58). Washington, DC: American Enterprise Institute for Public Policy Research.

Helmer, J. (1981). The presidential office: Velvet fist in an iron glove. In H. Heclo & L. M. Salamon (Eds.), *The illusion of presidential government* (pp. 45-81). Boulder, CO: Westview.

Hofstadter, R. (1965). *The paranoid style in American politics: And other essays.* Chicago: University of Chicago Press.

Karl, B. D. (1969). Presidential planning and social science research: Mr. Hoover's experts. In *Perspectives in American history* (Vol. 3, pp. 347-409). Cambridge, MA: Harvard University, Charles Warren Center for Studies in American History.

Kaufman, H. (1956). Emerging conflicts in the doctrine of public administration. *American Political Science Review, 50,* 1057-1073.

Kettl, D. F. (1993). Toward new governance: Making process a priority. *The LaFollette Policy Report, 5,* 1-2, 18-19.

King, G., & Ragsdale, L. (1988). *The elusive executive: Discovering statistical patterns in the presidency.* Washington, DC: CQ Press.

Light, P. C. (1991). *The president's agenda: Domestic policy choice from Kennedy to Reagan* (rev. ed.). Baltimore, MD: Johns Hopkins University Press.

Light, P. C. (1992). Watch what we pass: A brief legislative history of civil service reform. In P. W. Ingraham & D. H. Rosenbloom (Eds.), *The promise and paradox of civil service reform* (pp. 303-325). Pittsburgh: University of Pittsburgh Press.

Long, N. (1949). Power and administration. *Public Administration Review, 9,* 257-264.

Lowi, T. J. (1985). *The personal president: Power invested, promise unfulfilled.* Ithaca, NY: Cornell University Press.

Mansfield, H. C., Jr. (1981). The ambivalence of executive power. In J. M. Bessett & J. Tulis (Eds.), *The presidency in the constitutional order* (pp. 314-341). Baton Rouge: Louisiana State University Press.

McGregor, E. B., Jr. (1988). The public sector human resource puzzle. *Public Administration Review, 48,* 941-950.

McWilliams, W. C. (1980). Democracy and the citizen: Community, dignity, and the crisis of contemporary politics in America. In R. A. Goldwin & W. A. Schambra (Eds.), *How democratic is the constitution?* (pp. 79-101). Washington, DC: American Enterprise Institute for Public Policy Research.

Menand, L. (1993, May-June). The future of academic freedom. *Academe, 79,* pp. 11-17.

Miroff, B. (1988). The presidency and the public: Leadership as spectacle. In M. Nelson (Ed.), *The presidency and the political system* (2nd ed.) (pp. 271-291). Washington, DC: CQ Press.

Moe, R. C. (1990). Traditional organizational principles and managerial presidency: From phoenix to ashes. *Public Administration Review, 50,* 129-140.

Moe, T. M. (1985). The politicized presidency. In J. E. Chubb & P. E. Peterson (Eds.), *The new direction in American politics* (pp. 235-271). Washington, DC: Brookings Institution.

Morrow, W. L. (1984). Woodrow Wilson and the politics of morality: The 1980s and beyond. In J. Rabin & J. S. Bowman (Eds.), *Politics and administration: Woodrow Wilson and American public administration* (pp. 251-262). New York: Marcel Dekker.

Nathan, R. P. (1983). *The administrative presidency.* New York: John Wiley.

National Commission on the State and Local Public Service. (1993). *Hard truths/tough choices: An agenda for state and local reform.* Albany: SUNY, Nelson A. Rockefeller Institute of Government.

Nelson, M. (1990). Evaluating the presidency. In M. Nelson (Ed.), *The presidency and the political system* (3rd ed., pp. 3-28). Washington, DC: CQ Press.

Neustadt, R. E. (1960). *Presidential power: The politics of leadership.* New York: John Wiley.

Newland, C. A. (1984). *Public administration and community: Realism in the practice of ideals.* McLean, VA: Public Administration Service.

Newland, C. A. (1987). Public executives: Imperium, sacerdotium, collegium? Bicentennial leadership challenges. *Public Administration Review, 47,* 45-56.

Office of the Vice President, National Performance Review. (1993). *From red tape to results: Creating a government that works better & costs less.* Washington, DC: Government Printing Office.

Osborne, D., & Gaebler, T. (1992). *Reinventing government: How the entrepreneurial spirit is transforming the public sector.* Reading, MA: Addison-Wesley.

Peters, T. (1993, September). Thriving in chaos. *Working Woman,* pp. 42-45, 100-108.

Pfiffner, J. P. (1988). *The strategic presidency: Hitting the ground running.* Chicago: Dorsey.

The President's Committee on Administrative Management. (1937). *Report of the committee with studies of administrative management in the federal government.* Washington, DC: Government Printing Office.

Rector, R. (1988). H.R. 5195 and H.R. 5196: Civil service changes that set back the clock. *Heritage Foundation Reports,* Issue Bulletin No. 143.

Redford, E. S. (1969). *Democracy in the administrative state.* New York: Oxford University Press.

Rimmerman, C. A. (1993). *Presidency by plebiscite: The Reagan-Bush era in institutional perspective.* Boulder, CO: Westview.

Rockman, B. A. (1993). Tightening the reins: The federal executive and the management philosophy of the Reagan presidency. *Presidential Studies Quarterly, 23,* 103-114.

Rohr, J. A. (1986). *To run a constitution: The legitimacy of the administrative state.* Lawrence: University Press of Kansas.

Rohr, J. A. (1989). *The president and the public administration.* Washington, DC: American Historical Association.

Rose, R. (1988). *The postmodern president: The White House meets the world.* Chatham, NJ: Chatham House.

Rosenbloom, D. H. (1993). Have an administrative Rx? Don't forget the politics! [Editorial]. *Public Administration Review, 53,* 503-507.

Rossiter, C. (1960). *The American presidency.* New York: Time Incorporated.

Rourke, F. E. (1992). American exceptionalism: Government without bureaucracy. In L. B. Hill (Ed.), *The state of public bureaucracy* (pp. 223-229). Armonk, NY: M. E. Sharpe.

Salamon, L. M. (1981). Conclusion: Beyond the presidential illusion—Toward a constitutional presidency. In H. Heclo & L. M. Salamon (Eds.), *The illusion of presidential government* (pp. 287-295). Boulder, CO: Westview.

Sanera, M. (1987). Paradoxical lessons from "In search of excellence." In R. Rector & M. Sanera (Eds.), *Steering the elephant: How Washington works* (pp. 163-179). New York: Universe Books.

Seidman, H., & Gilmour, R. (1986). *Politics, position, and power: From the positive to the regulatory state* (4th ed.). New York: Oxford University Press.

Seligman, L. G., & Covington, C. R. (1989). *The coalitional presidency.* Chicago: Dorsey.

Selznick, P. (1957). *Leadership in administration: A sociological interpretation.* New York: Harper & Row.

Shogan, R. (1991). *The riddle of power: Presidential leadership from Truman to Bush.* New York: E. P. Dutton.

Smoller, F. T. (1990). *The six o'clock presidency.* New York: Praeger.

Storing, H. J. (1980). American statesmanship: Old and new. In R. A. Goldwin (Ed.), *Bureaucrats, policy analysts, statesmen: Who leads?* (pp. 88-113). Washington, DC: American Enterprise Institute for Public Policy Research.

Taylor, J. R., & Van Every, E. J. (1993). *The vulnerable fortress: Bureaucratic organization and management in the information age.* Toronto: University of Toronto Press.

Thompson, V. A. (1965). Bureaucracy in a democratic society. In R. C. Martin (Ed.), *Public administration and democracy: Essays in honor of Paul H. Appleby* (pp. 205-226). Syracuse, NY: Syracuse University Press.

Truman, D. B. (1951). *The governmental process: Political interests and public opinion.* New York: Knopf.

Tulis, J. K. (1990). The two constitutional presidencies. In M. Nelson (Ed.), *The presidency and the political system* (3rd ed., pp. 85-115). Washington, DC: CQ Press.

U.S. General Accounting Office. (1993). *Improving government: Need to reexamine organization and performance.* GAO/T-GGD, 93-9. Washington, DC: General Accounting Office.

U.S. General Accounting Office. (1992). *Quality management: Survey of federal organizations.* GAO/GGD-93-9BR. Washington, DC: General Accounting Office.

Updike, J. (1992). *Memories of the Ford administration: A novel.* New York: Knopf.

Waldo, D. (1984). *The administrative state: A study of the political theory of American public administration* (2nd ed.). New York: Holmes & Meier.

Wamsley, G. L. (1990). The agency perspective: Public administrators as agential leaders. In G. L. Wamsley, R. N. Bacher, C. T. Goodsell, P. S. Kronenberg, J. A. Rohr, C. M. Stivers, O. F. White, & J. F. Wolf, *Refounding public administration* (pp. 114-162). Newbury Park, CA: Sage.

Wamsley, G. L., Bacher, R. N., Goodsell, C. T., Kronenberg, P. S., Rohr, J. A., Stivers, C. M., White, O. F., & Wolf, J. F. (1990). *Refounding public administration.* Newbury Park, CA: Sage.

Waterman, R. W. (1989). *Presidential influence and the administrative state.* Knoxville: University of Tennessee Press.

Watson, J. H., Jr. (1993). The Clinton White House. *Presidential Studies Quarterly, 23,* 429-435.

Wildavsky, A. (1991). *The beleaguered presidency.* New Brunswick, NJ: Transaction Books.

Williams, W. (1990). *Mismanaging America: The rise of the anti-analytic presidency.* Lawrence: University Press of Kansas.

Williams, W. (1993). George Bush and executive branch domestic policymaking competence. *Policy Studies Journal, 21,* 700-717.

Wills, G. (1987). *Reagan's America: Innocents at home.* Garden City, NY: Doubleday.

Wills, G. (1991, June 13). The man who wasn't there. *The New York Review,* pp. 3-7.

Woll, P., & Jones, R. (1980). The bureaucracy as a check upon the president. In H. A. Bailey (Ed.), *Classics of the American presidency* (pp. 363-370). Oak Park, IL: Moore Publishing.

Yates, D. (1982). *Bureaucratic democracy: The search for democracy and efficiency in American government.* Cambridge, MA: Harvard University Press.

9

Refusing to Get It Right

Citizenship, Difference,
and the Refounding Project

CAMILLA STIVERS
The Evergreen State College

What sort of project is the "Refounding Project?" Critics have tended to see it as an effort to diminish politics and justify administrative power in the public realm. Consider, for example, Herbert Kaufman's argument that the Blacksburg Manifesto "imperil[s] democratic government" (Wamsley et al., 1990, p. 315), or Philip J. Cooper's verdict that "the argument included in the Blacksburg statement is destructive of the Republic" (Wamsley et al., 1990, p. 313), or the view expressed by Fox and Cochran (1990) that the Manifesto turns politics into "epiphenomenal noise" (p. 106).

Certain statements in the Manifesto and in its sequel, *Refounding Public Administration,* particularly if taken out of context, do seem to support the critical view that the Refounding Project's aim is to reduce governance to administration, to the exercise of expert, professional leadership for rational decision making and the maintenance of order. To illustrate:

> The only possible source of governing impetuses that might keep our complex political system from either a dangerous concentration of power on the one hand, or impotence or self-destruction on the other, is a public administration with the necessary professionalism, dedication, self-esteem, and legitimacy to act as the constitutional center of gravity. (Wamsley et al., 1990, p. 26)

Here, one might conceivably say, is the quintessence of the antidemocratic: The Public Administration as institutional hero, shepherding the public interest, that fragile creature, between the twin evils of totalitarianism and chaos.

From one angle, then, critics have a point: The Refounding Project can be read as a move to displace politics (public struggle, conflicting values) in favor of order (in this case administratively achieved), an aim with a long tradition in Western political theory (Honig, 1993). From a different perspective, however, the texts of the project can be read as, collectively, an encounter with politics and an effort to rethink administration in its light: not to reconcile public administration to a given set of political dynamics, because, as I want to argue, such a reconciliation would itself be antipolitical, but to "re-found" (re-conceive, re-birth) public administration in a manner that shows how administration can be, not the be-all and end-all of governance, but still legitimately "political." In at least this respect, I shall suggest, refounding public administration is fundamentally different from "reinventing government" (Osborne & Gaebler, 1992).

My sense of the Refounding Project, after having been a critical associate for more than 10 years, is that the Blacksburg philosophy is both coherent and permeable, perhaps more so on the latter count than many of its critics (and perhaps its authors, too) are aware, and that its openness is one of its greatest assets as a normative theory of public administration. With each reading of the Manifesto and its successor essays, I encounter ideas that are "always there" *and* perceive new spaces of openness, of potential contest. Recently that "settled-open" or "solid-fluid" experience has begun to seem less a personal idiosyncrasy than a response to something meaningful in Refounding Project discourse: that is, its form and rhetoric appear to express a crucial insight about the relationship between politics and administration in a constitutional polity, but one that may sometimes be overlooked.

Any theoretical edifice erected in support of such a polity must reflect two dynamics that are inevitably at odds with each other. One is the search for order, continuity, and the satisfaction of needs; the other is the urge to dislodge existing arrangements for the sake of righting their imperfections (Honig, 1993). The first impulse aims to settle things, to get it right, the second to disrupt in order to make better. The Refounding Project texts reflect both, though critics tend to see only the former because (I believe) they focus on the project's urge to be definitive, and neglect the many places where the force of the argument depends, paradoxically enough, on there being no possibility of getting it right. My aim in this chapter is to raise the profile of this latter disruptive impulse, which, as Honig observes, is fundamentally political. This impulse needs heightening, in my view, because in its engagement with the tension between politics and administration the project (understandably enough) begins from administration and moves toward politics, and has yet to reach a point where the two could meet as equals. The thrust of this chapter, then, will be to highlight those aspects of the Refounding Project that "refuse to get it right," and suggest conceptual moves that will strengthen this aspect of the project's theoretical dynamic.

The unsettled places in the Refounding Project mean that one could come at what I want to argue is its heart from a number of angles. One could find a way in, for example, starting from authority, or the public interest, or agency, or legitimacy. I choose to start from the idea of citizenship, partly because this was the opening by which I initially found my own way into the Manifesto, but also because the notion of citizenship offers the opportunity to foreground certain theoretical potentials that are important in strengthening the project's political dynamic and that offer resources that both the field's prevailing political accountability model (hierarchical executive authority answerable to the legislature) and "reinventing government," as well, fail to deliver.

In my view, *Refounding Public Administration* calls for a conceptual scheme and practice in which politics and administration are in contested relationship (and because the relationship is a continuing contest, and politics *is* contest, politics has the edge). The legitimate desire to provide moral and theoretical support to beleaguered bureaucrats should not be permitted to obscure this need by stressing the merits of system steerage so much that the democratic possibilities of politics are occluded. Politics cannot depend solely on legislative accountability; it also requires a strong form of citizenship in order not to be overwhelmed by the administrative tendency toward self-aggrandizement (rooted in the undeniable allure of social and economic stability), which continually threatens to take control of, even—perhaps inadvertently—to smother, its precarious partnership with politics.

Throughout the course of Western thought, citizenship has been a fundamental aspect of politics, even in the weak form inherited from Lockean liberalism, more obviously so in the strong, civic republican variety traceable to Aristotle. Citizens embody the agonistic urge to contest, to call existing arrangements into question, including—perhaps especially—the results of administrative rationality. Not surprisingly, administrators tend to view active citizens with, at best, mixed feelings. Yet administrative governance, if it is to be governance rather than management, must embrace the otherness, the openness, of the disruptive political impulse, that is, of active citizenship. Left solely to legislative accountability, democratic politics becomes too attenuated to counter the professional need to get things right and therefore to shut down dialogue. The administrative state needs active citizens because it needs a viable democratic politics if it is to remain a state rather than to continue to harden into a mere management mechanism.

In order to play this role in a theory of administrative governance, however, the idea of citizenship itself is in need of rebirth. The history of citizenship reflects its own persistent impetus toward closure, exclusion, and uniformity, one that now requires us to think differently about who citizens are and what the practice of citizenship entails in order to widen rather than narrow the space of politics in the administrative state. In an earlier iteration of the Refounding Project (Stivers, 1990a), I argued for a strong understanding of the citizen role, one based on the Aristotelian idea of the citizen as someone who rules and is ruled in turn, who sets aside self-interest in order to share in decision making in aid of the public good. Compared to liberalism's citizen, a bearer of rights who consents to be governed in order to pursue self-interests as freely as possible, it still seems to me that the active, Aristotelian citizen is a better model, because it emphasizes the performative and agonistic aspects of democratic politics. The trouble is that, when one examines even participatory citizenship closely, one finds that as widely understood it operates in an exceedingly constrained public space from which a great many qualities and considerations have been barred. It is this closure I want to subvert in order to invigorate politics in the administrative state.

Reframing Citizenship

Since Aristotle, we have known what a citizen was in contrast to what a citizen was not. Issues such as whether citizenship encompasses women, whether to admit or exclude the foreign-born, whether the sphere of citizenship requires the labor of "others" excluded on the basis of their sex and/or race—all have been central questions during the long process through which we have come to understand citizenship, and all still pose practical and theoretical problems today. By now, the exclusion of women, slaves, and the foreign-born from the Athenian polity of Aristotle's day is too well known to need cataloguing here, as are the contortions liberal theorists had to perform in order to grant women citizenship in theory while withholding it from them in practice (see, e.g., Clark & Lange, 1979; Eisenstein, 1981; Okin, 1979; Pateman, 1989; Pomeroy, 1975; Saxonhouse, 1985). What might be helpful, however, is to point out how such exclusions have shaped ways in which certain defining characteristics of citizenship have been understood and practiced. I would like to discuss two of these: the nature of the citizen's authoritative public speech, and the public-private distinction itself.

A central feature of citizenship has been the right to speak publicly, whether it was the liberal citizen's constitutive, contractual "Yes" to the state, thus granting it legitimate authority, or the civic republican's right to share in authoritative public deliberations. Yet gender and ethnic background have restricted access to civic speech since ancient Greece. In the Athens where citizens ruled, women were not only barred from the public space but physically restricted to the inner recesses of the household (Keuls, 1985). Even "citizen" women (wives and daughters of citizens) had no right to speak in public. Aristotle argued that the proper functioning of the polity depended on the household and advocated relegating women and slaves to the latter on the basis of their inferior natures. The exclusion of women from public speech persisted throughout subsequent Western history; they represented the illicit intrusion of the domestic into political life. Only comparatively recently, for example, have women in Western democracies won the right to vote, been elected to public office, headed public agencies, and served equally on juries, and they are still markedly underrepresented in public life in proportion to their numbers in the population.

Slaves and other foreign-born persons were also excluded from Athenian citizenship. As Held (1987) notes, the formation of a slave economy made possible the flowering of Greek urban culture; the growing sense of identity and solidarity in Greek cities drew clear lines between insiders (citizens) and outsiders (slaves and foreigners). U.S. history reflects the same concern over the racial or ethnic boundaries of the political community. From the colonial era onwards, the difference between slavery and free citizenship was a particularly meaningful dimension of American political life. Robinson (1971) notes that "[w]henever the colonists felt that an established and familiar pattern of governance was being disturbed, the cry of 'slavery' rose almost automatically to their lips" (p. 60).

Given the existence of widespread chattel slavery in pre-Revolutionary America, it is likely that "slavery" was more than a colorful political metaphor; it was also an ever-present object lesson. In his study of colonial Virginia, Morgan (1975) observes:

> The presence of men and women who were, in law at least, almost totally subject to the will of other men gave to those in control of them an immediate experience of what it could mean to be at the mercy of a tyrant. Virginians may have had a special appreciation of the freedom dear to republicans, because they saw every day what life without it could be like. (p. 376)

Both Shklar (1991) and Karst (1989) suggest that one of the most significant aspects of the Supreme Court's infamous Dred Scott decision was that it denied membership in the American community not only to slaves but to all black people on the basis that they had not been members of the "people of the United States" referred to in the preamble to the Constitution. Shklar, in fact, argues that the history of citizenship has never been as much about empowerment as it has been about inclusion in the polity.

Patterson (1991) maintains that it is no accident that both the United States and ancient Athens grounded their democracies in slavery and the exclusion of women:

> We, the politically free body of men, always, it would seem, tragically require the *them* who do not belong: the ignoble, the nonkith, the nonkin, the people we do not marry, the alien within—the serf, the Jew, the slave, the Negro, the people who cannot vote—who demarcate what *we* are, the domestic enemy who defines whom *we* love. (p. 405)

Its apparent logic—the constitutive requirement that some persons be excluded from public speech in order that others may be assured of their inclusion—uncovers a deep paradox in the heart of citizenship: Despite its having been asserted in liberal philosophy as a universal principle in which all may share equally, certain "others"—women, people of color—have been and continue to be defined as different in order to justify continuing substantive inequality among members of the polity, who supposedly share a "universal" status. What have been seen as innate differences serve to ensure that correspondingly unequal rights and public obligations are considered justified and appropriate rather than unjust (Vogel, 1988). In U.S. history, women's peculiar nature rationalized the restriction of their political role to "republican motherhood," that is, nurturing citizen-like qualities in their husbands and sons rather than deliberating or voting (Kerber, 1980), and justified the enactment of "protective" legislation to regulate the conditions of their employment, as if men did not need similar protection from harsh working conditions. These arguments persist today in such controversies as the proper extent of women's involvement in combat or their access to public military academies like The Citadel.

Similarly, slaves were seen both as persons and as property in order that they should have the worst of both worlds: They could be bought and sold as property, but convicted of crimes as persons. Such treatment in law was justified on the basis that dark-skinned persons were innately inferior. Today, race is a suspect category in law, yet, as West (1992) argues, white Americans still see African Americans, the descendants of slaves, as "problem persons"—not quite persons in the same sense as themselves—rather than as persons with problems.[1]

The key question here is, What sort of identity does citizenship status entail? Must all citizens speak with the same voice? As a principle, the coherence of citizenship appears to require "identical" citizens, whose differences are politically insignificant; yet insisting on citizenship as a status in which all participate identically obliterates all the variations in life circumstances that shape the very practice of citizenship. "To be equal is to be the same; to be different is to be inferior" (Ferguson, 1988, p. 68)—there is the dilemma. Can we conceive of processes that involve citizens in administrative affairs, as the Manifesto recommends, in such a way that the ability to give voice is open not to an abstract, universal "all" but to different real humans in all their plurality?

A second problem with citizenship as traditionally conceived (whether the tradition be liberalism or civic republicanism) is the strict boundary between public and private realms it appears to require. The very idea that the citizen role is a public one, in which decision making addresses the public interest over private concerns, shows how central to our notion of citizenship the idea of publicness is. Yet our commonsense understanding of this public-private division, as a split between government and business, obscures another boundary: the one between civil society (containing both government and business) and the household. Liberalism's emphasis on protecting private property from government power has hidden this other division from view and as a result has depoliticized the household entirely.

As women have been granted the franchise and other rights that approach formal equality with men, the lingering contradiction between formal public equality and actual domestic inequality has become increasingly difficult to rationalize: "Liberal principles cannot simply be universalized to extend to women in the public sphere without raising an acute problem about the patriarchal structure of private life" (Pateman, 1989, p. 129)—that is, about inequities in the sexual division of labor. The traditional resolution of this difficulty has been to see household arrangements as natural and therefore beyond justice. The well-known feminist credo, "The personal is political," calls into question just this idea that it is natural to consider one half of humanity equal in one sphere of life and unequal in another.

The Refounding Project so far has ignored the difficulty involved in admitting women to the public sphere: once defined by the domestic, a woman cannot speak for the universal public interest without divesting herself of her particularity—without becoming Public Man (Landes, 1988). We have used the idea of the public interest as if the public space throughout history had been equally open to men and women. Yet the universality of the public interest has always been questionable, though accepted as given. In Western thought, household concerns, and women along with them, have been excluded in order for the space of the political to be distinctive.

Race is similarly problematic. For example, as Smith (1989) notes, civic republican ideas about the need to promote citizen virtue served to rationalize, both in ancient republics and in the American South, assigning the most menial, arduous, dangerous, yet apparently necessary work to a group of people—slaves—considered unfit for citizenship. Today, society's dirty work is still disproportionately done by people of color, and increasingly by an underground army of illegal aliens in fields and sweatshops, made vulnerable to the predations of unscrupulous employers by their fear of discovery and deportation; in other words, by their lack of citizenship.

Organizations are still dependent on women to bear the double burden of domestic and paid work, and the trend toward policies like publicly supported child care and paid family leave is exceedingly slow. The U.S. economy as a whole relies on the poorly paid labor of vulnerable, undocumented workers, "needed" by employers in order to preserve their profit margins but excluded from most social welfare provisions. The Refounding Project needs to reexamine the extent to which its conceptual framework is structurally enabled by relegating groups of people to lives so driven by survival exigencies that they have little or no tangible opportunity to climb on the citizenship bandwagon. The current schizophrenic policy dialogue in which middle-class women are subtly blamed for not being home enough, and poor (especially black) women are castigated for being home too much, reflects the instrumental way in which "different" people are treated. We need to rethink the nature of the public.

In order to rebirth a notion of citizenship that equips it to reinvigorate the political impulse in the Refounding Project, there appear to be at least two conceptual requirements. We need a plural rather than a universal understanding of the nature of citizen identity, and we need to unsettle the hard and fast public-private boundaries that equate "private" with "private business" and cast the domestic realm into apolitical darkness. Both moves would help to disrupt the project's urge to achieve closure, an urge that obscures the dependence of One Right Way on the wrongness of all other ways. The project needs to strengthen its political energy by developing an understanding of citizenship in the administrative state that furthers openness, plurality, and contest. Both impulses (order/closure and struggle/openness) are legitimate parts of the overall Blacksburg enterprise, as indeed of the administrative state itself; the strategy of further opening up the project's conceptual framework to politics simply aims to revivify the impulse I take to be the more vulnerable of the two under current conditions—particularly given our location as teachers and practitioners of public administration, which as a field seems generally to have been more readily seduced by the administrative than the political.

The elements of the Refounding Project in need of subverting are exemplified in characterizations of "The Public Administration" (Wamsley et al., 1990, p. 34) as a "counterweight" to "disturbing [political] tendencies" (p. 33); as the prime source of public sector authority and legitimacy (p. 35), whose "core" is "generic management technologies that comprise its 'administrative capacity' " (p. 36); whose "agency perspectives" are rooted in "specialized knowledge, historical experience, time-tested wisdom, and . . . some degree of consensus as to the public interest" (p. 37); as "cooling, containing, and directing foil to the capitalist marketplace" (p. 44); as a "balance wheel in the constitutional order, using . . . statutory powers and professional expertise to favor whichever participant in the constitutional process needs . . . help at a given time" (p. 47); as animated by "transcendent purpose" (p. 51). It is elements like these that evoke reactions like Cooper's and Kaufman's (cited above), which charge the Refounding Project with being antidemocratic; at moments the Manifesto does sound as if it has moved beyond lauding the public administration for making the trains run on time (bad enough, in that politics appears irrelevant) to praising it for having special competence to define the content of the public interest in particular situations (worse, in that administrative expertise expands from technical skill to political judgment).

Yet there is another set of factors in the text of the Manifesto that complicates the critics' too-easy assessment. If foregrounded and explored, ingredients such as the following may make possible an iteration of the Refounding Project less hostile to democratic politics:

- the idea that the American Dialogue contains a "fundamental *tension*" between liberty and order, and that the contest between the two has "worn *different* masks at different times" (Wamsley et al., 1990, p. 34) [all italics in this list are mine]

- the observation that the Agency Perspective is the product of a *struggle* to "achieve and enact some kind of consensus" (p. 37)

- the caution against "over-reliance on techniques like policy analysis, program evaluation, and decision science" (p. 38)

- the notion of the public interest as a *process* ideal rather than a substantive achievement, and the emphasis on the responsibility of public administrators to nurture that process (p. 40)

- the stress on *tentative* approaches, curiosity, dialogue, skepticism about "grand designs," and learning (p. 42)

- the recognition of the *ambiguities* in the notion of the politics-administration dichotomy (p. 42), which in some ways exists and in some ways does not (a contradiction that Cooper enjoyed pouncing on, without realizing that—by refusing to resolve this apparent paradox—the Manifesto serves the very political principles he so wishes to rescue)

Where the Manifesto's impulse toward openness and contest reaches perhaps its flood tide is this statement:

> The Public Administration should be neither monolithic nor homogeneous. It must assume a rich diversity of perspectives born of differentiation and specialization and ought to welcome constructive criticism from within and without. Differing perspectives ought to be granted a legitimacy, that is, they ought not to be judged as *ipso facto* self-serving, but as a part of the constitutional heritage of robust public dialogue. In this respect the Public Administration is an analog to the pluralism of the larger political process with all the attendant assets and liabilities plus one: the opportunity and the moral obligation to strive explicitly to achieve the broadest possible public interest, something theories of pluralism trust to an invisible hand. Thus the conflict among the differing perspectives of The Public Administration is a valuable part of the creative tension so essential to a healthy American dialogue. (Wamsley et al., 1990, p. 46)

This passage seems to me the Manifesto's clearest statement in opposition to administrative interests, in that the urge to be systematic and uniform appears basic to the administrative enterprise yet the authors insist that the public administration be pluralistic and immersed in controversy, that is, that we renounce the hope of getting it right. If we take the above statement seriously, it seems to invite us to explore the ramifications of diversity, of pluralism, in administrative governance processes. By exploring the two questions outlined above in light of this overture from the Blacksburg perspective, what "difference" can we make?

━ Refounding the Refounding Project

The Manifesto's call for the public administration to embrace a form of pluralism may offer an approach to reframing our understanding of the citizen's identity and voice. The allusion to pluralism is not without problems, however, given the thin form of citizenship that mainstream American pluralist thought has offered.[2] Although based on the idea that individuals in society have multiple memberships and identities, of which one, "citizenship," is constituted in the struggle of interest groups, American pluralism—through its emphasis on "the social"—attenuates the influence of economic class on its analysis and reduces government to the status of an arena for group competition. The individual, though multi-aspected, becomes a rational preference-orderer, and the public interest is defined as whatever emerges from the struggle among interest groups. Although grounded in the recognition that politics is fundamentally about differentiation and struggle, mainstream pluralism remains unsatisfactory: It takes the construction of identities and interests for granted; it assumes that the individual can and should rationally resolve his [*sic*] multiplicity; and it accepts the results of competition as, by definition, the public interest in rather blithe "whatever is, is right" fashion.

A more appealing form of pluralism might emerge if we could bracket interest and identity formation—that is, call into question how they are constituted in continuing social and political processes (McClure, 1992, p. 124). Rather than accepting at face value the notion that people come to see themselves in certain ways, we might contest identity formation in order to undercut the idea that citizenship is a universal status, which people must leave important parts of themselves behind in order to assume. In other words, instead of taking race- and gender-based identities as given, we could question the social, political, and economic processes through which they are constituted. They would then become aspects of citizen identity instead of elements to be purged from it. We would then see citizenship as a constructed rather than given political identity, one that has multiple facets (any one of which can take precedence depending on the situation at hand) and is in continuous enactment in a wide variety of tangible public spaces rather than one abstract, rarified realm. Given the relatively few opportunities for public dialogue in the contemporary American polity, administrative agencies then come to be seen as significant sites for such performative identity development, and the role they play in either constricting or expanding the range of legitimate citizen identities a matter of considerable urgency.

This view of citizenship as a performative practice is much like the one put forward by Hannah Arendt (1958), who saw "action" in public in front of fellow citizens as creating the actor's identity. Several recent commentators (Honig, 1992, 1993; Jones, 1993; Mouffe, 1991, 1992a, 1992b) agree that Arendt saw the self as multi-aspected ("There is difference in identity" [quoted in Honig, 1993, p. 82]) and that this plurality was the source of energy for and a condition of free action. For Arendt, free action witnessed by others creates "new relations and realities" (quoted in Honig, 1993, p. 78) rather than perpetuating existing ones, and gives birth to the actor rather than merely expressing his preexisting characteristics. Arendt argued that "who" one is must be determined by others as the result of public performance.

The difficulty of simply adopting Arendt's perspective as a model of citizenship for public administration, however, is her firm distinction between public and private. For Arendt, the private realm has to do with "what" we are, the public gives us "who" we are. The actor in public forsakes "what" it is in the private space of material needs and interests (Arendt, 1977). As Brown (1988) has observed, one problem with this scheme is that it seems to leave nothing for public dialogue and action to be about; but an additional difficulty is that the purity of Arendt's public realm threatens to purge difference: for those whose identities in some deep sense *are* their embodiment, as has been true throughout Western history for white women and for men and women of color, there is no negotiating the public-private barrier that Arendt's theory insists on (Honig, 1993). Thus although Arendt helps us toward an understanding of identity as constructed rather than given, and of politics as inherently plural and enacted, performed with and in sight of others, we need an understanding of the public that does not require the abandonment of embodied identity. Otherwise most of the central concerns of excluded "others" must be parked at the door into the public space.

The germ of such an understanding appears to lie in Arendt's belief that openness is the sine qua non of politics. For her, the will to system wipes out politics by closing down spaces of contestability (Honig, 1993). The viability of action in public—of governance—depends not on resolving issues and settling disputes but on openness to new alternatives, to new beginnings—to what Arendt called "augmentation." A proper republic empowers its citizens through committing itself to continual world building, in which citizens join (Arendt, 1977). Thus foundings are only legitimate to the extent that practices of augmentation bring that beginning into the present, make it not merely our legacy but our own ongoing construction and performance (Honig, 1993).

Legitimate authority in public, therefore, is not a matter of command and obedience but a process of historical connection (Jones, 1993) through which the present is made meaningful through augmentation—through "re-founding," in fact: making a founding (like the Declaration of Independence and the Constitution) not something settled once and for all, thus closing off the space of free action to all who come after it, but a process of continual renewal and rebirth.

Honig (1993) argues that achieving this perpetual openness, which is the essence of the political, requires viewing the line between public and private as itself disputable: "If action is boundless and excessive, why should it respect a public-private distinction that seeks, like a law of laws, to regulate and contain it without ever allowing itself to be engaged or contested by it?" (p. 119). Unsettling the line between public and private means that "nothing is ontologically protected from politicization" (Honig, 1992, p. 224). The line becomes not an essence but itself a performative production. In other words, what constitutes a public issue becomes arguable, instead of given by definition.

In order for the Refounding Project to do what Arendt believed politics must do, join in making the political world continually new, we must understand administration as "action," therefore as essentially contestable. We must see public administration as taking place in a public space whose boundaries are under continuing challenge. No questions, no identities, no situations are *by definition* off limits. The question of what counts as political is itself a political question. If so, the question of whether or not there is such a thing as the politics-administration dichotomy is an essentially contested question, and the Manifesto's refusal to settle the matter of the dichotomy's existence strengthens the hand of politics in the continuing tension between the two. Further, the project of refounding public administration itself has political significance: the idea of refounding asserts that there always will and should be a contest over the line between system and struggle, between expert knowledge and argument. As the Manifesto itself asserts: "conflict among the differing perspectives of The Public Administration is a valuable part of the creative tension so essential to a healthy American dialogue" (Wamsley et al., 1990, p. 46).

Understanding the boundaries around the administrative state (therefore distinctions between public and private) as subject to contest is consistent with many other aspects of the Blacksburg argument: the public interest as a process guide rather than substantive reality; the agency perspective as constantly enacted and struggled over rather than taken-for-granted consensus; the preference for tentative approaches and organizational learning over techniques like policy analysis and decision science that purport to get it right once and for all. All these conceptual elements, implicitly at least, function to call into question attempts to depoliticize administration, to exclude administrative activity from the public space, whether the depoliticizing takes place by means of Wilson's (1887) politics-administration dichotomy or according to more contemporary theories, such as those that conceive of public administration as a "business" or exhort it to "reinvent" itself by emulating private enterprise. When Blacksburg theorists argue that public administration and private business are fundamentally *un*like each other, they aim not to separate politics and administration but to join them in creative tension.

In order to maintain the tension, however, the more fragile partner, politics, needs help: the help afforded by a plurality of actors in contested relationship in a range of flexibly bounded public spaces, not by an undifferentiated mass of universal Men in sterile dialogue within a policy arena tightly sealed off to unruly outsiders. The administrative state, to remain a state (the site of struggle, debate, and dialogue), needs active citizens whose identities are under construction within its (flexible) boundaries and who can contest the administrative and professional urge to be definitive arbiter of the public good. What this means is that a central governance responsibility of the public administration is to foster opportunities for diverse citizens to join in self-constituting action in public, including in agency arenas.

An example of the administrative state as a practical site of identity formation is found in Scandinavia, where "the lack of 'separateness' and the corresponding mutual permeability of state, market, family, and public sphere[,] the intermingling of different principles of rationality within one and the same institutional context" (Hernes, 1988, p. 209) have transformed needy women from passive recipients of welfare benefits, as in the American model, to important bargaining partners. Hernes argues that the looser boundaries between private and public in Scandinavia have facilitated negotiations between women and the state and empowered women as citizens. Women receive benefits because they are women; in this respect their gender identities are recognized. But as citizens, they negotiate with and therefore share in shaping the public programs from which they benefit; in this sense they are equal citizens. Here women as citizens are both different and equal, a situation made possible because the line between public sector, private business, and domestic realm remains flexible enough for citizens to be able to see governmental largesse not simply as a market corrective but as the expression of a theory they participate in constructing about the nature of the state and of citizenship itself.

Instead of compartmentalizing various aspects of our lives, perhaps we could conceive of every situation as at least potentially "an encounter between 'private' and 'public,' between an action or an utterance to procure an imagined and wished-for substantive satisfaction and the conditions of civility to be subscribed to in performing it" (Michael Oakeshott, quoted in Mouffe, 1992a, p. 237). From such a perspective, the pursuit of individual and group aims, many of them to be sought by entering into relationships of various kinds with administrative agencies, would offer countless opportunities not only for securing tangible goods but also for the production of varied citizen identities. Administrators would be responsible not just for adjudicating among competing claims, though this is an inevitable part of their public obligation, but for creating the conditions under which citizens can construct "who" they are.

Perhaps administrators' most fundamental duty, however, must be to a "grammar of political conduct" (Mouffe, 1992a, p. 231) consisting of democratic principles of freedom, equality, and the public interest, principles over which the struggle to achieve tangible interpretation in particular situations is continuous. The Refounding Project's most basic normative ground is its allegiance to an open understanding of the public interest rooted in continuing constitutional refounding, and its insistence that the public interest is *essentially* undefinable and yet attainable in particular situations in the sense that actions can be coherently legitimated by reference to it. Critics of the Manifesto rightly fear that administrative power too easily rationalizes its own interests as "the public interest." Active citizens, however, save administration from mistaking bureaucratic politics for Politics, in the sense that only in dialogue with citizens can administrators construct an "agency perspective" that represents a defensible understanding of the public interest. It is in relationships with active citizens that the public administration becomes legitimately political: not through the achievement of consensus, which is almost never possible, or through striving for intimacy more appropriate to friendship than citizenship; but rather through the maintenance of ongoing public-spirited dialogue, which even at its most acrimonious remains the only vehicle enabling administrators and other citizens to "make a world" together (Stivers, 1990b).

▬ Refounding Versus Reinventing

Much has been made recently of the idea of "reinventing government." The original Osborne and Gaebler (1992) volume has been followed by the Gore Report (Office of the Vice President, 1993) applying reinventing notions to the federal government, and the Winter Commission has made a similar effort for state and local government (National Commission on the State and Local Public Service, 1993). Superficially, the Refounding Project would seem to have much in common with efforts that style themselves as a "reinvention" of government; yet at a deeper level the two are only alike in unimportant respects, such as the assonance of the two terms. By now, these reinventing attempts have met with well-deserved criticism (see, e.g., articles in the March-April 1994 issue of *Public Administration Review*). Yet the difference between "reinventing government" and the Refounding Project needs clarification. As David Rosenbloom (1993) has pointed out: "mainstream public administrative theory has been the *product* of dominant political moods, movements, and coalitions. In some respects, therefore, 'orthodox' public administrative theory has been the political ideology of dominant political groups" (p. 1; emphasis in original).

Rosenbloom sounds a theme introduced half a century ago by Dwight Waldo's *The Administrative State* (1948) but never taken as seriously in the field as it should be: that is, that a theory of public administration is a theory of politics.

Recent critiques of the "reinventing" literature have recognized it as a political theory, despite its efforts to present itself as simply a management strategy. For example, Moe (1994) points out that the Gore Report recommendations, which essentially follow Osborne and Gaebler's (1992) lead, are a fundamental departure from the "executive management paradigm" underlying most of the thinking about the role of the administrative agency in the American system of governance, particularly as reflected in earlier commission reports such as Brownlow, first Hoover, and Ash. That theory sees bureaucratic hierarchy as the major element in assuring, by centralizing accountability in the chief executive, that administrative action is responsive to mandates legislated by representatives of the people. As Moe (1994) correctly observes, the entrepreneurial model characteristic of "reinventing government" replaces this centralized accountability mechanism with a "highly pluralistic organization and management structure" that in the interest of "customer satisfaction" puts an inventive, results-oriented organizational culture ahead of law and due process (p. 115). "Reinventing government" thus cloaks a theory of governance in organizational language in which "outcomes" take precedence over political values like justice. "The mission of government agencies," Moe (1994) argues, should be "determined by the representatives of the people, not agency management" (p. 119).

Interestingly enough, Moe finds fault with "reinventing government" on the same basis as critics have taken issue with the Refounding Project: Both are charged with departing from the administrative management paradigm, which depends on organizational chain of command and administrative subservience to the legislature in order to protect "democratic" values. This is essentially the position taken by Herman Finer (1941) in his well-known debate with Carl Friedrich (1940). But the Refounding Project and "reinventing government" depart from the Finer perspective in quite different directions, even though they are charged with the same crime, if crime it be. "Reinventing government" is content to waive the issue of accountability almost entirely, in favor of results, thereby vitiating the political impulse in the tension between politics and administration. Thus, for all its talk of creativity and inventiveness and its public-spirited rhetoric, "reinventing government" serves the interests of administrative stability, professional control, and budget cutting. Political values are seen as hindrances to entrepreneurialism. "Reinventing government" aims, in fact, to get it right: to meet goals, to attain maximum cost-effectiveness, to satisfy the customer.

In contrast, the Blacksburg Manifesto takes the Friedrich path. Both Friedrich (1940) and the Blacksburg philosophy rely on the public-interestedness of administrative discretion and reject a chain-of-command understanding of authority, not only on ethical grounds but also on the practical basis that, try precise laws and swift sanctions though we will, there is no way to control the actions of bureaucrats precisely enough to make the administrative management model live up to its billing. Without public-spirited bureaucrats, accountability to the people is doomed. In following Friedrich's lead, however, the Refounding Project inherits and perpetuates the downside of this perspective, which is its propensity to romanticize the commitment of public administrators to a public interest that *they* are held responsible for defining in practice. Thus, as I have argued in this chapter, by stressing the public administrator's special capacity to define the public interest, the Refounding Project has given administrative prerogative too free a rein, and thereby made itself vulnerable to the same criticisms as have been lodged against "reinventing government," though the political dynamics of the two are worlds apart.

━ Conclusion

Contra Marini (1994), I would argue that the basic impulse of the Refounding Project is at least potentially democratic, but Marini is right to question whether current political and administrative practice—along with most normative public administration theory—deserves the term. What I have aimed to show here is that, with all its flaws, the Refounding Project is more open to evolving in a democratic direction (in the original sense of "rule by the people") than most observers have noted, and indeed, than most other theories available in the field. Participants in the Refounding Project, diverse though we are (and despite what Marini says, we are not only aware of our diversity, we value it), share a perception of administrative governance as paradoxical, dialogic, constitutive of public life, marked by argument and struggle, and in perpetual unfolding. What our perspective needs (I still want to argue) is active citizens, in order to attain an understanding of accountability that neither relies on the hierarchical administrative management paradigm, canonizes administrative judgment, nor translates accountability into "customer satisfaction."

By giving up the hope of getting it right, the Refounding Project has taken an entirely new path, one that opens onto democratic vistas for public administration. With active citizens, we could move further in that direction.

━ Notes

1. In the aftermath of the first trial of police officers accused of beating Rodney King, I recall reading in a newspaper article on Simi Valley, the site of the trial, an interview with a white resident who, in an effort to demonstrate his lack of racial prejudice, stated unself-consciously that when he encountered a black neighbor out walking, "I say hello to him just like he was a real person."
2. My discussion of pluralism relies heavily on McClure's (1992) excellent analysis.

References

Arendt, H. (1958). *The human condition*. Chicago: University of Chicago Press.

Arendt, H. (1977). *On revolution*. Harmondsworth, England: Penguin Books.

Brown, W. (1988). *Manhood and politics: A feminist reading in political theory*. Totowa, NJ: Rowman & Littlefield.

Clark, L.M.G., & Lange, L. (1979). *The sexism of social and political theory: Women and reproduction from Plato to Nietzsche*. Toronto: University of Toronto Press.

Eisenstein, Z. (1981). *The radical future of liberal feminism*. New York: Longman.

Ferguson, K. (1988). Subject-centeredness in feminist discourse. In K. B. Jones & A. G. Jonasdottir (Eds.), *The political interests of gender: Developing theory and research with a feminist face* (pp. 66-78). London: Sage.

Finer, H. (1941). Administrative responsibility in democratic government. *Public Administration Review, 1*, 335-350.

Fox, C., & Cochran, C. E. (1990). Discretionary public administration: Toward a Platonic guardian class. In H. D. Kass & B. Catron (Eds.), *Images and identities in public administration* (pp. 87-112). Newbury Park, CA: Sage.

Friedrich, C. J. (1940). Public policy and the nature of administrative responsibility. *Public Policy, 1*, 3-24.

Held, D. (1987). *Models of democracy*. Stanford, CA: Stanford University Press.

Hernes, H. M. (1988). The welfare state citizenship of Scandinavian women. In K. B. Jones & A. G. Jonasdottir (Eds.), *The political interests of gender: Developing theory and research with a feminist face* (pp. 187-213). London: Sage.

Honig, B. (1992). Toward an agonistic feminism: Hannah Arendt and the politics of identity. In J. Butler & J. W. Scott (Eds.), *Feminists theorize the political* (pp. 215-235). New York: Routledge & Kegan Paul.

Honig, B. (1993). *Political theory and the displacement of politics*. Ithaca, NY: Cornell University Press.

Jones, K. B. (1993). *Compassionate authority: Democracy and the representation of women*. New York: Routledge & Kegan Paul.

Karst, K. L. (1989). *Belonging to America: Equal citizenship and the constitution*. New Haven, CT: Yale University Press.

Kerber, L. K. (1980). *Women of the republic: Intellect and ideology in revolutionary America*. New York: Norton.

Keuls, E. C. (1985). *The reign of the phallus: Sexual politics in ancient Athens*. New York: Harper & Row.

Landes, J. B. (1988). *Women and the public sphere in the age of the French revolution*. Ithaca, NY: Cornell University Press.

Marini, F. (1994). Echoes from no-person's land: Reflections on the political theory of some recent dialogue. *Administrative Theory and Praxis, 16*(1), 1-14.

McClure, K. (1992). On the subject of rights: Pluralism, plurality, and political identity. In C. Mouffe (Ed.), *Dimensions of radical democracy: Pluralism, citizenship, community* (pp. 108-127). New York: Verso.

Moe, R. C. (1994). The "reinventing government" exercise: Misinterpreting the problem, misjudging the consequences. *Public Administration Review, 54*(2), 111-122.

Morgan, E. S. (1975). *American slavery, American freedom: The ordeal of colonial Virginia*. New York: Norton.

Mouffe, C. (1991). Democratic citizenship and the political community. In Miami Theory Collective (Ed.), *Community at loose ends* (pp. 70-82). Minneapolis: University of Minnesota Press.

Mouffe, C. (1992a). Democratic citizenship and the political community. In C. Mouffe (Ed.), *Dimensions of radical democracy: Pluralism, citizenship, community* (pp. 225-239). New York: Verso.

Mouffe, C. (1992b). Feminism, citizenship, and radical democratic politics. In J. Butler & J. W. Scott (Eds.), *Feminists theorize the political* (p. 369). New York: Routledge & Kegan Paul.

National Commission on the State and Local Public Service. (1993). *Hard truths/tough choices: An agenda for state and local reform.* Albany, NY: Nelson A. Rockefeller Institute of Government.

Office of the Vice President, National Performance Review. (1993). *From red tape to results: Creating a government that works better and costs less.* Washington, DC: Government Printing Office.

Okin, S. M. (1979). *Women in Western political thought.* Princeton, NJ: Princeton University Press.

Osborne, D., & Gaebler, T. (1992). *Reinventing government: How the entrepreneurial spirit is transforming the public sector from schoolhouse to state house, city hall to Pentagon.* Reading, MA: Addison-Wesley.

Pateman, C. (1989). *The disorder of women: Democracy, feminism, and political theory.* Stanford, CA: Stanford University Press.

Patterson, O. (1991). *Freedom: Vol. 1. Freedom in the making of Western culture.* New York: Basic Books.

Pomeroy, S. B. (1975). *Goddesses, whores, wives, and slaves: Women in classical antiquity.* New York: Schocken.

Robinson, D. L. (1971). *Slavery in the structure of American politics 1765-1820.* New York: Harcourt Brace Jovanovitch.

Rosenbloom, D. H. (1993). Prescriptive public administration theory as a product of political dominance. *Administrative Theory and Praxis, 15*(2), 1-10.

Saxonhouse, A. (1985). *Women in the history of political thought.* New York: Praeger.

Shklar, J. N. (1991). *American citizenship: The quest for inclusion.* London: Harvard University Press.

Smith, R. M. (1989). "One united people": Second-class female citizenship and the American quest for community. *Yale Journal of Law and the Humanities, 1,* 229-293.

Stivers, C. M. (1990a). Active citizenship and public administration. In G. L. Wamsley, R. N. Bacher, C. T. Goodsell, P. S. Kronenberg, J. A. Rohr, C. M. Stivers, O. F. White, & J. F. Wolf, *Refounding public administration* (pp. 246-273). Newbury Park, CA: Sage.

Stivers, C. M. (1990b). The public agency as *polis:* Active citizenship in the administrative state. *Administration and Society, 22*(1), 86-105.

Vogel, U. (1988). Under permanent guardianship: Women's condition under modern civil law. In K. B. Jones & A. G. Jonasdottir (Eds.), *The political interests of gender: Developing theory and research with a feminist face* (pp. 135-159). London: Sage.

Waldo, D. (1948). *The administrative state.* New York: Ronald.

Wamsley, G. L., Bacher, R. N., Goodsell, C. T., Kronenberg, P. S., Rohr, J. A., Stivers, C. M., White, O. F., & Wolf, J. F. (1990). *Refounding public administration.* Newbury Park, CA: Sage.

West, C. (1992, August 2). Learning to talk of race. *New York Times Magazine,* pp. 24-26.

Wilson, W. (1887). The study of administration. *Political Science Quarterly, 2*(2), 197-222.

10

Understanding Social Process

The Key to Democratic Governance

LISA WEINBERG
University of Washington

The Refounding project seeks to demonstrate the legitimacy of public administration as a participant in the governance process and to fashion a more activist role for it in the realization of the public interest. The two are interrelated, of course, and not just because legitimacy is a precondition to its more activist role. The success of public administration in that role will derive from, and contribute to, the public trust so essential to its legitimacy. It is not surprising, then, that the centerpiece of this project has been the "agency perspective," which posits a different type of relationship between those who work in public agencies and the public they ostensibly serve. The exact nature of this relationship remained unclear in the Blacksburg Manifesto and the original *Refounding* volume, however, an ambiguity highlighted by Camilla Stivers in her contribution to the present volume (see Chapter 9).

Contributors to this volume, most notably Stivers and Dennard (Chapters 9 & 11, respectively), take up that aspect of the Refounding project, continuing to explore the nature and demands of the relationship between agency and public. Indeed, the chapters by these two authors can be seen as complementary; whereas Stivers examines how "active citizenship" can enliven "administrative governance," Dennard calls for public administration to serve as "creator of a political environment." What is striking about the respective approaches of these authors is that each envisions the experience of participation as transformative for the individual. Stivers argues for a new concept of citizenship, one that is "a constructed rather than given political identity," unfolding in a process of "continuous enactment," what she calls "performative identity development." Dennard's vision of a more democratic public administration entails no less than a change in "administrative consciousness," one that will engender in the individual administrator a sense of "his or her own efficacy."

The Refounding project thus is about more than a different role for public administration in the governance process; it is about a different way of coming together in political community, grounded in a different understanding of social process and the place of the individual within it. This is apparent in the chapters by McSwite, Stivers, and Dennard (see Chapters 7, 9, & 11, this volume, respectively), each of which contains a critique of prevailing models of citizenship, public administration, and the public interest, respectively, revealing the inadequacy of each in meeting the challenges of contemporary social conditions. In this chapter I take on the issue of social process directly, presenting an alternative conceptualization that provides a vehicle for understanding contemporary experience and redirecting future efforts.

My inspiration in this undertaking comes from the work of Mary Parker Follett. Recently celebrated as "the prophet of management" (Graham, 1995), a notable portion of Follett's work focuses instead on governance. Her sense of the potential, as well as the reality, of political community is nicely captured in the following passage:

> It seems to me that the greatest contribution a citizen can make to the state is to learn creative thinking, that is, to learn how to join his thought with that of others so that the issue shall be productive. If each of us exhausts his responsibility by bringing his own little piece of pretty colored glass, that would make a mere kaleidoscope of community. (Follett, 1919, p. 581)

Follett's "little piece of pretty colored glass" is a wonderful metaphor for the particularistic interests that drive American politics, a political community constituted by the accommodation of interests rather than their integration. But she suggests that to do otherwise, "to join his thought with that of others so that the issue shall be productive," will require more of the individual. Importantly, what Follett has in mind goes beyond the mastery of technique; "creative thinking" entails more than the acquisition of skill. Instead, truly coming together in community calls for an alternative ontology, a different way of thinking about the relationship of individual and group.

For Follett, "the fallacy of pluralism is not its pluralism, but that it is based on a non-existent individual" (Follett, 1919, p. 580). Indeed, she sees difference as "the essence of society," but it is a "*related* difference" (Follett,

1918/1965, p. 33; emphasis added). What she contests is the presumed autonomy of the individual. For Follett, individuality resides with the "centre of consciousness," and that consciousness is impoverished to the extent that it exists in isolation. Just as an individual's identity is realized as part of the group life, so too the character of the group life is determined by the nature and quality of the individual's participation.

Follett provides us with a vision of political community grounded in social process. In the remainder of this chapter I will elaborate on this vision and consider how it can inform the Refounding project. First, I will more fully describe Follett's view of social process, an understanding of human interaction that serves as the anchor for her work regarding governance as well as management. Then, I will draw on family systems theory[1] to illustrate *how* the interpersonal dynamics that fuel interaction determine the nature of "group life" or organized activity, and to what effect. I will conclude the chapter by considering the implications of this understanding of social process for the *Refounding* project.

▬ Circular Response

Mary Parker Follett uses what she calls "the doctrine of circular response" as the basis for her theory of organizing, *organizing* broadly conceived to include the management of public and private organizations, the conduct of labor relations, and the governance of communities. The idea of circular response, implicit in much of her work, receives its fullest articulation in her book *Creative Experience* (1924). In that volume, Follett describes circular response in terms of three "fundamental principles": (a) that response is not to a rigid or static environment but to a changing one; (b) that the environment is changing because of the activity between it and people; and (c) that response is always to this activity of relating rather than to the environment or person alone.

For Follett, organization or community is "wholly dynamic"; she exhorts us to "think no more in terms of social institutions but of social activities" (Follett, 1924, p. 207). According to the doctrine of circular response, people are forever creating and recreating their environment. And because of the interrelation between people and their environment, they too are being recreated as they contribute to a changing environment. But it is not the environment alone that shapes people and their behavior: "We now see behavior not as a function of environment, but as a function of the relation between self and environment. The activity is a function of itself interweaving with the activity of which it is a function" (Follett, 1924, p. 72). Response is always to a relating, organized activity unfolding through a process in which stimulus and response are interdependent.

Follett (1924) conceives of organized activity as "the functioning of a self-creating coherence," expressing it well when she writes, "You can tear it to pieces if you will and find subject and object, stimulus and response, or you can refuse to; you can claim the right to see it as a rational interplay of forces, as the functioning of a self-creating coherence" (pp. 74-75). Organization as "self-creating coherence" is to be found in activity, and in a "whole-a-making" rather than activity between "parts" and a "whole" (Follett, 1924, p. 102). Although this generative dynamic itself is inevitable, the nature of the emergent "whole" is not; the emergent whole could be "a mere kaleidoscope." Follett thus offers the following "first test" of organized activity:

> Whether you have [an organization or community] with all its parts so co-ordinated, so moving together in their closely knit and adjusting activities, so linking, interlocking, interrelating, that they make a working unit—that is, not a congeries of separate pieces, but what I have called a functional whole or integrative unity. (Fox & Urwick, 1973, p. 71)

It is important to distinguish between Follett's references to a "self-creating coherence" and an "integrative unity," for the former represents what necessarily is, the essence of social process, whereas the latter indicates only what might be, "integrative unity" being just one way in which people come together, just one mode of interaction.

━━ Modes of Interaction

According to Follett, integration (or integrative unity) is one of three "principles of human association," the other two being compromise and domination. Compromise is the prevailing principle of association, or mode of interaction, a principle that like domination precludes integration. Integration is an alternative to compromise and domination, one that can fuel rather than undermine progressive experience. As Follett (1919) describes it,

> The most familiar example of integrating as the social process is when two or three people meet to decide on some course of action, and separate with a purpose, a will, which was not possessed by anyone when he came to the meeting but is the result of the interweaving of all. In this true social process there takes place neither absorption nor compromise. (p. 576)

Integration is the joining together of ideas "so that the issue shall be productive," rather than each of the participants simply bringing their "little piece of pretty colored glass" to the meeting.

One of the concepts by which Follett is best known, "the law of the situation," can help illuminate what it takes to realize an integrative unity. In attending to the process by which organization or community is constituted, the law of the situation posits that it is necessary to work always with the evolving situation. In her paper "The Giving of Orders" (Fox & Urwick, 1973), Follett explains that because the situation is always changing, the order—or that toward which one's efforts are directed—must keep up with the situation; the order must repeatedly be "drawn fresh from the situation." This is analogous, of course, to the emphasis on continuous improvement in total quality management (TQM). Whether informed by Follett or TQM, the point is the same: Activity should be guided by a study of the situation rather than by a logic external to it.

Because organized activity emerges in the process of interaction, the situation inevitably involves more than one person. According to the doctrine of circular response, it entails "the adjustment of man and man" as well as "the adjustment of man and situation" (Follett, 1924, p. 122). Follett's use of the word *adjustment* assumes the existence of differences, a diversity that for her is life's most essential feature. But in the process of integrating differences she seeks more than mere adjustment, which suggests compromise. Rather, integration is a matter of invention, the creation of something new, allowing the situation to offer up possibilities that previously did not exist.

An integrative unity demands that people have a consciousness of the situation, an awareness of the part their own activities play in it as well as a willingness to remain open to that situation as it evolves. There can be no taking of sides or positions. Integration requires the examination of the situation irrespective of sides, for it is only through such a process that the "facts" of the situation can be truly revealed. Furthermore, this process of inquiry must be undertaken jointly, uniting all concerned in a study of the situation. According to Follett, "the best preparation for integration . . . is a joint study of the situation" (Fox & Urwick, 1973, p. 61). Interestingly, she also asserts that "the basis of all cooperative activity is integrated diversity" (Follett, 1924, p. 174). Just as integration requires cooperation, cooperation requires integration, the two bound together in a single seamless process.

Once again we encounter the doctrine of circular response, for a consciousness or attitude conducive to integration can emerge only in the process of interacting with others. Perhaps at her most poetic, Follett (1924) explains it this way:

> Through circular response we are creating each other all the time . . . reaction is always reaction to a relating . . . I never react to you but to you-plus-me; or to be more accurate, it is I-plus-you reacting to you-plus-me. "I" can never influence "you" because you have already influenced me; that is, in the very process of meeting, by the very process of meeting, we both become something different. (pp. 62-63)

In the context of this discussion, to be made different means to be available (or not) to relate in an integrative fashion vis-à-vis the situation; it requires a certain orientation to the situation and to those others with whom the situation is constituted. Moreover, being made different in this way not only occurs in the process of relating, relating itself must be well grounded in the situation. As Follett observes, "We cannot have any sound relations with each other as long as we take them out of that setting which gives them their meaning and value" (Fox & Urwick, 1973, p. 60). The quality of the relations that constitute organization or community thus determines its nature, determines the extent to which an integrative unity is possible. And the nature of that organized activity, or the quality of the relations that constitute it, influences the consciousness that people bring to the organizing process.

Consciousness and Organized Activity

Though Follett speaks to the methods for achieving integration, most notably a joint study of the situation, she does not sufficiently address what it actually takes to engage in such a study. Nor does she fully explain what inclines people toward the two other principles of human association, compromise and domination, neither of which is any less of a "self-creating coherence" than integration. Critical questions that remain include: (a) How does one realize the consciousness of situation required for an integration, a consciousness that itself comes into being in relationship; (b) What happens in the absence of such a consciousness; and (c) How does the absence of such a consciousness contribute to patterns of association characterized by compromise and domination? Although Follett's work is suggestive, it is incomplete. Family systems theory provides a psychological perspective, nicely supplementing Follett's work and providing some answers to these questions.

Family systems theorists adopt a perspective similar to Follett's, describing patterns of interaction in terms of the relations among family members rather than their individual "natures." Similar to the dynamic captured by Follett's notion of circular response, family systems theorists conceive of individual emotional functioning as a typically unconscious but mutual adjustment to the emotional states of others in a relationship system. These theorists thus share with Follett an interest in activity, focusing on functioning and interaction rather than personality and illness. Importantly, family systems theorists believe that the same patterns of emotional functioning apparent in the family operate in other settings as well.[2]

How does one realize the consciousness of situation required for an integration? One of the building blocks of family systems theory, the concept of "differentiation," is instructive in answering this question. An individual's level of differentiation refers to the extent of emotional separation from the family of origin, but also influences how the individual relates with others outside the family system. Differentiation is a function of two counterbalancing life forces, one that moves the person toward individuality, the other toward togetherness. To be differentiated means that the person can function autonomously whenever it is important to do so (Kerr & Bowen, 1988). It entails being an emotionally separate person, equipped with the ability to think, feel, and act for oneself.

According to the theory, the human intellect enables a person to limit the influence of the emotional system on her or his behavior. As Kerr and Bowen (1988) explain, "Objectivity and the associated autonomy from one's environment derive from the capacity to recognize the difference between emotional, feeling, subjective, and objective responses and to act based on that recognition" (p. 71n). The level of differentiation represents the intermix of emotional and intellectual functioning within a person (Bowen, 1978). The higher the level of differentiation, the more able a person is to distinguish (or differentiate) emotion and intellect, and choose between what she or he feels and thinks as a guide for behavior. Conversely, at lower levels of differentiation emotion and intellect are so "fused" that a person's behavior is dictated by the emotional content of the system.

To be differentiated does not mean to be cut off from what one feels and the energy that derives from it. Nor does emotional separation preclude emotional closeness: "The ability to be in emotional contact with others yet still autonomous in one's emotional functioning is the essence of the concept of differentiation" (Kerr & Bowen, 1988, p. 145n). Differentiation entails a consciousness that enables a person to act *on* what he thinks and feels rather than reacting *to* the emotional forces at play in the system.

The concept of differentiation can extend our understanding of the consciousness required for an integration, or more simply what it takes to be available to the situation. For Follett, it entails adopting "a conscious and responsible attitude toward experience," recognizing the evolving situation, one's role in it, and its impact on the self (Fox & Urwick, 1973, pp. 50-51).

In the context of an emotional system—whether constituted by family members, colleagues, or participants in the governance process—it means that each of the people involved must achieve the emotional separation necessary to be able to draw on the intellect in order to discern the situation and their place in it. In doing so, each person needs as well to assume responsibility for his functioning in the situation, instead of placing blame or otherwise attributing his behavior to others in the system, what Murray Bowen (1978) refers to as being "responsibly responsible for self." Though being clear about one's responsibility *to* others, a person should not assume responsibility *for* others, respecting the differences that others necessarily bring to the situation. This too requires substantial emotional separation or differentiation.

What Happens in the Absence of Such a Consciousness?

Differentiation is a relational concept; it occurs in relationship to others and influences the overall level of differentiation in a system. Family systems theorists make a distinction between "basic" and "functional" differentiation (Kerr & Bowen, 1988). Whereas the basic level of differentiation is established during the early years of childhood, functional differentiation is dependent on the relationship process and thus varies over time. The factor that most contributes to functional differentiation is the presence or absence of anxiety or emotional tension in the relationship system.

When anxiety is high, people become emotionally reactive. To be reactive means to react unthinkingly to the emotional content present in the system, what Murray Bowen (1978) describes as an "emotional reflex." The process of adjustment earlier likened to circular response, in which each person adjusts to the emotional state of others in a system, allows anxiety to travel among them, so that anxiety in one person eventually manifests itself in another. When anxiety is low, people can be more thoughtful. This tends to stabilize functioning, minimizing the pressure people put on one another and enabling autonomous action.

Just as the presence of anxiety influences the level of functional differentiation, the level of basic differentiation influences the presence of anxiety. Family systems theorists posit an inverse relationship between a person's basic level of differentiation and the presence of chronic anxiety (Kerr & Bowen, 1988); the lower the level of differentiation, the less adaptive the person is under stress, and the higher her or his average level of anxiety. The qualifier *chronic* is important, because unlike acute anxiety, which occurs in response to a real threat and tends to be of limited duration, chronic anxiety has little to do with extant life circumstances and therefore is much more persistent. Indeed, rather than a reaction to actual events, chronic anxiety quickly takes on a life of its own independent of external events, thus containing its own momentum.

Reactivity removes people from the realm of the situation. When people become reactive they assume roles or adopt positions that bear little relation to the situation itself. They define themselves, or their roles or positions, in relation to one another and the emotional forces animating their interaction. Each person becomes defined in opposition to the other, assuming complementary but opposite roles or adopting opposing positions. In the absence of more differentiated behavior, their cycle of interaction serves only to reinforce these roles or positions and the pattern of relating to which they contribute.

Once people enter such a pattern of relating, their actions are governed by a logic associated with the roles or positions adopted and the emotional forces that fuel them, not the demands of the extant situation. Real and substantive differences, the interplay of which is necessary for an integration, are obscured by the more superficial ones related to roles or positions, and these latter differences are played out according to an emotional rather than a situated logic. When people become defined in terms of superficial differences, they are unable to address their substantive differences, their pattern of interaction preventing them from challenging the assumptions in which their roles or positions are grounded. Indeed, by acting in accordance with these roles or positions people reinforce such assumptions.

How does the absence of differentiation contribute to patterns of association characterized by compromise and domination? According to family systems theory, the more action is prompted by anxiety, the greater the pressure for togetherness. This pressure for togetherness manifests itself in efforts to think and act alike. Under these circumstances, people are less tolerant of differences and thus less able to allow one another to be themselves (Kerr & Bowen, 1988). When some people become anxious, they become more intent on changing others, increasingly convinced that theirs is the one best way. In reaction to such pressure for oneness, people either resist or capitulate, predisposing them to dominate or compromise.

Resistance typically takes the form of defining oneself in opposition to the other, responding to the pressure for togetherness by distinguishing and distancing oneself. Follett recognizes the potential for this when she observes, "The more you are 'bossed' the more your activity of thought will take place within the bossing pattern, and your part in that pattern seems usually to be opposition to the bossing" (Fox & Urwick, 1973, p. 57). A sustained effort to change another, to get the other to do something he would not on his own choose to do, thus tends to prevent just such a change. Murray Bowen (1978) reports that when anxiety is high there is a general tendency among people to revert to cause-and-effect thinking, blinding them to their own contribution to the situation. To the extent that each defines himself in opposition to the other, the interaction amounts to no more than a contest of wills. Each feels he must prevail over the other. The outcome, then, is either domination or polarization.

Whereas resistance entails the definition of self in opposition to the other, compromise requires that people make concessions in order to reach an agreement. Follett recognizes the cost of compromise to the individual, that "the individual is to give up part of himself in order that some action may take place" (Follett, 1924, p. 163). Family systems theorists refer to this giving up of self as "deselfing" (Bowen, 1978), when, under pressure from another, a person sacrifices the self (what one thinks and feels) in order to preserve harmony in their relationship. Compromise like domination is fueled by reactivity, a reaction to the emotional content of the relationship system rather than an action grounded in knowledge of the situation. Interestingly, Follett suggests that even reasoning with a person, "convincing them intellectually," may not be sufficient for integration (Fox & Urwick, 1973). This is because their interaction, although ostensibly in the realm of the intellect, continues to occur independent of the situation and thus is propelled by the emotional forces at play in the relationship system.

Developing the Capacity for Integration

Integration requires the revealing of differences, it entails the appreciation—not the elimination—of diversity as life's most essential feature. Integration thus requires that the people involved take a differentiated stand in the situation, discerning how they are contributing to the situation and remaining open to that situation as it evolves. Follett says as much when she recounts a conversation with a friend regarding integration: "A friend of mine said to me, 'open-mindedness is the whole thing, isn't it?' No, it isn't; it needs just as great a respect for your own view as for that of others and a firm upholding of it until you are convinced" (Fox & Urwick, 1973, p. 48). Though an openness to the needs and concerns of the other is essential for integration, so too is a sense of what one thinks and feels in the situation. Without being so grounded, it is too easy to deself under pressure from the relationship. Without being so grounded, it is impossible to achieve the emotional separation needed to draw on the intellect in order to discern the situation and one's place in it.

Integration requires that people be able to attend to the process of their interaction in a differentiated fashion. Indeed, the ability to consult the situation begins with the ability to attend to the more fundamental business of relating. The reason for this is that the outcome of this process of interaction and change (circular response) is "the release of energy which produces new energy" (Follett, 1924, p. 209). Whether the energy released in this process is positively or negatively charged, whether it fuels progressive or regressive experience, depends on the nature of the interaction.

When people are able to remain differentiated in the process of interaction, they are available to meet the situation as it evolves, promoting within them the capacity for future integrations. Although she acknowledges that reality is sometimes otherwise, Follett advances a progressive vision of social process, one grounded in an appreciation of the dynamic relation that exists between the individual and the whole. As she envisions it, "The individual by his responses to the social fabric contributes that which so enhances it that the stimuli proceeding from it to the individual enhances his reactions and he has more to contribute than before" (Follett, 1924, p. 128). In other words, the development of the individual and that of the whole are interdependent. Importantly, what Follett refers to as the "productive power of the collective life" depends first on "its nourishment of the individual." Only then does she consider, as a "second test" of the productive life, whether "the contributions of individuals can be fruitfully united" (Follett, 1924, p. xii). Her priorities seem appropriate, because achieving such an integration (fruitfully uniting the contributions of individuals) requires a certain consciousness on the part of the individuals involved. Elsewhere in *Creative Experience,* however, Follett asserts that "the integrity of the individual is preserved only through integration" (Follett, 1924, p. 163). Once again, then, we encounter the inseparability of part and whole, that the nourishment or development of the individual ultimately depends on an integration, just as an integration depends on a developed individual.

Ironically, a person's efforts to become more differentiated initially may promote anxiety in the relationship system. Efforts at differentiation are experienced as disruptive to the system, and people react to such disruption in ways that generate anxiety (Kerr & Bowen, 1988). Uncomfortable with a disturbance to the balance of the emotional system, and the anxiety that attends it, people act to stabilize the system, to restore it to its previous equilibrium. Follett (1924) expresses both an awareness of and concern for this inclination toward equilibrium, seeing it as an obstacle to integration because it maintains the status quo rather than realizing the potential inherent in the situation. And by maintaining the status quo, an emotional rather than a situated logic governs interaction, limiting the differentiation of participants in the process and contributing to regression.

Regression is a concept articulated as part of family systems theory, a phenomenon that according to Bowen (1978) occurs societally as well as within the family. He characterizes regression as follows:

> When a family is subject to chronic, sustained anxiety, the family begins to lose contact with its intellectually determined principles, and to resort more and more to emotionally determined decisions to allay the anxiety of the moment. The results of the process are symptoms and eventually regression to a lower level of functioning. (p. 386)

Like the condition of chronic anxiety, regression feeds on itself, creating what Kerr has referred to as an "anxiety spiral" (Kerr & Bowen, 1988). Most symptomatic of regression is the prevalence of decisions designed to allay the anxiety, decisions intended to control the situation. These efforts at control come from outside the situation, generated and guided by the emotional content of the relationship system. The benefits are necessarily temporary, however, for such efforts to allay anxiety only further fuel the regression, diminishing the capacity of individual and system to function effectively. Just as an integration contributes to the development of a capacity for subsequent integrations, regression undermines just such a capacity.

▬ The Possibility of Democratic Process

If public administration is to assume a different and more activist role in making American governance more democratic, if it is to facilitate a process by which the public interest truly will be discovered, it must find a way to do so in the context of contemporary social conditions, the postmodern condition. For White and McSwain (O. C. McSwite, Chapter 7, this volume), the postmodern perspective brings us to the proverbial fork in the road, offering alternative paths that lead in dramatically divergent directions. If we proceed down one path, positive change in social and political life becomes possible. Such change would occur through the creation of "communities of *meaning* (not values) around public agencies, meanings that would keep agencies turned to purposes emerging from and grounded in the public interest." Actualizing such a community would entail bringing together the "multiple, partial, and momentary truths" of community members into a "tentative pattern" through a "group process grounded in authentic communication." Action based on these "tentative patterns" would be "experimental" and "iterative," the outcomes of which would become the basis for future consideration and iterative action.

The other path leads to what they call "technicism," a condition that is "already upon us." Under technicism, public agencies as well as the political process that directs them lack any connection to the people they ostensibly serve. Instead, "When social problems escalate to the point where they seem out of control, political pressure builds for the implementation of technical, certain, efficient, mechanical, brute force solutions" (McSwite, Chapter 7, this volume). This condition is indicative of regression. Anxiety, generated by a sense that social problems are out of control, prompts decisions intended to control the situation and, in so doing, allay the anxiety. But the decision, the so-called solution, comes from outside the situation, allaying anxiety temporarily but fueling regression to a lower level of emotional functioning. In the absence of differentiation, interaction is characterized by compromise at best, but more likely, by domination.

What would it take to move from a condition devoid of situated meaning to one grounded in "communities of meaning," communities in which people engage in "authentic communication" and act on the basis of "tentative" solutions? From the perspective on social process elaborated in this chapter, I would argue that it requires two basic shifts in consciousness. One has to do with an understanding of the situation as ever-emergent, the other with an appreciation for the essential interrelatedness of human beings. The first would enable action based on tentative solutions, the second would facilitate "authentic communications."

The first shift in consciousness has to do with our willingness to remain open to the situation as it evolves. It is not just a matter of public administration letting go of an identity grounded in expertise. It will require an acceptance on everyone's part that there are no absolutes, that solutions are always tentative. But "refusing to get it right," to borrow Stiver's phrase (Chapter 9, this volume), requires differentiation, a grounding in a sense of oneself and one's place in the situation that will not be undercut by more regressive tendencies. Regression feeds on fear and anxiety, emotions that incline people toward absolutes. Differentiation enables people to resist such tendencies.

The second shift in consciousness, then, is related to the first, the extent to which people are able to cede control to the process—the process by which the situation in that moment is realized—is dependent on the extent to which they are able to achieve differentiation. Family systems theorists attribute the ability to remain differentiated to a way of thinking rather than a "technique" of relating, "a way of thinking that translates into a way of being" (Bowen, 1978; Friedman, 1985). That way of thinking requires people to see interpersonal relations in terms of the interdependence implicit in processes of interaction, replacing cause-and-effect thinking with a systemic perspective. And it is that shift in consciousness that will enable people to engage authentically with one another. This will require that all parties to the process recognize their interdependence while respecting each others' individuality, attending to the business of relating in order to realize effectively the potential inherent in the situation.

Notes

1. As articulated by Murray Bowen and others adhering to his formulation of a psychological theory of the family as a system.
2. Indeed, Murray Bowen (1978) uses his personal experiences to describe how the emotional processes associated with family functioning are manifested among psychiatrists in the clinical work setting. However, he as well as others (Friedman, 1985; Hirschhorn & Gilmore, 1980; Kahn, 1979; Merkel & Carpenter, 1987) point out that an organization is not a family, and that the differences between them can be significant.

References

Bowen, M. (1978). *Family therapy in clinical practice*. New York: Jason Aronson.

Follett, M. P. (1919). Community is a process. *Philosophical Review, 28*(6), 576-588.

Follett, M. P. (1924). *Creative experience*. New York: Longmans, Green.

Follett, M. P. (1965). *The new state: Group organization the solution of popular government*. Gloucester, MA: Peter Smith. (Original work published 1918)

Fox, E. M., & Urwick, L. (1973). *Dynamic administration: The collected papers of Mary Parker Follett*. Great Britain: Pitman Publishing.

Friedman, E. H. (1985). *Generation to generation: Family process in church and synagogue*. New York: Guilford.

Graham, P. (1995). *Mary Parker Follett: Prophet of management*. Boston: Harvard Business School Press.

Hirschhorn, L., & Gilmore, T. (1980). The application of family therapy concepts to influencing organizational behavior. *Administrative Science Quarterly, 25*, 18-37.

Kahn, M. (1979). Organizational consultation and the teaching of family therapy: Contrasting case histories. *Journal of Marital Family Therapy, 5*(1), 69-80.

Kerr, M. E., & Bowen, M. (1988). *Family evaluation: An approach based on Bowen Theory*. New York: Norton.

Merkel, W. T., & Carpenter, L. J. (1987). A cautionary note on the application of family therapy principles to organizational consultation. *American Journal of Orthopsychiatry, 57*(1), 111-115.

11

The Maturation of Public Administration

The Search for a Democratic Identity

LINDA F. DENNARD
California State University at Hayward

Politics . . . the systematic organization of hatreds.

Henry Adams, *The Education of Henry Adams*

The common good is addressed by largely unhistoric acts.

George Elliott, *Middlemarch*

■ The Dawn of a New Age

The prescriptions for normative public administration made by the Blacksburg School have developed in a historical period when the core assumptions governing the management identity of the field have been brought into serious question (Cleveland, 1988). It is no longer enough simply to propose yet another managerial reform. It is instead a time in which the very identity of public administration must be transformed. Indeed, the evolving postmodern culture is creating the context in which such a transformation is not only warranted but possible.

What is now widely termed the "modernist" epoch is a historical collection of organizing principles for the modern administrative mind. This framework has emerged largely from Enlightenment philosophies. These philosophies create mental constructs that have come to define the nature of social relationships—the machine of Descartes; the Hobbesian social contract; and Darwin's theory of natural selection, for example (Heller & Feher, 1991; Taylor, 1989). Modernist principles based on these metaphors for social relationships emphasize the need for the instrumental regulation and control of human behavior in the achievement of prescribed and often technical outcomes. It is these principles that are coming under close scrutiny as another epoch emerges—one whose central theme appears to be the reemergence of democracy as both a national and global theme (Walsh, 1990; Walzer, 1988). This new epoch is being created not only by an emerging science of chaos with its emphasis on relationship and self-organizing, but by those social and political theorists seeking to revive humanism in a technological age (Prigogine & Stengers, 1984; Stanley, 1992; Wheatley, 1992). From movements and ideas as diverse as conservative new populism, the green movement, physics, privatization, communitarianism, feminism, cultural nationalism, and spiritual renaissance, a new singular theme emerges—one of alienation from the power-driven institutions of government (Fowler, 1991; Gould, 1984; Pateman, 1989; Spretnak, 1986).

Modernism, however, remains resilient in public administration because it is not simply a set of ideas or a methodology, but rather a state of administrative consciousness. Modernism is the mental framework with which all administrative questions connect and the conceptual matter from which their answers are formed. Yet the postmodern milieu is challenging public administration to face its democratic responsibilities and address its own growing identity crisis.

The Blacksburg School can contribute to the productive outcome of this crisis but it must come to recognize the full nature of the changes that public administration needs to make. The changing times make extending the dialogue of the Blacksburg School crucial, but they also place a profound responsibility on those institutionalists within the Blacksburg School who normally consider only the broad sweep of administrative relationships. They now must also be concerned with empowering each individual administrator as a unique epicenter of change in a democratic system. Arguments like those of the Blacksburg School must be able to transcend modernism, not simply reform it.

The Public Administration Identity Crisis

The prevailing modernist administrative mind-set might also be described as an ontological outlook—the way in which individuals and their cultures understand their relationship to each other and to their world (Taylor, 1989). For public administrators to hold firmly to the identity given them by the modernist concern for technicist social management, for example, they must also view human relationships as being in constant need of regulation, mediation, and control.

Indeed, its identity as a modernist institution has instilled in public administrators a deeply and sincerely felt responsibility for regulation of the democratic project and an almost religious devotion to the task of maintaining a secure equilibrium of the status quo as a "safe" haven for democracy (Kaufman, 1985; Leiserson, 1942; Schubert, 1989; Simon, Smithburg, & Thompson, 1950). To act responsibly, according to modernist principles, however, administrators must also be willing to endure the distrust and enmity of citizens whose resentment of bureaucracy is legendary. A modernist identity assigns administrators the dubious and often unrewarding task of regulating society for "its own good."

But the condition of the American culture demands that we courageously reconsider this role. We cannot simply blame the divisive malaise of postmodernist culture on current intellectual and cultural efforts to transcend modernism (Jameson, 1991). To do so is to miss the fact that the conditions we find ourselves in are largely the artifacts of the excesses of modernist thought. Indeed, what may seem to be the disintegration of conventional wisdom in postmodernism may also be understood as an evolutionary struggle to define a new, more humanistic era that may transcend these excesses rather than merely reform them. Yet such new potentialities appear to be more like threats than opportunities to public administration because of its own deeply embedded sense of self, which is modernism personified. It is perhaps that point in historic change, perhaps a state of secular grace, when everything seems both possible and impossible at once (Argyros, 1991).

Whatever is happening in postmodernism, it is clearly not a time for public administrators to watch as bystanders, casually adjusting their work routines to whatever comes along. We are being presented with the historic opportunity to participate in epochal change. We cannot simply use our antiquated sense of social responsibility as a shield against this potential. Remaining on the sidelines as the social critic and watchdog regulator affects the ability of both public administration and the society it serves to change meaningfully in accordance with these times. Indeed, to continue to see ourselves as mere observers, rather than participants, makes the emerging American and global culture seem unnecessarily threatening to the very existence of public administration.

The identity of public administration, however, need not be set in stone. The importance of the Blacksburg argument for a constitutional public administration, for example, goes beyond discovering legal legitimacy for the field. It is a recognition that public administration did not fully form with Woodrow Wilson's managerial edict at the turn of the century but instead has roots in the very founding of our nation. These roots suggest the possibility of *other* identities for public administration than the one inspired by managerialism. Like the Constitution from which it gains its legitimacy, public administration can take on new meaning and purpose in changing contexts (Cook, 1992; Rohr, 1990). The constitutional connection, rather than serving merely to reify public administration as another power structure of government, may well give public administration the generative foundation from which to develop a different, more democratic identity. Yet for public administration to tap this potential it must be more conscious of what it adapts to as a modernist institution.

■ The Limits of Adaptive Government

The hegemony of Western political and social thought, now generally regarded as the modernist ontology, has been unmasked by numerous social critics in this century as the reified framework from which the modern administrative state emerged (Giddens, 1990; Melossi, 1990; Pippen, 1991). According to these analyses, the bureaucratic state is a manifestation of that social construction that best represents a millennium-long development in human consciousness—one that embodies a decline in a Jeffersonian-style faith that individuals, acting in community, can bring about social progress (Taylor, 1992). Modernism is instead characterized as a powerful obsession with technocratic processes concerned most with the control of human inadequacies in the instrumental pursuit of preordained outcomes (Boggs, 1993; Mills, 1978).

It is this technocratic, control-oriented model of modernism that has become a specific identity for public administrators, one that seems to be perpetually at odds with democracy. Indeed there have been many in the history of the field who have earnestly doubted that public administration could realistically be efficient and effective if it was also charged with securing the open political dialogue and citizen action needed to support truly democratic government (Abrahamsson, 1977).

The bureaucratic identity, however, was well suited to the legal-rational ontology of modernism. Indeed, the Founders of the Constitution were deeply influenced by the Hobbesian social contract, itself a key metaphor of the modernist epoch, which assigns government the role of the aloof mediator of human conflict (Wolin, 1990b). As constitutional scholar Joe Cropsey has put it, "America is modernism working itself out" (Strauss & Crospey, 1963). To James Madison it was social regulation that seemed to make democracy possible at all, given the imperfect state of human nature. Over time, public administrators became the tools and the technical process by which this social regulation occurred (Leiserson, 1942; Siedman & Gilmour, 1986). Too, the concerns for the control of administrative discretion and the institutionalization of management procedure that marked administrative reform at the beginning of the century were in harmony with the emerging regulatory nature of Western civilization and the development of capitalism (Best & Connally, 1992; O'Toole, 1984).

It thus can be said that public administration was initially an adaptation to its historical context. Indeed it has come to define its responsibility chiefly in terms of its ability to be adaptive (Kaufman, 1985). But adaptation formatted by the constant of modernist ontology has not kept government in evolutionary process so much as it has continually reaffirmed its narrow managerial identity. The appropriate identity for one era, however, is not necessarily appropriate for another. Indeed, the adaptability of public administration, at least as it has been exercised from a modernist framework, may now be its greatest fault.

Changes introduced from the environment, for example, are most often seen in Darwinian terms, as impositions from a hostile external population (Kaufman, 1985; Schubert, 1989; Selznick, 1957). Adaptation based on this defensive posture reinforces the core modernist identity that gave rise to the adaptation as a means of securing institutional stability in a turbulent environment (Taylor & Gutman, 1992). Adaptation by a modernist public administration, then, is not necessarily a democratic response, but rather is a defense of the modernist state as the guardian of democracy. Unfortunately, this defense also creates hostile and competitive relationships between citizens and their government; relationships that then seem to justify further regulatory government.

It is this relationship between administrative adaptive processes and the creation of a negative political culture that is seldom recognized by administrators who frame their responsibility only in the regulatory language of the social contract rather than in democratic terms. The idea of natural selection that fuels this defense of a regulatory state derives from Darwin and Enlightenment physics. Natural selection embodies the concept that organisms seek a homeostasis—that is, they seek to maintain a static equilibrium in their environment through the redistribution of power (Ho & Saunders, 1984). In government, for example, this equilibrium is achieved by minimizing conflict among those who are competing for survival in the political environment (Melossi, 1990). In time, this need to minimize conflict incorporates an imperative for efficiency. That is, efficiency comes to be equated not only with saving time and resources, but also with the equitable reallocation of resources as a means by which conflict is reduced. By supposedly reducing conflict through procedural equity, efficiency appears to be the seminal liberal act in stabilizing society and making democracy possible (Wolin, 1960). Indeed, the majority of public discourse is often about procedure—how to talk to bureaucracy in terms it understands and how to get things done given the nature of bureaucratic government (Moe, 1989).

Public administration's ability, then, to reduce all environmental phenomena to the requirements of the efficient allocation of resources is also the means by which the social contract is made operational in a dynamic and conflicted political environment. Indeed, it often appears that despite its adaptability, public administration must be forced to change against its will—as if, for the benefit of social stability, it were defending democracy on some isolated island against the dangers implicit in the assumed struggle among citizens for domination (Dennard, 1995; Simon, 1992).

An organic metaphor, however, illustrates the limitations of this defensive position. It now appears to New Science, for example, that viruses may use the threatening elements in their environment in creative ways. Vaccines meant to eradicate certain viruses might also be the matter the target virus uses to extend its natural life, so that our most instrumental "wars" on particular diseases may actually give those diseases what they need to mutate into survivable forms (Garrett, 1994). To extend this metaphor to public administration, we might consider the bureaucracy in the aftermath of the bureaucrat-bashing Reagan administration. The crisis situation created by Reagan's slash-and-burn war on public administration did not, as expected, reduce the size of the bureaucracy. Indeed, the public administration—through its adaptive processes—may have used the negative policies of the Reagan era to enlarge itself through program adjustments (Bickers & Stein, 1991).

The modernist metaphor of "war" as an effective management tool has generally lost any power it might have to affect social change. It has begun to appear instead that in our war on drugs, or crime, or other social deviance we have created a culture of violence and a government particularly well adapted to surviving war and little else. This is made more frightening by considering that the money we spend on prisons is quickly outstripping our ability to pay for education. War has the unsettling effect of focusing all energy and resources on an adaptation to what is wrong in the system rather than on the potential for something different. A new identity for public administration (and for government in general) must embrace the consciousness that we create our futures by what we put into the moment.

This problem of negative adaptation, however, does not necessarily get resolved by purely structural changes—like the eradication of hierarchies or tighter regulations on administrative behavior. In fact, adaptation itself is not the fundamental problem of bureaucracy. The problem is more the organizing principles with which the adaptive behavior is employed. The same creative/adaptive process with different organizing principles could create a democratic environment in the same manner modernism has created a bureaucratic and divisive one. Adaptive behavior is a process that defines the nature of the structure it nurtures on the basis of the organizing principles employed in the adaptation (Jantsch, 1979).

Likewise, the bureaucratic problem is not necessarily the problem of hierarchies, either. A hierarchical structure premised on modernist patriarchal control will create a different culture than one premised more on relationship and interdependence. It is possible, for example, to imagine a hierarchy that serves democracy as an interrelated and interdependent whole by engaging its members in the creation of new, *different* equilibria appropriate to changing contexts (Jantsch, 1979). This "integrated" hierarchy is democratic because it cooperatively, rather than defensively, accommodates changes in the environment through collective, creative action—rather than being continually concerned with recreating old equilibria by instrumentally reducing difference and conflict according to one model of efficiency or conflict management (Jantsch, 1979).

The key distinction between a control hierarchy and an integrated hierarchy is not structural but *relational*. Citizens, in this scenario, are not fighting for access to the bureaucratic hierarchy, they are instead integrated (rather than adaptive) members of it. The result could be the difference between an agency that is accountable through its hierarchical structure and democratic at the same time and one that struggles to keep democracy under control.

If public administration continues to understand its environment from the reference point of the social contract, or its companion theory of natural selection, however, even the most authentic democratic reform will become part of the bureaucratic identity by way of adaptive behavior. It is perhaps better to have public administration adapting to citizen or political demands than it is to ignore them. But a defensive adaptation does not constitute a realization of the democratic common good as much as it reinforces the undemocratic control principles with which the adaptation is made.

The Modernist Administrative Identity

This adaptive modernist persona can be expressed in four overlapping identities dominated by a modernist ontology. They affect an individual administrator's perception of his or her ability to act democratically within public institutions. These identities manifest themselves as (a) The Scientist, (b) The Patriarch, (c) The Computer, and (d) The Victim.

Taking these identities one at a time creates a map for transcending modernism through personal action at every level of public administration. In fact, personal action is perhaps the only way that the whole consciousness of modernism can be addressed. Modernism places the center of action in things, laws, technology, programs, and strategic plans. It can only be changed by that which it lacks—individual human initiative and human relationship.

The Scientist

The need to break up the administrative environment into parts and to reorganize the parts into more manageable classifications reflects the emergence of reductive science as the mediator of human action in modernist times. Identifying and then classifying the elements of a social problem serves to streamline the process of problem solving and decision making. Yet what this enduring practice has produced are public administrators unwilling and incapable of addressing the social order as a whole. Instead, they become entangled in fixing pieces of the puzzle without a clear sense of the active relationship among those pieces (O'Toole, 1984). A corresponding sense developed from this practice is that the sum of the parts of society is equal to the whole. What is missing in this view, however, is an awareness of those nonlinear processes of loving, empathizing, forgiving, healing, and community that create, renew, and maintain cultures.

This need to reduce all phenomena to manageable parts is also Newtonian: reflecting the idea that the universe is composed of forms competing for a limited supply of energy according to immutable and mechanical "natural laws." This sense has developed several imperatives for the administrative identity: (a) It makes it appear that all interaction between citizens and their government is a potentially dangerous use of resources; (b) It makes it appear that nothing happens in these mechanical exchanges except that which can be instrumentally and empirically extracted; and (c) It makes it seem that all social problems can be solved through a means-end adjustment of parts and resources according to preexisting models, while ignoring the relationships created by the very assumption of competition.

Chaos physics, however, makes this an archaic model for administrative identity. Simply put, New Science sees the turbulence in life processes not as signaling the demise of the system, but rather as the seedbed for system renewal. That is to say, that system turbulence is our cue that the system can no longer maintain a particular pattern of behavior. It is only an end-game if we try to control the turbulence as a means of maintaining the old, dysfunctional pattern. Our most instrumental attempts to maintain order in social systems (like war, for example) only increase the turbulence because they address the chaos rather than the imbalance that produced it. But more devastating, perhaps, is that such actions force the system to correct itself according to the circumstances it is trying to transcend—thereby embedding practices that the system clearly cannot sustain. To embrace the potential of this New Science, however, public administrators must see themselves as part of a self-organizing system whose order is implicit in the turbulence of its diverse relationships (Briggs & Peat, 1989; Wheatley, 1992).

Yet in modernist thought the individual is not often seen as being connected to a larger community of relationships (Rorty, 1985). A welfare recipient is, rather, a "case," one that meets a certain profile and therefore evokes a particular legalistic response. What is supposedly equitable and conflict-reducing in this formula is that all persons are treated in the same dehumanizing manner. In this way, equity becomes inseparably linked to efficiency and conflict management and therefore the perceived need for suppression of difference as a source of conflict (Webster, 1992). This aspect of the scientific persona has been particularly hard to dispel because it has merged scientism and the social contract with a moral sense of liberal justice and administrative responsibility (Rawls, 1971). By reducing themselves to the role of experts, however, administrators have also reduced citizens to the roles they play to support this bureaucratic drama—the poor, the sick, the criminal, the alien, the consumer (Rorty, 1985; Wolfe, 1989).

Yet the role of the objective expert who keeps democracy safe is tightly wired into the administrative psyche. It is a source of power and prestige—key elements of a "successful" modernist identity. It is no doubt frightening for administrators who have framed their sense of Self as modernist to transfer power to nonexperts—despite the fact that such a move would free the administrators themselves from a state of arrested personal development.

The Patriarch

For most of this century, what debate there has been over the identity of public administration has been largely about how to improve upon the model of bureaucracy conceptualized by Max Weber. How are workers made to work more efficiently within bureaucratic structures? How do we exceed the limitations of bureaucratic life? In either instance the model has been presumed to be a hard reality, and therefore the potentialities of public administration have been bounded by the discourse over the strengths or weaknesses of a single model (Bolough, 1990; Melossi, 1990).

The hero in this scenario has been Chester Barnard's patriarchal, "moral" manager who masters a difficult and chaotic reality by arresting his own development and "staying above the fray." He mediates the dark, but necessary, realities of bureaucracy by problem solving, independently inculcating meaning into workers' lives, and by staying in control of all variables (Barnard, 1938). He is type-cast in the lonely role of defending democracy without participating in it. The patriarch embodies the politics/administration dichotomy that assigns a politically detached role for public administration in an attempt to remove it from the corrupting forces of partisan politics (O'Toole, 1987). However, this disposition has not insulated bureaucracy from partisan corruption so much as it has insulated government from the positive influence of citizens (Stivers, 1990).

Patriarchal detachment also comes from the sense that two parts of the same whole can be separated and made subject to different operational laws. That is to say, it appears that we can have democracy without a democratic government. Indeed, it is perceived that democracy is only possible if government regulates relationships in a manner that reduces the potential for conflict and increases efficiency (Schon, 1971). Yet this detachment denies the positive, healing influence that citizens and administrators could have on each other if there were fewer preconditions to relationship. But the bureaucratic model was never the only model possible for public organizations. Instead, it was perhaps the only one that could be imagined from a modernist sense that all human activity could be confined to the borders of its own logic.

The Computer

From a modernist perspective it is entirely possible to dismiss everything that is said, done, or felt in a citizen interaction except the accomplishment of the task at hand. That is to say, that a multidimensional situation can be reduced to a single cybernetic dimension for reasons of efficiency and expediency. Administrators are often trained to be sensitive to the principles of the management of things, technology, and resources (Boggs, 1993; Brown, 1989), but seldom are they encouraged to learn how to do more than manipulate human behavior to meet the needs of these management principles.

Modernism produced the methodology of behaviorism that reduced the range of human emotions to those that could accommodate modernism—emotions managed by experts seeking to reduce social conflict. Therefore, the emotions we seem to understand best are anger, frustration, resentment, and distrust—emotions attached to the failure of others to meet our expectations and that therefore seem to rationalize litigation, reform, and retribution as social discourse (Dennard, 1995). Because behaviorism is concerned with teaching people to respond appropriately to consequences, even emotions like empathy or love are seen to be attempts to avoid negative consequences or to garner rewards. Because of this, the best of human altruism is cynically assumed to only be self-interest in disguise (Wolfe, 1989).

Human emotions, however, manifest an incredibly complex process within which humans transcend current circumstances to create new states of being (Murphy, 1992). A fully personal encounter between human beings can heal individuals and the relationships that constrain them. Healing, grieving, loving are all processes that citizens, untrained in the ways of bureaucratic rationality, carry with them as potential avenues for change. This potential is democratic because it embodies our common humanity and the self-development and identity formation that are basic to that humanity (Taylor & Gutman, 1992).

Yet it is an administrator's trained sense that much of what happens in his or her environment of a feeling nature is to be discounted (Simon, 1992). This disconnection, however, diminishes the possibility of change occurring in *each* action of the administrator, however ordinary. Instead, change is seen to come only as the cumulative effect of thousands of administrators and complex programs applied instrumentally, rationally, and efficiently to the problem. But such a vision of change reduces the individual administrator to a often helpless cog in the logic of the political machine.

The Victim

The reluctance to wrestle with its own identity has left public administration in the nearly impossible role of mediating among all the interests and power-holders within the vast American system without a clearly articulated sense of democratic purpose. Public administration in response often casts itself as the hapless victim of these political realities.

Yet public administration has seldom recognized its own role in the creation of the American political culture. It has instead allowed itself to become the scapegoat for social ills, but without developing the corresponding sense that it could or should do anything to change the culture other than what has been asked of it legally and procedurally. Public administration has been the "fixer" of problems rather than the creator of a positive political culture in which citizens engage collectively and individually in the resolution of their own problems. Public administration is therefore at a turning point in its own development and, like all human enterprises, must make an active choice about the continuation of its own refinement or suffer a permanent decline— not only in its own prestige and relevance but also in the decline of American and global culture. *Public administration must choose to practice democracy and therefore create it.*

Yet the managerial ontology makes it appear that we are so constrained by the power relationships in our environment that the responsibility for change does not lie with us, but with all those other actors in the system who use us to define what's wrong in government while cynically asking for more and more compliance. Changing government certainly *is* a shared responsibility. But the changes proposed here are not dependent on legislation or power redistribution, but upon the integrity and self-awareness of individuals within the public service. Indeed, a more self-aware assumption of democratic responsibility within public administration is needed before the Blacksburg plea for normative government can be understood as anything more than a self-interested call by public administration for more administrative discretion and power (Golembiewski, 1991; Marshall & White, 1990; Rainey, 1992).

Public Administration as a Democratic Institution

A new identity for public administration begins from the insight that democratic responsibility is not in the regulation of human relationships in an undemocratic manner. Public administration's greater responsibility lies in the creation of conditions in which democracy can be realized. Yet we are so far from discerning this responsibility that calling citizens "customers" is now viewed as a major step toward reconnecting public administration to the lives of its citizens (Osborne & Gaebler, 1992). But this impoverished view of citizenship is only indicative of just how distant public administrators are perceived to be from the real world of citizens.

Reforms perceived as democratic, like better "customer" service or the Blacksburg call for more citizenship and public dialogue, are likely to become simply bureaucratized—modified to fit the regulatory identity of public administration. Further, for individual public administrators to subordinate their own sense of democratic responsibility to a modernist concern for regulation is to legitimate similar undemocratic behavior in the citizens they serve. Indeed, a government whose officers act in a manner that is less than fully democratic not only angers citizens by its officious manner, it also forces citizens to adapt to its efficient and impersonal discourse while at the same time tearing them loose from their sense of values, morality, and community in order to compete in the political "arena" (Waltzer, 1991). If citizens are competitive, mean-spirited, and instrumental with each other, they have learned it from us.

Yet much of what individual public administrators do is without any physical contact with individual citizens. This fact in itself, however, does not relieve public administrators from responsibilities of democratic administration. The effects of a power-driven government have helped create a power-driven citizenry and politics, and without physical contact with each and every member of the social order. In an interrelated society, the assumptions with which we manage at all levels of government have a direct bearing on the nature of the culture we serve. What if administrators at all levels stopped asking themselves *only* how an event or new demand can be made to fit the existing pattern of power or the legalistic and procedural relationships in government? What if we asked, How do I go about my work in a democratic manner? How do the policies I recommend contribute to the capacity of citizens to act meaningfully? How does my management style encourage democratic behavior among my staff and between staff and citizens? How do I convey the sense to politicians and presidents that I am a Constitutional Officer in service to democracy?

For example, the street-level bureaucrat, who is the manifestation of his or her own agency culture rather than just an independent actor, has an immediate effect on the political culture. The police officer who patrols the community in a computer-equipped car, wearing body armor and carrying an arsenal of weapons, conveys a particular disposition about the citizens he or she serves. Indeed, a decidedly undemocratic picture of the nature of government itself is conveyed. What is the responsibility of a citizen when confronted with this technological metaphor for government? Are sullen and angry compliance, fear of authority, and a passive acquiescence to the power of technology acts of responsibility that further democratic development or are they simply *necessary* responses?

Yet despite its identity crisis, public administration is still the best positioned of all public institutions to effect major democratic change. It has the ability to connect social, economic, and political arenas, and it can marry the tasks of "running a constitution" with democratic organizing principles in a way that both maintains the society, achieves its human aspirations, and ultimately transcends itself in evolution. This unique and vital role for public administration as a democratic institution, however, can be accomplished only by a deeper understanding of the human, rather than technical processes at work in public life. These human processes are most easily understood and executed at the individual level through relationship.

Most profoundly, public administrators must assume active responsibility for the realities of their profession. This means we must come to accept the importance of procedural ambiguity in giving citizens the space to self-develop through their own efforts. We must also come to cherish cultural complexity as the means of maintaining and renewing democracy. These phenomena cannot continue to be treated as problems to be solved, but instead must come to be seen as essential aspects of democratic life. We must use our position and power to enhance citizenship and rejuvenate the democratic system as much as we have used it to defend the state. We must gain a sense of our strength and purpose from being the self-conscious connection between people and their government—the human-centered process whereby democracy is realized and made meaningful.

It is simply no longer meaningful to see the critique of government as being only the need for "faster and friendlier" service. It is possible to reduce all claims on government to a call for more efficiency, but to do so we miss the opportunity this era provides us. It is possible, again considering things from a multidimensional perspective, that a plea for more efficient dispatch of critical social programs is also an indictment of the failure of expert managerial public institutions to empower individuals to act on their own behalf. Instead we have reduced this potential by merely training citizens to take on government and interest groups like tribal adversaries. Recent social and political phenomena such as mandatory sentencing of repeat offenders ("three strikes you're out"); the ATF's siege on the Branch Davidians in Waco and violence both by police and against them in inner cities can all be understood as the consequences of the inability of citizens, legislators, and administrators alike any longer to envision a democratic government.

It needs to be emphasized here that this observation is *not* the preamble to an argument for bootstrap economics. The problem of regulatory government is not in finding ways to motivate citizens in their climb up the economic ladder according to the rational principles of capitalism. The problem is a government that will not acknowledge and be influenced by the unique contributions each citizen can make to the resolution of his or her own concerns—whatever their social or economic condition. Transcending this problem requires public administrators who are *willing* to make a distinction between compliance by citizens with bureaucratic norms and the creative, developmental interaction between citizens and their government.

Self-regulation is perhaps difficult for public administrators to imagine because it threatens their modernist identity. In part, this is because the identity crisis of public administration is really that it has *no* clearly articulated identity separate from the tasks its performs. In essence, there is often no clear separation between public administration and the regulations it implements. In this manner, regulations are not tools employed by self-aware constitutional officers. Regulations *are* the government. Therefore, to suggest a change from a regulatory identity is also often construed as an attack on public administration's deeply felt sense of personal responsibility to the technical role it plays (Bruce, 1989).

▬ Evolution: The Continuing Process of Democratic Relationships

Public administration, in deference to its modernist roots, has come to identify itself with the products of the political process rather than with the process itself. In this manner it comes to see itself as the mediator among warring factions that threaten its potential to be efficient in the achievement of outcomes. Yet it would be the democratic purpose of public administration to eliminate the battlefield altogether by engaging itself in an overt effort to reconcile members of society—rather than merely mediating between winners and losers in the market and regulating those, like the chronically poor, who are not contenders in the war but the casualties of it (Kozal, 1991).

However, this reconciliation is *not* the same as resolving differences by finding an agreeable bottom line. Instead, this reconciliation involves fostering the attitude of universal acceptance of citizens without the assumption that all conflict can or should be made subject to compromise. In other words, the focus is on reconciling relationships because of the potential they represent to create new meaningful states for citizens, rather than on the reduction of conflict (Wheatley, 1992).

To a modernist, compromise is the way to restore equilibrium in a system in which both energy and knowledge are finite (Simon, 1945). A more democratic identity would allow public administrators to see that the conflicted interactions between citizens are less energy consumptive than they are generative of both knowledge and power. Citizens and their government are in *coevolution* in this regard; creating and re-creating society in recognition of both interdependence and individuality. The process that is enhanced in this coevolution does two things: (a) it maintains the social conditions in which meaningful human evolution can continue over time; (b) it creates *new* equilibria that express the core democratic organizing principles in contextually relevant ways.

To be in coevolution, however, means that public administration must feel itself to be connected to the citizenry in a more intimate way than through policy mandates. It must also come to feel that there is an implicit order in human relationships that supersedes and is extant with contextually specific policy goals—that is, a human-centered democracy is not something we move toward incrementally as we eradicate all obstacles in our path to an ideal, rather the potential for democratic action is *always* there. Democracy is therefore a choice we make in the present, not necessarily one we plan to implement in the future. The democratic public administrator acts in the moment, knowing that different futures are nurtured there.

Yet recognizing that we have the capacity to change our society in every action requires us to let go of the idea that all possibilities are contained in the narrow space between competitive opposites. For example, as Dwight Waldo (1989) says, the American administrative state is the child of the struggle between our roots in Roman authoritarianism and those in Greek democracy. Given its birth in the afterglow of the Enlightenment and the dominant language of the social contract dogma, it is perhaps no wonder that this struggle for the identity of public administration has evolved toward authoritarianism over the years (Wolin, 1990a). But the answer to this imbalance is not necessarily just to infuse government with more Athenian ideals in order to right the scales between the two. This prescription narrows the possibilities to what can be bargained for between the two conceptions of government—that is, democracy can never be realized because it must first answer to the demands of a functional and rational authority. The most hopeful scenario in this formula is a government that occasionally, when coerced, responds in a democratic manner.

But there always have been other possibilities than "its the best we can do given human nature" democracy. Through citizens and their shared relationships we have the power to *create* other realities—ones closer to our aspirations than to our fears. The most important metaphors of this new age are those expressing interrelationship and interdependence. These are especially important for public administration because they begin to let administrators and academics see that it is impossible to separate government from its people; that they come to reflect each other whatever the dogma in government is at the time. The emerging metaphors of postmodernism suggest that, in relationship, we can practice democracy as a daily habit and therefore create democratic conditions, regardless of the historical, ontologically interwoven past. Indeed, it is time simply to forgive the past and move forward re-creating and reconciling our society as we go.

Yet it is difficult for a time-oriented, politically sensitive administration to allow a democracy conditioned on relationship even when such a democracy would sustain regulations and perhaps even reduce the need for them (Dewey, 1954; Follett, 1940/1952). The conceptual problem of time for the modernist public administrator is this: that processes that cannot be measured in linear time and therefore be held up for evaluation, must be trivialized or simply ignored (Dennard, 1995; Simon, 1992). Yet human relational processes, which would both sustain and enliven a stable democracy, are timeless because they occur whatever the historical context, ideology, or structural boundaries (Argyros, 1991; Fraser, 1990). It is from the intersection of the historical context with what can be called the constant of evolutionary relationships that new, contextually relevant phenomena emerge (Ho & Fox, 1986; Jantsch, 1979).

Evolution in this sense is more an act of democratic and communal *creativity* than merely a reactive response to an environmental threat or historical opportunity. It is dependent on love, respect, forgiveness, empathy, and a sense of solidarity among human beings over time, rather than a solidarity of contextually bound interests that maintain their unity only to have the strength to dominate others. This democratic process is cultural "evolution by process" rather than a behavioral "evolution by consequence" (Ho & Fox, 1986; Ho & Saunders, 1984; Simon, 1945; Skinner, 1981).

In New Science, evolution is no longer understood to be a rational march of progress along a straight line of history toward an idealized, singular, and often technical goal—but rather a cooperative and creative contextual response to changing circumstances that accommodates the relationships and individuals involved. This change in the ontological understanding of evolution dramatically redefines social relationships—from fear-based, power-oriented battles, to cooperation among individuals who each have something unique to contribute to the renewal of the human project in the process of their own self-development. In other words, the aspirations of democracy are realized in the relationships that in turn re-create a democratic reality from which a democratic future emerges.

Yet clearly a despairing view of human potential has dominated political life since the Founding. Madison's cynical view of human nature would fit well into the emerging hegemony of Western thought and eventually with competitive Western economics (Best & Connally, 1992). Madison's conception of power counterbalancing power is distinctly modern and anticipated both Darwin and Marx. The effect, however, has been the distortion of *the potential* of the Constitutional order to be democratic, because the organizing principles of the Constitution became defined in modernist terms. It is still the prevailing view of how government works (Kaufman, 1985; Schubert, 1989; Simon, 1992). Yet the potential of the inherently cooperative government (which John Rohr describes as being the intent of the Founders) and a democratically "civil society" it can generate is not lost (Rohr, 1990; Walzer, 1991).

Human nature, like administrative identity, is really a potentiality rather than a bounded structure contained in the narrow space of linear opposites (Lifton, 1993). An identity based on the need to mediate the bleak process of natural selection and domination, however, forces this potentiality into negative channels rather than along more sustainable paths through love, trust, and acceptance. Indeed, if the pathologies of interest group politics and inner-city violence are any indication, a modernist identity perpetuates the negative citizenship it seeks to ameliorate. As the child and conduit of the system of blended powers, public administration must choose a path. It can choose to remain a beleaguered codependent of power politics or can instead choose to become a self-conscious agent of democratic transformation.

▆ Public Is Not the Opposite of Private

The fusion of modernism and market principles creates a bind for public administration that can only be transcended by the realization that government is not merely the opposite of the market. Indeed, it is perhaps a modernist trap to assume that all arguments against regulatory government are also arguments for fewer constraints on capitalism (Bahro, 1986). It has become the modernist assumption that a *model* of competitive economics is responsible for creative growth in society rather than a democratic government in cooperation with citizens who are seeking grander things than more consumer choices. It is perhaps difficult for a modernist to imagine human relationships that might produce less divisive models than those of capitalism or even those of idealogies that are mainly an adaptation to what is wrong with capitalism—like socialism or communism, for example (Boggs, 1986). Yet it is likely that the excesses of modernism will be transcended only by legitimizing other forms of relationship than competitive economics and not by conducting public life as an endless battle to find an equilibrium between capitalism and our social responsibilities.

The method for legitimating democratic relationships, however, is not to try to balance the market by an infusion of more democratic "controls." It is *not* a new compromise that is sought here. The answer may instead be to revive the strength of the democratic community by embracing different organizing principles than those of the market, and thereby create a less ideological social model that is more appropriate and more sustaining of the human project than the market can be. This does not eliminate the market or make it the focus of reform, but instead reseats the market as only one interdependent manifestation of a broader democratic reality rather than the adaptive opposite of public life.

▬ Democracy as Coevolution: The Turbulent Mirror

By imagining the creative space beyond opposites, public administration can begin to redefine its sense of responsibility to the democratic project. First, we can recognize that citizens are not necessarily helped in their efforts by simply teaching them how to gain access to government by being well organized according to modernist presumptions of competition and domination (Radin & Cooper, 1989). Simply teaching citizens the rules of an undemocratic process does not create democracy. Indeed, it often perpetuates the Darwinian notion that all politics and social interaction are about domination and therefore simply recreates that bleak state of affairs. In this same vein, public administrators can reframe their responsibility by separating their own identity from the identity implicit in legalistic discourse. Rules and regulations can be used instead by self-conscious public administrators to initiate public involvement without defining it.

Second, administrators must quit seeing participation as something only citizens do. The modernist perception of the world conveys a sense that social interaction is set into motion by purely rational intent; that whether or not citizens are influenced by government, or vice versa, depends on someone in authority deciding that this influence will happen (Stivers, 1990). Citizens are "out there" and we are "in here," and we are separated by very formal, opaque procedural and legal structures. Yet these boundaries are only mental constructs that even science no longer supports as "hard" realities. An intimate relationship exists between living things that physicists Briggs and Peat (1989) describe as the "turbulent mirror." This turbulence is the natural interaction of interrelated life in a continual process of maintenance, renewal, and transcendence. To put it another way, there is "life" in life that will always span those boundaries that we arbitrarily build from the basis of rational models (Prigogine & Stengers, 1984). The realization of this intimacy makes it both possible and necessary to reconsider what traditionally has been meant by representation and participation in government.

For example, the historical argument for more democratic government has relied on empowering citizen participation in decision making, or on creating a more demographically representative public administration (Cook, 1992; Rosenbloom & Krislov, 1981). However, such arguments begin from the modernist assumption that the social world can be divided into parts and that the parts each have their own operating principles and spheres of influence. It has always appeared, therefore, that how citizens participate in government, apart from elections, would depend on how well the bureaucratic system could accommodate them (Abrahamsson, 1977). This has come to mean that if the bureaucratic system operates according to the principles of efficiency and regulation, then citizen participation must be regulated in an efficient manner as well. It is this compromise between bureaucracy and democracy that has generated the pathologies of interest group liberalism (Lowi, 1969). In this manner the most noble of human efforts can be reduced to the administrative byproduct of Herbert Simon's "satisficing" behavior—the reduction of environmental potentialities to what is possible within the regulatory framework of public administration.

A similar dilemma is created by modernism for the idea of the "representative bureaucracy." From a minimalist understanding of this reasoning, the diverse elements of society would have their specific *interests* represented in the day-to-day actions of government. From a broader democratic perspective, the diversity would change government and create new identities for both government and the political culture. But modernist public administration has only been able to accommodate this broader ideal insomuch as it could be measured in a rational and predictable way (Carter, 1991). As a result, diversifying a modernist public administration may have made the bureaucratic expertise more representational, but no more democratic. New people are still saddled with an old, one-dimensional bureaucratic identity, and government is only minimally changed by the difference and potential diverse people manifest (Webster, 1991).

The issue of participation might better be understood as the reengagement of government with its people. This, however, is not a problem that can be solved by the instrumental application of laws, procedure, or ideological values alone. Reengagement must also be the *participation* of public administrators themselves in their environments as conscious actors in a democratic system. Indeed, feeling this intimate connection to citizens may provide the meaning and sense of purpose that is lacking for many administrators in these days of bureaucrat bashing.

Indeed, if we listen more carefully and less defensively we will hear our own concerns as administrators echoing back to us from the political culture we have helped create. If citizenship has waned, so has a sense of meaning and purpose within public administration (Volcker, 1987). There are administrators who often despondently testify that, as individuals, they have little control over their own destinies when faced with the intricate and powerful machinery of government. It is this disposition that makes it difficult for individual administrators to connect with a sense of calling or profession in the manner prescribed by the Blacksburg School. The emergence of the identity required for either a sense of calling or of profession is dependent on an individuals' ability to act in their environment in meaningful and ultimately personal ways. It would seem ridiculous to suggest, however, that this sense of personal malaise within government is curable by more efficiency. Why should we assume the same prescription would hold for a troubled citizenry?

The Blacksburg School will realize its vision of public administration more readily if administrators' natural sense of humanity—and the meaning and purpose that arises from it—can be enlivened. In this regard, the efforts of the Blacksburg School to establish the roots of public administration in the Constitution has more implications for the field than just giving it legal legitimacy. In fact, the development of a democratic identity for public administration is inhibited somewhat by the arguments supporting its legitimacy. Constitutional legitimacy may rightly support the place of public administration in government and give credence to its authority. Yet without a recognition of the need for a new democratic identity with which to temper the discretionary acts of public administrators, the Blacksburg prescription can easily be mistaken for another claim for government power and little else.

Yet a constitutional connection also can be the rationale for writing regulations and implementing programs with a sense of the broader concerns for democracy, not merely the fulfillment of an ideological agenda mandated by the political environment. Constitutional legitimacy, in the way the Blacksburg project speaks of it, is inseparable from democratic responsibility. In this regard, we must begin to see our accountability as being much broader than mere technical success.

Yet the seeming reluctance of the field to embrace this broader sense of democratic responsibility is not because government is run by hoards of "control freaks" who feel no compulsion to be democratic. It is more likely that government is run, as Charles Goodsell (1993) documents, by people who care deeply about their work and their country. What is missing is that administrators have not found their democratic voice, but instead too frequently define their responsibility only in fearful, bureaucratic terms. This narrow sense of responsibility to technical outcomes and power relationships alone makes democratic principles seem like idealistic fairy tales. Indeed, the question of changing public administration often dead-ends with the so-called real world of the present.

▬ Real-World Blues

This real world of administrative life is riddled with political games and people vying for power and interest. It is beset by corruption, greed, ambition, inequity, petty crime, and narcissism. It *is* real, and that point cannot and will not be contested here. But these hard realities of modernist public administration are not justified simply because they exist. Nor can they be changed by structural reform or an instrumental or legal redistribution of power and resources without further institutionalizing the modernist organizing principles that made them realities. Quite simply, fighting fire with fire only produces more fire. The familiar comment of Albert Einstein is relevant here—"You can't solve a problem with the same consciousness that created it" (Wheatley, 1992, p. 3).

Likewise, promoting a new democratic identity for public administration does not mean that public administrators can simply employ a "higher" set of values in going about their business. Values themselves do not guarantee a sense of the importance of democratic citizenship but can often serve as the rationale for more regulation based on the need to better control social realities through reified ideology. Perhaps more important, from a modernist sense of responsibility, these values would be made to "fit" into a stabilized equilibrium of market interests. That is, democratic values are likely to be "bureaucratized" and therefore cause the further erosion of citizens' relationship with their government. Either way, public administration would once again be only the conduit of a compromised democracy, not an active cocreator in the practice and realization of democracy.

One can argue that the Constitution is a set of values, but it is not the values per se that bind a government with its people, as much as it is the relationship and shared responsibility they symbolize. The Constitution symbolizes this connection of public administration to the citizens they serve and provides the rationale for maintaining that connection in a positive and generative manner. This necessarily assumes that administrators must be able to make judgments within their systems of constraints about what action best maintains these relationships and which therefore maintains the ability of the nation to evolve, change, and realize its most aspirational dreams of a democratic society.

The conditions that call for administrative action and expertise—poverty, drug abuse, crime, unemployment—are also very real. But so are the citizens caught up in these realities, and real also are processes of development and social evolution they carry within them. If public administration continues to see citizens only as problems to solve or unsavory realities to endure, they cannot connect to those human relationships that have the capacity to heal these despairing realities. They can only regulate them. Democracy and the responsible citizenship it engenders simply cannot be realized through undemocratic relationships. Insisting that they can creates a "real" world where no one really wants to be, but to which we are bound for the lack of imagination and courage.

The dilemma of these "real-world" arguments for academics has been that if we answer pleas to be prescriptive according to the real world of public administration, we often are also being asked to "be practical" when doing so simply reinforces the status quo. Likewise, as educators we often acquiesce to market pressures to give students the practical tools they need to survive the government as it is, rather than the personal capacity to change it (Brown, 1989; Kettl, 1993). In these troubled times, however, there are critical choices—not merely market adaptations—to be made by academics and administrators alike.

These choices must get past the "real-world" defense that administrators "are just doing what citizens want them to do." This defense simply misses the point that what citizens demand may often as not be what public administration tells them is possible. Citizens do want and deserve efficient and effective government but must they always trade their individuality, their community, and their democratic aspirations to get it? Public administration and academia can lament the sorry state of American citizenship or we can recognize our own part in creating these negative conditions and open a new door of potential for all of us.

▄▄ Who Changes First?

Pubic administrators do not have all the responsibility for healing the deep wounds in the political culture. We are, after all, responsible to a broader system of relationships, laws, mandates, and norms. Nor can it be argued that these constitutional constraints should be altered in any way. It is also recognized that the general perception of the rest of government and citizens that public administration is only a managerial technology must also change. Academics have an important, democratic role to play in this regard.

The focus here is on how public administration can change itself as a catalytic act of responsibility to the entire political system. It is in a unique position of being strategically located within the governmental system, yet characterized by constitutionally decentralized and subservient power. Turning our full attention to citizens allows us to accomplish what must be a transformation of public administration through democratic relationship, rather than merely an adaptation to power politics. The system will not change simply with the redistribution of power or through the mediation of more power struggles. It will only change by employing that which it lacks—love and respect for citizens and for each other.

This prescription, then, is not a call for the reform of procedure, the collapse of the hierarchy, the equitable regulation of power relationships, the inculcation of values, the reengineering of processes, the recognition of customers, the downsizing of agencies, or any other managerial reform to which public administration has become expert in accommodating. Instead, it is a recognition of the difference one administrator can make in the American culture by conducting himself or herself as a self-aware constitutional officer serving his or her fellow citizens.

━━ Public Service as Democratic Therapy

Reconsidering more earnestly the service aspect of our profession may open a more meaningful discourse for administrators than the perpetuation of a negative democracy for the sake of social stability. In Greek, service means "therapy." The metaphor of therapy helps us visualize how an act of service might also be a transforming event, one in which democratic relationships are nurtured and a shared sense of communal responsibility is conveyed. Service as communal therapy legitimatizes acts that are not only task oriented but also serve to maintain and renew the political culture (Gawthrop, 1993). This is not therapy that seeks to fix or correct a bad behavioral habit through the administration of expertise, however. It is not confined to "sessions" and a couch. Rather, democratic therapy recognizes a citizen as a person who can and should be engaged in his or her own development. It is nonjudgmental. It is empathetic. It is concerned with the whole of social relationships to which the individual is connected. It is focused on a process of change and renewal, rather than on the validation of power relationships or roles.

Therapy, as service, is concerned with meaning, not in creating it for the citizen, but legitimizing the self-discovery process by which meaning contributes to individual maturation. It is these acts of recognition and compassion that will allow administrators to make the human connection with each other and with the environment they serve. When this connection is made, the potential of the human enterprise to change and rectify its own imbalances is endless. In fact, the cure for ailing citizenship is also the prescription for healing the wounds of public administration left from more than a century of modernist ontological dogma. The prescriptions proposed here are for democratic government. They are largely acts of personal commitment for individual administrators.

━ The Prescriptions

Practice Self-Development as Democratic Responsibility

The responsibility of a democratic public administrator is to be very competent at a technical skill but also to be a self-aware person who understands and appreciates the nature of the human project. Simon's powerful idea that a fulfilled person was also a rationalized one simply denudes the human character of its basic heroic nature (Simon, 1992). What the new epoch can offer public administration, through its science, philosophy, and its doubt of pure truth, is the inspiration that there is meaning in the human struggle that cannot be dismissed in the expedient pursuit of goals. By perpetually looking for those circumstances and that behavior that reaffirms our basic modernist assumptions about human nature we reduce ourselves to one-dimensional "characters" and we pull the rest of society down with us. As individuals we must come to be surprised and therefore changed by our environments.

It is no longer appropriate, if it ever was, to tell administrators to "leave their personality on the doorstep" (Barnard, 1938). Without personal involvement it is not possible for administrators to practice democracy, because they cannot experience it themselves. Self-development through an engagement with democracy assists administrators in discovering their sense of calling to the public service, which carries with it a powerful sense of responsibility and love for citizens.

Address the Whole Through Individuals

Addressing the whole of society recognizes that the boundaries between government and its citizens are largely artificial. One way to understand this is to recognize that the "parts" of the system are people, not problems to be solved, tasks to be completed, or models to enact. Each person is connected through relationship to a larger sphere of relationships and commitments, so that serving one person can change a much broader sphere than what can be imagined by assessing the linear effect of one outcome. The common good will always be broader than the specific, contextual goal. The common good will always be that which addresses the whole society in a manner that allows the entire chain of relationships connected to any one person or interest to progress. This also must be true of relationships within public administration. An interconnected and interdependent society does not stop at the doorstep of bureaucracy. If we have created a powerful negative democracy by the reenforcement of greed, competition, and violence, what might we do if we openly embraced the positive emotional, spiritual, and communal life of citizens?

Practice Democratic Authority

Democratic authority is practiced by listening to all citizens for what they have to say, thus empowering their sense of personal efficacy and helping them discover their own sense of values and purpose. Dialogue with citizens is only authentic when an administrator is listening. Dialogue is only democratic when an administrator is listening authentically for the multiple dimensions present in any human interchange. Public dialogue is only meaningful if it produces new space in which diverse elements of society can interact with meaning and purpose. This, however, is not the same thing as finding an equitable bottom line or common interest. It is dialogue that ignores interests and roles and connects the people as human beings in a process of creating new social space and individual identity.

Within public administration this means that policy-level managers and all those above and below must listen more to street-level bureaucrats. Also, policy implementation procedures should not make it unduly difficult for those on the enforcement end of bureaucracy to practice democracy. This requirement may be as simple as granting street-level bureaucrats the time to interact with citizens in ways other than through the management of outcomes, or by making program evaluation requirements that recognize the meaningful human processes at work in every situation.

Citizens are also empowered by being able to have control over what happens in their communities. Turning government over to private bureaucracies does not necessarily make democracy. It simply transfers responsibility for democracy to a segment of the polity least concerned with human issues. Individual citizens are no more empowered and democratic government has given away its most important trust. Countering this trend toward privatization of democratic responsibility requires a particular act of self-consciousness on the part of public administration—an admission that the proper place for democratic government is government itself. The individual administrator makes the case for democratic government each time he or she recognizes and engages the humanity of citizens. The market, on the other hand, only recognizes citizens for their functionality to its enterprise.

Administrative discretion is another issue of democratic authority. The reality is and has perhaps always been that whether or not it is perceived as legitimate, discretion exists as a fact. It would seem more fruitful if administrators spent less time defending their discretion and more time refining it as moral judgment (Dennard, 1994). It is in discretionary acts that an administrator can accommodate the many dimensions of public life.

Accept Citizens as They Are

Modernism is built on the belief that a perfect society can be created through the marriage of technology and reason. The means to this end has been the control of individual behavior in accordance with a rational blueprint for perfection. This dream was particularly strong during the 1950s and 1960s when it appeared that with an understanding of human behavior coupled with the technology of science, we had at last realized the Cartesian dream and mastered our environment (Gleick, 1987). In the late 20th century, however, our society has come to express doubt in the ability of human beings to master anything so precise as utopia. The widespread cynicism about this era might not just be from cultural nihilism but from grief, shame, and depression over the lost promise of a scientific utopia, designed, controlled, and managed by experts.

The vision of a utopic world free from all human struggle was perhaps never a realistic one. But even to think it was possible or even appropriate has helped create a negative society, one most concerned with compliance and the correction of deviation. Citizens are seen as problems because they often fail to meet the minimal standards imposed on them by a bureaucracy seeking to achieve procedural social equity as a manageable equality. Poverty, disease, and human trauma have come to be identified with the persons themselves, rather than being the conditions in which persons find themselves—in the same manner an administrator narrows his or her own potentiality to change the circumstance to what seems functional to the accomplishment of a task.

This constant critique and evaluation according to static, utopic, and largely economic models has had a devastating effect on the population. The nihilism in inner cities is attributable, at least in part, to the sense among the poor, the unemployed, the sick that they have lost the rest of their identity and the meaning their experiences might contribute to society (West, 1991). These conditions cannot be transcended by more blame. In the long run it does not matter who is to blame, if, in the process of finding out, we destroy the potential of a human system to renew itself.

One of the legacies of modernism and its idiosyncratic sense of perfection, for example, is that unless a procedure can be seen to fix a problem in a predictable manner over time it is somehow unworthy of consideration. Small incremental steps in problem solving are favored as a way to accommodate political forces and maintain accountability. Further, because these steps are seen to be connected in a simple cause-and-effect manner, it is perceived that anything nonlinear will only distort the final and complete fix of the problem (Lindblom, 1965). The administrative sense develops, then, that not only is it unlikely that an individual can make a difference in the system, but that if an individual independently addresses a problem it will make it more difficult to realize the projected outcome. The irony of this logic is that before action to correct a problem is deemed possible the conditions under which the correction is to be made must, in effect, be sterilized of their human content. Yet this practice separates administrators from the emotional and relational reality they are attempting to change and attaches their attention instead to the realization and correction of a one-dimensional model (Simon, 1992). And in making conditions for change procedurally perfect, countless opportunities are missed for real-world accidents, accidents in which administrators and citizens can find an opening, pursue a potential, and make a contribution; accidents in which individuals can connect with the human process of healing and maturation (Teilhard de Chardin, 1964).

Our devotion to this false objectivity had made it appear that citizens, like the poor, have nothing to tell experts about the problem of poverty because the citizens seem to embody the "problem" in the same way the administrator embodies the "solution." Yet it is too easy to pass these phenomena off as somebody's "problem." In an interrelated society there are no such single scapegoats for social problems. Indeed, if our most severe problems emerged in modernism, it is not likely they can be cured at all through regulation or behavioral management. They may be more amenable to love, compassion, listening, and healing. Perhaps the chief criterion for public service in these days of social despair is a deep love, respect, and unconditional acceptance of all citizens.

Come to Terms With Suffering

In public administration we have served our liberal sense of humanism by connecting our efficient allocation of resources to the act of reducing suffering among citizens. But this aspiration does not in itself make suffering meaningless. To convey to citizens that their poverty, for example, is a meaningless occurrence in their lives because it places them below some standard of normality, is to deny the individual and the nation the opportunity for development afforded by the experience of poverty. This does *not,* however, in any way mean that we should continue to institutionalize poverty for the insights we might gain from other people's suffering, it is more a recognition that all human events are multidimensional. Yes, we relieve suffering whenever and wherever we can, but we cause more suffering if we do not also allow citizens to gain meaning from their experience (Frankl, 1969; Soelle, 1984). Indeed it is this meaning that could inform administration about how to end poverty if we would simply listen.

This failure to recognize other people's suffering and instead to standardize it as a statistic or category has also had the effect of insulating administrators from the emotions that might produce new evolutionary insights about poverty or crime, or about the individual administrator, or indeed about the nature of government itself. We are taught instead that our emotions will "overwhelm" rather than inform us. But this approach has reduced emotions, like the people attached to them, to merely unproductive by-products of history rather than the bridges to democratic relationship. If individuals cannot act on their feelings, cannot feel compassion or revulsion or despair, then they cannot connect to human process. In public administration this disconnect has linked the fulfillment of our responsibilities with our ability to move away from the human condition in order to work out the perfect, rational solution to it.

But in an attempt to control all circumstance from a critical distance, government has robbed administrators of the richness of an emotional attachment to citizens and it has robbed citizens of the comfort of an empathetic government. Thomas Jefferson said citizens were to be loved. He perhaps did not mean that they should be loved only when they had been made to fit the icy criteria of a pain-free life. Sometimes, in the spirit of service, the most powerful thing an administrator can do is to recognize the pain of another human being.

Helping the American culture heal the wounds of a failed behavioral project and reconciling the relationships that have been devastated by the modernist push for rational perfection is perhaps a working definition of public service that fulfills the Greek ideal of therapy. It is also the way that the culture and government mature through the experiences of its citizens.

Assume Responsibility for Answering the Hard Questions

A modernist identity consciously discourages administrators from asking deeper questions about their role in the human enterprise. Why do we act? What is human nature? What purpose is there in government? What is ethical behavior? What is my personal role in the democratic project? Yet by individually struggling with the answers to these questions, administrators enhance their own self-development. They also reconnect themselves with the human project through its global philosophies, its history, and its timeless aspirations. The vision of a public administration composed of people who are deeply involved with and conscious of their humanity—its multicultural art, music, poetry, philosophy, and politics; its struggle to answer the hard questions of life—is perhaps the democratic vision of government that exists in potential in the arguments of both Jefferson and Hamilton, if not in our historical experience so far. It is a vision that creates a sense of dynamic interchange between government and its people that continuously moves the democratic and human project forward.

Public administration educators must also ask the same hard questions. It is no longer enough to teach administrators how to survive and manipulate their environments. We must encourage their personal development in a manner that allows them to transcend the battleground of their environment and practice democracy. Perhaps the most alarming observation of the Volcker Commission report on the public service in 1987 was that 70% of those polled in a study of federal workers said they would not encourage their children to enter the public service (Volcker, 1987). This is understandable if the best we can offer them as academics is armor with which to brave the onslaught on democracy. Whether we call it a profession or a field or a discipline, a vocation or a calling, public service should mean something to those who are engaged in it—not just for the sake of these individuals but also for the sake of the people they serve.

▬ Summary

By calling for a more normative public administration grounded in the Constitution, the Blacksburg School lays a powerful framework from which to begin a dialogue about the continued evolution of American public administration and indeed the American State and Citizenry. The School, however, is impeded in its efforts by its tendency to give slight attention to the individual administrator, who acts from a modernist sense of responsibility, as the primary player in the administrative system.

The School celebrates the unique role of public administration in government, but it can be helped in this recognition by a further clarification of the democratic meaning of its prescriptions. Democracy evolves from a public administration in which individual citizens self-consciously serve other citizens in a shared human process of change and development. Public administration cannot meet its constitutional responsibilities by simply increasing its ability to survive the power politics of an ideologically driven chief executive or legislature. Indeed, accepting the premises of that battle makes public administration permanently vulnerable to its own worst modernist idiosyncracies.

The strengths of public administration are unique to itself. They come from its particular position of service to government and to citizens. This position becomes demoralizing when it appears to individual administrators that they are merely cogs in a machine. It becomes pathological when they act the part. This crucial democratic position takes on meaning when it is possible for administrators to see that in each action, however small or mundane, democracy can be realized.

References

Abrahamsson, B. (1977). *Bureaucracy or participation: The logic of organization.* Beverly Hills, CA: Sage.

Argyros, A. (1991). *A blessed rage for order: Deconstruction, evolution, and chaos.* Ann Arbor: University of Michigan Press.

Bahro, R. (1986). *Building the green movement* (M. Tyler, Trans). Philadelphia: New Society Publishers.

Barnard, C. I. (1938). *The functions of the executive.* Cambridge, MA: Harvard University Press.

Best, M. H., & Connally, W. E. (1992). *The politicized economy* (2nd ed.). Lexington, MA: D. C. Heath.

Bickers, K. N., & Stein, R. M. (1991). *Federal domestic outlays, 1983-1990: A data book.* Armonk, NY: M. E. Sharpe.

Boggs, C. (1986). The green alternative and the struggle for a post-Marxist discourse. *Theory and Society, 15,* 869-899.

Boggs, C. (1993). *Intellectuals and the crisis of modernity.* Albany: State University of New York Press.

Bolough, R. W. (1990). *Love or greatness: Max Weber and masculine thinking, a feminist inquiry.* London: Urwin Hyman.

Briggs, J., & Peat, F. D. (1989). *Turbulent mirror: An illustrated guide to chaos theory and the science of wholeness*. New York: Harper & Row.

Brown, B. (1989, March/April). The search for public administration: Roads not followed. *Public Administration Review,* pp. 215-216.

Bruce, W. (1989). A response to C. J. McSwain and O. F. White, Jr.: Transfiguring the golem: Actions speak louder than words. *Public Administration Review, 49*(2), 197-200.

Carter, S. (1991). *Reflections of an affirmative action baby*. New York: Basic Books.

Cleveland, H. (1988, May/June). Theses of a new reformation: The social fallout of science 300 years after Newton. *Public Administration Review,* pp. 681-686.

Cook, B. J. (1992). The representative function of bureaucracy: Public administration in constitutive perspective. *Administration & Society, 23,* 403-429.

Dennard, L. F. (1994, December). Negative democracy and the American character. *International Journal of Public Administration,* p. 12.

Dennard, L. F. (1995). Neo-Darwinism and Simon's bureaucratic antihero. *Administration & Society, 26*(4), 464-487.

Dewey, J. (1954). *The public and its problems*. Chicago: Swallow Press.

Follett, M. P. (1952). *Dynamic administration: The collected works of Mary Parker Follett* (Henry C. Metcalf & H. Urwick, Eds.). New York & London: Harper & Brothers. (Original work published 1940)

Fowler, R. B. (1991). *The dance with community: The contemporary debate in American political thought*. Lawrence: University Press of Kansas.

Frankl, V. (1969). *Man's search for meaning: The will to meaning, foundations, and applications of logotherapy*. New York: World.

Fraser, J. T. (1990). *Of time, passion, & knowledge: Reflections on the strategy of existence*. Princeton, NJ: Princeton University Press.

Garrett, L. (1994). *The coming plague: Newly emerging diseases in a world out of balance*. New York: Farrar, Straus & Giroux.

Gawthrop, L. C. (1993, February). *Ethics & democracy: A call for barefoot bureaucrats.* Inaugural lecture. Delivered on the occasion of the acceptance of the Tinbergen Chair professorship at Erasmus Universeit Rotterdam, the Netherlands.

Giddens, A. (1990). *The consequences of modernity*. Stanford, CA: Stanford University Press.

Gleick, J. (1987). *Chaos: Making a new science*. New York: Viking.

Golembiewski, R. T. (1991). [Review of the book *Refounding public administration*]. *The Journal of Politics, 53*(4), 1187-1191.

Goodsell, C. T. (1993). *The case for bureaucracy*. Chatham, NJ: Chatham House.

Gould, C. (1984). *Rethinking democracy: Freedom and social cooperation: Politics, economics, and strong democracy*. Berkeley: University of California Press.

Heller, A., & Feher, F. (1991). *The grandeur & twilight of radical universalism*. New Brunswick, NJ: Transaction Books.

Ho, M.-W., & Fox, S. W. (1986). *Evolutionary processes and metaphors*. Chichester, UK: John Wiley.

Ho, M.-W., & Saunders, P. T. (1984). *Beyond Neo-Darwinism: An introduction to the new evolutionary paradigm*. London: Academic Press.

Jameson, F. (1991). *Postmodernism, or the cultural logic of late capitalism*. Durham, NC: Duke University Press.

Jantsch, E. (1979). *The self-organizing universe: Scientific and human implications of the emerging paradigm of evolution*. Oxford, UK: Pergamon.

Kaufman, H. (1985). *Time, chance, and organizations: Natural selection in a perilous environment*. Chatham, NJ: Chatham House.

Kettl, D. F. (1993). Toward new governance: Making process a priority. *The LaFolette Policy Report, 5*(2), 2, 18-19.

Kozal, J. (1991). *Savage inequalities: Children in America's schools.* New York: Crown Publishers.

Leiserson, A. (1942). *Administrative regulation.* Chicago: University of Chicago Press.

Lifton, R. J. (1993). *The protean self: Human resilience in the age of fragmentation.* New York: Basic Books.

Lindbloom, C. E. (1965). *The intelligence of democracy: Decision-making through mutual adjustment.* New York: Collier-Macmillan.

Lowi, T. J. (1969). *The end of liberalism: Ideology, policy, and the crisis of public authority.* New York: Norton.

Marshall, G. S., & White, O. F., Jr. (1990). The Blacksburg Manifesto and the postmodern debate: Public administration in a time without a name. *The American Review of Public Administration, 20*(2), 61-76.

Melossi, D. (1990). *The state of social control: A sociological study of concepts of state and social control in the making of democracy.* New York: St. Martin's.

Mills, C. W. (1978). *The sociological imagination.* Oxford, UK: Oxford University Press.

Moe, T. (1989). The politics of bureaucratic structure. In J. E. Chubb & P. E. Petersen (Eds.), *Can government govern?* (pp. 267-329). Washington, DC: Brookings Institution.

Murphy, M. (1992). *The future of the human explorations into the further evolution of human nature.* New York: Tarcher.

Osborne, D. E., & Gaebler, T. (1992). *Reinventing government: How the entrepreneurial spirit is transforming the public sector.* Reading, MA: Addison-Wesley.

O'Toole, L. J. (1984). American public administration and the idea of reform. *Administration & Society, 16*(2), 154.

O'Toole, L. J. (1987, January/February). Doctrines & developments: Separation of powers, the politics administration dichotomy, & the rise of the administrative state. *Public Administration Review,* pp. 45-59.

Pateman, C. (1989). *The disorder of women: Democracy, feminism, & political theory.* Stanford, CA: Stanford University Press.

Pippen, R. B. (1991). *Modernism as a philosophical problem: The dissatisfaction of European high culture.* Oxford, UK: Basil Blackwell.

Prigogine, I., & Stengers, I. (1984). *Order out of chaos: Man's new dialogue with nature.* New York: Bantam Books.

Radin, B., & Cooper, T. (1989, March/April). From public action to public administration: Where does it lead? *Public Administration Review,* pp. 167-170.

Rainey, H. G. (1992). [Review of the book *Refounding public administration*]. *Journal of Policy Analysis & Management, 11*(1), 147-154.

Rawls, J. (1971). *A theory of justice.* Cambridge, UK: Cambridge University Press.

Rohr, J. (1990). The Constitutional case for public administration. In G. L. Wamsley, R. N. Bacher, C. T. Goodsell, P. S. Kronenberg, J. A. Rohr, C. M. Stivers, O. F. White, & J. F. Wolf, *Refounding public administration* (pp. 52-95). Newbury Park, CA: Sage.

Rorty, R. (1985). Postmodern bourgeois liberalism. In R. Hollinger (Ed.), *Hermeneutics & praxis.* Notre Dame, IN: University of Notre Dame Press.

Rosenbloom, D. H., & Krislov, S. (1981). *Representative bureaucracy and the American political system.* New York: Praeger.

Schon, D. (1971). *Beyond the stable state.* New York: Random House.

Schubert, G. A. (1989). *Evolutionary politics.* Carbondale: Southern Illinois University Press.

Siedman, H., & Gilmour, R. (1986). *Politics, position, and power: From the positive to the regulatory state.* New York: Oxford University Press.

Selznick, P. (1957). *Leadership in administration.* New York: Harper & Row.

Simon, H. A. (1945). *Administrative behavior.* New York: Macmillan.

Simon, H. A. (1992). *Models of my life.* New York: Basic Books.

Simon, H. A., Smithburg, D. W., & Thompson, V. A. (1950). *Public administration: The struggle for existence: Organizational equilibrium.* New York: Knopf.

Skinner, B. F. (1981). Selection by consequence. *Science, 213,* 50-54.

Soelle, D. (1984). *Suffering.* Philadelphia: Fortress Press.

Spretnak, C. (1986). Postmodern populism: The greening of techno-cratic society. In H. C. Boyte & F. Riessman (Eds.), *The new populism: The politics of empowerment* (pp. 156-164). Philadelphia: Temple University Press.

Stanley, M. (Ed.). (1992). *Technicism, liberalism, and development: A study in irony as social theory.* Syracuse, NY: University of Syracuse Press.

Stivers, C. (1990). The public agency as polis: Active citizenship in the administrative state. *Administration & Society, 22*(1), 86-106.

Strauss, L., & Crospey, J. (1963). *History of political philosophy.* Chicago: Rand McNally.

Taylor, C. (1989). *Sources of the self: The making of the modern identity.* Cambridge, MA: Harvard University Press.

Taylor, C. (1992). *Ethics of authenticity.* Cambridge, MA: Harvard University Press.

Taylor, C., & Gutman, A. (1992). *Multiculturalism and politics of recognition.* Princeton, NJ: Princeton University Press.

Teilhard de Chardin, P. (1964). *The future of man.* New York: Harper & Row.

Volcker, P. A. (1987). *Public service: The quiet crisis* (The Francis Boyer Award Lecture). Washington, DC: National Commission on the Public Service.

Waldo, D. (1989). Politics and administration: On thinking about a complex relationship. In R. C. Chandler (Ed.), *A centennial history of the American administrative state* (pp. 89-112). New York: Free Press.

Walsh, D. (1990). *After ideology: Recovering the spiritual foundations of freedom.* New York: Harper's.

Walzer, M. (1988). *The company of critics.* New York: Basic Books.

Walzer, M. (1991, Spring). A better vision: The idea of a civil society, a path of social reconstruction. *Dissent,* p. 298.

Webster, Y. O. (1992). *The racialization of America.* New York: St. Martin's.

West, C. (1991, Spring). Nihilism in black America: A danger that corrodes from within. *Dissent,* pp. 221-226.

Wheatley, M. J. (1992). *Leadership and the new science: Learning about organizations from an orderly universe.* San Francisco: Berett-Koehler.

Wolfe, A. (1989). *Whose keeper: Social science and moral obligation.* Berkeley: University of California Press.

Wolin, S. (1960). *Politics and visions: Continuity & innovation in Western political thought.* Boston: Little, Brown.

Wolin, S. (1990a). Democracy and the discourse of postmodernism. *Social Research, 57,* 5-30.

Wolin, S. (1990b). Hobbes and the culture of despotism. In M. G. Dietz (Ed.), *Thomas Hobbes and political theory.* Lawrence: University of Kansas Press.

12

Thinking Government

Bringing Democratic
Awareness to Public Administration

JOHN H. LITTLE
University of Maine

──── The project of refounding public administration in a way that legitimizes it and clarifies the role of public administration in our system of
governance was begun by the authors of the Blacksburg Manifesto in the
1980s. Most of the discourse stimulated by that project has concentrated on
surface issues of public administration and has neglected an underlying issue,
one that frames much of our discourse about the field. This is unfortunate
because the Blacksburg Manifesto and the *Refounding* book that followed it
made an important but incomplete start toward reframing the way we think
about governance itself.

I believe that the field cannot be successfully refounded unless its underlying conceptual grounding has been reframed in a way that ties theory and
practice together, equips it with practical means to cope with the complexities
of governance in a postmodern society, and enables administrative structures
and systems to adapt to the needs of a socio-technical environment that is
changing at an ever-accelerating rate. To accomplish such a reframing, we
must consciously revise the way we think about governance. This conceptual
grounding is formed and influenced by the metaphors we use to think about
our system of self-governance.

A variety of underlying metaphors are used, consciously or otherwise, to
think about the design of government and the processes of governance. Two

327

such metaphors dominate: government as a *machine* and government as an *organism.* We tend to rely on either or both of them when we think, write, and talk about government and about public administration. Both metaphors lead toward dichotomous thinking such as the fact-value distinction or the idea that politics and administration are separate actions. Reliance on these metaphors has led the field of public administration into an intellectual trap. Despite common agreement that such dichotomies are problematic at best, the prevailing metaphors simply do not support their elimination. There is, however, a third metaphor, one of government as a *brain,* whose use leads to the collapse of the dichotomies, clarifies the role of public administration, and provides a basis for linking contemporary public administration theory with practice and with the design of administrative systems supportive of normative theories.

Thinking About Governance: The Role of Metaphors

Everyday life is pervaded by metaphor (Lakoff & Johnson, 1980). Language, especially the ability to form abstractions, is built upon metaphor, and our understanding of the world is colored and influenced by metaphors, which are essential to understanding abstract ideas.

The importance of metaphor to thought is especially great when we try to understand the exceedingly complex interactions of physiological and neurological processes that constitute human beings. This complexity is further compounded when many human beings interact with each other as they form organizations, governments, and other social institutions. The attempt to understand and influence social complexity has led to the use of systems-oriented metaphors, which have deeply influenced our perceptions of social and political realities.

Systems Metaphors

A systems perspective is an attempt to organize and understand the complexity of the world. The idea of system is deeply ingrained in the way we view the world. We divide the world arbitrarily into systems—quarks, atoms, molecules, machines, organisms, intelligent organisms, individuals, groups, institutions, cultures, societies, humanity, oceans, atmospheres, gaia, planetary systems, galaxies, universes, and other aggregations of interacting somethings. Every thing that we think about is both a system and an element of a higher system.

The term *system* is so widely used in our society that it is easily discounted as shallow, meaningless, or without content. I do not have this broad use of system in mind, however, but a much narrower and richer conception of system that does not simply refer to things *in* the world, but suggests systematically organized conceptions *of* the world. As such, they are abstractions that are not real and do not actually exist. Instead, systems are creative thoughts about reality evoked and organized via systems metaphors (Flood, 1993; Flood & Jackson, 1991). Systems metaphors, in this view, are filters through which we view the world, not expressions of the world itself.

The predominant systems metaphor, in use at least since the Reformation, is the *mechanistic* metaphor. The idea that social institutions are somehow analogous to machines leads us to think of social institutions as deterministic and predictable entities that are susceptible to "design" and "engineering." In more recent times, *organismic* metaphors have become common, leading to ideas of social "organisms" that are born, grow, struggle for survival, and die.

Perhaps the most influential recent reporter on metaphors in organization theory and advocate of their usefulness in understanding organizations has been Gareth Morgan (1982, 1986). Morgan, citing previous work by Emery and Trist, points out how thinking based in the traditional *mechanistic* metaphor typifies the bureaucratic approach to control. As complexity and turbulence in the environment increase, the need for control mechanisms increases along with controls for the control mechanisms, and so on until the whole process becomes impossibly unwieldy. The rise of regulatory organizations as a major portion of the public sector of all modern societies can be seen as an attempt to use *mechanical* government to deal with society's complexities. According to Morgan (1982), "The bureaucratic, control-oriented ethos which underlies the drive to overcome problems through a redundancy of parts, is not well equipped to deal with conditions of turbulence" (p. 529).

An alternative way to deal with the problem is to reduce the formation of chaotic changes in the environment, rather than to attempt to control them after the fact. This can be done by somehow achieving a greater consensus on values, thereby making collaboration and collective action more likely and reducing the turbulence caused by uncertainty and unilateral action. Such an approach would be similar to the way in which cooperating organisms manage to shape their environments, rather than simply responding to them. This line of thought leads Morgan to the suggestion that nonmechanistic metaphors, such as those based in the idea of an "organism," or even of a "brain," can offer useful ways to frame our thinking about how to deal with complex, turbulent, chaotic environments.

System Metaphors and Public Administration

Public administration theory has been dominated, with a few exceptions, by a view of governance as either a *mechanistic* or an *organismic* process ever since the founding of the field as a self-conscious entity in the 1920s. The *mechanistic* metaphor, when applied to organizations, can be exemplified by the scientific management approach to organizations as enunciated by Taylor, by Fayol, and by Weber. Scientific methods are used to design jobs so things are done in the most efficient manner. For this purpose, tasks are broken down into parts and observation and measurements are used to describe the worker and the job, much as the parts and functions of a machine would be described. Management is the process of planning, organizing, commanding, controlling, and coordinating these parts using engineering principles. The organization is seen as a closed, bureaucratically hierarchical system.

Similarly, a machine model of governance divides governance into two functions, politics and administration. Politics is the mechanism through which the people express their purpose and decisions are made, whereas administration is done by government in an instrumental organization composed of discrete parts arranged in a hierarchy. Governance as a *machine* leads to the view that government is an entity—a machine—that can be designed, understood, and controlled. Such a machine is composed of parts that interact in known ways. The machine can, therefore, be understood by examination and understanding of each of those parts, and it *must* be seen as a bureaucratically controlled entity.

The *organismic* metaphor when applied to organizations is the metaphor of Parsons, Selznick, Katz and Kahn, Barnard, Roethlisberger and Dickson, Herzberg, McGregor, and Perrow (Flood, 1993, p. 82). The view of organizations as living systems implies both that organizations are complex systems made up of parts that can be understood only as a whole, and that their primary aim is to survive. Organismic organizations have functional parts, or organs, with needs that must be satisfied, but overall control is still necessary for harmonization and to ensure overall survival. Seen through the filter of this metaphor, organizations are open and adaptable systems with inner needs satisfied by transforming inputs into outputs. Although the system is open in this respect, there is no clear relationship between its inner needs and the outside world; it has no mechanism for revising the inner needs as the outside world changes. When used to influence the way we think about government, the *organismic* metaphor implies, as does the machine metaphor, that government is composed of organs with discrete or specific functions, and that government is ultimately a bounded system that interacts in only very specific and limited ways with its environment. The metaphor supports the idea that governmental agencies act to fulfill their own needs and that the public's goals for government, therefore, can be externally imposed only through exercise of rigid hierarchical control.

The *organismic* metaphor ignores the issue of politics versus administration, because organismic models have no goals or values, as such, other than survival. To the extent that the *organismic* metaphor is relied on, theories about the role of public administrators have avoided normative issues and relied on ideas such as neutral competence. Neutral competence is consistent with a conceptual view of governance as an organic, open system, composed of functional administrative cells that must survive and attempt to maintain a steady state, despite the vicissitudes of the political environment that impinges upon the organism.

Because each cell is, itself, an open system to some extent, external influences can leak into individual administrative organizations. This understanding leads to recognition that politics and administration are never entirely separable. Theory framed in the *organismic* metaphor is incapable, however, of fully dealing with normative goals for governance in a democratic society. Such goals, by their very nature, may be ephemeral, indistinct, or contradictory. We must either ignore the issue (under the guise of neutral competence) or look to another metaphor.

The *brain* metaphor adds to the *organismic,* open systems view an emphasis on the importance of reflexive interaction with the environment. The metaphor emphasizes the abilities to communicate and learn, and to establish, modify, or eliminate goals based on that learning. The brain is capable of learning to learn. Use of the metaphor implies acceptance of dynamic rather than static aims and objectives, and emphasizes self-questioning, rather than merely self-regulating, government. This metaphor suggests that organizations consist of flows of information and means for responding to, or acting on, that information. The more information that must be dealt with, the more flexible the organization must become if it is to maintain its ability to respond appropriately. The *brain* metaphor stresses holism, connectivity, redundancy, and simultaneous specialization and generalization.

The metaphor also implies an observing system for which learning is not simply a mapping of external content, but what the system does to transform its environment (Foerster, 1970). Organizations, when seen through the filter of the *brain* metaphor are self-referential and self-generating systems that are also self-observing and self-aware (Beer, 1981, p. 24). From the perspective of the *brain* metaphor, organizations are structurally recursive, that is to say, they are composed of suborganizations and are, themselves, suborganizations of larger organizations, all of which share an underlying functional structure, although their surface features are substantially different.

The Brain as a Metaphor for Postmodern Society

Of the three systems-oriented metaphors (*machine, organism,* and *brain*), the *brain* metaphor is the one most strongly evoked by the characteristics of postindustrial, postmodern society as depicted by postmodern critiques of objectivity. Where modernism pictures an objectively knowable and stable world, postmodernism sees ideas about the world, and the world itself, as unanchored, unstable, and changing chaotically. Modernism postulates a world of structure that is not just understandable but controllable by reason. Postmodernism finds the world to be unstructured, consisting only of process. Attempts to stabilize the world are seen as futile attempts to suppress the insuppressible or to control the uncontrollable.

Postmodern society as it is emerging exists in a highly individualized, networked, digitized, and even virtual world of instant and world-wide communications, in which ideas and organizations coevolve, adapt, speciate, and mutate, and in which order emerges from an underlying flux and chaos along paths whose possibilities are predetermined but whose actualities are not (Kelly, 1994). In this view, the role of individuals in the social world is analogous to that of neurons in the brain. Both interact constantly with multitudes of similar individuals in dynamically unpredictable ways, so that intelligence or overall direction and control emerge from the combination of process and underlying structural principles, much as the action of a swarm of bees seemingly emerges from a hive mind composed of all the individual bees interacting with each other.

According to Kevin Kelly (1994), the executive editor of *Wired* magazine and apostle of virtual-real cyberculture, complexity emerges from natural systems according to "The nine laws of God" governing the incubation of something from nothing (p. 468). These laws refute the possibility of central, top-down control in favor of bottom-up, simple-to-complex, diverse, and adaptable systems that have multiple goals and that seek not only persistent disequilibria but change that changes the change process itself. This is not unlike the current picture that cognitive science has developed of the brain as a network of agents that leads to a society of mind (Minsky, 1985).

Similarly, the *brain* metaphor is well suited for understanding new forms of organization. In the postmodern organization, Weberian bureaucracies and Taylorism give way to

> flatter hierarchies, decentralized decision making, greater capacity for toler-
> ance for ambiguity, permeable internal and external boundaries, empower-

ment of employees, capacity for renewal, self-organizing units, and self-integrating coordination mechanisms. Leadership in these new organizations seems to reflect a shift from maintaining rational control to leadership without control, at least in the traditional sense. (Daft & Lewin, 1993, p. ii)

Just as existing organizational theories, based largely on *machine* and *organism* metaphors, are inadequate to explain these new organizational forms, existing concepts of social organization are similarly inadequate to explain or to help us understand postmodern societies. Our understanding of the social institutions and organization around us is no longer well served by relying on too-simplistic systems metaphors with which to ground our theories. We must begin the difficult task of learning to put *brains* into our ideas about the world.

▬ Democratic Awareness

Using the *brain* metaphor to think about the process of governance allows us to think of government and the governed as they really are—complexly and massively interconnected in interdependent ways that defy analysis or full understanding. This metaphor supports a view of government that is neither a closed machine "operated" by its environment, nor an organism "stimulated" by or "responding" to its environment, but a brain that "models," "understands," "encompasses," and in an important sense "is" its environment. Government is a closed system, but that closure includes, not excludes, the environment, most especially the citizenry. It is the continuous product of its society, just as its society is in large part the product of governmental actions. Government modifies or scraps goals, or creates new ones, and recreates itself continuously in the light of new experiences. In the end, government as a *brain* is government with a *mind,* one that is intersubjectively entwined with its environment.

In a similar fashion, the *brain* metaphor evokes an image of public administration as inextricably embedded in the system of governance. Just as government as a system is indistinguishable from its environment, administrative organizations and agencies are indistinguishable from government. Indeed, because governmental action comes only via those administrative entities, it can be only those entities that create and sustain the system of governance. While aims, goals, policies, or decisions may—at least in theory—originate anywhere, there *is* no government without action.

The Brain as a Metaphor for Democratic Governance

If recent thinking of cognitive scientists is to be believed, the brain consists of an immense system of networks that form an ecology, or society of mind, composed of smaller, simpler agents that operate with considerable independence in terms of what they do and how they do it, but whose actions are coordinated by other simple agents (Minsky, 1985). Simple agents doing comparatively simple things network together in hierarchical layers that themselves network into layers, and so forth until the *brain* as an entirety becomes *mind*. There is no top-down control, no "ghost in the machine," that makes decisions. Decisions emerge, somehow, out of the summation of all these simple processes acting together.

Similarly, government emerges out of the summation of all the simple processes of governance acting together. Democracy, according to this metaphor, is the opportunity of the public to influence, contribute to, and interact with each of those processes, whereas, from the perspective of *machine* and *organism* metaphors, democracy deals with the ability of the citizenry to act either directly or through elected representatives to make top-down decisions for government. This view leads directly to the dichotomization of people and government, of politics and administration, and of policy making and policy implementation.

Just as it is commonly acknowledged that centralized control of economic systems is at best ineffective, it is increasingly apparent that centralized control of policy or decision making of all sorts is problematic. In similar fashion, traditional ideas of centralized democratic decision making can be called into question. The *brain* metaphor points toward means for overcoming these problems by allowing us to look at the democratic process as one that influences government at every level. Issues of democratic governance cease to be issues of how citizens can better express their preferences to Congress, or how interest group preferences can be reconciled with the public interest at the agency level. Instead, democratic governance implies that the public participates, or has the opportunity to participate, in the governance process at all levels. Democratic governance has to start with the simplest governmental action taken by the lowest agent of governance—the individual public employee. If this is to be so, that individual agent must have the discretion, authority, training, and motivation to act in a way that not only permits, but encourages, citizen participation. As the actions of networks of agents are coordinated by other agents or networks of agents, these actions also must include citizen input, consideration, and participation. Decision making by Congress and the president are simply the higher levels of coordination, and not the sources of top-down control. In this manner, government includes the people, and governmental actions advance policies that emerge out of the process of governance, not something externally imposed or centrally controlled.

Systems Metaphors and the Blacksburg School

The so-called Blacksburg school of public administration theory commenced officially with publication of "The Public Administration and the Governance Process" (Wamsley et al., 1987), also known as the Blacksburg Manifesto. The Manifesto, written in reaction to widespread criticism and denigration of the public service, attempted to legitimize public administration by reconceptualizing it away from its (mechanistic) identity as bureaucracy to a new, institutional, identity as "the Public Administration." The Manifesto and the subsequent book *Refounding Public Administration* (Wamsley et al., 1990) were attempts to lay the groundwork for a refounding of the field. The argument was that the first founding on the politics/administration dichotomy and the more recent dominance of behaviorism, positivism, and managerialism had led the field into its current dead end. They proposed a neotraditionalist approach grounded in structuralism and directed toward defining a legitimate role for public administration in governance.

The message of *Refounding* is that the "legitimate" role of public administration can be found in a concept of "agential leadership" wherein administrators consider themselves trustees of the constitutional order, acting as a "balance wheel" between competing branches of government in accordance with an "agency perspective." This perspective is the result of the institutional knowledge and experience that uniquely equips the staffs of agencies with what approaches consensus as to the public interest with regard to that agency's function (Wamsley et al., 1992).

A close reading of the Blacksburg Manifesto and of other published statements of the Blacksburg position, suggests a variety of systems metaphors embedded in the thinking of the authors,[1] but the *brain* metaphor is clearly in evidence. For example, the authors of *Refounding* appear to equate institutionalism or neoinstitutionalism with structuration theory (Cohen, 1987; Giddens, 1979). Neoinstitutionalism (which holds, for example, that organizations are strongly influenced by the institutional fields in which they exist) is based in structuration theory and can be identified with the *brain* metaphor.

In an essay titled "A Legitimate Role for Bureaucracy in Democratic Governance" (Wamsley et al., 1992), the authors draw attention to the fact that the English word *govern* derives from the Greek noun *kybernatas,* meaning "helmsman." *Kybernatas* is also the root of the English word *cybernetics.*[2] They cite Lowi's argument that political science has embraced a myth that the American political system is an automatic and self-correcting process (*organismic* metaphor) that has no need for governance. *Governance,* as used in the essay, however, seems to imply the active processes of selecting and modifying goals that are involved in a *brain* metaphor, rather than the less complex process of maintaining homeostasis implied by the *organismic* metaphor.

The Blacksburg authors argue that there are two competing ideologies about governance (Wamsley et al., 1992), pluralist democracy (*organismic* metaphor) and administrative efficiency (*machine* and *organismic* metaphors). As an alternative to either of these two ideologies, they propose a normative framework for a bureaucratic role in governance. That involves an agency perspective, a broad understanding of the public interest, and an interpretation of the constitutional governance process. The agency perspective relies heavily on a *brain* metaphor that is reflected in the idea of an agency as a learning organization that develops and follows an institutional concept of the common good.[3] This perspective asks the public administrator to search for a sense of the public interest that is restricted to the realms of the agency and its policy community and that is grounded in their history, micropolitical economics, values, and cultures (Wamsley, 1990a, p. 154). These concepts of agency perspective and public interest appear to be agency-centered versions of Vickers's "appreciative systems" (Vickers, 1965, 1983), which are based in part in the *brain* metaphor.

The Blacksburg interpretation of the Constitution concludes that the public administration is subservient to no single branch, yet is responsible to all (Wamsley et al., 1992, p. 77). Under this concept, the legitimacy and role of the public administration does not derive from the design or aims of elected officials, nor from any explicit mandate of the Constitution, but rather from the enacted order that emerges from the underlying order that is embedded in the Constitution. The public administration as an institution, in fact, has a special trusteeship role for the maintenance of the *constitutional order* that the framers of the Constitution intended as an expression of the will of the people (Wamsley et al., 1992). This clearly structural interpretation of the governance process is consistent with a *brain* metaphor.

Despite its move away from *mechanistic* and *organismic* metaphors, however, the Blacksburg perspective is still heavily influenced by them. The idea that the public administration is part of a distinct function of governance, even when given an institutionalist flavor, depends on a metaphor that segregates governance into discrete *pieces* or *organs.* Moreover, the concept of "agential perspective" seems to imply that agencies should be thought of as distinct organs of government—open to the environment in a limited sense, but not interrelated with other agencies (other organs of government). The primary internal relationships are with the two governmental "organs" with "hierarchical" control over the agency, the president and the legislature. When these two "organs" are in conflict, agential leaders should tilt toward one or the other, in order to act as constitutional balance wheels.

Refounding, then, can be seen as having started movement in the direction of reframing the field of public administration in terms of the *brain* metaphor, although such movement may not have been clear to its authors at the time. It remains to consider the Refounding project more explicitly through the lens of that metaphor.

Legitimacy, Dichotomies, and Metaphors

The concern with the legitimacy and role of public administration that produced the Blacksburg Manifesto and *Refounding Public Administration* (Wamsley et al., 1990) was a reaction to public distrust in bureaucrats and in administrative government overall. Such lack of legitimacy is not restricted to the bureaucracy, however, but extends to government overall. Public confidence in government in general has reached an all-time low.

This reduced public sense of government's legitimacy relates closely to a perception of governance as something done by a government and not as an inherent social process. As such, it reflects the prevalence of *mechanistic* and/or *organismic* metaphors in public thought about the matter. Both metaphors lead to reductive views of reality, which is to say, they lead to the view that any particular system can be subdivided into functional elements or parts. These parts of the whole system can, in turn, be fully understood in relative isolation from the rest of the system to which they belong. This idea is so deeply ingrained in Western thought that we tend automatically to subdivide our society into functional elements and attribute to each element an independent existence free of interference from other functional elements (Churchman, 1968).

For thinking framed in terms of either metaphor, governance becomes "the government," a separated, functional element of society. Society, in effect, bifurcates or dichotomizes itself into a "private" and a "public" sector, which, in turn, is divided into "administration" and "politics." This bifurcation goes back, at least, to the Greeks. These reductions and dichotomizations result in the conceptual divorce of society's members from the inherent processes of governance. Governance, a process inherent in social existence, becomes synonymous with government, a machine or organism separated from the society it "controls."

When the *brain* metaphor is used as a filter to examine our notion of governance, however, the thinking changes. From the perspective of the *brain* metaphor, the system of federal government devised by the Constitution is a system that relies on a strategy of limits and constraints, rather than of ends and goals. It is within the degrees of freedom permitted by the Constitution that society self-organizes toward reasonable consensuses. The consensus, however, is not necessarily stable or complete, and self-organization is an ongoing process, not a discrete event. Governance organizes itself around that consensus. The instrumental organization of governance, the government, needs to learn, adapt, and self-organize continuously in response to these changes. Within the government, individual agencies and institutions, and the subunits that they comprise, must also self-organize in response to self-criticism and learning, as the entire process incorporates itself holistically, and recursively,[4] into all of the relevant aspects of governance, without regard to officially declared boundaries. Government as seen through this filter is necessarily democratic governance, because boundaries to the governance process do not really exist.[5] "Public administration," if it refers to anything at all, refers to particular levels within the governance system's recursive structure, and not to inherent differences in function from other entities of governance.

Public administration deals with the execution of public affairs. If that is so, however, *where,* in a recursive model of governance, does such execution lie? Does it reside at the level of the American people, which according to our theory of governance are sovereign? Does it reside in the government as an all-encompassing organization? Does it reside in Congress, the president, and Supreme Court, or does it reside in the departments, agencies, or in still lower recursions? Does it reside in the individuals that compose each and/or all these? If governance is recursive as suggested by the *brain* metaphor, there is no way to decide. The execution, or the actions, of governance occur, as far as we can tell, in *all* these recursive levels simultaneously. Public administration, in other words, cannot be distinguished from governance itself. They are synonymous. To talk about public administration is to talk about the process of governance.

Similar arguments readily deal with apparent dichotomies such as politics versus administration, and policy versus implementation. "Politics" and "policy" are distributed, along with "administration" and "implementation," throughout all of the recursions that compose the system of governance. They are all interrelated with higher and lower recursion levels, and are all integrated and interrelated with the environment at each level, to the point that they are indistinguishable. True, we can discuss aspects of a particular policy, as it exists at an instant, within one recursion level, but those aspects are clearly fleeting and partial. We cannot assume, from the perspective of the *brain* metaphor, that we have captured government's policy by examining it from the perspective of one recursion level or at one point in time. The dichotomies are epiphenomena of the *mechanistic* or *organismic* metaphors, which either disappear or become trivial when the *brain* metaphor is dominant.

The Public Administration

Wamsley et al. (1990, p. 34) characterize "the Public Administration" as an institution of government. They use the phrase in an attempt to move away from the negative connotations and organizationally based meaning of the word *bureaucracy* and toward a reconceived, more legitimate, view of the operational, or administrative, components of government as active players in society and in governance. What is apparently meant by the phrase *the public administration* is an institution associated with performance of governance, which is distinct from, but that can be thought of as logically equivalent to, the Congress, the president, and the courts, albeit constitutionally subservient to them all.

The Blacksburg Manifesto describes public administration as centered on the executive branch but including any portion of any branch to the extent that it is charged with execution of the laws (Wamsley et al., 1987, p. 299). What they have defined as the Public Administration is, in terms of the *brain* metaphor, a composite of *separate* viable[6] systems, not a *unified* viable system. There is no single viable system that can be identified as either Bureaucracy or the Public Administration.

There is no sizeable group of government employees, organized or otherwise, who identify themselves first and foremost as "the Public Administration," just as there is no group that considers itself as the Bureaucracy. Public employees may characterize what they do as public administration, and consider their profession as public administration, but their identification is with a profession or with their agency, not with a system called the public administration. It is this concept of identity that is essential for identification as an institution. The use of the term *institution* can be confusing, because it can refer to social or cultural practices, organizations, or relationships. As used here, it is taken to refer to an institution based in an organization, and not simply to the practice of public administration. "Institution," therefore, is intended to imply an organization, together with the information about, and relationships with, its environment that allow it to have closure, to be autopoietic, and to have and maintain an identity. An institution, in this sense, is an organization seen as a viable system.

The conclusion that there is no viable system identifiable as the public administration implies that *Refounding* cannot accomplish its task as it is presently defined, which is to legitimize and clarify the role of the public administration in governance. Legitimacy surely requires more than simply proposing a new term for *bureaucracy* in the hope that it will not also imply, to the public mind, "a system of administration marked by officialism, red tape, and proliferation."

The Role of Administrative Agencies

Despite the fact that there is no public administration for which a role can be identified, a model of governance based in the *brain* metaphor does identify roles for administrative agencies and for the public administrators who staff them. Departments, agencies, and other administrative components of government are themselves viable systems. Each of these systems has a unique identity, is interconnected to its environment, and exhibits all the characteristics normally associated with an institutionalized organization. It is these systems that *produce* government. There can be no government without such systems, because all actions of government eventually flow through them. Public administration is involved with governmental action and administrative organizations are government's means for action. Instead of "the Public Administration" as a replacement for "bureaucracy," and a focus for study, there is simply "the Government."

It may be difficult to accept the idea that it is the departments and agencies that produce government, and not government that produces agencies. This concept, nevertheless, is the logical result of the idea that government is a closed viable system. *Closed,* in this usage, is not the narrow concept of "isolated from the environment" that is commonly used by open- versus closed-system theorists. It is used, here, in the broader sense of a system that contains within itself all the information and structure necessary for self-generation, articulation, and maintenance (Maturana & Varela, 1980; Zeleny, 1981).

In this sense of closure, relevant portions of the environment are as much parts of the viable system of government as are Congress and the president. It is the interaction of an agency with its narrow environment—other agencies and institutions of governance, interest groups, media, clients, and so forth—that *changes* that environment. Changes in the narrower agency environment *are* changes in the broader environment, because that narrow environment is an integral part of its broader environment. The broader environment is at least partly determined by the cumulative influence of individual governmental operations on local environments. It is the interactions of the broader environment with government that *change* government. It is the interaction of government at all levels that produces governance.

Environment, as it is used here, must be understood as far more than mere popular opinion. It encompasses the entire environmental context, insofar as it is relevant, *including* public opinion, but also those things that form, influence, and constitute our society, including values, culture, history, precedent, stakeholder reactions, interest group pressures, science, technology, the economy, international issues, and so on. Expressed in the simplest possible terms, what public agencies do and the way that they do it influence, if not create, the environmental and systemic context that *ultimately* influences, shapes, and determines government's policies. This is true not only in the immediate sense of policies that the administrator's agencies are expected to carry out, and the resources they are given, but in the broader sense of governmental policy in general.

Agencies are subservient to the political direction of elected officials, and elected officials are ultimately subservient to the electorate. The electorate, however, forms its views, opinions, and attitudes within a context formed by the *actions* of government, which are taken by agencies and departments. In this sense, government is a closed system, in the broad sense of closure.

Each agency or department, in turn, is similarly closed, because an agency is itself a viable system at a lower level of recursion. The interactions of all governmental departments and agencies with their immediate environments (which, in turn, are the result of interactions at lower recursions) merge to influence the larger environment that is part of the closed system of governance. Though agency environments include those portions of the citizenry that are generally thought of as clients, interest groups, or the media, they are by no means limited to them. Their environment also includes the broader citizenry, who form impressions of how useful, effective, and relevant the agencies' actions are, and who, in their turn, influence, shape, or constrain the ways in which clients, interest groups, and the media interpret and react to agency actions. Ultimately, lower recursions in the agency are composed of *individuals*. These individual public administrators are, themselves, viable systems. In the end, it is these individuals, interacting with their own environments, with each other, *constrained* by the requirements and controls imposed upon them by higher levels, which also motivate and empower them, who create government.

This understanding of closure and governance leads to the conclusion that the role of public administration, and of public administrators, is not simply to execute policy developed by others, but to *produce* government. This is done by interacting with the environment at all levels. Agencies and public administrators act upon their environments and are, themselves, acted upon by them. It is this interaction that *is* government, and those involved in that interaction are involved in governance.

■ Toward Governance With Purpose

Every system that corresponds to the *brain* metaphor has an aim or purpose. Such an aim can be thought of in two distinct ways. In the first, or *descriptive* sense, the aim of a viable system is simply what it does. There is no teleological implication involved. The second way to think about the aim of a system is in *prescriptive* terms. If we decide what a particular viable system should do—what its aim should be—we may attempt to *design* the system and its subsystems to support that intended aim and to *modify* those designs, as necessary, in the attempt to achieve that aim. This teleological selection of aims is arbitrary, but the range of possibilities is not unlimited. Every viable system is embedded within a larger viable system that has its own aims, both actual and intended, that impose constraints on allowable aims. Every viable system also contains other viable systems embedded within it, and these lower-recursive-level systems have their own aims, which *also* act as constraints. The achievement of a particular aim is determined by the design of communication channels that allow the viable unit to communicate with its environment, to communicate within itself, and to communicate with higher and lower levels. An essential part of this design includes the ability of those channels to bring the aims of the viable unit into closer alignment with the aims of higher and lower recursions. In the process of achieving this, however, the teleological aspects of purpose are largely lost. With so many aims, both actual and intended, at so many interconnected levels, all adjusting or aligning themselves with those of higher and lower recursions as well as interacting in a learning response to changes in the environment, there is no way to identify a causal intent that can be said to be the teleological purpose for which a system exists. We can, however, arbitrarily decide on an aim or purpose for a particular system (or recursion) of interest. In doing so we must be acutely aware that we do so only to assist ourselves in examining or understanding some aspect of the system, and that our purpose is one we ascribe to (or wish for) the system, and nothing more. In the case of systems that include government and American society we must also remember that we ourselves are parts of those systems, and that our idea of intended purpose is conflated with all the rest. Notwithstanding these caveats, the careful selection of a purpose, or aim, can be useful in our analysis.

To examine the prescriptive implications of the *brain* metaphor for public administration, it is first necessary to select an appropriate aim for our system of governance. Note that what is needed is a purpose—or group of purposes—that includes the whole system of governance, and not one addressing specific policy prescriptions. It must summarize, in some fashion, the apparent intent of government's higher recursion—the people. Such a statement of purpose is well known, and widely accepted, as Lincoln's statement that "government of the people, by the people, and for the people shall not perish." This aim contains both an expression of *viability* (shall not perish) and an expression of *values* that the vast majority of citizens hold concerning government. Moreover, as we will see, the aim that government of the people, by the people, and for the people shall not perish relates very closely to issues of concern to public administration theorists: legitimacy, representativeness and accountability, and the public interest.

Legitimacy: Government of the People

The public's sense of governmental legitimacy is decreasing. Two indications of this are seen in popular demands for Congressional term limits and in growing public expression of concern with the influence of special interests. Other indications are the current tendency to elect presidents who depict themselves as "outsiders," and the public outcry that government overall is fraught with "waste, fraud, and abuse." Polls show that the public's confidence that government usually does the right thing has decreased dramatically. Nevertheless, the *brain* metaphor implies that legitimacy ultimately depends on more discretion for public administrators, not less.

The "agency perspective" was an attempt to reconceptualize and legitimate the role of the public administration around an argument that "the popular will does not reside solely in elected representatives, but in a constitutional order that incorporates a remarkable variety of legitimate titles to participate in governance" (Wamsley et al., 1992, p. 77). The public administration is, according to this view, entitled to legitimacy by virtue of its grounding in statute and in constitutional order. Each officer of the government may be considered a "representative" of the people, no matter whether that person was elected, appointed, or otherwise selected for office. This theory, which Rohr (1990) argues was the Federalists' interpretation, gives agencies a *theoretical,* or rational-legal, claim to legitimacy for governance, but rational-legal claims are not enough to establish legitimacy.

If the implications of the *brain* metaphor are to be accepted, the constitutional approach to legitimacy is incomplete at best. As we have already seen, public administration cannot be clearly separated from government in general. Government's legitimacy, however, ultimately comes from the people, who assign authority to the formal government, allocate its resources,[7] and hold it accountable. Legitimacy for the government must derive from the people, and not from the Constitution.[8] In the end it is the people acting as a nation of equals, and not the Constitution, that determines legitimacy. It is at least conceivable that the people, having decided the present government no longer meets their needs or desires, could revoke the Constitution and initiate a convention to write a new one. In the end, the American public's sense that their government is of the people is about as good a definition of legitimacy as we have.

One implication of the *brain* metaphor is that government's results, over the long term, derive from complex interactions at all levels. The public's general impression of government, therefore, cannot be ascribed to a unique causal agent. If any aspect of government detracts from public confidence, or fosters the impression that it is not of, by, and for the people, it lessens the public sense of the legitimacy of all government. On the other hand, good management at each level of government is required to ensure that that level functions in ways that facilitate the viability of the system and achieve its aims. It is the composite result of good governance applied at the agency level, and at other recursion levels, both higher and lower, that builds legitimacy.

The implication of the *brain* metaphor is that legitimacy is closely related to administrative discretion. If an agency has too much discretion (or misuses it), the "system" may become unstable, decreasing its legitimacy. The most likely result of this decreasing legitimacy is a reduction in the discretion allowed the system—bringing it back to stability. Another possible result is its disappearance entirely, as it becomes no longer viable.

If an agency has too little discretion, on the other hand, the agency becomes unresponsive to its environment. When it is unable to respond or adapt to its environment, that agency's legitimacy decreases, as does the legitimacy of government in general. One likely result of this decreasing legitimacy is a further reduction in the discretion allowed the system in a misguided hierarchical attempt to *force* responsiveness. Here, however, the system is not returned to stability, but driven ever farther into illegitimacy. This may *also* result in the agency disappearing (eventually) as it becomes unviable. While a particular agency comes to be seen as less and less legitimate, this also decreases the legitimacy of government overall, making the problem still worse. Agencies (and public administrators, if they understand these effects) should see that their personal viabilities are closely tied to the need for discretion and to the use of that discretion in ways that *increase,* not *decrease,* legitimacy. They would act in ways they believed would maintain and increase the legitimacy of both their agency in particular and government in general over the long term. They would consider, in using their discretion, whether their responses to short-term requirements would also stand the test of long-term legitimacy.

Representation and Accountability: Government by the People

Two central issues in the administration of democratic government are ensuring that it is the people in a democratic society who govern through their representatives, and ensuring that government is ultimately accountable to the people. A variety of approaches have been proposed for increasing the sense of representation or participation. Most of them involve the bureaucracy, as either the source or the conduit, for increased representation for individuals and interest groups. Among these approaches are the formation of bureaucratic organizations to represent the interests of specific groups and interests (corporatism), and representation via citizen participation. The former, based in interest group politics, produces a sort of symbiotic relationship between agencies and specific groups and organizations, for example, the Department of Agriculture and farmers. The latter emphasizes the use of citizen committees and advisory groups.

An elaboration of the latter approach, proposed by Stivers (1990), sees public administrators and citizens sharing practice:

> Relationships between public administrators and citizens that constitute a community of citizenship can be fostered by laws, regulations, policies, procedures, and ongoing actions that share responsibility with citizens in conduction of agency affairs. Within given legislated mandates, administrators can use their discretion to approach rule-making and the design of agency processes so that not just clients and interest groups but members of the general public participate as fully as possible in policy making and in implementation. Such arrangements do not entail privatization, or the divestiture of public responsibilities, but rather substantive cooperation between citizens and administrators in which citizens are seen as co-governors and co-decision makers, not simply as consumers or providers of services. (pp. 267-268)

The feeling of being unrepresented leads to demands for greater governmental accountability and increases dissatisfaction with government in general. For years, political candidates have succeeded by emphasizing antigovernment and antibureaucratic agendas aimed at increasing the accountability of the bureaucracy to the public. Actual attempts to increase accountability, however, have invariably focused on increasing the political accountability of governmental operations to Congress and the president. These attempts reduce the discretion available to public administrators by increasing the restrictions imposed through control and coordination systems. Restrictions have often taken the form of ever more specific and restrictive regulations imposed upon the public, which public administrators must enforce, whether or not they make sense in a particular set of circumstances. The result has been a *decrease* in the ability of government to apply common sense to the actions of government and a corresponding *increase* in the public's sense that government is too intrusive, out of control, unresponsive, unaccountable, and illegitimate. Increased political accountability to both the president and Congress has been an integral part of attempts at governmental reform since the early days of the Republic. The action, and the intent, of these reforms has been both to decrease the independence of government's operational organizations and to make them more accountable to the political system in an attempt to increase control over governmental operations (Rourke, 1980).

The public's sense of being represented, that government is "by the people," can be increased through *increasing,* not decreasing, the ability of government to be responsive to individual differences, situations, and preferences. This can occur only if departments and agencies become less centralized, bureaucratic, authoritative, and hierarchical, not more so. Contrary to Lowi's (1969) argument against decentralization and bureaucratic discretion, increased accountability to the public must come directly via government's actions, and not indirectly through increased congressional and presidential restriction on that action.

The Public Interest: Government for the People

An understanding of the role of administrative departments and agencies as the producers, or autopoietic self-organizers, of government also leads us to a new understanding of "the public interest." *Autopoiesis* refers not to planned or designed properties of a system, but to properties that "emerge" out of the dynamics of the system as it interacts with its environment. It is impossible to predict or fully control the outcomes of autopoietic, self-organizing processes that emerge from the dynamics of the process itself.

Self-organization can, however, be either inhibited or facilitated. The cost of inhibiting self-organization tends to be quite high. Viable systems that cannot self-organize in response to changes in their environment lose their viability—they cease to exist. Government and the viable systems that it comprises have only two options. They may act to maintain the existing order, by inhibiting the processes of self-organization, and risk losing viability. Alternatively, they may enable unpredictable changes by facilitating them through fostering and maintaining the kind of dialogues and relationships that can permit the emergence of public policy.

If an aim of governance is to ensure that government acts in the public's interest, and if government is a closed viable system that produces itself, then "the public interest" cannot be simply the decision of a few representatives or officials. It must be an emergent property of the system. Public administrators, or other government officials, can act only in ways that either block or facilitate emergence; they have little control over *what* it is that emerges. They contribute to that emerging policy by contributing their sense of the public's interest to the dialogue, and they sustain it by acting according to the emerging view of public interest as they see it from their perspectives. Moreover, because government is a viable system recursively embedded in a larger viable system—society—it is the public's *perception* that government's actions are in the public's interest that maintains government's viability. The problem for government overall, and public administrators in particular, is not to decide what the public interest is, but to act in ways that facilitate the emergence of a public sense that government's actions are in the public interest.

━ Democratically Aware Public Administration

The idea of the agency perspective (Wamsley et al., 1987) holds its greatest potential when it is clearly seen through the lens the *brain* metaphor provides. The agency perspective contends that public agencies as *institutions* are repositories of something approaching the public consensus as to the public interest in its particular area of concern. They are the organizational entities that can maintain the kind of dialogue and relationships that allow the emergence of public policy and some semblance of the public interest. Nevertheless, the agency perspective falls short when it ignores the implications of an underlying *brain* metaphor. The public administrator should not see him- or herself "as an agent acting on behalf of others, yet doing so in a vigorous and thoughtful manner" (Wamsley, 1990a, p. 115), but rather should see him- or herself as an agent *through which* others are allowed to act. The difference may seem subtle, but it is critical. Public administrators, if they are to be the agents of governmental change, must cast themselves not in the role of governmental parents who act "on behalf of others," or as "stewards" who act for others, but as "instruments" through which the public acts for itself. This view of administrators as instruments is reminiscent of that suggested by Stivers (1990), in which active citizens and administrators interact through dialogue to develop public policies. Stivers's view is important because, in effect, it calls for an increase in the responsiveness of government to its citizens.

Stivers, however, neglects the importance of *design*. Administrators must do more than engage in dialogue with citizens and find ways to share responsibilities with them. Administrators must be *active* and *intelligent* instruments. They must design the systems and processes for which they have responsibility so that they, and those systems at lower levels, can support the minimal *aim* that government of the people, by the people, and for the people shall not perish, while maximizing the ability of the system to respond to its environment. They must allow specifics of policy to *emerge* out of lower recursions, confident that their designs for organizational communication and control systems are supportive of the overall aim of government. Administrators must see government as composed of a *recursive network,* and not as a hierarchical bureaucracy. In such a network, which interacts with citizens at all levels, decision making is not top-down or bottom-up, but emergent from the process of governance at all levels. It is *this* perspective that can allow the governmental *mind* to act with intelligence and knowledge in the public's interest over the long term.

Notes

1. The application of an organismic metaphor to governance by public administration theorists leaves ample room for "political" metaphors to assume the role of "environment."

2. It is not surprising that the published works of the "Blacksburg School" would show evidence of several systems metaphors. This can be true for either (or both) of two reasons. First, few people, consciously or otherwise, can think or write about any system as complex as "governance" or "public administration" without hints of several metaphors being in evidence. Second, where multiple authors are concerned, each author, even when in general agreement with the others, will tend to have a preferred or "favorite" metaphorical "lens" with which to approach a problem. This effect should be particularly evident where each author has written a different chapter of a book, such as was the case with *Refounding Public Administration* (Wamsley et al., 1990).

3. *Webster's New Collegiate Dictionary* defines *cybernetics* as follows:

[Gk *kybernetes* pilot, governor (fr. *kybernan* to steer, govern) + E *-ics*]: the science of communication and control theory that is concerned esp. with the comparative study of automatic control systems (as the nervous system and brain and mechanical-electrical communication systems.).

Cybernetics can be associated with either an "organism" (hemostatic autopilot) or a "brain" metaphor.

4. See especially Wamsley (1990a). Wamsley, unfortunately, reverts to the purely mechanical metaphors of "mainspring" and "balance wheel" to illustrate his argument.

5. The concept of "recursion" is very similar to what Jantsch (1980) called "multilevel autopoiesis." "Autopoiesis refers to the characteristic of living systems to continuously renew themselves and to regulate the process in such a way that the integrity of their structure is maintained" (p. 7). According to Jantsch,

> In a multilevel dynamic reality, each new level brings new evolutionary processes into play which co-ordinate and accentuate the processes at lower hierarchical levels in particular ways. Therefore, reduction to one level of description is never possible. In order to understand self-organization and especially the phenomena of life it is not only necessary to recognize different levels, but also to understand the relations between them. (p. 242)

"Recursion" implies a hierarchy of structure, interdependence, interaction, coordination, and evolution, but not necessarily one of bureaucratic control, decision making, or authority.

6. The non-Governmental governance process includes governance-related actions by entities or individuals that are not a part of "official" government. This includes contractors to official government, the media and press, various lobbying groups, nonfederal governmental entities and officials, and the like. All of these are (or potentially are) part of the holistic, or recursive, nature of governance as seen from the frame formed by a brain metaphor.

7. Viable systems are systems that, although recursively embedded in other systems, are capable of independent existence. They have everything needed to survive and maintain their identity. In particular, they

> have the ability to make a response to a stimulus which was not included in the list of anticipated stimuli when the system was designed. They can learn from repeated experience what is the optimal response to that stimulus. Viable systems grow. They renew themselves— by, for example, self reproduction. They are robust against internal breakdown and error. Above all they continuously adapt to a changing environment, and by this means survive quite possibly in conditions which had not been entirely foreseen by their designer. (Beer, 1966, p. 256)

8. Though the allocation of resources to government by the people may not be readily apparent, strong public resistance to the allocation of *added* resources to government is in evidence by the fact that the percentage of GDP that goes to government at the federal level has been remarkably stable in recent years, despite large deficits.

References

Beer, S. (1966). *Decision and control.* London: John Wiley.

Beer, S. (1981). *Brain of the firm* (2nd ed.). Chichester, UK: John Wiley.

Churchman, C. W. (1968). *The challenge to reason.* New York: McGraw-Hill.

Cohen, I. (1987). Structuration theory and social praxis. In A. Giddens & J. Turner (Eds.), *Social theory today* (pp. 273-308). Stanford, CA: Stanford University Press.

Daft, R. L., & Lewin, A. Y. (1993). Where are the theories for the new organizational forms: An editorial essay. *Organization Science, 4*(4), i-iv.

Flood, R. L. (1993). *Beyond TQM.* Chichester, UK: John Wiley.

Flood, R. L., & Jackson, M. C. (1991). *Creative problem solving: Total systems intervention.* Chichester, UK: John Wiley.

Foerster, H. von (1970). Molecular etiology, an immodest proposal for semantic clarification. In G. Ungar (Ed.), *Molecular mechanisms in memory and learning* (pp. 213-248). New York: Plenum.

Giddens, A. (1979). *Central problems in social theory: Action, structure, and contradiction in social analysis.* Berkeley: University of California Press.

Jantsch, E. (1980). *The self-organizing universe: Scientific and human implications of the emerging paradigm of evolution.* Oxford, UK: Pergamon.

Kelly, K. (1994). *Out of control.* Reading, MA: Addison-Wesley.

Lakoff, G., & Johnson, M. (1980). *Metaphors we live by.* Chicago: University of Chicago Press.

Lowi, T. J. (1969). *The end of liberalism: Ideology, policy, and the crisis of public authority.* New York: Norton.

Maturana, H. R., & Varela, F. I. (1980). *Autopoiesis and cognition.* Boston: Reidel.

Minsky, M. (1985). *The society of mind.* New York: Simon & Schuster.

Morgan, G. (1982). Cybernetics and organization theory: Epistemology or technique. *Human Relations, 33*(7), 521-537.

Morgan, G. (1986). *Images of organization.* Newbury Park, CA: Sage.

Rohr, J. A. (1990). The constitutional case for public administration. In G. L. Wamsley, R. N. Bacher, C. T. Goodsell, P. S. Kronenberg, J. A. Rohr, C. M. Stivers, O. F. White, & J. F. Wolf, *Refounding public administration* (pp. 52-95). Newbury Park, CA: Sage.

Rourke, F. R. (1980). Bureaucratic autonomy and the public interest. In C. H. Weiss & A. H. Barton (Eds.), *Making bureaucracies work* (pp. 103-112). Beverly Hills, CA: Sage.

Stivers, C. M. (1990). Active citizenship and public administration. In G. L. Wamsley, R. N. Bacher, C. T. Goodsell, P. S. Kronenberg, J. A. Rohr, C. M. Stivers, O. F. White, & J. F. Wolf, *Refounding public administration* (pp. 246-273). Newbury Park, CA: Sage.

Vickers, G. (1965). *The art of judgement.* London: Chapman & Hall.

Vickers, G. (1983). *Human systems are different.* London: Harper & Row.

Wamsley, G. L. (1990a). The agency perspective: Public administrators as agential leaders. In G. L. Wamsley, R. N. Bacher, C. T. Goodsell, P. S. Kronenberg, J. A. Rohr, C. M. Stivers, O. F. White, & J. F. Wolf, *Refounding public administration* (pp. 114-162). Newbury Park, CA: Sage.

Wamsley, G. L. (1990b). Introduction. In G. L. Wamsley, R. N. Bacher, C. T. Goodsell, P. S. Kronenberg, J. A. Rohr, C. M. Stivers, O. F. White, & J. F. Wolf, *Refounding public administration* (pp. 19-29). Newbury Park, CA: Sage.

Wamsley, G. L., Bacher, R. N., Goodsell, C. T., Kronenberg, P. S., Rohr, J. A., Stivers, C. M., White, O. F., & Wolf, J. F. (1990). *Refounding public administration.* Newbury Park, CA: Sage.

Wamsley, G. L., Goodsell, C. T., Rohr, J. A., Stivers, C., White, O. F., & Wolf, J. F. (1987). Public administration and the governance process: Refocusing the American dialogue. In R. Chandler (Ed.), *A centennial history of the American administrative state* (pp. 291-317). New York: Free Press.

Wamsley, G. L., Goodsell, C. T., Rohr, J. A., White, O. F., & Wolf, J. F. (1992). A legitimate role for bureaucracy in democratic governance. In L. Hill (Ed.), *The state of public bureaucracy* (pp. 59-86). Armonk, NY: M. E. Sharpe.

Zeleny, M. (1981). *Autopoiesis: A theory of living organizations.* New York: North Holland.

13

A Public Philosophy and Ontological Disclosure as the Basis for Normatively Grounded Theorizing in Public Administration

GARY L. WAMSLEY
Virginia Polytechnic Institute and State University

Recently I had the misfortune to open a book I had coauthored nearly 30 years ago at the beginning of my academic career. I was dismayed to read the following words, which I could just as well have written today:

> The search for a theory of public administration over the decades has taken on aspects of a quest for the Holy Grail or a hunt for the mythical unicorn. The search has been filled with zeal and piety, but seldom has it been made clear what it is that is sought, nor have the searchers been altogether certain of its existence. (Wamsley & Zald, 1976, p. 1)

So many years; so little progress!

I cannot think of a book or article, including my own work, that I would be comfortable in referring to as embodying *a* theory of American public administration, or *a* theory of democratic American public administration, and certainly not a normative theory in either case. I say this thoughtfully and in spite of my awareness of what I consider the closest thing to such an effort by Vincent Ostrom (1974) in his book, *The Intellectual Crisis of Public Administration,* and of a fine chapter by Robert Denhardt (1990) titled "Public

351

Administration Theory: The State of the Discipline," and my admiration for a prescient article written by Dwight Waldo (1952) when I was still in high school, titled "Development of a Theory of Democratic Administration."

On the first page of Waldo's (1952) article I have underlined in red one of those insights for which he is justly famous. It reads, "If administration is indeed 'the core of modern government,' then a theory of democracy in the twentieth century must embrace administration" (p. 81). This book and this chapter are premised on Waldo's insight inverted and altered a bit: *Administration is the "core of modern government," and theorizing about American public administration, its practice and praxis*[1] in the 21st century, needs normative grounding in a public philosophy drawn from values of the Constitution, the philosophy of pragmatism, and democratic theory.

▬ Still Wrestling With Theory

I used the term *theorizing about* in the previous sentence rather than speak of "a theory" because I am no longer confident that a single theory of public administration can be or should be sought. At one time it seemed clear enough what the characteristics of a theory were and what purpose it served. Only a few years ago I would have begun by confidently distinguishing between philosophy and theory. The former I would have described as more comprehensive in scope—purporting to explore some of humankind's more profound questions. These can range from the most sweeping, such as "What is the nature of the universe?"—which borders on cosmology and physics, and "What is the nature of God and how can we know of God?"—which borders on theology and natural theology, to a range of garden-variety philosophical questions such as "What is the nature and meaning of 'reality,' 'love,' 'truth,' 'beauty,' 'history,' 'time,' and so on." Ranging still further across the "profound-to-mundane" continuum, we would find questions that have always been of concern to humans and their existence, like "What is the good life? How do we go about achieving it? Who should rule?" Ralph Hummel (1993) brings things to an even tighter focus on human-centered concerns when he states that philosophy has traditionally asked three questions—"Who is Man? What can he know? What must he do?" Overlooking the need to state these questions in a more politically correct fashion, they serve as an example of philosophical concerns at the far end of the continuum from the cosmological.

But is there in fact an end to either side of the continuum? Jun (1994) reminds us that serious matters—existential questions—can be found in the seemingly mundane questions that never mention the word *philosophy,* for example, "What is the meaning of these routine activities that I perform every day?" (Jun, 1993). Perhaps, therefore, we should not be so quick or so confident about drawing a line between the profound and mundane or philosophy and theory, and in this chapter I will propose that public administration ground itself in a particular kind of philosophy that I believe warrants a place on the continuum of philosophical concerns outlined above—a public philosophy.

Once, however, I would have glibly tried to make a distinction between philosophy and theory by simply saying that theory is less ambitious in scope and deals with some aspect of philosophy's broader concerns, such as economic theory, political theory, a theory of justice, or even a theory of public administration. I would have also said that theories can suggest patterns of testable relationships among variables that might be usefully spoken of as a model, that the usefulness of such models can be enhanced by metaphor, and that they should produce testable propositions or hypotheses.

Today, I am no longer confident of the feasibility or advisability of trying to adhere closely to these thoughts in theorizing about public administration. I, like many of my generation, was professionally socialized to George Homans's dictum that "the only inescapable office of theory is to explain," (p. 811) by interrelated and proven propositions derived from theory and models and that answered the question "Why?" Supposedly one went from explanation to prediction, and then, presumably on to the eventual possibility of controlling social, political, and economic phenomena. The naïveté of such assumptions embarrasses me today.

I now recognize that theory has several other "inescapable offices." It often performs several functions, sometimes simultaneously. It can guide description, raise questions, hypothesize relationships, purport to explain, suggest causality, and prescribe norms/values/behavior. I have also come to see that all theory is normative in some way and to some degree, even those whose adherents claim them to be "objective," "empirical," or "scientific." For such theory rests upon certain assumptions about the universe and reality, and upon certain norms or conventions called science that we have used for some time now in discovering and validating what we have been willing to call "truth."

Nonetheless, until recently it seemed plausible to me to speak of *a* theory of public administration, despite the lack of it in our field. In the first *Refounding* volume (Wamsley et al., 1990), I said that I was convinced that we had stumbled into the task of building a theory of public administration or a theory of the American state. And so we had. But as we have moved beyond the "naive realism" associated with extreme behavioralism and positivism, and begun the transition from modernism to the postmodern era, creating something that can be called a theory has become much more complex, less feasible, even less desirable.

Public administration has had difficulty with theory for several reasons. First, because we have tended to see theory and practice as dichotomous or even antithetical; of course, they are not. One cannot exist without the other; one has no meaning without the other. Obviously this is also true of praxis, which involves reflexivity between theory and practice and vice versa. The second reason for our difficulty with theory lies in the distinctive American political context—its lack of a positive conception of the state, its constitutional design of separate institutions that must share power if governance is to occur, and the apparent need of contemporary politicians to use public administration as a scapegoat for systemic problems that they either cannot understand or refuse to confront responsibly. This context has resulted in a false consciousness concerning the nature of public administration and its role in the political system. That is to say, such things as the societal primacy accorded the economy and business by our ideology, the history of public administration's founding as given to us, and the belief on the part of elected politicians that they must dominate public administrators and the belief that they can profitably use them as a scapegoat, all combine (generally without much conscious intent) to produce a false consciousness on the part of practitioners and academics in public administration (Perdue, 1986).

Politicians, citizens, and public administrators themselves have found it necessary or expedient to declare that administration is distinct from and subordinate to politics and involves "mere management" or execution of policies developed in other institutions of government with greater perceived legitimacy. Existing alongside this subordinate role conception has been the contradictory conception of "bureaucracy" as too powerful and a threat to democracy. The lack of reality in both these conceptions has been pointed out repeatedly, but without discernible impact on practice or—for that matter—on theorizing. The apparent need on everyone's part to retain the false consciousness concerning public administration has simply been too great.

The third problem has had to do with the fact that most of us who teach and research in the field have been educated in traditional academic disciplines. We therefore have had difficulty understanding that public administration is *not* a traditional discipline, and that to make it one would risk destroying its worth and relevance, not to mention its excitement and challenge. We have not understood that the theoretical needs for an interdisciplinary field that serves a sociopolitical practice are much different, and the potential for explanatory theory are much more limited. It may well be that *a* theory of an explanatory nature is neither feasible nor desirable. Equally important, an applied field related to a profession has a need for explicit normative grounding that shapes theorizing—defines problems, provides norms for practice, and questions for research.

The conception of public administration was adopted from Western European sources. The field of public administration, however, began with norms, methods, and techniques borrowed from, or more accurately, associated with, the field of business or created to apply to both business and government. Then borrowing again from organizational sociology and psychology, the field tried to develop middle-range explanatory theories in the positivist tradition that once again were believed to be equally applicable to business and government. And, more recently, we have been theorizing about public administration from a wide range of approaches (Stokes, 1994) and paradigms (Burrell & Morgan, 1979) or perspectives, though a sizeable portion of the field continues to hold that there is little difference between business and public organizations, and to operate under a conventional wisdom little changed from the days of administrative management in the late 1930s (Bozeman, 1987; Dudley & Wamsley, in press).[2]

We have been working without a full understanding of what we are about (our place in the power structure, i.e., we suffer from false consciousness) and we lack an appropriate normative grounding that might ameliorate that condition. The norms we borrowed from business and the Progressive Reform movement have been wrong for us. Neither the techniques from business, the values of reform, middle-range organizational theory, nor wide-ranging reinterpretations from different paradigmatic perspectives have brought about any kind of theoretical or paradigmatic consensus. Their impact on practice has been problematic at best.

Theory has also been such a problem for public administration because the quest for efficiency, which has been so important in business management and which public administration has been expected to emulate, is only one of the many purposes of public administration. Equally if not more compelling has been the need to determine the right thing to do at a given point in time and the right way to do it when acting as an agent for *multiple* principals in a complex, chaotic, and contentious political environment.[3] Efficiency should not be the last consideration, but certainly one that comes well after serving our fellow citizens, upholding constitutional values, and the creation of relationships that evoke human and democratic development.

The "scientific" quest for the 3-Es (economy, efficiency, effectiveness)—for increased output—is not simply misguided because it puts primary emphasis on the wrong values for public administration in a democracy, where the prior concerns should be for responsiveness, representativeness, and responsibility.[4] It is *wrong* because it is dangerously incomplete without normative grounding. It can produce not only more toxic waste cleanups or social security checks, but also slaughtered Jews as in the Holocaust, "relocated" Japanese Americans as in the United States during World War II, or "disappeared" regime opponents as in Argentina, Chile, El Salvador, and so on. The 3-Es are measures of the efficacy of means given agreed-upon or specified ends, but they do not provide a satisfactory measure of the *appropriateness* of either the means or the ends. Such a measure of appropriateness is important for all government but essential for a democratic constitutional republic. Without it such a government has no raison d'être.

Theorizing Without Trying to Develop a Theory

Thus our major difficulty with theory has been that we have stumbled about struggling to "retrofit" a 20th-century hierarchical institution (bureaucratic public administration) that draws on the norms of business and the tradition of Rome, to a republic of 18th-century design that has been democratically modified in the tradition of the Greek city-state and that is not hierarchical in design or operation. We have told ourselves, and allowed others to tell us, that we should administer this entity as we would a hierarchically organized business. Small wonder no dominant theory has emerged from such a tangled intellectual thicket, and it should not surprise us that the study, praxis, and practice of the field lack legitimacy. The surprise is that any of us still have our sanity and sense of humor.

Our troubles with theory have blocked development of *a* theory and it has been theor*izing* in which we have been engaged, and theorizing that Denhardt has reviewed so well—not theor*ies* of public administration. For the most part, this theorizing has consisted of each of us trying to convince the others that our approach—positivism/functionalism, hermeneutics, phenomenology, critical theory, radical humanism, or rational choice—is the most likely candidate to become *the* paradigmatic approach that will generate *the* theory and spin off models and testable propositions, or generate insightful analysis that can best describe, understand, explain, and predict public administration.[5]

We must not mistake theorizing for having presented a theory, and we need to begin to examine the possibility that we should no longer be looking for *a* theory of public administration. Indeed, our inability to develop one may be a blessing in disguise. Theorizing, as opposed to building *a* theory, may be quite sufficient if we could agree on what we hope for or what we believe the practice and praxis of public administration *should be* in a democratic, constitutional republic in the postmodern era.

More Meaningful Dialogue
Through Ontological Disclosure

Agreeing on what we hope for or believe public administration "should be" will not be easy—it may not even be possible. But I am convinced the effort alone will be more meaningful, and we will progress further, than if we continue to pummel each other with different paradigmatically based "approaches" and claims to building *a* theory without acknowledging the normative issues or philosophical questions hidden in the discussion.

I propose that our theorizing will begin to lose some of its confusion and murkiness if we engage in ontological disclosure and begin by stating where we stand on such matters as human nature, the nature of reality and how we can "know" it, and therefore what we want our society, politics, and public administration to be. Surely we will better serve our practitioners with this approach, and the relevance of what we academics are struggling with will become more apparent to them.

O. C. McSwite (in press) points out that overwhelmingly academic discourse is predicated on the presumption of irresolvable differences: We spend most of our time disagreeing on what we believe are epistemological grounds, while we mask or refuse to deal with deeper ontological differences. We unconsciously "agree to disagree" because: (a) we are very uncomfortable and feel vulnerable with discourse on an ontological level; and (b) we are not at all sure that the nascent profession of public administration and the interdisciplinary applied field of public administration are at all compatible with our democratic constitutional political system. McSwite suggests that we, by mutual but unconscious agreement with other actors in the American political system, have taken the role of "designated victim" (pp. 11-12). If McSwite is right, the picture is bleak for both public administration academics and practitioners, indeed it is bleak for the entire republic. I prefer to act as though it is not true.

I believe we must begin to disclose our ontological stance, but a fair challenge on this point is, "If we can't agree on epistemological grounds, how can we even communicate on ontological grounds, let alone agree?" My response would be that we do not have to come to agreement, but we can and should be discussing the real and fundamental sources of our differences—differences that really matter, not differences that add to our false consciousness.

One of the commentators on an early draft of this chapter exclaimed, "You mean you want us to do *philosophy?*" The answer is yes—of a sort (more on that later). But I am asking a good bit less than that when I ask that we simply be reflective and self-aware enough to recognize what is wrong with our discourse and to attempt to correct it. If we cannot handle that, then there seems little hope for us, our field, or our democratic republic.

Along with some of my colleagues in the Blacksburg project, I increasingly believe epistemological differences are a red herring, or our disagreement over them a pathology of our academic profession that stems from the transition from the modern to postmodern era.

I believe that if we begin pragmatically by taking what we know to be the problems of our political system, our institutions of government, and our governing process (and our body of knowledge on these matters is vast), and if we set forth how we believe they *should* operate (and that is what the Blacksburg project is about), we can build a normative grounding—a public philosophy from which to theorize, practice, and engage in praxis. Furthermore, we will obviate the need for *a* theory or *an* epistemology. Settling on *one* becomes irrelevant.

A key aspect of such an effort should be to draw on the philosophy of pragmatism, the hallmark of which is experimental problem solving. If we have consensus on a normative grounding, and we turn our various approaches to problem solving—matching approaches to the problems, then disagreement over epistemology is rendered moot (see below for a further discussion of the importance of pragmatism to theorizing in public administration).

One other element might enable us to achieve ontological disclosure. That would be to experiment with our modes of academic discourse; trying modes and formats that are more process-oriented in nature than we currently use. Possibilities might include: writing in the first person; longer and more intense conversations between fewer persons as opposed to large conventions, panels, and papers; ontological appendices to our papers and books.[6] Too idealistic? I hope not.

False Consciousness, Ideology, and the Problems of a Normative Grounding

The field of public administration suffers from false consciousness on two dimensions: first, on the societal, both academicians and practitioners generally lack consciousness of our actual place in the societal and political order, as opposed to our conventional wisdom concerning our place. We are similarly lacking in cognizance of our true interests and how we are at times used to serve the interests of others; and second, on the dimension of studying the phenomena we lump under public administration—academicians generally lack consciousness of our immersion in normative and philosophical questions and their relevance for us. We generally believe and present ourselves (though if pressed we know better) as being "scientific" or "social scientific" and therefore "objective." Naturally, the two dimensions of false consciousness are not unrelated—indeed, they are mutually reinforcing.

Our ability to work our way out of our miasma and find a common normative grounding depends on our being able to suspend, however briefly, our false consciousness, and this depends on our ability to make a distinction between ideology on the one hand and philosophy, a public philosophy and theory, on the other. Ideology, to put it as broadly as possible, is a common aspect of human existence, "a particular expression of social life" (Urban, 1982, p. xii). It refers to "a more or less coherent set of ideas which are generated by real conditions of conflict or contradiction obtaining in society. Such ideas reflect this conflict, but in a refracted manner, so as to render it resolvable at the level of symbols" (Urban, 1982, p. 5). Ideologies, then, "simultaneously reveal and conceal something about the conditions which give birth to them and, insofar as they conceal or obscure these conditions in thought, they tend to stabilize or perpetuate them in reality" (p. 5).

For example, our American ideology holds that all people are equal before the law; but that obscures the contradiction that lies in the fact that *for the most part* the possession of wealth reduces the risk and severity of punishment; the contradiction is resolved in symbols and processes that are heavily symbolic (blind justice, constitutional right to a fair trial and to be represented by counsel). Ideologies emerge in societies (largely unconsciously) to enhance coherence. Naturally they work to advantage those in positions of dominance over others by eliciting quiescence or compliance. Ideology is an instrument of action or a mediator between action and reflection; its function is definitely *not* to evoke reflection but rather to render reflection superfluous.

Although we may never completely escape the effects of ideology, a normative grounding need not have the "veiling" effect of ideology. It need not block reflection. It can simply help frame and prioritize questions and efforts in a way that is especially important to an applied interdisciplinary field. A normative grounding or regrounding for theorizing about American public administration, however, must be more than a list of "ought to bes" and "should bes." It should be in effect a public or civic philosophy; a prescriptive, teleological, or aspirational subset of the broader political culture. Its prescriptions amount to a prioritization of political culture with reference to the operation of the political system and government. A public philosophy is based on perspectives shared by elites and informed segments of the public, and accepted by the rest of the public as to how our political and governmental institutions *should,* and for the most part do, operate to perform the functions of the political system. Unless it is to face serious challenges, it must be consonant with dominant (or if the system is in flux, with potentially dominant) values found in the Constitution and related founding papers (The Declaration of Independence, The Federalist Papers, The Anti-Federalist Papers), selected Supreme Court decisions, landmark statutes, and values reflected in dominant democratic theories.

Robert Bellah et al. believe that a normative grounding, a public philosophy, can only be achieved by "renewing an older conception of social science, one in which the boundary between social science and philosophy was still open" (Bellah, Madsen, Sullivan, Swidler, & Tipton, 1985, pp. 297-298). They look to Tocqueville as an exemplar and refer to his "synoptic view, at once philosophical, historical, and sociological, that narrowly professional social science seems not so much incapable of, as uninterested in." They label their efforts "social science as public philosophy" (p. 298). Although they are members of a traditional discipline (sociology), it seems that the connection they found it necessary to reestablish is precisely the normative grounding for theorizing about public administration that we need.[7]

Academics in public administration must engage in social science, but a social science given direction and meaning by the values expressed and emergent in ongoing theorizing that in turn is grounded in a public philosophy. This presents a unique problem for the field of public administration, one that is at best implicit in America's dominant public philosophy, most often simply referred to as pluralism. Theodore Lowi's (1979) label, "interest group liberalism," is harsher, and though it is more descriptive in some respects, it lacks in others; that is, the aggrandized power and expectations lodged in the presidency and other chief executive officers.

Although that public philosophy (and any potential alternatives) would be inoperable without public administration, it is scarcely acknowledged except negatively in the ongoing discourse. Of course at the level of operant behavior, public administration is acknowledged because every actor in the political process seeks to blame, reform, reorganize, reinvent, cutback, but above all control and *use* it for their own purposes. There is therefore a considerable disparity between our public philosophy, which fails to deal with it, and our political modus operandi, which relies on it and uses it as designated bête noire. What we need is a public philosophy that openly and positively acknowledges the positive role of public administration in governance.

My colleague John Rohr has expressed reservations concerning a public philosophy. According to Rohr, public administrators, whether academics or practitioners, should take the regime values found in the Constitution as our starting point in the way the American lawyer or legal scholar takes the common law as a starting point over the continental or code law system—or the medical doctor takes as a base assumption that the profession must pursue health over sickness.[8]

The point is well taken. Public administrators cannot go back to a philosophic square one as a guide for action; for that matter public administration academicians cannot do so every time they write or teach, either. But there are several reasons why I feel we must develop a concept called public philosophy.

First, we cannot simply change our ideology by direct conscious effort. Through changing our public philosophy it may be that our ideology will slowly change, but ideology is not the best strategic target if one seeks change. In addition, *ideology* has acquired a host of negative connotations over nearly half a century or more of Cold War. Second, in discussing the problems of perceiving ourselves as a discipline rather than an applied interdisciplinary field, we have seen the problems of trying to develop *a* theory or theorizing. That effort keeps us trapped in the functionalist/positivist project of trying to explain, predict, and control. Third, the concept of political culture or regime values as those have currently been developed are without differentiation or valence so that they do not prescribe action in specific situations and contexts.

A public philosophy thus gives shape to regime values and political culture. It is, in effect, the accepted prioritization of those values by governing elites, the informed public, and more broadly the general public; stable and enduring but also changing and emergent. It is based on: certain assumptions about human nature; what politics and society should be about in a democratic, constitutional republic; and the nature of reality, reason, and knowledge with particular reference to politics and administration.

Public philosophy occupies the intellectual space between philosophy in all its breadth (including values and norms), and theory, which has come to have such functionalist, positivist, and explanatory connotations. And although a public philosophy is also affected by the false consciousness created by ideology like any other aspect of a society, still it connotes reflection and inquiry, whereas an ideology is meant to overcome both and commit persons to a line of thought or action. If there is to be any chance of even momentarily or partially suspending false consciousness, it will more likely be done under the banner of a public philosophy. It is fitting that the normative grounding for theorizing in public administration should be in a public philosophy—a concept based on norms, values, and prescriptions. But equally important, philosophy connotes inquiry *and* a pursuit of knowledge. The latter and equally important dimension of philosophy suggests norms and values do not have some once-and-for-all, highly specific, trans-contextual meaning. For example, equality, or separation of powers are values that are suggestive of meaning, but only suggestive. Their meaning must be worked out again and again in changing historical moments and circumstances. Even if one were to take the rather narrow view that these are defined only or primarily by the courts, students of the law know that the opinions of the courts are neither monolithic nor immutable, though the "magic" of the legal process is to make them seem both. The concept of public philosophy offers both inquiring and normative connotations and traditions.

Though one can argue that public administrators cannot engage in philosophizing, even of the public philosophy variety, I would agree with David K. Hart (1984) that public administration academicians and practitioners can and must engage philosophy, at least of the public philosophy variety and probably beyond. Public administration, government, and governing are all an inescapably moral enterprise. We cannot become philosophers but we cannot escape dealing with the philosophic aspects of public administration. A democratic, constitutional republic requires having a certain measure of confidence that citizens can handle such a challenge.[9]

Thus normative grounding in the form of a public philosophy is an important preface to all our so-called approaches to public administration because it gives us a unity and focus. Without placing one approach over another it helps frame the questions we expect an approach to address, or the values we expect our practice to uphold, and it is thus at the heart of the reflexivity that is central to praxis. Each of our many approaches raises important issues and provides valuable insights into multifaceted social reality, but a public philosophy can be the important means of bringing those approaches to bear on that social reality.

The Significance of Our Misfounding, Misgrounding, and Being a Field

Misfounding and Misgrounding

As Hannah Arendt (1977) has reminded us, foundings are of surpassing importance in shaping a regime's values and mode of governance, or—in the terms I will be using—its public philosophy and its mode of governance. Certainly this was true of the founding of the United States of America, and unfortunately it is true of the founding, or better said, the misfounding of the self-conscious study and practice of public administration. As we have retrospectively created the history of our field (and we *have* created it), we have placed its founding at the turn of the century in the Reform Movement. But E. N. Gladden (1972) has traced public administration back to prehistoric times, and Van Riper (1987) has shown that it is a patent absurdity to even entertain the idea that it began with Woodrow Wilson's little noted article in an 1887 issue of the *Political Science Quarterly*.

We have been simply and egregiously wrong in our retrospective creation of our national history and founding with regard to public administration (Van Riper, 1987). In doing so we have unwittingly misgrounded our theorizing efforts. We have saddled ourselves with a reform mentality (O'Toole, 1984), and with the values of science, rationality, and efficiency that might be appropriate for business in a capitalist economy within a setting of liberal democracy, but which are inappropriate as primary emphases for public administration in the circumstances in which it finds itself, and for the role to which it must aspire if America is to have effective governance in the postmodern era. Our practice has struggled forward with this albatross-like legacy of efficiency and reform around its neck grasping at the "fad du jour" (e.g., reforming, reorganizing, and now, reinventing government), and our theorizing has involved far-ranging searches for approaches such as critical theory or radical humanism that we have had difficulty relating to the work life of practitioners.

A Field, Not a Discipline

It is critically important that we recognize our misfounding and misgrounding because we are *not* a traditional or typical academic discipline of the social science variety. Whether they should or not, traditional disciplines attempt to detach themselves from society, its problems, and human agency enough to convince their adherents that they are committed to "inquiry," something above the turmoil and messiness of the world. Essentially it is an imagined position of the potentially "omniscient observer" or the "eye of God." Such disciplines tend to be driven by their agreed-upon epistemology and related methods of analysis. They ask questions that arise within their dominant paradigm, but when they must decide among questions to pursue, their primary focus is on those that meet their epistemology or "ways of knowing" and to which their methods of analysis can provide plausible answers. They then concentrate on ever more finite and detailed subjects considered relevant, and questions deemed important, within the realm defined by their dominant paradigm and epistemology.

The development of knowledge in the traditional discipline can be thought of as pyramidal in shape. Starting with a broad and general base of knowledge, usually with a dominant paradigm and theory, the discipline builds upon it and works on increasingly narrow theoretical subsets or models directed to defined and finite problems and questions at the apex. The contrast between our field and a traditional discipline was once made clear to me by one of my daughters who was majoring in microbiology. She had read an article I had written on contrasting patterns of Air Force socialization (Wamsley, 1972) and asked how it was that I got involved in such a variety of subjects. "My major professor has been studying one strain of E-coli bacteria for 22 years!" she exclaimed. She later went on to study in an applied interdisciplinary field—medicine—and learned first hand the difference between it and the discipline of microbiology. All this means is that the shape of knowledge development in public administration is more like an *inverted* pyramid or array of smaller inverted pyramids, the bases of which overlap at the top.

An applied interdisciplinary field is different from a discipline in other ways. It has an inescapable symbiotic relationship with practitioners of a profession (or would-be profession) from which it cannot distance itself. It is involved in the socialization and education (and some career training), both initially and on a continuing career basis, of practicing professionals. That relationship should be supportive, but constructively critical. We should be able to tell practitioners what "even their best friends won't tell them," as an advertisement for mouthwash used to say.

An applied interdisciplinary field may or may not have a dominant paradigm or epistemology and methods. But because it has special responsibilities for professional socialization and education, and an obligation to maintain an ongoing relationship with a profession, an applied field's attention is more often directed by problems and questions encountered by practitioners. It also means that the field is involved with, and concerned about, not only individual practitioners but practitioners in the social construct we call institutions.

The Excitement and Challenge of Being a Field

Because many of us were educated in traditional disciplines, and we spend our careers in institutions dominated by the norms of such disciplines (universities), we generally bemoan the conditions that go with being an applied interdisciplinary field while ignoring the opportunities, excitement, and challenges that are thus presented. The challenges are daunting, but they are also exciting. They were captured in an aphorism of Martin Landau's that every public policy is an hypothesis, every public program is an experiment, and public administrators must conduct each experiment under the worst possible conditions. One could extend the aphorism further by adding that the hypothesis (the policy) was developed as a result of a struggle among persons holding different paradigms, ideologies, perspectives, and interests. The winners are determined to prove the hypothesis is correct; the losers equally intent on proving it wrong. The experiment's (the program's) design reflects the points of exhaustion in the battle by both the winners and losers of this hypothesis struggle; each trying to structure the experiment so that the outcome will be the one they want. The conductors of the experiment (the public administrators) will have to conduct the experiment, despite the built-in design flaws, interventions, harassment, and even sabotage, with a great show of optimism and confidence while seeking to demonstrate their own objectivity, scientific expertise, and rationality. They will also have to make an elaborate manifestation of dedication to economy and efficiency despite the fact that the experiment is probably operating on too few resources to succeed even if the design were not tragically flawed. Should some worthwhile outcome emerge from all this, the original opponents in the hypothesis struggle will declare them invalid or fraudulent and the winners will claim much more success than reason can support.

This tragi-comic spectacle spun from Landau's aphorism, suggests several things about theorizing for our field: (a) that the complexity of it all limits the value of the positivist conception of theory; (b) that the participants are in desperate need of normative support in the form of professional values; and (c) that a single theory that seeks to explain it all will be of less value than a variety of perspectives and approaches with inquiry guided by a shared normative grounding.

The extended aphorism epitomizes the challenge inherent in the practice, study, and praxis of our field. It illustrates that we have no choice but to range across the width and breadth of human endeavor and knowledge, from the microscopically technical, treatable as matters of "objective reality," to grandly macroscopic matters of theology and philosophy that are inescapably normative and moral in nature. In one field we encompass the extremes of the theorist and the practitioner or implementor. Patricia Shields, paraphrasing James Gleick, has pithily captured the distance that lies between those two roles that we must span:

> Theorists are thinkers, implementors are craftsmen. The theorist operates in a pristine place free of noise, of vibration, of dirt. The implementor develops an intimacy with matter as a sculptor does with clay, battling it, shaping it, engaging it. The theorist invents his companions, as a naive Romeo imagined his ideal Juliet. The implementor's lovers sweat, complain, and fart. (Gleick, 1987, p. 125, quoted in Shields, in press)

The Analogy of the Medical Field

Roughly three decades ago Dwight Waldo said that public administration's exemplar should be medicine. I strongly disagreed then (Wamsley, 1976), but as usual he was largely right and I was largely wrong.[10] Medicine is an applied interdisciplinary field (microbiology, biochemistry, pathology, psychology, biophysics—even the disciplines are hybrids or variants of basic disciplines). The field of medicine is engaged in providing professional education for practitioners. As an analog it suggests the value of coherence around shared values and at the same time cautions us concerning the liabilities and limitations of such coherence.

The strength of the medical field has been a common ontological stance in modernism and natural science and epistemological consensus in positivism and empiricism. Without opening up a larger discussion I cannot finish, I would suggest that its strength may also be its weakness or limitation. That is, medicine has been slow to accept and some would say it has shut itself off from a variety of potentially valuable additions to the spectrum of health care by its limited conception of science. Alternative approaches to medicine have steadily increased in efficacy and potential value as a part of health care— chiropractic, osteopathy, homeopathy, holistic medicine, and Eastern medical practices such as acupuncture. What I feel we can glean from the medical analog is *not* that we in public administration must find consensus on epistemology or a shared ontological stance, but rather, that we can learn what it means to be an applied interdisciplinary field associated with a practicing, if nascent, profession. To me it suggests that we should seek coherence in a common normative grounding; that is, a public philosophy rather than in a common ontology or epistemology.

The medical analogy should sharply remind us of the academy's responsibility to practicing professionals. Most academics in public administration do not think the matter of whether or not we are a discipline is important, but *if* they do, they assume or believe we should be a discipline. We, and our society, pay a heavy price for that misguided choice. It means abandonment of our obligations to the nascent profession and to our government and society; it means we are drawing our salaries under false pretenses; and it means that we are more likely to ignore institutions and thereby badly misunderstand the world we say we want to explain and understand.

We need multiple paradigms and approaches and eclectic theorizing, which can provide different "lenses" for seeing our subject from different perspectives. For we must deal with the whole of human nature in a way that medicine has not, setting aside for the moment the question of whether or not it should. And humans are not of a common mind as to human nature, nor is such consensus a likely prospect. Furthermore, we must deal with humans at the level of greatest opacity—the tangle of motives and intentions, of projections, ideals, dissembling, and self-delusion called politics. We need ongoing dialogue on these matters, not an imagined "final solution to the theory problem." This openness by design, of which ontological disclosure would be a keystone, can lead us to ask and answer different questions, and enable us to expand our knowledge and understanding of public administration while maintaining a supportive but constructively critical relationship with its practitioners.

That happy prospect for our applied interdisciplinary field also requires an explicit normative framework or grounding: not just for the study of public administration, but for its practice and praxis as well. As noted earlier we currently have a grounding, but it is largely unrecognized and ill-suited for the role into which we have been thrust. It is drawn from liberal democracy and business, and emphasizes science, instrumental rationality, and efficiency. It is both damaging and delegitimating, given the role we are called upon to play; a role that is supposedly only one of neutrally competent management, but that in fact is fundamentally political (in a nonpartisan sense), involving the upholding of constitutional values and the formulation, implementation, and adjudication of policy. Public administration by its nature has never been and can never be anything else. We must now find a way to refound and reground ourselves that legitimates that circumstance and our role in governance of a democratic, constitutional republic in a postmodern era.

Transcending the Role of Designated Victim for a Legitimate Role in Governance

The term *governance* deserves some explication. It is seldom used in American literature or rhetoric, and its absence is as understandable as it is lamentable (Wamsley, in Hill, 1992). Historically, our public philosophy has reflected a strong faith in an invisible but presumably benign hand at work in our political system—not unlike our faith in the providential nature of the economic market. We seem to believe that through contention, bargaining, or a process of natural selection the best policy ideas will prevail without political elites having to make tough choices, disappoint anyone, or strain unduly to create perceptions of transcendence.

The advent of the "zero-sum society," in which a gain for one interest is another's loss, has been exacerbated by competition in a global economy (Thurow, 1980). Americans have become increasingly anxious about their economic well-being and that of their children. These forces are causing our politics to become increasingly ideological and vitriolic as politicians have been pushed into difficult choices, frustrations have grown, and the civility of discourse declined (Putnam, 1996; Walzer, 1991).

The increasingly negative attitudes toward public administration are directly related to this growing frustration. Politicians redirect this frustration, fear, and anger toward public administration. Each party has seen public administration as the instrument of the other party's nefarious intent, and all have sought to blame it for the lack of resources to meet all the demands of political factions and interests without raising taxes or increasing debt. Because the vast majority of politicians have rejected the latter two possibilities and have been excruciatingly reluctant to reexamine the most expensive of our entitlement programs (e.g., medicare, social security, veterans benefits, farm and corporate subsidies) it leaves them with little to blame but "bloated bureaucracy" (which has scarcely grown in personnel at the federal level over the past three decades) and the inefficacious poor.[11]

Our political elites have not "governed" according to most dictionary definitions of that word. The definition that I have used in the past was "to maintain a straight course toward an objective in the interest of the individual and the whole" (Wamsley in Hill, 1992). The metaphor from which the word *govern* is derived is "steering," but American governing elites with their existing public philosophy have done little steering. From the ramshackle development of the "system" of expensively "perverse incentives" we call health care at the national level, to the ugly space-consuming blight we call "urban and commercial development" at the local level, no one has been willing to admit being at the wheel—only the allegedly beneficent invisible hand of the market, or so our political leaders would have us believe. The supposed lack of steering has, of course, always redounded to the benefit of some more than others, but political elites have simply been able to obscure that embarrassing reality with the aid of a rising standard of living for most of us (Phillips, 1990). Few politicians have been willing to say no as well as yes to the efficacious, or develop the skills to engender win-win solutions in which people feel they are sacrificing for some common or greater good.

Our politicians will increasingly face situations requiring a more intensive and skillful effort to create perceptions of win-win solutions, or perceptions that losses are a necessary sacrifice for the common good. These are tasks politicians have simply not had to face and for which they lack a repertoire of ideas. As Christopher Bosso (1991) has pointed out we could scarcely have a "national creed" more ill-suited for the world we are now entering. Our culture glories the rugged individual, the "independent plainspoken, virtuous and tough risk taker" who battles "entrenched corporate interests or intrusive government." Unfortunately, such a person is rapidly becoming as rare and maladapted as a being from another planet (pp. 7-8). Bosso offers an engaging description of the world we live in and how it contrasts with the Huck Finn or Mr. Deeds world of our creed. But he comes finally down to the point that

> The hard truth of the next century is that *our problems will be common problems,* national and international problems, requiring communal solutions on a scale and duration that Americans in peacetime are neither accustomed to nor comfortable with (p. 9).

Given our existing public philosophy and mode of politics, the task seems impossible. It may help a bit, however, if we begin amending our expectations of governance in a postmodern era by modifying our definition of governance itself. Though not without its virtues, the teleological character of the steering definition may be not only typical of the modern era but unrealistic even for that era. Moreover, it neglects some matters that have been considered important since the time of Plato and Aristotle. It also seems to me that we must redefine governance in the postmodern era—an era of kaleidoscopic change filled with both potential and incoherence—an era in which relationships may be crucial.

In a light that is therefore both postmodern and high modern let us reconsider Webster's "steering" definition. To begin with, it may be too demanding teleologically given the limits upon human agency in social constructs as large and complex as a nation-state or even a state in our federal system, and given the baffling complexity of today's policy problems. More important, it may place too much emphasis on steering toward at least implied "goals." For it may be that although the ultimate destination matters, it matters less than, and indeed is not achievable without, the relationships citizens share with one another and with their government during the voyage. *Governing, in other words, may be the ability of political elites to create circumstances that evoke the kinds of relations among citizens that allow us to maintain a collective coherence, establish our identities individually and collectively, and generally foster conditions that ultimately permit us to discover ourselves and the meaning of our lives. Good governance by this definition is about evocation of human potential more than steering a course. Good governance should also enable us to occasionally transcend, renew, or recreate ourselves individually and collectively in ways that maintain democracy while fostering human development and fulfillment.*

John Kirlin (1995) makes a similar point when he states—

> Democratic polities must focus on the sustained capacity of the political system itself to make and act on collective choices, on opportunities for effective citizenship and political leadership, on ensuring a limited govern-

ment, on nurturing the civic infrastructure necessary for collective action without public authority, on providing the institutional structures necessary for operations of the economy and on protecting individual freedoms and rights.

These Kirlin says are the foci of governance and address "the big questions" of public administration which should be our concern rather than matters at the level of public "management" and public organizations (Kirlin, 1995, p. 3).

Not only Kirlin but Robert Putnam (1993), Christopher Bosso (1991), Michael Walzer (1991), and Lester Salamon (1981) emphasize the need for public administration to see governance as involving far more than government and the role of citizen as something far beyond passive consumership of services. These authors make the point that governance and public administration must be concerned with the whole range of instruments and institutions available to a modern society for collective action. These include not only government but the market, non-profit and voluntary institutions—"the rich tapestry of institutions that comprise the civic infrastructure" (Kirlin, 1995, p. 5).

Public administration must transcend the roles of instrumental management, broker of interests, and obedient servant of a partisan CEO or legislative majority. These invariably make us the victim in partisan warfare. Transcendence must begin with a normative grounding out of which we can shape a new identity. To the extent that our political system is capable of governance as steering, we should aspire to a leading role in it. If, as seems more likely, a postmodern conception of governance is called for—one that is more a matter of evocation of relationships than achievement of goals—then we should aspire to play a leading role in that as well.

Presently, we are without an appropriate logic-in-use or conventional wisdom, self-conception, values, symbols, rhetoric, education, and skills. We are simply not equipped to participate in governance even if we *were* accepted as having a legitimate role, and no matter how governance is defined. I believe the things we lack for our role can only be provided by starting not with a return to a more "down-to-earth" management approach, a different kind of approach to organizational theory, or application of some totally new approach, but rather by starting with a new public philosophy that can provide a better normative grounding.

Historically Situating a New Public Philosophy

I am convinced that a normative grounding for theorizing (i.e., public philosophy) must be "situated" so that it is both historically and contemporaneously relevant. In other words, it should reflect our history with more rather than less accuracy, reveal the problems with the older public philosophy, serve to mitigate long-standing historical problems and questions, depict with some accuracy the current context, and have the potential to guide actions and mitigate contemporary problems as well as those in the foreseeable future.

As the painstaking scholarship of John Rohr (1986), David K. Hart (1984), Louis Gawthrop (1994), Jeffrey Sedgwick (1983), Nigro and Richardson (1987), and others before them has shown us, public administration or its functional equivalent was definitely a part of the debate at the Founding of our nation. Indeed, Sedgwick has shown that it was unhappiness with lax administration under the Articles of Confederation that led to the Founding. Public administration of the 18th and 19th centuries has not been readily recognizable to us in looking back because it lacked the scope, the reform trappings, and the concept of a civil service system that we have come to associate with public administration. Beach et al. (in press) have shown us the extent and importance of colonial public administration and Rohr (1986) makes it clear that in our early development good administration was simply equated with effective governance. Its importance is manifest in the fact that "administration" was mentioned in the *Federalist Papers* the most frequently. And because the Founders equated effective administration with effective governance, it needed no mention in a Constitution created to assure the same.

Even though public administration was largely implicit in our Constitution, public administration was, and remains, a fundamental though largely implicit or negative part of pluralism, our dominant public philosophy, and an explicitly negative part of our mode of politics (Hill, 1991; Milward & Rainey, 1982). Although pluralism is a key aspect of our dominant public philosophy, I will use the label of Federalist or Hamiltonian-Madisonian because it is more descriptive.

At our founding the language of Thomas Jefferson, Thomas Paine, Samuel Adams, and Patrick Henry, which had inspired revolution (and doubtless continued after the war to inspire or inflame elements of the population like revolutionary veteran Daniel Shays) had to be brought to ground in the language of a document of governance. The Declaration of Independence spoke of all men being created equal; the Constitution made elliptical provisions for slavery without ever using the word. The Declaration spoke inspiringly of the pursuit of happiness; the Constitution speaks more mundanely of the protection of property without mentioning happiness. To the dismay of many of the Anti-Federalists, the passions of the revolution were thus placed within the cooler constraints of the Constitution. What emerged as the dominant public philosophy was a combination of some of Hamilton's thinking with regard to a strong national government with "energy in the executive" and Madison's ingenious Newtonian mechanics for the institutional control of factions. That is the core of continuity in our public philosophy that runs from the ratification of the Constitution to this day.

Federalist or Hamiltonian-Madisonian Public Philosophy

The Federalist part of our public philosophy and related stream of discourse focused on the "functional requisites," so to speak, of "an extended commercial republic" or a "fiscal-military state" of at first continental and later global, dimensions—a growing, industrializing, modern nation-state with the need to maintain ordered liberty at home, promote its commerce, and protect its international interests. It has resulted in a steady increase in the power of the president (and probably of governors and mayors) under Hamilton's notion of "energy in the executive" given added impetus by misinterpretation of that notion and the notion of "unity of command" from classical administrative management. It also provided the rationale for subsidization of business and industry in an allegedly capitalist economy under the banner of national interest or geopolitical necessity. Similarly, it provided the rationale for development of a standing army and navy and the imperialistic acquisition of territory.

The Hamiltonian-Madisonian public philosophy has repeatedly provided rationale for the way our politics and government have evolved: in the Progressive Movement; the movement for an executive budget; for Wilson and Goodnow's politics-administration dichotomy; for classical administrative management; and perhaps it has influenced the emergence of the plebiscitary presidency and the currently popular "reinventing government" movement, though these might have appalled both Hamilton and Madison.

Overwhelmingly the Hamiltonian-Madisonian, or Federalist, public philosophy has been predominant and Anti-Federalist thought marginalized. George Will (1992) points out the irony in the way we honor Jefferson with an elegant memorial in our nation's capital, but there is none for Hamilton. "However, if you seek Hamilton's monument, look around," says Will. "You are living in it" (p. 167) (Will's comment applies equally well to Madison—we live in his "monument" as well).

Since the turn of the century, Hamilton-inspired public administration has consciously collaborated with forces that would aggrandize the president and with Madison-inspired pluralism to remain the dominant strand in our public philosophy. It has done so with ultimate detriment to its self-interest as a field of study and practice as well as to the interest of the nation as a whole. It has styled itself as the "neutrally competent" instrument of the chief executive's will with its legitimacy based (as in business) in expertise, science, and instrumental and economic rationalism. At the same time it has, with less open acknowledgment, been a crucial prop for pluralism by mediating among interest groups. Lowi (1979) goes so far as to say that it is public administration that enabled pluralism and interest group liberalism to absorb and replace capitalism as the public philosophy.[12]

That brings us to a closer consideration of pluralism, the other equally important strand within the extant Hamiltonian-Madisonian public philosophy and related stream of discourse. Pluralism has provided the political underpinning for the strong Hamiltonian national government with its administrative core. It has served to describe, explain, prescribe, and justify the prominent role of powerful interest groups in our political system, and has reassured us that pluralism is compatible with, even desirable for, the kind of nation Hamilton envisaged—an urbanized, industrialized, popular republic with a status of world power.

The roots of pluralist thought are found in Madison's brilliant essays in *Federalist* 10 and 51, in which he argued that liberty could be maintained and the "mischief of faction" controlled in a "compound and extended republic" with multiple competing interests and a government of elegantly structured institutions with contrapuntal powers. Just as Adam Smith's "invisible hand" of competition had beneficent effects for the market, its political equivalent would (if one stretched the logic far enough) not need virtue, or proximity of relations, but instead would rely on the competitiveness of people, which would be held in benign equilibrium by "institutional physics"—ambition checking ambition. The pluralist stream of discourse has a long lineage manifest in works that either extol the virtues of pluralism: James Madison, Charles Merriam, Arthur Bentley, David Truman, and Robert Dahl; or those who have raised concerns or attacked it such as Herbert Croly, Peter Bachrach, and Theodore Lowi.[13]

Public administration has rationalized its heavy involvement with, and mediation of, interest groups with the pluralist's argument that as long as interest countered interest democracy would still flourish, no matter how powerful the groups and no matter who might lose or be left out of the process. Some writers in the field, such as Avery Leiserson (1942), went so far as to suggest that public administration must inevitably act as the arbiter of interests, and that the compromises it affected among groups were a fair approximation of the public interest. Today the body of criticism of pluralism has grown, though it seems to have done little to change pluralism's dominance as public philosophy, political theory, or ideology. But at least we in public administration have become increasingly uncomfortable with Leiserson's reassuring conclusion concerning our role in determining the public interest.

There is growing concern that the pathologies of pluralism combined with our Hamiltonian tendencies toward a stronger national government with power centered in the presidency and a large bureaucratic core at its heart have produced effects that threaten the stability, and even the existence, of our political system. These effects include: weak and ineffective parties engaged in irresponsible partisan gamesmanship, overcentralized and clumsy bureaucracies, and alarmingly ubiquitous and powerful interest groups. These political effects combine with others derived from consumer capitalism: social fragmentation and dislocation; rampant individualism and decline of social responsibility. And both political and economic effects are exacerbated by: (a) declining real family income; (b) the emergence of a postindustrial and global economy with all its anxiety-producing impacts on citizens; and (c) the decline in civic life resulting from commodification and marketing of candidates; increasing ideological shrillness; and ethnic, gender, and racial tensions. Our Hamiltonian-Madisonian public philosophy is overdue for reexamination and adjustments.

Anti-Federalism or Jeffersonianism

There is, of course, another stream of discourse that has been with us since our colonial and founding periods, but muted, marginalized, and largely reduced to rhetoric: the Anti-Federalist or Jeffersonian.[14] It has been primarily concerned with how we can achieve or maintain a government close enough to the people *and* of a meaningful human scale that it can sustain democracy and community. The Anti-Federalists worried that in the process of building a strong national government and a great commercial empire we might lose social ties of community and governments of a proximity and scale that allowed both development of the individual and meaningful relationships among citizens and between government and citizens. We might, in other words, gain liberty, empire, and power, but lose the shared meaning, identity, and significance that is the soul of democratic community and of human existence.

We honor Jefferson, largely for the brilliance of his democratic rhetoric in the Declaration of Independence, but neither he nor other Anti-Federalists were able to put together as coherent and persuasive a vision of what American government should be as the Federalists did. This does not mean, however, that the Anti-Federalists' case was without merit. It served to strengthen and democratize the Constitution by the inclusion of the Bill of Rights. There were other more subtle threads of Anti-Federalist thought that were and are of value.

The Anti-Federalist case for the virtues of classical republicanism are fainter, more intermittent, and interwoven with the arguments for democratization. Nonetheless they can be seen in the Anti-Federalists' response to the *Federalist Papers,* the Jacksonians or Democratic Republicans, Jackson's rationale for the so-called Spoils System, the Populists, and various experimental utopian communities of the 19th century; in the writing of John Dewey, Mary Parker Follett, and New Dealers like David Lilienthal and Rexford Tugwell; and in such contemporary writers as Philip Selznick and Robert Bellah. A distinct subset of theorists in public administration, the Traditionalists described in the introductory chapter of this volume, also assumed the potential for a national community, and argued against public administration's sublimation to the "science" of "administrative management" and against its becoming an extension of the chief executive. It is the idea of community and the values of dialogue and a closer relationship between citizens and their government that is important, not whether these were local or national in locus or scope.

Today the concerns raised by the Anti-Federalist stream of discourse seem all too warranted. More than ever Americans seem to be searching for the social bonds and shared meaning of community that our political system has failed to sustain. We in public administration particularly, but our nation as well, must give more attention to such concerns, to counter our uncritical acceptance of the correlated Hamiltonian and Madisonian lines of thought. The study of public administration must play a key role in developing a better balanced public philosophy—the basis for a new mode of governance and a normative grounding for theorizing about it and a different modus operandi for politics.

America's Reaction to the Frustrations of Hamilton-Madison Public Philosophy and Mode of Politics

At the very time this challenge confronts us, I contend that our political system is undergoing a reaction to the pathologies of the Hamiltonian-Madisonian public philosophy and its derivative mode of governance, and that this is happening without our understanding the real source of our problems. Hamiltonian thought justified a large federal government with centralized, hierarchical bureaucracies with the size and acuity of dinosaurs at its core, which make a mockery of effective policy implementation; and Madisonian thought has justified interest group liberalism that has weakened our parties and made it impossible for us to form coherent national policy. Our policy outcomes are either particularistic and distributive, win-lose, or least-common-denominator-of-agreement solutions that frustrate all of us. I would offer the Clinton administration's health care policy debacle as a case in point.

The reaction to the Hamiltonian-Madisonian public philosophy and political modus operandi encompasses a heterogenous lot. There are New Republican "revolutionaries"—Newt Gingrich, "Flat Tax" Forbes, and "populist" Pat Buchanan—and New Democratic politicians (the latter labeled "Republican Lite" by detractors) who have seized upon the mood of fear and anger to proclaim that there must be a "revolution" or "no more business as usual" in Washington. Some in both parties say that there must be downsizing, right-sizing, dismantling, decentralization, and devolution of the national government. Each side wants to "get government off of people's backs" *except* in instances in which *they* deem government intervention appropriate. Trying to identify such persons or groups as Left or Right, or even Democrat or Republican, seems increasingly difficult, not because passions have diminished but because of the lack of fundamental ideological or philosophical consistency. The same person who is willing to have government diminished in one capacity is adamant that its power be sustained or expanded in another.

For some politicians in both parties it is a chance to pass off problems and expenses to some other level of government or the private or not-for-profit sector; for some it means turning government operations into contracts with private firms that will presumably reward them with votes or contributions; others participate in downsizing and cutting from a more thoughtful position based on the conclusion that the national government has reached the limits of its effectiveness because of size; because it has been fiscally incapacitated by high debt level and the inexorable growth of entitlements; or because they have concluded that state governments are now more responsible, professional, closer to the problems, and therefore able to develop effective solutions. And finally, for some it is simply a time to try once again to bring the "latest, exciting business practices to government" so it can be "reinvented." The wave of reaction thus encompasses persons as diverse as Jesse Helms, Bill Clinton, Newt Gingrich, and Tom Osborne, each operating from different assumptions and different understandings.

Whether this reaction is labeled Neo-Liberalism, Neo-Populism, New Democrats, or New Right, I believe it is an anomic reaction to the dominant public philosophy and mode of politics and it seriously muddies the conceptual waters at a time when we desperately need more clarity. That both Newt

Gingrich and Bill Clinton can claim they are "turning government around" and doing so in the name of Thomas Jefferson, says much about the conceptual confusion and ideological inconsistency underlying the reaction. Much of the confusion has arisen because we have tried to frame the reaction to the problems of our political-administrative system in contemporary Democratic-Republican or Liberal-Conservative ideologies and slogans. This simply can no longer be done in a meaningful way (Luttwak, 1994; Reich, 1991). Both parties are operating with outmoded shibboleths, stereotypes, and mantras crafted for a political economy that has disappeared and an era now behind us (Reich, 1991).

Unfortunately, it is wishful thinking to believe that such a phenomenon, even though built on such contradictory grounds, would collapse of its own weight. The thing that must be hoped for is that politicians will work to develop a better understanding by the public of the implications of the often contradictory strands of thought encompassed in the reaction. At the heart of such an understanding must be a coming to terms with the fact that the collective demands of interest group liberalism cannot be met without raising taxes or worsening our debt situation. We are simply living well beyond our means and no downsizing of personnel or elimination of "waste" is going to solve the problem. The thing that must be hoped for is that this phenomenon can be analyzed and that understanding can be developed of the implications of the often contradictory strands of thought encompassed in this reaction to our extant public philosophy.

Public Administration's Role in
Finding a More Balanced Public Philosophy

The Blacksburg Project and the
Traditionalist Stream of Discourse

The magnitude of the challenge we face is not unique for public administration. The history of our field is one of epic struggles of this magnitude. Nor is the kind of thinking we propound radically new or far-fetched.

Those of us involved in the Refounding project are contributing to and drawing upon a stream of discourse that is logico-meaningful for us and particularly relevant to our efforts to develop a normative grounding for our disparate theorizing about public administration and for our practice and praxis. Elsewhere, White and McSwain (1990) have labeled this stream "the Traditionalists" and it is discussed in more detail in the introductory chapter of this volume. It represents a stream of discourse consonant with the development of a normative grounding open to all the approaches to public administration seen in the literature of the field.

The "Traditionalists" were a group of scholars (many of them scholar-practitioners) whose involvement in the practice of public administration during the New Deal and World War II led them to question some of the central tenets of classical administrative management, for example the politics-administration dichotomy, the primacy of the value of efficiency, positivism and rationality, and so on. They were beginning to develop a meaningful intellectual challenge to the dominant scientific management/administrative management stream of discourse when it was overtaken and marginalized by the events of World War II and the behavioral movement in the social sciences. Theorizing then diverged into myriad streams not the least of which was neo-classicism or "decision making" led by Herbert Simon, but also functionalist organizational sociology, organizational psychology, policy analysis, bureaucratic politics, and eventually to the "new public administration," and today, public management and public choice.

Though badly marginalized (by events, not the quality or importance of their work), the Traditionalists steadfastly sought to mitigate (a) the field's misfounding in "scientific management" and in concepts borrowed from business management; (b) its false consciousness concerning the role it plays in the American political system; and (c) the corrosive power of radical individualism by holding to the belief that community both mattered and was feasible. The Traditionalists generally saw agencies as social assets and also saw the advancement of an agency's well-being as consonant with the public interest, as long as its ambitions were held in check by controls imposed by Congress and the political executive. In their thinking, effective public administration was to be pragmatic in attitude, experimental in method, and focused on the public interest, which was viewed as an important concept, not just an artifact of rhetoric or metaphysics. They valued experience, intuition, and values as much as they did science and instrumental or economic rationality, and they therefore viewed case studies as a valuable means of teaching and learning. But most importantly, this stream of discourse sought to conceptualize public administration as fulfilling a nonpartisan but fundamentally political role in the governance process. Its contributors have been positive about the potential role of public administration in overcoming some of the most serious problems and limitations of our existing governmental institutions, and about finding an alternative basis for governance that can offset some of our system's growing pathologies.

I believe the Blacksburg project is extending the Traditionalist stream of discourse in our contention that public administration should be equally or more concerned with governance as evocation than it is with management, with our greater concern for collaboration achieved through dialogue than decision making/command/control, with our emphasis on the values of the Constitution as well as the words of the laws or their interpretation, and with our concern for a capacity to evoke democratic and communitarian values in addition to serving "customers" well. The values of the "Traditionalists'" stream of discourse, developed outside of and in opposition to the misfounding of our field, are the appropriate ones from which to build refounding and for normatively regrounding the theorizing, practice, and praxis of public administration in a way that will result in its being perceived as legitimate—not in a legal sense, but in the political and governance sense. Interestingly, the Traditionalists' ideas seem better suited for the postmodern era than the earlier period that saw their emergence and marginalization.

Thus we are merely restoring a blocked channel of discourse that had been headed toward development of a normative grounding that should be prefatory to, and deserves at least as much discussion as, the merits or problems of the various approaches we have been seeking to apply to public administration. We feel that each of these approaches has its merits and shortcomings and that these will become clearer when the questions they raise are "based," "framed," or "shaped" by a normative grounding in public philosophy, one that strikes a better balance between the Federalist and Anti-Federalist traditions.

Philosophic Pragmatism and Strong Democracy: Key Ingredients for a New Public Philosophy

Two of the several sources I am convinced we must draw upon in developing a more balanced public philosophy and in refounding a more democratic public administration are: (a) the philosophy of pragmatism; and (b) democratic theory. It is a measure of the difference between philosophy and a public philosophy, and an indication of the way philosophers play a role of social critic, that the writings of the classical American philosophers—Walter Lippman, William James, and John Dewey—have been sharply critical and at odds with many aspects of our old and dominant public philosophy.

All of these philosophers were pragmatists concerned with the problems of democracy and public life, and, in varying degrees, they stood against the trend toward utilitarian individualism and positivist scientism that has been fundamental in buttressing the Hamiltonian-Madisonian public philosophy. A smattering of their thoughts show their compatibility, indeed their essentiality, to the Refounding project as it has come to span the threshold between the High Modern to Postmodern eras. For example, Dewey and James both emphasized the constancy of change, the necessity of learning, and of experience in combination with a loosely defined experimental model and the use of naturalistic logic (an interplay of deductive and inductive reasoning) in the development and testing of ongoing working hypotheses (Shields, in press). Peirce (1931-1935) emphasized that science, which became such a large part of that public philosophy from the latter part of the 19th century onward, was a social enterprise; Royce (1969) wrote that a "community of interpreters" constantly reinterpreted the past in light of the present reality in a continuing conversation about spiritual truth and moral good; and Mead wrote at length concerning the social development of the self. All of these are relevant and topical for public administration in its efforts to fulfil its duties in the face of postmodernism.

Bellah et al. (1985) contend that these philosophic pragmatists staked out a "paradigmatic position of communicative reason" (see pp. 297-321) that is essential to what Robert Dahl has called "the third transformation of democracy" (Dahl et al., 1994). I agree with both Bellah and Dahl; America's classical philosophers have laid the critical basis for a better balanced public philosophy, and Dahl in his latest works has come to acknowledge the inadequacies of pluralism, which must give way to what is increasingly called a "process" approach.

White and McSwain (1990) have suggested that the philosophy of pragmatism holds promise as one of the major intellectual underpinnings for a public administration that must learn to function in a postmodern world. I am convinced they are correct in that matter.

Patricia Shields (in press) points out that the pragmatists saw theory and experience as symbiotically linked "through practical consequences associated with the experiences." "Learning and knowing" are thus connected as are "learning and action." Shields also points out that for the pragmatists truth was not rigidly defined but traced by its "respective practical consequences" (Shields [in press] quoting James, 1907, p. 201). James stated that the "truth of an idea is not a stagnant property inherent in it. Truth *happens* to an idea. It *becomes* true, is *made* true by events. Its verity is in fact an event, a process" (James, 1907, p. 201, as quoted in Shields, in press). "Effective truth is associated with a plan of action—mediates between experiences—connects the old to the new, welds theory and fact—is provisional, just the starting point used to address the next day's problem" (Shields [in press] drawing on Flower & Murphy, 1977, p. 681).

There are many other aspects of pragmatist philosophy that are consonant with postmodernism and on which we can fruitfully draw—its holistic view of the world and phenomena within it, and its ability to incorporate dualisms and seeming contradictions. Shields says the "fundamental elements of pragmatism are context, the problem, experience and consequences" and theory is "useful because it can connect all four." Here Shields is using "theory" in the way I use "theorizing"—in a tentative, experimental, and pragmatic way.

Here I can only suggest the possibilities to be drawn upon in developing a better balanced public philosophy that can serve to normatively ground public administration. In one enlightening passage of her paper on pragmatism and public administration, Shields draws on a metaphor introduced by James in 1907 to show the value of pragmatism in relating theory to practice. And, incidental to our purposes here, it shows how an applied interdisciplinary field such as ours does not and should not have *a* theory but should use pragmatism to justify accessing all theories and enlisting them in problem solving. Shields says James depicted pragmatism as lying "in the midst of theories like a hotel corridor. All the rooms (of theory) open out to it and all the rooms can be entered. Pragmatism owns the corridor and the right to move freely from room to room (Shields [in press] drawing on James, 1907, p. 54).

Shields continues—"Using pragmatic logic one would not expect a unifying PA theory." Shields then says "PA is organized around the principle that theories are useful and should be judged by their usefulness in solving problems." I wish this were so and hope that it soon will be, but clearly I think this is something to which we must aspire. Shields (in press) continues, "Unity (of theory and practice) is achieved because the pragmatic administrator *owns* the corridor, walking from room to room using the theories that address ongoing problems. Ownership of the corridor joins theory and practice. Public administration can find unity in the ownership." (I would say they can find unity in a public philosophy well grounded in pragmatism). Shields concludes, "It is the sense of *ownership* that provides an organizing principle." Because it seems unlikely we can come together over epistemology, perhaps we can unite on public philosophy.

Finally, Shields (in press) reminds us that perhaps the best known of the pragmatists, John Dewey, maintains "that actions and their consequences should be guided and assessed by ends or 'ends in view.' " Dewey came "to see democratic values as critical to defining these 'ends in view.' " Shields concludes "that PA's working hypotheses and PA's assessment of consequences should be grounded in democratic values and the public interest."

"Strong Democracy" and Public Philosophy

Let me turn now to the other major source upon which I feel we must draw in developing a normative grounding: democratic theory. John Kirlin (1995) makes a point that ought to be a challenge to all of us—"one schism in the study and practice of public administration concerns the starting point: is it public bureaucracy or a democratic polity (p. 1)?" That should be an intellectual equivalent of a slap in the face. Of course it should be a democratic polity, but foolishly we most often make our starting point public bureaucracy.

With Kirlin's slap in the face in mind, let me turn to Benjamin Barber's valuable ideas on "strong democracy." He sets forth the kind of democracy toward which I feel America must move in the postmodern era, and the kind of democracy with which a more democratic public administration will be symbiotic.

Barber's (1984) book *Strong Democracy* acknowledges the positive things we have gained by liberal democracy or "thin democracy," the kind of democracy that follows from a Hamiltonian-Madisonian public philosophy or "interest group liberalism" with its emphasis on the individual and privatistic ends. But more important, he makes it achingly clear what we have lost through following that civic philosophy too slavishly. Liberal democracy derived from Locke, Hobbes, and Mill is not a theory of political community, according to Barber. As he tartly puts it

> It does not so much provide a justification for politics as it offers a politics that justifies individual rights. It is concerned more to promote individual liberty than to secure public justice, to advance interests rather than to discover goods, and to keep men safely apart rather than to bring them fruitfully together. (p. 4)

Humans, in the view of liberal democracy, Barber (1984) notes, are like "captured leopards"—admired for "their proud individuality and for their unshackled freedom, but they must be caged for their untrustworthiness and antisocial orneriness all the same. Indeed, if the individual is dangerous, the species is deadly" (p. 21). He fruitfully describes three "dispositions" within liberal democracy: anarchism, realism, and minimalism. The first sees a human as a God, the second as a beast, and the third a beast with reason, but Barber reminds us that these are dispositions with a common origin and shared inadequacies. Liberal democracy remains "thin democracy," which has a profound negativity in its view of human nature: one of the major reasons it has proven vulnerable and fragile in the face of enemies and adversities.

Barber (1984) persuasively argues that there is an alternative vision of democracy that holds that the essence of "man is no abstraction inhering in each single individual. In its actuality it is the *ensemble of social relationships*" (p. 91). Barber describes it as a vision in which there is a choice between being citizens or being slaves, between being subservient to one another and nature or being able to transform subservience into interdependence through politics. It is a vision of democracy that sees the world as "social to its core," where we can "learn to become creative individuals *within* the families, tribes, nations, and communities into which we are born" (Barber, 1984, p. 91). That vision of democracy arises not from philosophical principles, but is engendered by the "political condition," which in turn is derived from "history, circumstance, and context" in which "real political actors, confronted with controversies and dilemmas issuing out of fundamental conflicts of interest and value in a changing society, are required to make responsible and reasonable choices" (p. 131) in the "absence of private or independent grounds for judgement" (p. 132).

According to Barber, these conditions should evoke *strong democracy, which he defines as "politics in a participatory mode" that "acknowledges (and indeed uses) the centrality of conflict in the political process," but resists the idea that it is intractable and vulnerable only to adjudication or toleration." "Instead," he continues, "it develops a politics that can transform conflict into cooperation through citizen participation, public deliberation, and civic education." "Strong democracy," Barber (1984) concludes, "begins but does not end with conflict: it acknowledges conflict but ultimately transforms rather than accommodates or minimizes it"* (p. 135).

This is not a value-free process, but it gives each participant's convictions and beliefs "an equal starting place." The degree to which they are accorded legitimacy is determined by the course of the public talk and action—the *process,* rather than by their "prior epistemological status" (p. 136). They do not just emerge legitimated, but also transformed—thus differing from bargaining and exchange in which "choice is a matter of selecting among options and giving the winner the legitimacy of consent." In transformation, "choice is superseded by judgement" and leads people to modify, enlarge, or invent options. As a result of "common talk" they are able to see the problem differently in light of "more common or public concerns" (p. 136), and to "imaginatively reconstruct their own values as public norms through the process of identifying and empathizing with the values of others" (p. 137).

Strong democracy thus goes beyond representation, bargaining, independent grounds for decision (surreptitious or acknowledged), or the "discovery" of some preexisting "hidden consensus." *It is based on "participation in an evolving problem-solving community that creates public ends where there were none before by means of its own activity and of its own existence as a focal point of the quest for mutual solutions" (p. 152). Public ends are "created by public participation in the process of deliberation and common action, both of which result in interests changing shape and direction."*

Hopefully, the foregoing sketch drawn from Barber (1984) offers readers some suggestions as to how both philosophic pragmatism and strong democracy can provide the basis for a more balanced public philosophy—a normative grounding for theorizing about public administration. Neither the Hamiltonian-Madisonian core of our public philosophy as distorted by capitalism and scientism, nor Jeffersonianism with its many ambiguities or misunderstandings can by themselves or in combination provide the basis for a more balanced public philosophy; it must be some new creative synthesis.

Philosophical pragmatism with its openness, problem solving, and experimentation, its evolutionary quality and flexibility toward truth with a small *t;* and strong democracy with its emphases on problem solving, participation, evolving process, and emergent community, can both provide key ingredients for such a new synthesis. I do not believe that it would be or should be altogether new. Many of the traditional virtues of republicanism can be seen in both pragmatism and strong democracy; certainly both echo many of the themes of the Anti-Federalists and the Traditionalists. One can make a strong case that our constitutional design, in its totality and in its consequence, is a "process" form of government.

One can read Madison's discussion of the economic basis of factions and think one is reading Karl Marx; or can read his discussion of how to balance interest against interest and set ambition against ambition and think one has picked up Machiavelli or Hobbes. But as a whole it was a government design that is not that far from some of the key ideas of the Anti-Federalists or Barber's strong democracy. It could only function if men and women of honor and civic virtue, acting upon self-interest *rightly understood,* would engage in *deliberation* and arrive at the collective good (Hart, 1984; Tocqueville, 1990). The government they designed could not possibly function effectively without deliberation that developed the "right understanding" of self-interest. We are seeing the proof of that as our Hamiltonian-Madisonian public philosophy has let such aspects of our founding discourse slip into oblivion, to be replaced by the assumption that our constitutional order is a kind of institutional sausage grinder into which unmediated interests are poured on the assumption that the machinery—with the assistance of some benign and invisible hand—will somehow produce the common good, or at least an output that will not result in dissidents stacking arms or building bombs. Since the Oklahoma City bombing, we are suddenly and frighteningly no longer sure of that latter point.

The notion has been lost that the common good is arrived at largely by deliberation for which the institutional machinery provides an appropriate context. Our Founders knew it was the deliberation, as much as the institutional machinery along with good administration, that would secure the Republic. We have come to rely too much on an assumed providence and the machinery and now both are cast in doubt. I submit that today we have at hand the conceptual ingredients to develop a better balanced public philosophy that can serve as public administration's normative grounding and the basis for a new mode of politics.

The Value of Explicit Normative
Grounding to Our Many "Approaches"

A more balanced public philosophy that can serve as a normative grounding for public administration and more ontological candor in our academic discourse will not mean adoption of some common paradigm or approach. A practice of a public administration that is evocative of human and democratic development and that lies at the heart of the governance process will generate more than sufficient questions and problems to which those of us who study it can apply our various approaches about which we have been writing and arguing (e.g., interpretivism, radical humanism, rational choice, etc.). But with normative grounding in a more balanced and pragmatic public philosophy concerned with strong democracy and problem solving we will be better able to appreciate that all have some value, depending on the level of analysis, question, or problem to be addressed; all our approaches represent some aspect of our multidimensional, socially constructed (or, if one prefers, socially perceived) reality.

All of the approaches encompass *parts* of the *potentially* shared vision of what we want, or what would be desirable to have in an American public administration that could be perceived as a legitimate institution of democratic constitutional governance. But as things stand now these are fragments of a vision—a vision that is not currently shared. If we could come together around a shared public philosophy, those ideas of what are or would be desirable could frame many of our questions, our efforts as practitioners and academics; help define our problems, guide our curiosity and inquiry as well as our work as practitioners. Now, however, these choices are being framed on the academic dimension of our field by competition among paradigms or "approaches," career pressures and ambitions, institutional cliques and snobbish, assumptions of irreconcilable epistemological differences, unconscious or recondite norms and values, or vague appeals to "advancing our knowledge" or "searching for Truth" (mind the quotation marks and the capital T) (Kickert, 1994; McSwite, in press; Stokes, 1986).

On the practitioner side, the normative choices are being shaped by: a public philosophy that has become dysfunctional, an outmoded conventional wisdom, irresponsible and ideological partisanship among elected officials, the bipartisan bureaucrat-bashing and antigovernment syndromes, interest groups, slavish adoption of business fads and values, and general demoralization and career angst.

These conditions are largely attributable to the fact that, in typical American fashion, we have put the cart before the horse. Without knowing what public administration has been historically, what it is now, and what we want it to be—before we have even conceived of a role in governance that would be seen as legitimate in our government of separate institutions sharing power—we have been busily applying first one and then another approach to this misfounded, ill-defined, and widely misunderstood subject in the name of understanding, explanation, and prediction. Some explicit normative grounding for the theorizing, practice, and praxis of public administration is surely in order, indeed overdue. It should be prefatory to (not more important than) other approaches and concerns.

A Sampler of Ontological Disclosure

My original intent in this part of the chapter was to be as frank about my ontological stance as possible, to indicate where I stood on epistemology and move on to speak candidly about how I saw our politics and government today and the place (or more specifically the predicament) of public administration in it. I hoped to experiment with ontological disclosure and see if it enhanced or disrupted what passes for discourse these days. It is now painfully clear to me, however, that the confines of a book chapter do not provide much room for such an ambitious enterprise.

I can only present a few samples of what I mean by ontological disclosure and some notes on a public philosophy. These are offered in a spirit of experimentation and of encouraging discourse. Some of it will reinforce and make clear why I have taken the positions I have in the preceding part of the chapter; and some of it will be suggestive of some of the content that a new and more balanced public philosophy might take. Clearly, however, I will have to pursue these topics in a more accommodating format at some future point.

I wish to add one prefatory comment. Over the years I have been proud to call myself a "pracademic," and I like to believe I have done enough administration, consulting, and organizational and policy analysis to merit the label. No matter how academic some of the foregoing and that which follows may sound, I have tried to write it bearing in mind the practitioner as the intended and ultimate recipient, if not through these printed words then translated or relayed through the words of others. In doing so I have tried to keep in mind the question with which the practitioner is always confronted. That question may come from the far reaches of philosophy wrapped in abstractions, but comes down to the practitioner in the form of: What should I say or do *next?* It is that immediacy, that compelling urgency to bring theory and reflection to bear in action, and in the wake of action to reflect and adjust theory, that makes the field fascinating and challenging to me, and I imagine and hope for many of you as well.

What follows "ain't purty," as some in Blacksburg might say. It lacks grace and its parsimony may mean that it is less clear or persuasive than a fuller treatment would be. However, rough and disjointed though it may appear, it does represent a sampling of the kind of disclosure in which I feel we in the field must engage, and it suggests some of the elements of a public philosophy in which to ground public administration. Finally, I must make clear that what follows samples *my* thoughts, *my* reflections, and *my* experience as a "pracademic"; in other words, *my* ontological stance at this time.

▇ A Sampler of Ontological Disclosure

All of us, even those who have studied organizations, institutions, and administration for an entire career, differ in our views of them, particularly those which are a part of government. This is probably true for several reasons, but primarily because we perceive so much to be at stake—taxes, welfare checks, air traffic safety, police and fire protection, education of our children, and so on, and so forth, but also because we work in organizations and our work is so integral to our self-identity and to our search for meaning for our lives. We invest so much of our time, selves, egos, ambitions, hopes, and fears in our "work." As Robert Lane has put it, "It is most often in the sphere of work, not consumption, that the greatest subjective well-being lies" (p. 6). Finally, so much is at stake in organizations because politics and government, which are organizational by nature, rest on an emotional substructure. As Murray Edelman (1967) has said: "Politics is for most of us a passing parade of abstract symbols, yet a parade which our experience teaches us to be a benevolent or malevolent force that can be close to omnipotent. Though they may strive to be "objective," students of organizations and public administration cannot escape having their views shaped by the powerful emotions that derive from such deep psychic investments" (p. 5).

But psychic investment is only the basis for the *intensity* of our differing views of organizations and public administration. What is the basis for the *difference?* Why do some of us see these phenomena so negatively and others so positively? The answer lies in our views of nature and of human nature: Serious theorizing about public administration must therefore start with these matters. Consider, if you will, the following notes con-

cerning my views on nature, human nature, and its relevance to organizations, and therefore to public administration.

— A fundamental difference among people probably lies in their view of nature. Some of us assume a fundamental order in nature which may seem to have pockets of disorder, but only (we assume) because we have imperfect knowledge. We assume that as our knowledge grows disorder recedes and more of the order of nature is revealed. Others of us assume a fundamentally different perspective: a nature which is basically disorder punctuated by pockets of order which we have largely created with our minds and projected upon disorderly nature. Since humans intend instrumental rationality in collectivities, these fundamentally different ontologies clash in matters such as strategic planning, budgeting, managing, controlling, etc.—fundamental questions of institutional life. Those who posit a world of order believe such things have more meaning and importance than those who posit a world of disorder. The latter believe that in a world of disorder, people must create their own order—their own reality, through social processes based on authentic relations rather than reified social structures that some of us impose on others of us.

— As for myself, I began adult life assuming a world of order with pockets of disorder which I expected to help clear up over the course of my lifetime. I have steadily fallen away from that ontological position and now assume a world of rich, if sometimes disturbing disorder that is alternately terrifying and beautiful. I am not prepared to say that the mainstays of institutional life or what we call management are meaningless. Rather I have come to feel that authentic relations matter far more than these. To the extent that those traditional mainstays can enhance authentic relations or grow out of such relations they can be of value if not reified into obstacles to authentic relations.

— At this point, we can still say that humans seem to have developed language and symbolic interactions to a significantly higher degree than other animals. Our mental capacity is developed along at least three major dimensions: memory to enable us to deal with the past, reason to deal with the present, and imagination to deal with the future. But more than these, humans also seem to have a greater capacity for reflection (to set ourselves apart mentally and contemplate a situation) and for reflexivity (to act upon the basis of our reflection and, having acted, to readjust our thinking on the basis of experience).

— Like other organisms we need to develop as individuals and strive to live as long as possible, but we seem to have a much greater consciousness of the inevitability and impending nature of our death. It is this consciousness of impending death and its effects upon us that is widely believed to be a major distinguishing feature of the human condition. More certainly, it can be said that consciousness of our impending death gives a special dimension to our lives, especially from middle age onward. Some would call that dimension ironic, some poignant, some tragic, others label it a permanent condition of "existential angst."

— I believe the "discovery of self" and the "search for meaning in our lives" are uniquely human characteristics that provide a complex, sometimes barely discernible and conscious—but nonetheless fundamental—factor in all our thought and action, including those related to organizational life and public administration. Although the quest for self-discovery and meaning must begin in developing our autonomy as individuals, because of our social nature it ultimately is achieved largely in and through relationships with others; that is—the quest is not monologic, rather, it is dialogic. Moreover, because the struggle for self-discovery and search for meaning involves others, it involves organizations and institutions.

— We humans strive for individuality and autonomy, but also for relationships and shared dependence. We are inescapably social beings and therefore much of our context is social. We both shape that social context and are shaped by it. So it is with our social constructs—our organizations or, more precisely, our institutions, including governmental—we shape them and in turn are shaped by them.

— Both our social nature and our drive for individuation create problems for us. Our experience as humans thus requires both the growth of individual autonomy and of social relationships to realize our fullest human potential to discover meaning in our lives. Our identity can only take shape and our self can only be found through others, and our ability to relate to others is dependent on a well-defined self.

— Much of the social interaction in the contemporary world occurs in and through the social constructs we call organizations, but this sets up a fundamental tension between the individual and organizations. We individuals seeking self-discovery and meaning for our lives need autonomy, growth, and opportunities for individual creativity. At the same time our social selves need: stability and coherence; to encounter authority; to learn to lead/follow/cooperate, disagree; and create together. There can be no denying that large organizations provide many people with a means of maturation and human development, but there is also no denying that given the way most of them are currently constituted they tend to thwart fully rounded human development. Nor is there any denying that public organizations too often engage in self-serving behavior and serve powerful interests and dominant elites too readily and too well.

— As social creatures, we can and do give up much of our natural agency and individual autonomy and usually willingly place ourselves under the influence of organizational cultures, symbols, and values. This can be done for both laudable and despicable purposes. Organizations are socially constructed realities that lead people to see themselves and the world in particular ways. They can influence people to commit selfless acts of heroism and/or senseless acts of barbarism. This adds a special dimension to the moral problems organizations create for human beings.

— Organizations generate their own inertia as a result of their emphases on stability, coherence, and regulation, or their tendency not to disturb entrenched interests. Some hold, therefore, that they impede necessary social, political, and economic change, thereby increasing human suffering. At the same time, others point to the inertia as a source of desirable "natural conservativeness" that keeps a society from disintegration and chaos. Still others hold that if there is to be social, political, and economic change and innovation it is, and must be, done through organizations or institutions. Each perspective sees organizations in a different moral light. Whether organizations block change or spearhead it, serve the broader public interest or the interests of dominant elites is probably dependent on other factors as yet poorly understood, rather than inherent characteristics of organizations. What would seem both appropriate and necessary is that organizations (especially governmental) be able to serve both the few and the many—the powerful and the weak, foster both stability and change—both coherence and emergence.

— American public organizations present special problems of inertia and innovation because they must operate within governments of separate institutions that must share power. American public organizations must be legally subordinate, responsive, and responsible to several institutions—that is, they must operate in a context of polycentric power in which they are an agent for multiple principals, and in which law is of special importance. Numerous forces in this political/legal context work toward inertia, but at the same time public organizations are expected to be instruments of change in dealing with some of society's most perplexing problems.

Human beings have a remarkable capacity for social construction or social perception. We create our selves, communities, organizations, institutions, and societies and reify them—endow them with varying "realities" and meanings. This creates ontological and epistemological problems for us as we seek to understand our various social constructs. People's sense of being, their concepts of truth and reality and how they can know them, vary sharply and widely. Consider the implications for public administration.

— Our capacity for natural agency and our propensity to pass judgments on ourselves and others means that understanding ourselves and our world is difficult at best and implies that circumstances allowing "objective" ways of acquiring and validating knowledge about social phenomena are limited. Students of organizations and public administration differ sharply, however, on just how difficult it is and how limiting the circumstances are. Some still have confidence in functionalism and positivism, which began with Descartes and the Age of Reason and eventually spread to social science in the mid-20th century. Persons of this persuasion believe that we can and must describe, understand, explain, predict, and control social phenomena in the same way some believe we can the phenomena of the so-called natural sciences. Others, in growing numbers, point to the asymmetry between observed behavior and intention or the meaning of behavior. There is also the matter of subjects dissembling, engaging in obfuscation, or being victims of false consciousness. And finally they hold that human nature makes it impossible for those studying social phenomena to divorce themselves from the objects of their study, and they point out that the effect of the observer upon the observed has been increasingly recognized in studying the phenomena of the natural sciences as well.

— A growing number of students of organizations and public administration insist that because of the nature of our subject, positivist-behaviorist or so-called objective methods of analysis must be augmented by or combined with the study of (a) subjective meanings that people attach to their own actions and the actions of others; (b) the intersubjective reality they create or discover among themselves; and (c) the interrelationship between these socially constructed realities and the physical world.

Others insist that we must understand the role of organizations and public administration in serving some classes and elites at the expense of others and doing so in the name of rationality, efficiency, and science. Still others insist that we must understand that the nature of organizations (most certainly those that are hierarchical) is inimicable to human spirit, development, and search for meaning. And, finally, there are those who believe that competition and self-interest are the most fundamental of human traits, the market the most constructive institutional embodiment of these traits, and acceptance of these "laws" is the best way to understand (and to design or improve) organizations, economies, and society.

— The dominant social theory (functionalism) that supports "objective" ways of knowing is also under increasing attack for its acceptance of existing social "facts" and value consensus as given and its focus on the study of the behaviors and beliefs required to sustain those conditions. It is thus charged with failing to comprehend significant changes in the normative structure of society or the potential or need for change. Functionalism is also criticized by some for ignoring the social construction of realities. Increasingly, students of organizations have come to see them as intersubjective realities that are in dynamic and simultaneous states of construction, decay, and repair. At a more fundamental level, functionalism—and science and technology from which it is derived—is increasingly criticized for alienating humans from their "inner selves," one another, their work, and from nature. And, finally, functionalism is charged with failing to accommodate relatively new postmodernist advances in the natural sciences variously referred to as chaos theory, quantum physics, advanced systems theory, or complexity theory.

Public administration as a field of study must be sensitive to these charges and the changes taking place in both the natural and social sciences. When doing so leads to better understanding or action that advances the human condition, we should be in the forefront of discussing the challenges of different epistemologies and methods that are rigorous, but that go beyond the limits of functionalism or logical positivism.

I believe that, ontologically, we must come to terms with the possible existence of multiple social realities in a field of study as broad and phenomena as complex as those encompassed in public administration. Although there may be a physical reality (at least at a certain level of analysis) that we experience and for which we have developed conventions of intersubjectivity we call science, and technologies that enable us to build skyscrapers and cure diseases, still there are conceivably as many *social* realities as there are people, social constructs, and situations. Despite the difficulty of studying and acting meaningfully in the social world, there nonetheless is a practical level at which we often experience that world and that is more than simply the projection of each individual mind—realities with characteristics and consequences our experience tells us are significant for us. If explored at a deeper level, the same is true in the natural sciences. One can experience reality at the level of a civil engineer or at the level of a quantum physicist. Whereas the ontology and epistemology of the former seems tangible and enduring, the physical world of the latter may dissolve into chaos or something beyond our comprehension.

It is useful to bear in mind at least three domains of reality that are useful to us: the "my" world of the individual, which we generally treat as subjective-expressive; "the" world of external nature, which we generally treat as "objective" and "factual"; and the "our" world of collectivities, which we generally treat as interactive intersubjective. The world of public administration as we experience it encompasses these realities and more—simultaneously and iteratively. That makes ontologies, epistemologies, and methods of analysis ever problematic.

Of primary importance among the many factors that influence our forms of government and governance are our conceptions and beliefs about human nature and sociability. Consider the following notes.

— Given the moral dimension of human existence, we tend to have varying outlooks on human nature—some seeing it as basically good or tending in that direction, others seeing it as basically "bad" or so tending. We also differ over how malleable (improvable or degradable) human nature is. Probably the most persistent view of human nature across cultures and eras has been one that sees it as being of limited malleability and characterized by a basic duality—that humans have the capacity for both good and evil, or that their better qualities are limited but can be expanded through growth, search for meaning, overcoming narcissism, or adherence to religious teachings.

— Given the persistence and prevalence of the duality view of human nature, we look to religion, varying socioeconomic arrangements and institutions, and particularly government either to control or to shape human nature, or to allow, foster, or evoke development of human nature's positive aspects. Which alternative verb is chosen is indicative of a person's view of human nature and which way it is tending. I describe myself as a *very* cautious optimist as to the improvability of human nature. I would agree with Madison that when one must rely on human nature for positive social outcomes, history has taught us the advisability of auxiliary precautions.

━━ Notes on a Public Philosophy for P.A.

— The purpose of government is viewed in a variety of ways, but generally in those societies aspiring to democracy it is seen as not only to control the darker aspects of human nature but also to allow and evoke the better. As societies secularize and modernize, the responsibilities of both controlling antisocial behavior and/or fostering an improved quality of life and human development fall more heavily upon government as other institutions such as village, clan, or tribe atrophy.

— Governments are generally expected to play a preeminent role in creating and maintaining conditions that nurture other institutions capable of controlling nature or influencing human development. They are, in other words, the framers of society's fundamental conditions, boundaries, and basic rules of association. Experience with varieties of despotism and degrees of totalitarianism has shown, however, that government alone is incapable, in the long run, of bearing sole responsibility for controlling human nature and/or fostering human development—or even for fulfilling our need for sociability.

— Governments aspiring to be democratic must first create honest, competent governments that citizens believe are concerned for their well-being. But beyond that, such governments must create "civil societies" in which un-coerced human association and relational networks—the "other institutions" that play an essential part in controlling human nature or fostering human development—can thrive. These "other institutions" include economic, familial, social-fraternal, religious, and those that are political in purpose but nongovernmental. They are expressions of our primal sociability—the means of freely associating, communicating with, and caring for one another in cooperation, conflict, competition, and compromise. If one believes human nature must be controlled, these institutions are essential to democratic government as a means of creating conditions of plurality and countervailing power, and by providing a host of other nongovernmental institutions that absorb potentially destructive energies or temper the darker side of our nature. If one believes that human nature is to grow, mature, and seek meaning, then the associations of a rich civil society provide the means of doing so.

— Honest, competent, caring government undergirded by a rich civil society, an economic system that meets basic needs and allows for a modicum of consumer choice, capital accumulation, and investor initiative, socioeconomic mobility, and a large and stable middle class are the necessary yet insufficient conditions of a democratic government, institutions, and public administration; in other words—a democratic state. A democratic state must of course perform the framing role spoken of earlier—providing "the setting of settings." It must, for example, devise and make operational with a minimum of coercion and a maximum of trust, a pattern of relations between the state and the economy, the state and church, the state and citizens, citizens to one another—relationships among governmental structures and processes and citizens (in other words, a democratic public administration).

But in the end the democratic state must not only provide the "framework for civil society," it must also be the upholder of the common good, the "instrument of the struggle" to create social, political, and economic conditions that: (a) improve the human condition psychologically, materially, and even spiritually; (b) protect and advance basic human/democratic values such as liberty and equality; (c) foster a balance between liberty and order; (d) enable citizens to define and meet the needs they have in common while protecting individual rights and liberties (especially as they bear upon the continued efficacy of democratic processes); (e) value diversity, tolerance, opportunity for free inquiry, open communication or dialogue, willingness to compromise, sense of individual significance, individual responsibility, participation, and concern for the whole; and (f) enable citizens to discover meaning in their lives and thereby realize their fullest possible potential as humans and as citizens in a democracy.

A government dedicated to these values and purposes has the best chance of evoking not only the trust and support of people but also the finest and fullest potential of both individuals and their community.

— American government was designed to achieve the purposes of limited republican (not democratic) government by constitutionally guaranteeing civil liberties against encroachment from governments and other sources, by providing for election of key officials, and by systematically fragmenting power within government—(a) among branches of government with different constituencies and legitimacy bases that must share power in order to govern; and (b) among levels of governments, also with different constituency bases, that perform both different and overlapping functions cooperatively and in conflict.

From the early 19th century onward we have made a series of adaptations (extension of franchise, development of parties/conventions/primaries, popular election of senators, etc.) that have been aimed at democratizing the republic. How successful we have been is debatable and depends on the criteria for judgment. Public administration (which in our Founding was seen as synonymous with good government) was implicitly but clearly important in the original republic, but its role and importance were not as clear in a democratizing republic. When democracy, mass immigration, and social turmoil resulted in machine politics and corruption, public administration was self-consciously conceived of as a part of an elitist reform movement, rather than something indigenous to our democratic republic's process of governance with its polycentric power. We must reconceptualize and refound it as the valuable core of governance in a constitutional, democratic republic—de jure responsible to all branches, de facto semi-autonomous but constrained by professional allegiance to constitutional values.

— American cultural mythology portrays the American economic system as "free enterprise capitalism" and as the major support for democracy. Though there may be some synchronicity between capitalism and democracy, they are by no means synonymous nor interdependent. Our political economy is in fact a mixture of free enterprise, government regulation, and intervention and limited social security programs. It generates great wealth for a small percentage of the populace, considerable class mobility and social security for most, but at the cost of the continued existence of a large number of very poor who are excluded by their circumstances from significant participation in mainstream economic, social, and political life.

Our economic system is more accurately described as consumer capitalism blended with aspects (relatively few and ungenerous by standards of Western democracies) of a welfare state—a blend that is capable of generating consumer demand through advertising rather than simply responding to such demand and that provides certain minimal social programs that mitigate some of the harsher aspects of capitalism. It narrows the definition and scope of democracy to proper procedures rather than a fuller democracy with greater participation and material equality.

Our economic system (or better said, our political economy) obscures the meaning of democracy by linking the ideas of citizenship with the role of customer, and confusing product and lifestyle choices with policy choices that affect the quality of our lives. Our political system operates (largely unconsciously, systemically, and on the basis of anticipated reactions) so that the privileged position of economic elites is seldom threatened; and the political efficacy of middle and lower classes is increasingly limited in a variety of informal ways and by seemingly "natural" circumstances as one descends the socioeconomic scale.

— In most democracies the governments have assumed a significant role in managing their economies, and political parties have taken positions that have resulted in amelioration of negative effects of the market and the articulation of public (collective) needs as a counterweight to private (individual) wants. In the United States this trend has not been nearly as extensive. There is still growing ideological contention as to the degree of responsibility government should assume in ameliorating the negative externalities of the market and meeting collective needs. Many of America's present problems seem unlikely to be solved without a better consensus on these issues and the development of some strong collective counterforce to the extreme individualism/consumerism fostered by our consumer capitalism. A strong democratic public administration concerned with the most effective means of accomplishing ends—regardless of whether this entails public, private, nonprofit, or a mixture—and primarily concerned with a positive relation to citizens that facilitates articulation of collective needs, growth of the individual, and the enhancement of the commonweal, could be such a force.

— Unlike other democracies whose public administration generally evolved from the monarchical household and which are supported by a concept of the state, the American institution, though always present, only at last emerged as an important and self-conscious institution in reaction to corrupt political machines. Consequently, public administration was linked with reformism, scientific management, and business efficiency rather than the Constitution and governance as other government institutions have been. What has come to be a critical institution of government was therefore *mis*founded, and though it is to a considerable degree a consequence of reformist symbol manipulations and partisan machinations, those associated with it largely still think of themselves and generally present themselves as "neutrally competent" subordinates of the chief executive, concerned primarily with efficiency, economy, and effectiveness, not unlike business.

— The legitimacy of all our governmental institutions and leaders is declining, but this decline has been most severe for public administration. The distinction between politics and administration is no longer (if it ever was) clear and does not provide grounds for definition of a legitimate role in governance distinct from, but equal to, that of elected officials. Nor does it provide grounds on which career officials can build cooperative interaction with appointed partisan political executives. In short, on these and many other grounds it is inappropriate for developing either a more democratic public administration or a more effective system of governance. What little legitimacy it has enjoyed was derived from the administrative management model and has become embedded in a conventional wisdom, or logic-in-use, that seems to defy change despite significant changes in our society, our government, and our knowledge of a host of matters impacting on public administration ranging from changes in society to new insights into organizational design and management practices.

Thus the institutional presidency and the field of public administration were closely linked through the 1950s and most of the 1960s. That relationship gradually deteriorated through the late 1960s and the 1970s until a nadir was reached in the Reagan administration. Much of this stemmed from the fact that partisan division of government increased during these years. In the wake of presidential and congressional mid-term elections, the executive and legislative branches were held by opposing parties 14 times from 1952 to 1994 and unified only seven times. This means it became contested ground in partisan warfare—the object of control by all, trusted by none.

Now more than ever public administration needs the appropriate normative theoretical underpinning it has never had and a new conventional wisdom or logic-in-use derived from it. That normative theoretical base must support a legitimate role for public administration and be grounded in democratic governance, constitutionality, law, and pragmatic philosophy rather than management concepts misplaced from business *(. . . to be continued at another time and place. . . .)*

▬ Conclusion

The above offers only the barest suggestion of what kinds of matters a better balanced public philosophy might address. It must be one that pulls us back from the escalating ideological shrillness in our politics, overcomes some of the worst deficiencies of pluralism, and brings about some abatement of both the expectations placed upon, and the powers being ceded de facto to, the president. It will not surprise the reader who has patiently come this far when I suggest that a more democratic public administration at the core of governance is one of the best ways to achieve such results.

Other Western democracies have largely put the extremes of ideology behind them. And though in several instances their politicians are seeking to avoid tax increases and to blame public administrators for the high cost of their welfare states, they have never gone so far as we have in devaluing, decapitalizing, and denigrating public administrators. It seems likely they never will in light of their positive traditions of the state and their general acceptance of their governments' role in socioeconomic matters.

Though we are unlikely to follow their example in establishing relatively centralized welfare states, we do have to come to a level of maturity that lowers ideological temperatures and recognize that amelioration of our wicked socioeconomic problems cannot be done by the market or government alone. Rather, this can best be done in the problem-solving spirit of American pragmatism and with government evoking conditions of human and democratic development rather than attempting to steer—government that has an effective and democratic public administration at its core. To put it bluntly, America is going to have to come of age—grow up—and when it does, we hope the ideas contained in this volume will be at hand and of use.

Notes

1. Jun (1994) takes his definition of *praxis* from Aristotle, for whom praxis meant a special kind of human activity devoted to political life as contrasted with contemplation or abstract reasoning (*theoria*). For Aristotle, political life as practical activity (praxis) implied performance of an activity with moral significance.

2. I maintain that the conventional wisdom for most practitioners is still that developed by Luther Gulick (1937) in the *Papers on the Science of Administration*. This, despite all that has been written, learned, and practiced differently since then.

3. One of the best analyses that shows how far a public organization is from business is Terry Moe's "The Politics of Bureaucratic Structure" (1989). In addition to the things they should be, public organizations are contested ground in partisan struggles to maximize one party's continued influence at the expense of opponents.

4. My colleague John Rohr suggests that before a government can be anything, it must have the qualities of justice and wisdom. Far be it for me to quarrel with this. I simply maintain a democratic, constitutional republic must be concerned with the 3-Rs over the 3-Es, though not unmindful of the latter.

5. Other approaches are equally important though they do not explicitly claim to be working toward *a* theory—policy analysis, public management, or public affairs. See Donald Stokes's *The Changing World of the Public Executive* (1994). Moreover, in our theorizing we apparently feel duty-bound to do our best to trash all other approaches before then presenting our own with roll of drums and flourish of trumpets. This may not be the most efficacious way to try to advance inquiry and understanding, not to mention practice and praxis. Though no one would suggest that all ideas or approaches are "born equal," if there are multiple realities, or multiple perspectives on different aspects of reality, then all other approaches do not have to be ritualistically denigrated in order for another good one to be useful. Our excuse for this ritualistic theoretical cannibalism has been that our field is pre-paradigmatic and an assumption that this is how academia "works." Perhaps we ought to reexamine our excuses and our mode of discourse (O. C. McSwite, in press).

6. For my entire career I have listened to people complain about the paper-giving panel format. Everyone seems to agree it is the worst format for authentic dialogue ever imagined. But for a variety of reasons, not the least of which is economics, no one seriously tries to change the format.

7. I realize the phrase "social science as public philosophy" will make many colleagues uncomfortable. Some will be concerned with reserving "philosophy" for a loftier realm and the likes of Aristotle, Hobbes, and others; others will be concerned that the term "social science" connotes a naive positivism that persists in believing the social sciences should and can mimic the natural sciences. I understand these concerns, but have not been able to solve all the limitations of our language.

8. Some persons might argue that we in fact have evolved from a health care into a "sick care" system. Our inattention to preventive medicine, our focus on "disease," and our heroic expenditures of money and energy in the final months of life could be cited as evidence.

9. One can also argue with some force that because we are educating persons for a profession that serves the state it is not feasible, or not appropriate, for public administration academics to attempt to "lift the veil" of society's false consciousness, either for their practitioner students or for themselves. But this could only be the case if we were not educators and researchers with a professional obligation to search for knowledge, but rather were only trainers transmitting knowledge rather than creating it; or if values were immutable and transcontextual in their meaning, and if we wished to produce professionals who are rigid, unreflexive automatons. Our student practitioners, however, need to be reflexive with the regime values of the Constitution, higher authorities, their experience, and with citizens.

10. I say "largely" only because I would not want us to adopt totally the medical school model. It has its pathologies. See the limitations created by the field's epistemological consensus in the text that follows.

11. It is not just coincidence that Aid for Dependent Children, Medicaid, and Women, Infants, and Children are always the first to feel the budget cutter's knife. The program recipients seldom write letters or threaten to withdraw campaign support.

12. A conclusion from which I demur for several reasons.

13. Interestingly, Robert Dahl (1994) has now begun to voice his concerns about the pathologies of pluralism. It goes without saying that the ideology of capitalism that separates politics from economics makes Hamiltonianism and Jeffersonianism feasible. It, and individualism just for socioeconomic differences and indeed inequities.

14. The assignment of the label of Anti-Federalist to Jefferson may raise some questions because he was abroad as Ambassador to France at the time most of the Anti-Federalist responses to the *Federalist Papers* appeared. He also served as Washington's Secretary of State. It is clear, however, that his sympathies were with the Anti-Federalists, and the Democratic Republican party he headed was the intellectual and political descendant of the Anti-Federalists.

━ References

Arendt, H. (1977). *Between past and future: Eight exercises in political thought.* New York: Penguin Books.

Barber, B. R. (1984). *Strong democracy: Participatory politics for a new age.* Berkeley: University of California Press.

Beach, J. C., Carter, E. C., Dede, M. J., Goodsell, C. T., Guignard, R.-M. M., Haraway, W. M., Morgan, B. N., Murthi, M., & Sweet, V. K. (in press). *Administration and Society.*

Bellah, R. N., Madsen, R., Sullivan, W. M., Swidler, A., & Tipton, S. M. (1985). *Habits of the heart: Individualism and commitment in American life.* New York: Harper & Row.

Bosso, J. (1991). Government and democratic governance into the twenty-first century. In J. C. Shea (Ed.), *Arguments on American Politics* (pp. 5-16). Pacific Grove, CA: Brooks/Cole.

Bozeman, B. (Ed.). (1987). *All organizations are public: Bridging public and private organization theories.* San Francisco: Jossey-Bass.

Burrell, G., & Morgan, G. (1979). *Sociological paradigms and organizational analysis: Elements of the sociology of corporate life.* London: Heinemann.

Dahl, R. A., et al. (1994). *The new American political disorder: An essay.* Washington, DC: Government Printing Office.

Denhardt, R. (1990). Public administration theory: The state of the discipline. In N. B. Lynn & A. Wildavsky (Eds.), *Public Administration: The State of the Discipline* (p. 351). Chatham, NJ: Chatham House Publishers, Inc.

Dudley, L., & Wamsley, G. L. (in press). Organizational design and government reorganization: Sixty years and we "still don't get it." *International Journal of Public Administration.*

Edelman, M. (1967). *Symbolic uses of politics.* Urbana: University of Illinois Press.

Flower, E., & Murphy, M. G. (1977). *A history of philosophy in America.* New York: Capricorn Books.

Gawthrop, L. C. (1994). In the service of democracy. *International Journal of Public Administration, 17*(12), 2195-2229.

Gladden, E. N. (1972). *A history of public administration.* London: Cass.

Gleick, J. (1987). *Chaos: Making a new science.* New York: Penguin Books.

Gulick, L. (1937). Science, values, & public administration. In L. Gulick & L. Urwick (Eds.), *Papers on the science of administration.* New York: Institute of Public Administration.

Hart, D. K. (1984). The virtuous citizen, the honorable bureaucrat, and "public" administration. *Public Administration Review, 44*(2), 111-120.

Hill, L. B. (1991, August-September). *The refusal of American politicians to take bureaucracy seriously.* Paper presented at the 1991 Annual Meeting of the American Political Science Association, Washington, DC.

Hill, L. B. (Ed.). (1992). *The state of public bureaucracy.* Armonk, NY: M. E. Sharpe.

Hummel, R. P. (1993). A call for a philosophy of administration. *Administrative Theory & Praxis, 15*(1), 52-54.

James, W. (1907). *Pragmatism: A new name for some old ways of thinking.* Cambridge, MA: Riverside Press.

Jun, J. S. (1993). What is philosophy of administration? *Administrative Theory and Praxis, 15*(1), 46-52

Jun, J. S. (1994). On administrative praxis: The concept of praxis. *Administrative Theory and Practice, 16*(2), 201-207.

Kickert, W. J. M. (1994). *Public governance in the Netherlands: An alternative to Anglo-American "managerialism."* Manuscript submitted for publication. (Contact author at Department of Public Administration, Erasmus University Rotterdam, P.O. Box 1738, 3000 DR Rotterdam, The Netherlands, for a copy.)

Kirlin, J. (1995). The big questions of public administration. *Public Administration Review.*

Landau, M. (1995). Conversation with author.

Leiserson, A. (1942). *Administrative regulation: A study in representation of interests.* Chicago: University of Chicago Press.

Lowi, T. J. (1979). *The end of liberalism: The second republic of the United States* (2nd ed.). New York: Norton.

Luttwak, E. N. (1994, November 27). Will success spoil America? Why the polls don't get our real crisis of values. *Washington Post,* pp. C1, C4.

McSwite, O. C. (in press). *The legitimacy issue in American public administration: A discourse analysis.* Thousand Oaks, CA: Sage.

Milward, H. B., & Rainey, H. G. (1982). Don't blame the bureaucracy! *Journal of Public Policy, 3,* 149-168.

Milward, H. B. & Wamsley, G. L. (1984). Policy subsystems, networks, and the tools of public management. In R. Eyestone (Ed.), *Public policy formation and implementation* (pp. 3-25). Greenwich, CT: JAI Press.

Moe, T. M. (1989). The politics of bureaucratic structure. In J. E. Chubb & P. E. Petersen (Eds.), *Can the government govern?* (pp. 267-329). Washington, DC: Brookings Institution.

Nigro, L. G., & Richardson, W. D. (1987). Self-interest properly understood: The American character and public administration. *Administration and Society, 19*(2), 157-177.

Ostrom, V. (1974). *The intellectual crisis in American public administration* (rev. ed.). University: University of Alabama Press.

O'Toole, L. J., Jr. (1984). American public administration and the idea of reform. *Administration and Society, 16*(2), 141-166.

Peirce, C. S. (1931-1935). In Hartshorne & P. Weiss (Eds.), *Collected papers of Charles Sanders Peirce, Vol. 5.* Cambridge, MA: Harvard University Press.

Perdue, W. D. (1986). *Sociological theory.* Palo Alto, CA: Mayfield.

Phillips, K. (1990). *The politics of rich and poor: Wealth and the American electorate in the Reagan aftermath.* New York: Random House.

Putnam, R. D. (1995). Bowling alone revisited. *The Responsive Community, 5*(2), 18-33.

Putnam, R. D. (1996, Winter). The strange disappearance of civic America. *The American Prospect,* pp. 34-48.

Reich, R. (1991, February). Notes on "The Real Economy." *The Atlantic,* pp. 35-52.

Rohr, J. A. (1986). *To run a constitution: The legitimacy of the administrative state.* Lawrence: University of Kansas Press.

Royce, J. (1969). *The basic writings of Josiah Royce.* Chicago: University of Chicago Press.

Salamon, L. M. (1981). Rethinking public management: Third party government and the changing forms of government action. *Public Policy, 29*(3), 255-275.

Sandel, M. J. (1996, March). America's search for a new public philosophy. *The Atlantic Monthly,* pp. 57-74.

Sedgwick, J. L. (1983, September). *Human nature and bureaucracy: Founding versus progressive views.* A paper presented at the annual meeting of the American Political Science Association, Chicago.

Shields, P. M. (in press). *Pragmatism: Exploring public administration's policy imprint.* Manuscript submitted for publication.

Stokes, D. E. (1986). Political and organizational analysis in the policy curriculum. *Journal of Policy Analysis and Management, 6*(1), 44-55.

Stokes, D. E. (1994, December). *The changing world of the public executive.* Paper presented at the Conference on Public Affairs and Management in the Twenty-First Century, New York.

Thurow, L. C. (1980). *The zero-sum society: Distribution and the possibilities for economic change.* New York: Basic Books.

Tocqueville, A. de (1990). *Democracy in America.* New York: Vintage.

Urban, M. E. (1982). *The ideology of administration: American and Soviet cases.* Albany: State University of New York Press.

Van Riper, P. P. (1987). The American administrative state: Wilson and the founders. In R. C. Chandler (Ed.), *A centennial history of the American administrative state* (pp. 3-36). New York: Macmillan.

Waldo, D. (1952, March). Development of theory of democratic administration. *American Political Science Review, Vol. XLVI,* 81-103.

Waldo, D. (1984). Woodrow Wilson and the "identity crisis" of public administration. In J. Rabin & J. S. Brown (Eds.), *Politics and administration: Woodrow Wilson and American public administration.* New York: Marcel Dekker.

Walzer, M. (1991, Spring). The idea of civil society. *Dissent,* pp. 293-304.

Wamsley, G. L. (1972). Contrasting institutions of the Air Force socialization: Happenstance or bellwether? *American Journal of Sociology, 78*(2), 399-417.

Wamsley, G. L., & Zald, M. N. (1976). *The political economy of public organizations: A critique and approach to the study of public administration.* Bloomington: Indiana University Press.

White, O. F., Jr., & McSwain, C. J. (1990). The Phoenix project: Raising a new image of public administration from the ashes of the past. In H. D. Kass & B. L. Catron (Eds.), *Images and identities in public administration* (pp. 23-59). Newbury Park, CA: Sage.

Will, G. (1992). *Restoration: Congress, term limits, and the recovery of deliberative democracy.* New York: Free Press.

About the Contributors

Thomas J. Barth is Assistant Professor of Public Administration at The University of Memphis, teaching and conducting research in public human resources, administrative ethics, and administrative theory. His work has appeared in a number of leading public administration journals, including *Administration and Society, Review of Public Personnel Administration, The Public Manager,* and the *American Review of Public Administration.* Prior to his academic career, he spent 10 years in Washington, DC, first as a Presidential Management Intern and then as a senior analyst in several federal agencies, including the Department of Health and Human Services and the Environmental Protection Agency. In addition to his academic work, he is also currently an active strategic planning consultant with a variety of government and nonprofit agencies.

Joy A. Clay is Associate Professor and Chairman of the Department of Political Science at the University of Memphis. Her research interests include administrative theory, health policy, strategic management, and continuous quality improvement. She has published articles in *Administration and Society, Public Manager, Review of Public Personnel Administration,* and *Environmental Review.* She has also done extensive community research on medical indigency and maternal and infant health.

Linda F. Dennard received her doctorate in public administration from Virginia Polytechnic Institute and State University at Blacksburg in 1993. She has taught at Western Michigan University at Kalamazoo and is currently on the faculty of the Department of Public Administration at California State University at Hayward. Her current research interests include democratic theory for public administration, social design for community and citizenship, bioeconomics, and evolutionary health care policy.

Larkin Dudley is Assistant Professor at the Center for Public Administration and Policy. Her research and teaching interests include privatization, organizational theory, and public management.

Richard T. Green is Associate Professor in the University of Wyoming Political Science Department. He teaches in the Master of Public Administration Program and conducts research in public administrative history, theory, and ethics.

Lawrence Hubbell is Head of the University of Wyoming Political Science Department. He teaches in the Master of Public Administration Program and conducts research in the areas of public personnel, organization behavior and development, and management psychology.

Larry M. Lane is currently Assistant Professor of Management at American University in Washington, D.C. He has previously served as Adjunct Professor of Public Administration at Virginia Tech and at Troy State University. He was a charter member of the federal Senior Executive Service and was Deputy Director of Personnel for the Department of the Interior. He writes frequently on public service issues and is coauthor, with James F. Wolf, of *The Human Resource Crisis in the Public Sector: Rebuilding the Capacity to Govern.*

John H. Little is an Assistant Professor of Public Administration at the University of Maine. He is a graduate of Virginia Tech's Center for Public Administration and Policy, where he has served as Adjunct Professor. He previously worked for over thirty years as an engineer and manager for the Navy.

O. C. McSwite is the pseudonym of Orion F. White, Professor of Public Administration at Virginia Polytechnic Institute and State University, and Cynthia J. McSwain, Associate Professor of Public Administration at the George Washington University. They have published widely on the subjects of social and psychological theory and organizational change. Their current research interests include the application of postmodern approaches (especially the psychoanalytic orientation of Jacques Lacan) to public administration. They are completing a book for publication next year, entitled, *The Legitimacy Issue in American Public Administration: A Discourse Analysis.* Together they have over 40 years of experience working as consultants with organizations of all types in the United States and internationally.

John A. Rohr is Professor of Public Administration at Virginia Tech's Center for Public Administration and Policy. His writings on public administration cover several fields including ethics, constitutionalism, and comparative studies. His most recent book is *Founding Republics in France and America: A Study in Constitutional Governance* (1995).

Camilla Stivers teaches public administration at The Evergreen State College, Olympia, Washington. She is the author of *Gender Images in Public Administration* (1993) and numerous book chapters and articles. She is at work on a book on the influence of gender on the emergence of public administration as an academic field during the Progressive era. She was a practicing administrator in nonprofit organizations for 20 years before coming to Evergreen.

Gary L. Wamsley is the founding director of the Center for Public Administration and Policy at Virginia Polytechnic Institute and State University. He is best known for his work as editor and contributing author of *Refounding Public Administration* (1990) and for his work with Mayer Zald, *The Political Economy of Public Organizations* (1976). He has been editor of *Administration and Society* since 1979. His expertise covers selective service, national security, emergency management, and budgeting. He has served as consultant to federal, state, and local governments.

Lisa Weinberg is Assistant Professor at the University of Washington's Graduate School of Public Affairs in Seattle, where she teaches courses on management and organization, budgeting, and intergovernmental relations. Her research interests include processes of organization, democratic participation, and community-building. She is currently working on a case study about labor-management cooperation at the Los Angeles Bureau of Sanitation.

James F. Wolf currently serves as Professor and Director of Virginia Tech's Center for Public Administration and Policy. He earned a doctorate in Public Administration from the University of Southern California's School of Public Administration. His research focuses on public administration, human resources management, and organizational change. He coauthored (with Lawrence Lane) *The Human Resource Crises in the Public Sector* (1990). For 20 years, he has been a consultant and trainer for organizational change programs. He has worked as a management and community development expert in Turkey and the Philippines. While at the University of Connecticut, he provided technical assistance to state and local governments. More recently, he has supported Virginia local governments' Total Quality Management programs and has mediated annexation disputes among local jurisdictions.